Joyce Lain Kennedy's CAREER BOOK

Joyce Lain Kennedy's CAREER BOOK

Joyce Lain Kennedy
Dr. Darryl Laramore

VGM Career Horizons
a division of *NTC Publishing Group*
Lincolnwood, Illinois USA

1990 Printing

Published by National Textbook Company, a division of NTC Publishing Group.

Manufactured in the United States of America.

Library of Congress Catalog Card Number: 87-83718

9 0 RA 9 8 7 6 5 4 3

To my husband, William Alvey Kennedy
—JLK

and

To my wife, Joyce Hutchison Laramore, and
my children, Nina, Christopher and Megan
—DL

CONTENTS

★ WORK TRENDS ★

★ FUTURE JOBS ★

★ GETTING HELP ★

★ SELF-AWARENESS ★

★ WORK AWARENESS ★

★ RESEARCH ★

★ GOALS ★

★ MAKING DECISIONS ★

★ STUDENT JOBS ★

★ COLLEGE PLANNING ★

★ COLLEGE DAYS/ADVANCED STUDY ★

★ OTHER EDUCATION ★

★ ADULT JOB SEARCH ★

★ WINNING ON FIRST JOB ★

★ CAREER MANAGEMENT ★

Acknowledgments

To our executive editor, *Ellen Roberts Weimer,* heartfelt thanks for your clarity of mind, analytical wizardry and knowing a convoluted sentence when you see one. This book would not have happened without you.

Editorial associate *Sarah Richards* labored with exemplary efficiency through stacks of statistics and studies, the volume of which would have anesthetized a lesser person.

Although many experts read appropriate pages, four valued colleagues gave us a treasury of helpful advice on large portions of the manuscript. Our lasting appreciation goes to *Dr. Kenneth B. Hoyt,* distinguished university professor at Kansas State University and former U.S. director of career education; *Bonnie Bekken*, editor of *Career World* magazine; *Steven S. Ross,* a journalism professor at Columbia University and leading technical careers authority; and *Laura Ruekberg,* vice president and senior editor of General Learning Corporation.

U.S. Department of Labor professionals were unstintingly gracious in providing us with key market findings, especially *Melvin Fountain, Neale Baxter, Neal Rosenthal* and *Michael Pilot. Dr. Vance Grant* of the U.S. Department of Education's Center for Educational Statistics kept us on the right path with more numbers than we knew existed.

At Sun Features Inc., *Sandra Riedel* worked with tireless cheerfulness over long weeks and even longer weekends struggling to win the word processing battle. She was victorious. *Muriel Turner* provided good humor and valuable assistance in keeping the word processing system on its best behavior. *Dyan Colvin* also let the word processing system know who was boss. *Helen Gaither* served as our grammatical safety net; to prove it, she has a large bin of excess punctuation marks salvaged from the manuscript.

Leonard Fiddle, executive vice president of VGM Career Books/NTC Publishing Group, asked us to write this book, and VGM editor *Michael Urban* brought the keenest of eagle eyes to bear upon it. In the art department, designer *Karen Christoffersen* and design/production assistant *Arlene Sheer* put beauty in the eyes of all beholders of this work.

The full list of those who helped prepare the *Career Book* would fell a forest. Our thanks and apologies to any we have omitted.

∞

To The Parent

It's no secret that you want the best for your child, an ambition more complex now than when you were beginning to find your way in life.

What isn't so well known is that you are a much bigger factor in your child's successful career launch than you probably realize.

In fact, you, the parent, are the *most* influential person in your child's career choice. Years of research in career selection have produced this important, unequivocal finding:

Young people are most influenced by their families —not by their peers, teachers, or counselors. Occupational attitudes are most shaped by what happens at home, not by what happens in classrooms and social settings.

This means you are the number-one resource and power for helping your young person target on a rewarding career, and focus on the educational investments that will best lead to that target.

Being number one in anything is a heavy responsibility and the concern you carry for your child's future is justified. The choice of career largely determines how your young adult will live and whether the sum of his or her life will be a plus or minus.

As the authors of the *Career Book,* our purpose is to help you, the parent, meet the challenge of providing young adults with the information they need to make sensible, satisfying decisions about their career and life goals.

What The *Career Book* Can Do For Sons And Daughters, Age 15–25

For young adults, finding answers to these questions is of lifetime importance:

- *What do I want to be?*
- *What must I do to get what I want?*
- *Once there, how do I move further ahead?*

Why do we say these questions are of lifetime importance? Because, in the modern world, job security is an illusion: factories close, government employees are dismissed, whole industries shift to other countries.

True security is in the understanding of how to make good career decisions, to get training and to find jobs. Once career *strategies* and *processes* are understood, an individual can face the workplace with confidence. In this sense, the *Career Book* is a kind of insurance policy for covering life satisfaction. Whether young people express it in these words or not, that's what they hope the future holds for them.

In an age when work will never again be the same, the *Career Book* guides young adults through the process of making relevant life-satisfaction decisions, for now and later. Specifically, readers learn how to

- acquire facts about the world of career options
- become more aware of their interests, abilities and values
- set goals and develop techniques to reach them
- make effective decisions
- involve their family and friends in career planning
- make appropriate educational choices
- identify marketable skills
- become an expert job seeker
- nail down success on the job

By providing a young adult with the information in the *Career Book,* you offer an opportunity to reach for true lifetime security and happiness.

YES, THE *CAREER BOOK* IS DIFFERENT

Most guidance books for young people aim at either high school students preparing for college admission, or at college students seeking careers.

The *Career Book* is for both groups, as well as for students not bound for college.

The *Career Book* ranges from concerns of untried teens who are just beginning to think about their futures, all the way to recent college graduates who are experiencing their early days on their first permanent jobs.

Because the book deals with developmental issues over a 10-year span (ages 15 to 25), both the sophistication of the text and the learning activities vary, and, in general, show increasing maturity as the guide progresses.

The enormous scope of the *Career Book* invites buffet reading: Your young adult can pick and choose topics that are critical at various stages of life. The format, too, invites dip-in and scoop-out involvement—information comes in concise, quickly absorbed portions. Most segments require no more than a few minutes to read, and most activities take no more than a few minutes to accomplish.

The scope, format and content of the *Career Book* intend that the guide will have a long shelf life in home libraries. Like the basic cookbook or medical handbook that's consulted again and again, the *Career Book* can be a trusted and valuable reference for use during the years ahead.

MAKE CAREER PLANNING A FAMILY AFFAIR

Young Adult:

I don't know what I want to do. Jeff is going into the Air Force, but he isn't sure he wants to spend the rest of his life in the service. I like to travel, but it's a pain taking orders all the time. I don't think military life is for me. Rachel wants to be an engineer, and I hear they make good money, but I don't know what they do.

Parent:

I think you ought to go to college as soon as you finish high school. Think about law school—or you're pretty good in math—engineers do okay, too. It's a tough decision. Your sister is still having trouble choosing her college major.

Who calls the shots when young adults plan their careers?

Ultimately, definitive career decisions must be the prerogative of your offspring. It's a mistake to maneuver a young person into a field you wanted, but didn't land in, or to see your young adult as an extension of your own skills package.

On the other hand, your ideas as an adult are likely to be more realistic, seasoned as they are by experience with the real world. This is why it is both your right and your responsibility to exercise leadership in the sense that Gen. George Marshall, who knew a thing or two about it, used the word.

Gen. Marshall described a leader as "a person who exerts an influence and makes you want to do better than you could."

In a Marshall-style leadership role, feel free to help young people gather information about careers; to help in self-discovery by sharing your observations with them about their traits and, if asked, by helping with such activities as preparing resumes and practicing job interviews.

Read through the *Career Book* and become familiar with its contents. It's not necessary to study these pages like a textbook, but know the sections well enough so that when issues arise, you can locate the pertinent information.

We hope you'll confer regularly with your young person about career planning. We urge you to pay close attention to those sections (5, 6, and 7) that deal with awareness, and which are tailor-made for family conferences.

We also hope you can eliminate sex bias in your thinking about a young person's future career. The *Career Book* is a guide for everyone, male and female.

With nearly half of our workforce already made up of women, statistics project that nine of 10 of today's girls will work for 25 to 45 years.

Unless young women, especially, acquire solid skills while they're in school, many will lead humdrum, low-paid job lives. Math, science and computer courses, for instance, will open a wide range of career options for those who are prepared; many opportunities will be eliminated for those who aren't. That is the word from Joyce Ride—mother of Sally, the nation's first woman astronaut.

Before putting on your Gen. Marshall career leadership hat, why not find out where you stand in your own career awareness?

Using one side of a piece of paper, list the careers you consider appropriate for your child. Turn over the paper and list the careers you would want available if you were isolated on a desert island or in space. Now quickly answer the following questions.

1. Do your lists differ?
2. Do you think some careers are important but inappropriate for your child?
3. Are you more interested in seeing your child follow a career satisfying to him or her, or one that will make you proud?
4. Would the list of careers that you think are appropriate for your child be different if his or her sex were different?
5. Do you believe that certain careers are inappropriate for women? What are they and why?
6. Do you consider some careers inappropriate for men? What are they and why?
7. What would your reaction be if your son or daughter chose one of these "inappropriate" careers?
8. Is your knowledge of careers sufficiently up to date so that you feel confident about your choices of "appropriate" and "inappropriate" careers?
9. Would you share your answers to these questions with your son or daughter?
10. Do you think you give your offspring useful advice about how to research a career?

Completing this exercise should help make you aware of your knowledge and attitude about possible career choices for your son or daughter. If you like your responses, fine. If you are not satisfied with your answers, you at least are probably more aware of your own biases, and like the young person who is so important in your life, can learn something from this book.

To People Concerned With Disabilities

What career choices are open to those who have physical disabilities or other limiting characteristics? *The choices are identical to those for the able-bodied population with one exception: An individual with a disability must look for ways to modify the sought-after occupation to accommodate a limitation.*

Because the *Career Book* recognizes that disability is a single feature—not the whole package—the career guidance information is mainstreamed for the millions of young people with disabilities. Where beneficial, targeted messages are addressed to students with special problems.

Wheelchair user William G. Stothers, assistant financial editor of the *San Diego Union* newspaper, explains the career-related viewpoint we hope readers will have: "No one wants to be disabled. But *it is okay* to be disabled."

—JOYCE LAIN KENNEDY
—DARRYL LARAMORE, PhD

To The Counselor

School Counselors
College and University Counselors
Vocational School Counselors
Private Career Counselors
Career Information Specialists
Librarians
Teachers
Psychologists
Members of the Clergy
Social Workers
Rehabilitation Counselors

—in other words—

Any professional to whom young people turn when they need help in choosing a career direction. This help may be given at any time during the decade of career launch: high school, postsecondary education/training, and the first job after graduation.

It's tough to be an adviser, caregiver and helper.

Dr. Glenn Frank, a former president of the University of Wisconsin, could have been listening to the same young people that you encounter every day when he delivered these thoughts during a baccalaureate address:

> *I know that all sorts of anxieties haunt your minds, anxieties about the first and further steps in your careers. And these normal anxieties that you would feel even if all skies were cloudless, have, I know, been trebled by the political and economic distraction through which your nation has been passing as you have pursued your training.*
>
> *What shall you do with these anxieties?*
>
> *I want to be honest with you. I do not want to minimize one whit the uncertainties that infest the economic affairs of your time. I do not want to raise in your minds a single hope that will be doomed to die unfulfilled. But I do want to stir in you, if I can, every hope that can be fulfilled.*

Stir every hope that can be fulfilled—spoken half a century ago, the meaning of these words remains a mission for contemporary advisers across the land.

As counselors, we often speak of the future even though we know the future doesn't exist—it is constantly evolving as events unfold. That's why it is such an enormous and sometimes overwhelming challenge to stir every hope that can be fulfilled for *each* student or client.

Never Enough Time

Having as our professional goal the purpose of helping people create the best possible future for themselves can be at once satisfying and frustrating. Certainly we would like to give undivided attention to each individual, helping that person conquer life, both in personal and public achievement. What stops us is the myriad of intertwining tasks that are part of our professional responsibility.

Having spent my entire professional life in counseling, I know how it is to frequently feel squeezed in dealing with the time bind of counseling schedules. I know how it is to be forced to devote hours to budgets or college admissions paperwork or participate in curriculum meetings when I feel that I should be helping students by

- developing strategies and activities to guide young people toward educational and career success
- teaching research techniques to help students meet demands of the 21st century
- assisting counselees to discover their aptitudes, skills, values and interests.

Time and accessibility. How can we counselors make ourselves available to all who need our guidance on career development and life planning?

We can't. The work schedule of the most dedicated counselor can collapse when the counselor tries to do it all.

Share The Work Load

This organized career development plan is a time stretcher to save you hours for your highest priorities.

The *Career Book* contains valuable information for students who are just beginning to think about lifestyles and learning to establish goals, as it does for those ready to enter college, vocational training, the military or the work force.

Depending on where the student/client is in the decade of career launch, you can direct the individual to the relevant section, following up as you deem appropriate.

You can choose various levels of interaction. We provide activities that require minimal face-to-face contact between you and the counselee, but allow plenty of opportunity for personal follow-up via a telephone call, hallway conversation or other brief encounter.

Besides one-on-one counseling, you may use the *Career Book* in small groups as a focus for discussion, or in large classroom learning experiences as a text.

As counselors, you're familiar with much of the career development literature and so we need not belabor the point that the *Career Book* is a comprehensive work tool.

As you read, you will see the *Career Book* takes the reader from self-awareness to decision-making to job market packaging, suggesting ways to develop self-confidence, assess values, discover talents, research options and land the right job.

The *Career Book* can help you be realistic with each counselee as you stir every hope that can be fulfilled.

—DARRYL LARAMORE, PhD

∞

To The Reader

An American Indian legend tells this story of an orphaned eagle.

A young warrior found a lone eagle egg. Meaning to be helpful, he placed it in the nest of a prairie chicken. The little eagle hatched with his stepbrothers and stepsisters, the prairie chicks.

Growing up friends, they pecked and clucked around the ground together, scratching for worms, insects and seeds. Eaglethood was one pleasant day after another—with no challenges.

When the eaglet flew, he imitated his prairie chicken family. With a lot of flap and little flight, the changeling eaglet never rose more than a few feet off the ground.

As the years passed the eaglet grew up, matured and grew old. Scratching the ground one day, the changeling eagle happened to glance up and there in the clouds was the most splendid bird he'd ever seen. He couldn't look away from the magnificent bird as it played tag with the sun. And yet the bird's gorgeous strong golden wings scarcely seemed to move as it commanded the sky.

"This is the most noble bird I have ever seen," clucked the changeling eagle to the senior prairie chicken. "I wonder what it is."

"Why that's an eagle, the chief of birds," said the senior prairie chicken. "But he's far above you. Keep scratching."

And so our eagle kept scratching the ground. He died never realizing he was not a prairie chicken.

If you want to be a prairie chicken, that's fine. If you'd rather be an eagle, that's good, too. What's most important is that you know what you want and how to get it. If you drift through life not ever really finding out who you are, you are certain to miss the thrill of soaring.

(Legend source: The Christophers, New York City.)

What's In This Book For You?

Readers ranging in age from 15 to 25 will soon have to answer these questions:

- *What do you have to do to make things go your way now and in the 21st century?*
- *What do you have to do to be everything you can be?*

We intend to help you figure out the answers to these questions.

Whether you are beginning to develop secret career hopes or already harbor serious ambitions, you need to start now making a plan for living life on your terms.

What you have to do is learn how to plan for the style of your life, realizing that your career choice is the magic that makes it happen.

Your career choice is the major factor in shaping your entire lifestyle. Your career determines what kinds of friends you'll have; how much money you'll make; where you will live; the type of home you can afford; how much and where you'll travel.

Your career choice will strongly influence how much leisure time you'll have and how you'll spend it; the sort of person you'll marry; and whether you'll look forward to healthy paychecks, or exist in fear of poverty and lay-offs.

View career choice not in isolation, but as the means to get what you want out of life.

Earlier generations frequently drifted into jobs, even careers, but you and other working adults in the 21st century—an era of ocean farming and telecommunicating with neighbors on the next continent—can't afford the luxury of relying on the chance discovery of a suitable career.

The strategy we suggest for planning your career future combines two basic moves:

- conceptualizing your future as you want it to be, and
- taking the action that turns dreams into reality.

To help you visualize what you want to be doing in the years ahead, we have created a series of "identity inventories" that spotlight individual interests, values, aptitudes, personality traits and lifestyle preferences. From these inventories, clues emerge leading you to identify occupations that will satisfy your dreams and goals.

We tell you how to set up a "future file" of job information. You will learn how to explore "career clusters" and how to establish a network of career resources in your community.

Arming you with a sense of career awareness is one way of helping you learn to control your work future. We also explain in gritty detail specific career actions: how to plan and make the most of your education; how to use student jobs to your own best advantage; how to star in job interviews and how to choose the all-important first job.

By mastering the process of career decision-making, you award yourself a long-term insurance policy. Once you understand the ins-and-outs of making good career decisions, you can repeat the process as often as necessary. You may experience half-a-dozen different occupations during your life. Why?

The workplace will change; electronic books, computers that mimic the human mind, business ventures in space, and other advances may appear sooner than is convenient and short-circuit your original career. Rather than fold your tent, you'll reactivate the career decision-making skills you learn here.

You, too, will change. As you mature, you may outgrow your current ambitions. Or your perspective on career goals may change. Activities that intensely interest you now may slip off your priorities list tomorrow.

We caution you to remember that intelligent career decisions recognize economic realities. Many people make bad decisions by studying subjects that lead to good party conversation but not to good jobs. When they graduate and are disappointed in the employment market available to them, their universal wail is, "Why didn't somebody tell me?"

We're telling you: Take the blinders off. Have a plan. Anticipate outcomes. Weigh the economic realities of your career decisions. Think about the money you'll make in a prospective career in relation to the life you want. (Money is not the most important thing in life—but it is flat and meant to be piled up.)

Another warning: "Best" careers are a myth. You may see lists of the 10 or 25 or 100 so-called "best" or "hottest" career fields for tomorrow. Ask yourself, "Best for whom?"

Ceramic engineering certainly would figure on such a list—it's a field alive with technical advancements. If you're a C student in math, however, you can chalk it off your personal "best" list.

The whole idea of absolute best careers is incorrect. Many variables make career choices as much of a guessing game as the stock market. *All* careers are subject to the ups-and-downs of the job market.

A decade ago, for instance, when physicians were in short supply, being a doctor was the key to the treasury. Now, newly graduated physicians are being jostled by other newly graduated physicians and most are having a bit of trouble becoming established.

Certainly you must pay attention to promising fields—and the *Career Book* will show you how to do that. But your interests and talents should forge your career choice. Simply looking for fast-growing fields isn't likely to pay off in the satisfaction department.

Like wind surfing, career decision-making is a set of skills you can learn. Once you master the movements, there's little to stop you from catching breezes of opportunity wherever you wish.

How To Use This Guide

Career decision-making takes place in bits and pieces over a long period of time. We have styled our book to reflect that fact.

The scope, format and content of the *Career Book* make it easy for readers to pick and choose topics that are critical at various stages of life. If you're in college, you can skip the pages that deal with college preparation. If you're in high school, you need not read the section about succeeding in college until you're headed for campus.

We have laid out the book so that it follows the same sequence that an organized career development plan follows. If you prefer to read in a straightforward, orderly fashion, instead of hopscotching through the book, that will work fine, too.

We know you want solid information packaged in a concise, quick-reading format and that is what we provide. All topic segments require no more than a few minutes to read, and most activities can be accomplished at one sitting.

As authors, we ask only one favor: For starters, read through the next few paragraphs to get an idea of what this guide has in store for you. That action alone will put your challenge in perspective.

In *section 1*, you'll meet people very much like yourself who propelled their ideas, talents and energies into huge success stories. We tell you how to get rich in America and note that anyone can be successful in some way.

Does the idea of taking risks scare you? *Section 2* gives you ideas on conceptualizing—establishing the proper mind-set for managing risk and achieving career success.

Even back when computers were as big as a room and an apple was something you ate, the work world was a trendy place. There are potent career shifts taking place today, too, and *section 3* tells you how to deal with the outside forces that may affect your career.

Like most of us, you probably have only a limited idea of all the careers available to you. *Section 4* offers an overview of selected occupations for this century and the next.

Are you aware of the many and varied sources of help available to assist you in a career search? *Section 5* explains who can help you and why you should not try to go it alone.

If you're unsure about your interests, aptitudes, skills and values, or don't really know how your personality type can affect your job satisfaction, read *section 6*. You must know yourself before you can find the career that provides the kind of life you want and that is compatible with your interests and abilities.

Like polishing a diamond in the rough, *section 7* shows you how to add brilliance to career plans. The secret: We reveal the most effective contemporary techniques for enhancing your career awareness.

If you have physical disabilities that are standing in the way of an exciting career, we show you how others overcame such difficulties and how their examples can provide concrete help for dealing with your own.

We ask you to consider whether your ideas are based on racial, ethnic or sexual stereotypes, and if you are excluding a career that should be high on your options list.

Section 8 gives you the most comprehensive crash course in print on researching a career. Extensive career and job market research is how you avoid unpleasant surprises.

Are you aiming too low or expecting too much too soon? In *section 9*, you learn to set goals that will make you reach and stretch toward your career objective.

Do you have trouble making decisions? The chicken kiev looks good, but so does the fresh fish; you can't decide whether to go to the concert or the movies this weekend; you accepted an invitation to a weekend at the beach, but really want to stay home. Master decision-making skills by following the seven-step formula described in *section 10.*

Everyone has to start somewhere and if you are 15 to 18 years old, begin now to get work experience. Even if you're beyond high school—in college, for instance—*section 11* explains the basics of how to find a job you want and how to make the most of the job you land. (Once you have grasped the principles, you'll find advanced information in later sections.)

Want to go to college? This is a far-reaching decision and *section 12* makes the process easier. You will need all the information you can get.

Section 13 deals with the college experience, including your choice of major. We suggest you build power skills for the future, and we help you look ahead to graduate and professional education.

Section 14 is a round-up of all the ways other than in college, including vocational-technical studies and military service, that you can acquire career know-how.

Section 15 focuses on your first full-time job, telling how to market yourself effectively in a competitive job market.

In *sections 16 and 17* you find out how to choose that all-important first job and how to successfully manage it. You also learn how to climb the corporate ladder.

So there you have it—a career book of the widest scope ever. Think of it as a trusted family friend to whom you can turn for answers to career questions. Within its pages, we try to give you the counseling you need to pinpoint, search for and land the career of your dreams in an age where work will never again be the same.

—JOYCE LAIN KENNEDY
—DARRYL LARAMORE, PhD

JOYCE LAIN KENNEDY'S CAREER BOOK

SECTION ONE

Why Not Go for Big Career Rewards?

T*he* Career Book *opens with a discussion of financial rewards* because money figures prominently in our lives. A Louis Harris & Associates poll shows that 63 percent of employed adults surveyed value a good salary as one of the most important job factors, even above job security (53 percent) and a chance to use one's mind and abilities (39 percent).

While it is true that for some go-getters, money is the main motivating force in the career process, most people believe that money isn't everything and we suggest you consider a range of career satisfactions.

In this section, you'll first be inspired by young action-oriented people who jump right in and do—and earn big incomes in the bargain. Next you'll discover some ways to get rich, including being your own boss or becoming a topflight corporate executive. Several fields noted for fat paychecks are reviewed.

On a less elevated, but more realistic plane, you'll glance at median earnings for typical workers.

You're asked to think about what success truly means to you and we warn you about the dark side of going after too much too fast.

The section closes with philosophical thoughts on work and a guiding principle to follow when you feel uncertain about a career choice.

Success at an Early Age

At 32, William H. Gates III looks like somebody's kid brother. He also has stock worth hundreds of millions of dollars.

Here's how it happened.

When he was 15, Gates and a high school friend grossed $20,000 a year from a company they created to provide computer analyses of traffic patterns for small towns.

Several years later, as a Harvard sophomore, he helped write a software operating program—the brains that make the machine work—for one of the earliest personal computers. The program was such a wow that Gates left college to start a company called Microsoft.

In 1981, Gates' big break came: IBM chose a Microsoft operating system for its personal computers. The company's sales increased from $32 million in 1982 to more than $140 million in 1985.

In 1986, Microsoft, headquartered in the Seattle suburb of Redmond, began selling shares on the stock market. Gates, founder and chief executive officer, kept stock worth $390 million.

In 1987, IBM chose Microsoft software for its new generation of personal computers, helping Microsoft yearly revenues to soar to more than $300 million.

In the volatile personal computer business, no company has a perpetual lock on leadership. But whatever the future brings—up or down for Microsoft—Bill Gates' achievement is spectacular.

Yet, it is not unique. This is one of the best of times in the history of the United States to make it big.

Why? Because of the economy's shift from heavy manufacturing to high tech and services, individuals don't always need costly factories and inventories, and can start new ventures on relatively little money.

Most people who achieve stunning success have graying hair, but others (you?) grab the brass ring at an early age.

They are the fast-starters, the dynamos that break at warp-speed from the starting gate, leaving the rest of the field far behind. When you hear about fast-starters, you have to wonder how they did it. Let's glance at a handful of them and see what we can learn about the sought-after rewards that propel these youthful superachievers to scale such heights.

An Album of Fast-Starters

Certainly there are other rich rewards in life beyond aspiring to the trappings of a swashbuckling capitalist. Rewards like feelings of self-actualization, making a real contribution to your planet and—well, having a whale of a good time doing what you're doing—are important too.

As you read each fast-starter's profile, try to guess which career rewards the person values especially—creative expression, a mega-income, power, recognition, social service, organizational achievement, pioneering efforts, or other satisfactions you can think of.

Gail Berman and *Susan Rose* were just 21 and new graduates of the University of Maryland when they decided to produce *Joseph and the Amazing Technicolor Dreamcoat* for Washington, D.C.'s Ford Theatre. Everyone told them it couldn't be done. They ended up with a Broadway hit and seven Tony nominations.

Tom Ryan and *Mike Kofoed* were both in their late 20s when their company, Leggoons, was grossing $10 million. Located in Omaha, Nebr., Leggoons was inspired by the Winnie-the-Pooh-patterned shorts the men wore painting curbs when they were college students. From a few people producing whimsical beach pants, the staff has grown to 15 office workers and two dozen sales reps.

Linda Alvarado was within sniffing distance of her first $1 million before she was 30. Her Denver-based construction company, Alvarado Construction Inc., now contracts about $45 million in business yearly. A new project, Alvarado Development, handles development from land acquisition to construction. Her motto: "You have to believe in your own ability to do it better."

Floyd Scholz of Hancock, Vt., is in his late 20s. From the time he was 24, his "avian sculptures," as he calls them, have been winning blue ribbons at national bird-carving shows and selling for up to $32,000 each. He began doing birds at 12 and is now one of the nation's top carving artists. He lives in a 13-room farmhouse, which, he says, "the birds bought for me."

Elizabeth Bernstein, a native of Long Island, N.Y., was 31 when the U.S. Supreme Court handed her a major victory, but she was in her 20s—and fresh out of Harvard law school—when she did the hard legal work that led to her shining hour. Rejecting establishment law, Bernstein chose to move to an Indian reservation in Arizona, where she worked for the Navajo Nation's justice department. She went to court to give Indians the right to tax companies doing business on their reservation. The victory for the Indians means tens of millions of dollars for Navajo schools, police and roads.

John Herman had been in business 12 years when he was 20 years old. He began by selling items from his uncle's specialty advertising business to friends, relatives and neighbors. At 16, he formed his own specialty advertising business. At 18, he was attending college and juggling eight employees. That year the John Herman Company grossed approximately $500,000. Two years later, the company merged and, although no longer involved in day-to-day activities, Herman remains a principal of the expanded company while attending the University of Miami.

Zara F. Rolfes at 29 was a General Motors manager. With advanced degrees in mechanical engineering and business, the impressive young woman started at the giant corporation designing Chevy crankshafts. From there she zoomed up to lead a team that is responsible for one of the industry's first airbag programs, and later was placed in charge of occupant restraint systems in three major GM car lines. We didn't ask her salary but her managerial position shows she's certainly traveling in the corporate fast lane.

Steve Kirsch built a better mouse and the computer market beat a path to his door. In the early '80s, a 24-year-old Kirsch, working in his Sunnyvale, Calif., living room, started Mouse Systems, a company to produce optical mice—controls used with computer keyboards. Six months later, sales broke the $2 million mark. Today the company Kirsch founded is a major producer of mice, although without the talented inventor. Kirsch moved on to form a software company, Frame Technology, but retains his stock in Mouse Systems.

Ginnie Johansen, at age 23, earned more than $100,000 yearly from Ginnie Johansen Designs Inc., a Dallas-based company she formed with her father. Today, the accessory company has earnings in excess of $15 million, its own manufacturing plant and 130 employees. Johansen Designs are displayed in 1,800 shops throughout North America with a line that now includes silk scarves, jewelry, hair ornaments, and fragrance, as well as the preppy belts that first started the company.

Raphael Collado and *Ramon Morales,* both in their early 30s, put their minority neighbors to work in one of the nation's most economically disadvantaged areas—New York's South Bronx. Their high-tech company, Protocom Devices, boasts sales in the $2 million range. Financially successful, yes, but Morales describes Protocom as a company with a mission, "showing people that they can participate in controlling their own destiny and take part in growth opportunities of the future."

Robin Keeney, of Washington, D.C., was 26 when she was named chief lobbyist for an important group, the American Land Title Association. Keeney polished her superb persuasion skills working as an associate lobbyist at two other trade organizations after graduating from American University with a liberal arts degree. In a city where power is everything, the high-performance young woman spends long hours on Capitol Hill trying to convince legislators that the positions she represents are the right ones. Daily she speaks with people whose faces are familiar on the evening news.

What Fast-Starters Have in Common

The most successful young achievers appear to have several characteristics in common.

- *Commitment to win.* Fast-starters burn with a fever of enthusiasm for their work. They have enormous energy in pursuing their profession. "If you want success, communicate vision—and don't let anything get in your way," offers Steve Kirsch.
- *Impatience to start.* Some young achievers drop out of college because they can't bear delaying their missions. Others, like John Herman, were in business before they finished high school. His advice to other young adults: "Putting things off is one of the biggest problems people have."

Although some do bypass college, by far the majority of achievers in life acquire higher education. But even there, their hunger for success shows. They typically begin their hard-charging drive by taking jobs or starting little business ventures on campus.

- *Strong persuasion skills.* Young achievers have the ability to make their ideas sound creditable. With virtually no executive experience, Linda Alvarado convinced a bank to finance her first construction jobs and a government agency to award her firm its early contracts.

If you're a fast-starter, we applaud your dust. If not, there's always later. Do begin now, though, to think about what would turn on the lights and turn up the music in your life—and the rewards you'd like to come your way.

If becoming a millionaire is high on your list of things to do, your interest will catch fire in the next discussion.

Getting Rich in America: The Agony and the Ecstasy

"How can I make big money in my career?" This is a question posed by many of you who are standing in the foothills ready to begin a mountainous career climb.

Interest in wealth is not new. Americans have always been a nation of strivers searching for the secret formula to make it big.

As writer Robert J. Samuelson said, "The idea that society is suddenly preoccupied with wealth as a measure of achievement is a statement of huge historic ignorance."

In the 1830s, Alexis de Tocqueville, a Frenchman who came here and wrote *Democracy in America* from a visitor's viewpoint, remarked: "The love of wealth is...at the bottom of all that the Americans do."

Without a rigid hereditary class system, de Tocqueville said that making money is the surest way for Americans to show success.

This Is an Ideal Epoch for Making Money

Welcome to the Opportunity Society! Millionaires are no longer a rare species.

The Internal Revenue Service estimates that since 1976 the number of Americans with a net worth of at least $1 million has better than doubled to more than 400,000 persons.

Other estimates are even more eye-popping. According to the calculations of various market researchers, there may be as many as a million millionaires in the United States. Since there is no central net worth reporting device, it's impossible to be sure how many people are in the tycoon class—but there are plenty, you can be certain of that.

Why This Is a Good Time to Get Rich

The center of economic gravity is shifting in the U.S. and other advanced nations from mechanics to electronics, from fossil fuel to renewable energy. We are growing out of the industrial age and into the information/knowledge age.

Although the engines of change occasionally become vapor-locked by recessions, they make it easier than usual to pile up money. Just as in the late 1800s when the industrial age was blooming, and in the 1920s when many major corporations were born, special factors are again at work.

- In this time when one era is closing and another beginning, awesome fortunes will be made as new technology replaces old.
- Because corporations are restructuring, demand is high for corporate miracle workers who are lavishly rewarded.
- Companies can be started on a tight budget.
- Start-up capital is fairly easy to obtain.
- With women working, new needs are arising for two-career couples.

In addition to these markers of opportunity, most of you were born into a smaller generation than that of your parents, an advantage we discuss next.

Factors That Help Determine Wealth

Age. How old you are and how many other people are in your age group is one of the factors that determine financial health. Generations with few members have an edge on large generations because there is less competition for entry-level jobs and, down the road, for management jobs. (Remember, though, management jobs are likely to come later, rather than sooner, because graduates of the near future still see the baby-boom population bulge standing in their way.)

Those of you born between 1965 and 1975 are in a small generation. Others are at the tail end of a larger group that population experts call the last-wave baby boomers (1956 to 1964). Even if you're a last-wave baby boomer, other factors can overcome your generational "disadvantage." You can make choices that will help boost your affluence, no matter which generation you belong to.

Education. Households headed by college graduates earn two-thirds more than the median for all households. With so many college graduates competing for the best jobs, you will lag behind if you do not obtain a degree or specific job skills.

Occupation. We later cover this topic fully, but do note now that any "wallet roundup" of occupations reveals vast earnings differences. Despite high income for doctors, lawyers and corporate executives, proprietors of small businesses have a much better chance of becoming millionaires than do professionals and executives.

Marital Status. A study by the University of Michigan's Institute for Social Research says marriage is more important to your pocketbook than are your education, skills or attitude toward work. A sample of 5,000 families tracked over 10 years shows that important financial gains and losses are related more to marriage and divorce than to individual characteristics. In the future, the financial well-being of both men and women will be linked to marital status, because two incomes are becoming increasingly important.

Personal Characteristics. Earlier we mentioned that fast-starters share several attributes such as commitment to win and strong persuasion skills.

Other characteristics of financially successful people of all ages include

- foresight
- native wit
- ingenuity
- willingness to risk
- hard work
- excessive energy
- self-confidence
- disciplined mind (intelligence, common sense and ability to concentrate for long periods)
- extroverted personality that cultivates influential people.

Luck. Most wealth watchers say you need luck as well as pluck to make it big. Great wealth occurs when the right person standing on the right street corner hops on the right bus at the right time.

Places. Where you live influences your opportunities. What are the country's hottest growth areas between now and the turn of the century? Here's a list of boomtowns for the year 2000 reported by *Money* magazine.

- *Washington, D.C.*—Population 3.5 million; projected growth 51 percent to 5.3 million and 1 million jobs, largely in professional services, high technology, and medical research; most of the growth expected in nearby Virginia and Maryland counties.

- *Rochester, Minn.*—Hometown of renowned Mayo Clinic, credited with "cosmopolitan atmosphere," Rochester is now undergoing a growth campaign; projected growth 60 percent to 159,000, with new jobs in medical technology.

- *Reno, Nev.*—Successful in attracting industry; projected population growth 43 percent to 320,000; lures for business are low wages, no personal income tax on wages or investment income, and nearness to West Coast markets.

- *Portsmouth, N.H.*—Moderate living costs and absence of sales and income taxes are luring companies here from Boston, 50 miles south; projected population growth 36 percent to 426,000 for Portsmouth, Dover, Rochester triangle; many lakes and the White Mountains are within 55 miles.

- *Austin, Texas*—Computer research and electronics are developing here, with 125 new companies or expansions in six years, partly drawn by prosperous University of Texas; projected population growth 48 percent to more than 1,000,000; most companies are along 70-mile Austin-San Antonio corridor.

- *Raleigh-Durham, N.C.*—A continuing growth area projected up 32 percent to 828,000 in 15 years. A magnet for companies is Research Triangle Park between the two towns and within 25 miles of University of North Carolina, N.C. State University and Duke University; growth expected from smaller and entrepreneurial businesses.

- *Santa Rosa-Petaluma, Calif.*—This winemaking area is attracting San Francisco exiles; projected population growth 33 percent to 433,000; Santa Rosa is robust.

- *San Diego, Calif.*—Research in genetics, medical diagnostics and oceanographics at University of California/San Diego, Scripps Clinic, Salk Institute and La Jolla Cancer Research Foundation has attracted related companies; a National Science Foundation $100 million research center with a Cray supercomputer is located at the university; projected population growth of 47 percent to 3,100,000 includes high-tech workers.

Riches: Yesterday, Today

During the 17th and 18th centuries, when our young nation was hungry for most products, the first majestic fortunes were earned by merchants and traders.

As the years rolled on and the age of machines arrived, fortunes developed from other sources. Merchants with seed money and business know-how invested in inventions and the cash rolled in; rarely did the inventors themselves get rich. Textiles, iron, real estate, furs, banking, railroads and the telegraph were fertile investment fields at that time.

In the late 19th century, steel, mining, oil, mass transit, machinery and equipment, retailing, tobacco and food processing created super wealth for some.

During World War II, millionaires blossomed from heavy industry and defense contracting; by 1950, new financial giants were springing from aerospace, real estate, mortgage lending, transportation, chemicals, consumer products and broadcasting.

In the 1980s, leading industries from which the super rich draw their fortunes are oil, real estate, construction, insurance, investment banking, stock brokerage and private investing.

What about tomorrow's fat cats? If you discount the theory that nothing succeeds like inheritance, there are several other schools of thought on acquiring wealth and we'll talk about those next. The authors wish they were speaking from firsthand experience but, alas, our knowledge stems from research and observation. Should the topic fascinate you, one of the most illuminating books is wealth watcher Jacqueline Thompson's *Future Rich,* published by Wm. Morrow & Co.

Tomorrow's Money Makers

How can you get rich, richer, richest? By following one or a combination of three basic approaches.

The first two pathways to wealth involve owning a business. One approach is the steady-as-you-go school in which you operate a company that satisfies such traditional needs as food, clothing, shelter and education. You plug along working long hours for many years, saving and investing prudently.

The second approach is the proprietary niche method in which you have a secret product/process, or are one of the nation's few suppliers of a particular item. On the West Coast, a man is raking in money for a metal part used on advertising signs that only he knows how to manufacture. Colonel Sanders had a secret recipe for fried chicken. A man in Missouri became a multimillionaire as one of the few suppliers of police billy clubs and broom handles.

In the third approach, you might be a key employee given stock as part of your compensation. This is the find-fields-on-a-roll strategy. The theory holds that gargantuan fortunes can be made from dealings with embryonic and emerging industries.

How can you know which will be the go-go fields of tomorrow? Science and business magazines regularly report trends to watch. On the next two pages are lists of ideas others have made on how to become a VWP (very wealthy person)—a sampling that is far from complete. The first deals with the here and now. The second is futuristic and speculative, focusing on what *could* develop.

Going Out on Your Own

Starting your own enterprise has always been and continues to be the most promising way to make a great deal of money. Overnight fortunes can happen in one of two ways: by selling stock in your company, and by selling out. Fortunes over the long term materialize by profitably operating the company. Here are several examples, drawn from reports in news magazines.

- Austin Furst moved from being financially well-fixed to very wealthy in 1986. That was when he sold 15 percent of his company, Vestron Video, to the public for $70 million. Furst and his family still have majority ownership, which makes them worth hundreds of millions of dollars on paper. Furst got rich by buying the film library from Time-Life Films, of which he was president, when the library wasn't profitable. Borrowing on his home and using his savings, Furst got his big break releasing the video that showed how Michael Jackson made "Thriller." Vestron sold a million copies of the tape and reaped $20 million.
- Fred Pryor moved from pulpit to podium when he established the Kansas City-based Fred Pryor Seminars. His daylong courses teach corporate managers how to turn in a better performance. In a recent year, the company grossed $15 million by providing 2,000 seminars on management topics.

Profitable Business Fields for the Here and Now

Here are some industries market researchers say offer wealth-creating career opportunities.

Genetic engineering. Altering genetic characteristics for a specific purpose is in its infancy but already producing human insulin.

Telecommunications. The marriage of computers to communications has produced local area networks, modems, high-speed video and data traffic, electronic mail and a host of other wonders.

Robotics. Computer-integrated manufacturing (CIM), of which robotics is a main part, is the best-known industry but entrepreneurs tomorrow could have robot armies painting houses and cars.

Real estate and finance. Land and processing money never go out of style. Beyond normal financial dealings, a rash of leveraged (on credit) buy-outs, activities of corporate "raiders," and company mergers and acquisitions have allowed speculators to earn billions of fast bucks for financial shufflings.

Business services. To avoid creating permanent overhead costs, companies are farming out some specialized duties to small, efficient service companies, such as those that do product design, employee training, stockholder reports and office relocation.

Importing. Owners of many small import firms benefit from cheap foreign labor and America's rush to buy foreign goods. Electronics and machine parts are especially profitable.

Health and fitness. Americans are spending hundreds of millions of dollars yearly to keep in shape. There's money in sweat.

Child care. Franchising or owning a chain of child care facilities can be profitable, particularly now that large companies are beginning to offer child care benefits to female employees with young children.

Wealth-Building Industries of the 21st Century

Which unborn industries will eventually become giants is anyone's guess, but Edward Cornish, president of the World Future Society, mentions some possibilities:

Space exploration. It will lead to all kinds of new industries with products made in factories in space.

Air purification. As air gets dirtier, the industry built on the cleaning of air will zoom in importance.

Life extension. As more is understood about the aging process, anti-aging therapies and businesses will sprout.

Underground construction. As surface space grows expensive in large cities and environmental height limits are imposed, a big future industry may lie under our feet.

Personal security. Rising crime, terrorism and electronic snooping have made people feel increasingly insecure. An armory of security gadgets is growing.

Packaged education. All kinds of educational courses are being put onto audio and video systems, so people can learn whatever they want whenever they want.

- Felice and Boyd Willat started a business in their garage. The business was a glorified date book called Day Runner. Sales recently exceeded $10 million yearly with $1 million in profits.
- After losing money for five years, Tom McLaughlin, a former IBM manager, saw his pet business idea succeed. Started on a shoestring, his firm, Technical Support Services, maintains IBM equipment. Recent company earnings: about $1 million a year.
- L. H. Sevin quit working for Texas Instruments to launch his own company, Mostek, a semiconductor business. Sevin became $8 million richer when he cashed in his chips by selling out to giant United Technologies. The problem was that Sevin wasn't happy with the bureaucratic constraints inherent in a large company. "After being a god for a while, it's not so interesting to be a prophet," Sevin told a reporter, and he bolted to establish a venture capital company.

Interest in owning your own business is so intense that at least 250 colleges and universities now offer courses in entrepreneurship.

Women, especially, are rushing to run their own shows. For every man who opens a new business, five women start their own companies.

Experts say that between one-third and one-half of all new businesses go belly-up within five years, or remain marginally profitable. Despite the rags-to-rags dark side of entrepreneurship, the ranks of independents are swelling. The number of self-employed now rings in at more than 10 million people—one of every 10 working Americans is on his or her own.

Here's a tip for setting up your own employment. It comes courtesy of Paul Dickson, author of *On Our Own: A Declaration of Independence for the Self-Employed* (Facts on File).

In starting a new business, follow the taxi principle—find out what it costs before you get in. Learn about the special taxes, licenses and regulations in advance. Double or triple the estimates of time and money it will take you to get off the ground.

Corporate Pay Goes Sky-High

Although starting your own business is a popular way to try to hit the jackpot, it's not impossible to get rich by working for someone else.

This is the age of corporate stars—the miracle workers whose companies pay them more than $1 million a year.

The top bosses—presidents, chairmen of the board, or chief executive officers (CEOs)—are in a class alone. Their pay and benefits dwarf the earnings of most people.

Just how well are the nation's topmost executives paid? Here are recent annual earnings rounded to the nearest thousand for the nation's highest paid chieftains.

Lee A. Iacocca Chairman, Chrysler Corp.	$20,542,000
Paul Fireman Chairman, Reebok Intl.	$13,063,000
Victor Posner Chairman, DWG Corp.	$8,400,000
John J. Nevin Chairman, Firestone	$6,355,000
Charles E. Exley Jr. Chairman, NCR Corp.	$6,295,000

(Source: *Business Week*)

Beyond the money, corporate kingpins enjoy private planes, country club memberships, chauffeured cars, stock options and more.

As corporate salaries escalate, controversy grows. Are executives really worth millions of dollars a year—sometimes hundreds of times more than their lowest paid employees?

Critics say such wide wage differentials are destructive, causing restlessness in the ranks and affecting an organization's ability to function effectively. Do you agree? disagree? Your answer can throw a little light on your interest in being a corporate chieftain.

Money Begets Money in Finance Careers

No doubt about it, where impressive financial returns are concerned, it's hard to beat the financial sector as a career option.

The business press daily reports on such individuals as investment bankers, securities traders, financial planners, securities analysts, securities sales representatives, and corporate chief financial officers (CFOs) who are making bundles in today's electric financial environment.

These people are heavy on facts, numbers and nerve. They range from daring corporate raiders who war in the stock market to seize control of companies, to international money traders who earn handsome incomes by correctly guessing how the world's currencies will yo-yo in money markets.

Never has capital been so abundant in so many different forms in so many places. No longer does American business limit its search for funds to local banks. Money markets around the world—in particular, New York, London and Tokyo—are increasingly computer-linked so that would-be borrowers can reach across the globe for the lowest interest rates and terms.

People who make major financial decisions, who come up with financing innovations, who show other people how to make money, and who shuffle money from one pocket to another can earn incomes in the six figures, even the sevens.

Investment bankers are an example of the astonishing financial rewards possible in moving money around. Despite the fact that a sudden wave of layoffs in late 1987 cast clouds over the glamorous investment banking business, the field is still rich with opportunity for bright, ambitious young people.

Even when investment boom times quiet down, companies often need huge amounts of capital for expansion. One source is the investment banker, who, for a fee, finds funds. The banker may put a cash-lean company in the fast-growth orbit by personally putting up the money, or find a group of high-ticket investors to provide it.

Apart from nepotism and old-boy networks, entry-level investment banking jobs go to MBAs—usually those who come from prestigious graduate schools and have specialized in finance. What investment firms look for is young people who have deal-making talents. What else is required to succeed in this field?

Lynn Gilbert, an executive search consultant in New York City, recruits for investment banking firms where individuals in their early 30s can earn more than $200,000 a year. She says you must be a confident risk-taker, thrive on a fast pace, have a strongly competitive personality and "live" your work.

Any takers?

The Rarified Reaches of Real Estate

Fortunes are made in real estate. Some are relatively small; others are mammoth.

Rookies hired by major commercial real estate firms are an eclectic group who often have college degrees in liberal arts or business, and some of the top producers have no degree.

Their backgrounds vary widely, ranging from secretary and city planner to government worker and hearse driver. The cement that draws them together is an intense desire to make a lot of money, fast!

Beginners usually get no salary, only a "draw" against future commissions of between $15,000 and $20,000 the first year. A big percentage of rookies don't last two years because they don't lease enough properties.

Commercial real estate is incredibly hard work. How would you like to make 400 calls to lease an office building without gaining a single nibble of interest to show for your efforts?

On the other hand, if everything works out, the payoffs can be *huge.* A former dental technician, who broke into the business as a receptionist at a Washington, D.C., commercial real estate firm 10 years ago, recently earned more than $1 million in commissions when she aced out the competition and leased a corporate headquarters building to a giant publishing corporation.

Residential real estate agents also suffer feast or famine. Most residential agents scrape by or do modestly well. Others—especially those who have found a niche, such as bank foreclosures or multimillion dollar estate sales—can buy their own Caribbean island.

Real estate development is another stairway that money stars climb. Developers build residential, industrial or commercial properties, arranging financing for their visions and ventures. Generally, real estate developers work on OPM—other people's money. Thus, the ability to visualize and to persuade are basic requirements in this work.

There are a number of occupations in this fast-fortune field—real estate exchanger, appraiser, finance specialist, and title insurance provider, to name a few. Moreover, some lawyers become real estate syndicators gathering money for investment, and some physicians become real estate investors in syndicates.

Some real estate agents build custom homes on speculation to sell to people who don't want to be bothered building their own homes; in the process, they try to earn more than $50,000 per house.

There are many avenues to a fat bank account in real estate.

Speaking of Doctors and Lawyers

Don't assume that doctors and lawyers have it made in the fortune department. Their success is far from guaranteed because of the large influx of new practitioners within the last decade.

Moreover, the lifestyle of professionals tends to be expensive—houses, cars and trips.

Even living well, doctors with certain specialties—radiologists, pathologists, neurosurgeons, plastic surgeons, orthopedic surgeons and anesthesiologists, for example—can pile up earnings because they often bring in more than $250,000 annually. General practitioners, family physicians and pediatricians are at the low end of the earnings scale.

Overall, physicians have the highest average annual earnings of any occupational group—over $118,000.

But are doctors *really* wealthy? That distinction belongs to the physicians who make wise investments with their surplus cash early on. An East Coast radiologist says he has made more money in his side business, building houses, than in his practice.

What about lawyers? By and large, attorneys don't tap into as much money as you might think. The average salary for lawyers in business, industry and non-profit organizations is $67,000, according to Abbott, Langer & Associates, a compensation consulting firm in Crete, Ill.

Young lawyers starting as associates in private practice earn an average $33,000 annually. Those who make partner—the average time is five years—can expect an eventual income of more than $100,000 a year.

At the top of the financial bracket are partners in major law firms. Law partners in New York City's Wall Street concerns may earn from $200,000 to $600,000 a year. Super lawyers pay taxes on seven figure incomes.

More Highflyers

Few people can join the elite corps of athletes and entertainers who earn headlines grabbing multimillion-dollar salaries, but many can compete for less-publicized positions that pay a respectable $100,000 or more annually. A few examples? University presidents, labor union officers and heads of major welfare organizations such as the American Red Cross. Of course, you can always aim to be the President of the United States and earn $200,000 plus a pleasant assortment of benefits.

What about women? Are there certain fields that seem to offer greener pastures than others? Retailing is the most salary-friendly to female executives, according to a study by the executive search firm Korn/Ferry International. The study shows that women executives at the vice-presidential level or higher in the retail field are pulling in average annual salaries exceeding $100,000.

When it comes to salaries for senior women, industrial corporations rank second, but also are in the $100,000-per-year league.

What Others Often Earn

From the success stories we've described, you'd think American salaries are shooting through the roof. Only for the standouts.

The median income for a full-time wage and salary worker was about $370 a week in 1987. Salary increases are averaging about 5 percent annually.

Lists such as the one that follows give clues, not definitive answers, about how much you might earn in a particular job. Numerous factors affect your pay, not the least of which is the profitability of the organization, how long you have held the job, the number of qualified people who would love to have your job, the region of the country and the industry where you work.

As an example of how widely the money can vary in an occupation, consider a self-employed gardener in posh Beverly Hills, Calif., who may earn $700 a week. Compare that sum to the $222 median weekly salary for gardeners noted in the salary sampling of wage and salary workers below.

The following federal government figures show 1986 median weekly earnings for selected occupations. Median means half the people in the occupation earn less, half earn more. The data were published by the Bureau of Labor Statistics, U.S. Department of Labor.

If you want a general idea of what an occupation's median pay is at the time you read this, add about 5 percent a year. This approach is not dead accurate but it's close enough for estimating what an occupation may pay when salary information is several years old.

Occupation	Median Weekly Pay
Construction	
Brickmason	$412
Carpet installer	$331
Carpenter	$348
Drywall installer	$374
Electrician	$473
Laborer	$301
Operating engineer	$410
Painter	$299
Plumber	$470
Insulation worker	$369
Roofer	$303
Health	
Dental assistant	$243
Dietitian	$336
Licensed practical nurse	$300
Pharmacist	$607
Radiologic (X-ray) technician	$383
Registered nurse	$460
Managerial and Professional	
Accountant & auditor	$478
Advertising manager	$680
Farm manager	$375
Financial manager	$584
Government administrator	$513
Personnel manager	$621
Purchasing manager	$633
Real estate manager	$375
Retail buyer	$397
School administrator	$610
Training specialist	$485
Underwriter	$500
Manufacturing	
Electronic equipment assembler	$271
Machinist	$419
Sheet metal worker	$432
Tool & die maker	$506
Mechanics and Repairers	
Aircraft mechanic	$505
Auto body repairer	$354
Auto mechanic	$324
Data processing equipment repairer	$514
Electronic repairer	$511
Heating, air-conditioning, refrigeration repairer	$390
Heavy equipment mechanic	$438
Industrial machinery repairer	$415
Millwright	$501
Office machine repairer	$376
Telephone installer	$568
Small engine repairer	$301
Office	
Bank teller	$231
Bill collector	$284
Bookkeeper	$287

(continued)

Occupation	Median Weekly Pay
Computer operator	$318
Date entry keyer	$277
Dispatcher	$347
Insurance adjuster	$356
Office supervisor	$404
Order clerk	$366
Personnel clerk	$317
Postal clerk	$479
Receptionist	$242
Secretary	$288
Sales (except retail)	
Advertising sales	$454
Business service sales	$453
Insurance sales	$418
Real estate sales	$457
Sales engineer	$492
Securities sales	$608
Sales (retail)	
Auto sales	$424
Cashier	$181
Clothing sales	$192
Counter clerk	$193
Door-to-door sales	$343
Furniture sales	$302
Hardware sales	$267
TV, stereo sales	$304
Service	
Baker	$292
Bartender	$214
Butcher	$299
Cook	$196
Correctional officer	$362
Firefighter	$464
Garbage collector	$238
Gardener	$222
Hairdresser	$208
Household child care worker	$ 91
Household servant	$147
Janitor	$247
Police officer	$558
Private guard	$266
Waiter, waitress	$164
Social Science and Communications	
Economist	$704
Editor	$425
Photographer	$392
Psychologist	$491
Recreation worker	$232
Social worker	$399
Teachers and Librarians	
College professor	$600
Elementary school teacher	$422
High school teacher	$437
Librarian	$423
Preschool teacher	$274
Technical	
Aerospace engineer	$708
Architect	$577
Biological and life scientist	$503
Chemical engineer	$721
Chemical technician	$459
Chemist	$601
Civil engineer	$618
Computer programmer	$519
Computer systems analyst	$631
Drafter	$412
Electrical engineer	$704
Engineering technician	$447
Mechanical engineer	$687
Operations researcher	$617

(continued)

Occupation	Median Weekly Pay	Occupation	Median Weekly Pay
Transportation		Taxicab driver	$272
Airplane pilot	$754	Truck driver, heavy	$371
Bus driver	$327	Truck driver, light	$281
Locomotive operator	$625		

(*Source:* The U.S. Department of Labor's Bureau of Labor Statistics)

Success Has Many Faces

Dressed in an expensively tailored designer suit, leather attaché case in hand, a confident-looking young woman strides toward a billion-dollar New York skyscraper. Hair squeaky clean and modishly styled, nails manicured and squared, her image plainly says: "I am a woman who matters."

Is she successful?

As a member of the sheriff's department, he works with violent street gangs in the barrios of Los Angeles. He dresses like a street person, drives a beater and often may be seen sitting on a park bench sharing a brown-bag lunch with a gang member. His image says: "I am a man who cares."

Is he successful?

What is success? An accomplishment that can be measured by status and material possessions? A state of mind?

In thinking about the meaning of success, consider both viewpoints.

Accomplishments That Can Be Measured

Rich and famous—it's the American dream. In that dream, success touches your shoulder with a sword, raising you to personal fortune, power and status.

People know who you are and what you can make happen. They look up to you, counting how many rungs you've climbed on life's ladder and guessing how many dollars you have in the bank. They know you shop at better stores, drive a foreign car that costs as much as a house, and have live-in help to keep your palace clean.

Perhaps you're a big executive in line for the company presidency, living in the best suburb, with two children in private schools, two VCRs and your own cabin cruiser.

Perhaps you're a high-tech entrepreneur whose company made $50 million its first year in business.

Perhaps you're a film superstar with homes in three countries and so much celebrity you can't walk down the street without being mobbed.

Or perhaps you haven't quite arrived at a lofty position but are a young urban professional—a yuppie—in hot pursuit of all the comforts and luxuries a thriving career can provide.

If you belong to the rich-and-famous school of success, begin your journey by realizing that it's okay to want what you want. Never feel guilty about what is a perfectly natural and healthy ambition.

Success: A State Of Mind

In this viewpoint, success is mainly a matter of personal inner fulfillment.

Holding an internal vision of success in no way rules out the possibility of stockpiling a personal fortune, but it does seem to be a characteristic of a special breed of Americans: the helpers, the caregivers.

To understand that not everyone goes for the gold in pursuing success, look at teachers, librarians, social workers, nurses, firefighters, military personnel, members of the clergy, and many, many others.

Test pilot Chuck Yeager was a modestly paid Air Force officer when he became the first flyer to break the sound barrier. The absence of a hefty monetary reward for his feat didn't dim inner feelings of accomplishment.

For personal rewards, career guidance colossus John Crystal suggests asking yourself two questions:

1. *What do I want to accomplish with my life?*
2. *How do I go about achieving my goal?*

If you realize your goal after knowing what you want to accomplish, that's success.

Success means obtaining your objectives and goals. These may vary from time to time, but you achieve success each time you reach one.

Others may or may not see you as a success, but you have the satisfaction of knowing you are living up to your promise.

Success: Uplinks and Downsides

By now you've figured out what we're driving at: Like beauty, success is in the eye of the beholder. Success is what you think it is, measurable achievement or state of mind.

Personally, we vote for a dose of both. Who wouldn't like to be earning $40,000 a year and living a fairly well-rounded life? On a grander scale, who wouldn't like to be the President of the United States, or a Nobel Peace Prize winner or one of the 10 richest people in the world? It's nice to have prominent spots on life's parade floats.

Face the possibility, though, that you may pay a high psychic price for success if it becomes naked ambition compulsively pursued.

Many young urban professionals are very serious about measuring their careers and about measuring material success. They have money and power, but some are reporting dissatisfaction, anxiety and physical problems. The trouble, says a Washington, D.C., psychoanalyst, is that young careerists want something more—fulfillment.

Dr. Douglas LaBier, author of *Modern Madness: The Emotional Fallout of Success* (Addison-Wesley), believes the trouble stems from conflict caused by compromises and trade-offs that must be made in pursuit of a smashingly successful career.

Conflicts? Compromises? This could mean working long hours at the expense of family and self. It could mean being cunning like a fox at the office to outdistance the competition at all costs. It could mean forgetting about personal attitudes to agree with the boss no matter what.

And when you're the boss there may be unpleasant trade-offs you never dreamed of. Do you recall in the earlier discussion of entrepreneurs we mentioned Tom McLaughlin, the man who made a mint servicing IBM equipment? In the struggle to establish a thriving business, McLaughlin and his wife separated. If he'd known his marriage would be a casualty, he says he'd never have gone into business for himself.

Throughout history conflicts have been interwoven with success. Older generations understood why they had to make sacrifices and compromises to be a big success at work. Why do young people have problems with that concept?

"Probably because of their psychological legacy," says LaBier. "In the '60s, there was an outpouring of desire to express oneself, to liberate oneself. In so doing, some people lost all sense of purpose and structure. Being a financial success was a bad thing.

"Then in the '70s, people wanted to be winners, to be successful. Now people still want to be successful but feel conflict about how much they've had to give up in the process," LaBier says.

So how are unhappy young careerists dealing with their frustrations?

LaBier, a senior fellow at the Project on Technology, Work and Character, says the coping process may be one of conspicuous accumulation of material goods.

Others take out their frustrations by adopting a consumerist approach toward relationships, handling people like commodities to be used and discarded.

Fulfillment. That's what everyone wants more of. One sure way to experience it is to know what you want and give chase. Each time you catch up to an objective or a goal, whammo! you're a success! And there's nothing better than a series of successes to put emotional substance in your life.

Please remember the benefits of state-of-mind success, as well as accomplishments that can be measured. It's not a lot of fun being a shark who spends all of each day circling prey.

Success: Win Some, Lose Some

Just as the best football players don't always gain yardage when they have possession of the ball, none of us plays a perfect "success game." We fumble and drop the ball once in a while.

Dwight David Eisenhower was no exception. The five-star general and President of the United States has been called the most successful man of the 20th century.

Even so, Ike occasionally stepped out of bounds in his charge toward greatness.

After being turned down by the Naval Academy, Ike was accepted at West Point. Not a spectacular student, he loved to play football but a knee injury destroyed his playing career. Ike was crushed. He lost interest in life at West Point, accumulated a mountain of demerits and graduated with a lackluster ranking of 61st in his class.

When informed by a West Point officer that he would not be recommended for a commission after graduation, Ike practically told the officer to take a hike, that it didn't matter—he might become a South American gaucho instead.

For reasons Eisenhower never understood, a few days later the officer reversed himself and offered the blasé cadet a commission. The rest is history.

Even champions have a few bad quarters during certain periods of their lives.

Can Success Make You a Better Person?

One of the world's all-time greatest writers thinks so:

> *The common idea that success spoils people by making them vain, egotistic, and self-complacent is erroneous; on the contrary it makes them, for the most part, humble, tolerant, and kind. Failure makes people bitter and cruel.*
>
> —W. Somerset Maugham

Today! Take Your First Step to Success!

Michael Korda, a successful author and editor, wrote an entire book on getting ahead. In *Success! How Every Man and Woman Can Achieve It* (Random House), Korda makes these points:

- "Once you understand that the will to succeed is natural, and that success is more pleasurable than failure, you will already have taken the first step toward becoming a success. You have to want it to get it, and you have to realize that if others can, so can you."
- "The techniques of success are available, and can be mastered by most people."
- "Learn the art of self-motivation. To succeed is to change, to grow, to *live*. Start living *today* and begin by taking the first courageous step—the step of deciding *now,* that *you too can be a success!*"

We agree with Michael Korda that winning is more fun than losing, that you can learn how to win, and that you may as well start now.

The success package belongs to those who unwrap it.

Work as a Philosophical Subject

Work is the core of most lives; who you are depends on what you do. Here's a quickie quiz to see how much you know about work.

The Quiz

1. Most people work for money.

   True False

2. The majority of people like jobs because they need other people.

   True False

3. Most people gain self-esteem from their jobs.

   True False

4. Work is activity that produces something of value for the worker and/or other people.

   True False

5. Work is still work whether it's paid or unpaid.

   True False

The Answers

All the statements are true.

People work basically for three reasons: money, social contact and self-esteem.

1. "The money is always there but the pockets change," said American writer Gertrude Stein. To get through this life paying for food, clothing, housing, medical care, education, transportation and a few luxuries, you'll need deep pockets. To many, money also has a symbolic value: It is a way of keeping score.

2. The majority of people are social creatures who dislike being alone. Sociologists say people want human contact for the feeling of belonging or loving. We need other people. We need to chat and interact with them. In a mobile society such as ours—where ties with family and friends may be weakened—the workplace may substitute for the community as we make acquaintances and friends at work.

3. Self-esteem means you feel good about yourself, and a big part of this rests on how you feel about your work. At its best, work is a way of relating to life and others. When you do a poor job, you feel as though you flunked a test. When you do a good job, you feel satisfaction and achievement. Your work defines you as a person. If you're not happy with what you're doing for approximately half your waking hours, you won't be happy with yourself.

4. Work creates value for society, as well as for yourself. Our civilization and standard of living are dependent upon a working society.

5. The efforts of unpaid volunteers and homemakers are valuable to society. Why shouldn't their activities be counted as work merely because money has not changed pockets?

Here we are at the bottom line: Why shouldn't you skip work to dance all night and sleep 'til noon? Have you ever heard of flat feet and bed sores?

Do Something You'd Do For Nothing

As you move through this book, zeroing in on your career choice, all the facts and feelings you'll uncover may at times leave you a bit confused.

Even idealists know that life's uncertain circumstances could make it necessary to forego your first choice of a career for one more attainable, but whenever you are trying to sort it all out, begin by following a beacon that has worked for countless career seekers:

Do something you'd do for nothing.

Do something you think will bring you satisfaction and the kind of pride in achievement that keeps you vitally absorbed in what you're doing. Do something that makes you glad to be alive. Do something you love to be doing.

Do something you'd do for nothing and you will have found a gateway to real and lifelong happiness.

SECTION TWO

A Positive Mind-Set Is Essential to Success

W*ithout a positive self-image, ability and hard work may not be enough* for future success.

How can you see yourself in the best light? Behavioral experts recommend "conceptualization" to people who have a strong desire to win.

Conceptualization? That's the big word we use to describe the imagery process that begins your career development.

In conceptualizing, you need to imagine who you want to be, what you want to do, where and with whom. A mental dress rehearsal helps you to set the stage for getting what you want in life.

This section calls to center stage the mind-set you must have to achieve career success and the role that risk taking plays in success.

Program Yourself for Success

To reach the top, you have to feel like a winner and envision yourself as a winner.

People who feel like losers and dim their minds with expectations of loss keep themselves from getting all they want out of life. They create their own negative destinies. No matter how much ability you have, if you do not fundamentally believe you have a chance of reaching a particular goal, you won't.

Moreover, some people unknowingly sabotage themselves day after day, year after year. Why? Because deep down they are convinced they are *not worthy* of achieving a goal. They do not value themselves as "okay" people. The reasons for this would require another book, but the point for career climbers is this:

If negative thoughts block the way, any goal is likely to remain beyond your grasp.

Choose to think about winning, not losing.

For instance, rather than worry, "I'll never get a good job," grab a sheet of paper and write down your sterling qualities; then think, "It is easy to sell myself to the right employer."

Athletes choose to think about winning, not losing. Cincinnati Reds player-manager Pete Rose told *Life* magazine about his winning ways:

> *I've played in more winning games than Joe DiMaggio played in games. And if I've played in more winning games than anybody in the history of baseball and if two and two isn't four, that's gotta make me the biggest winner in the history of sports.*

Rose's attitude is right on target.

Anyone who plays sports knows that a lack of self-confidence can put you on the short end of the score. The famous Notre Dame football coach Knute Rockne is reported to have said, "Show me a good loser and I'll show you a loser. Give me 11 lousy losers and I'll give you a national championship football team."

A strong self-image as a winner is vital to success. Choose to think well of yourself.

Concerning your goal: Remember that somebody has probably done it before and there's little reason why you can't do it now.

Winning Starts in Your Head

When we say that achieving success requires you not only to feel like a winner, but also to visualize yourself winning, we are speaking of "conceptualizing" success.

Conceptualizing, to us, is the opening round in career development. Blending fantasy and fact, conceptualizing is using your imagination to float pictures through your head about what you would like to be doing with your life in the years ahead.

A point of caution: Do not confuse conceptualizing with daydreaming. Both contain an element of fantasy, but daydreaming is *unfocused* imagination. Daydreaming is only wishful thinking, not a commitment to achieving a goal. Unlike daydreaming, conceptualizing is rooted in reality.

Conceptualizing is easy. It is like producing a film in your mind. You imagine a winning script and mentally shoot the physical action. You do it all in your head.

Suppose you want to be a successful home builder. Your script calls for the development of 200 homes on a sunny hillside. Picture yourself in these scenes:

Finding the land; buying it; hiring an architect; ordering cement poured; watching the framing going up; beaming with pleasure when the houses are ready to market; selling the first house; selling the last house; and smiling all the way to the bank.

Here's another example of using conceptualization: On the way to a job interview, imagine yourself in the role of the interviewee and mentally go through the paces of how you want the interview to progress. See yourself entering the interviewer's office, smiling, shaking hands, and making small talk to establish rapport. Concentrate on details as well as the large picture. A detail would be to visualize yourself speaking without your voice cracking. The large picture concludes with a job offer.

That's all there is to it—your mental movie, a form of thought that helps you reach your goal.

Superstar diver Greg Louganis—who has won two Olympic gold medals and an impressive number of U.S. national titles—agrees.

According to a story in *Reader's Digest,* he learned how to conceptualize at an early age—not in diving, but in dancing!

"My teacher would play the music we were to dance to," Louganis says. "She'd say, 'OK, now do the dance in your head.' If I missed a step in my head, I'd have to go back and repeat the exercise."

The mental skill transferred to Louganis' diving. "If I'm preparing for a major competition, I'll put some internal music on and go through a list of my dives, doing each one perfectly."

The more you conceptualize, the easier it will be to marshall the inner resources you need to be successful.

You can conceptualize any time, any place, including life's idle moments: traffic signals, movie theater lines, elevators, fitness walks, supermarket checkout lines, holding on the telephone.

Words other than conceptualization can be used to describe the imagery process—visualization, mental imagery, and success imagination, for example. Call it what you like, as long as you understand how it works and use the technique to start building your glowing future.

Conceptualizing Helps With Risk Taking

Fear of risk, more than any other single trait, binds people to boring lives. No adventure, no hills and valleys, no pains or gains.

Psychologists say that fear of risk is really fear of failing. It is fearing that in the distance between your reach and your grasp, something will go wrong.

Why are you afraid? The culprit is change. Change frames every picture of your life: maturing, studying, working, staying healthy, having relationships, traveling, the weather, technology—everything. Change is ever present and with it comes certain uncertainty—and risk.

Having some fear of risk is reasonable, mature and expected. A sense of caution when it comes to taking risks shows you are in robust mental health.

Still, we can use conceptualization techniques to desensitize ourselves to a paralyzing fear of risk taking. By mentally role-playing risks, we can size them up, become familiar with their range of options, uncover their frightening mysteries, and eventually put the risks into proper perspective.

Train your mind to consciously focus on the "risk of the day." Think it through. Imagine how the risk might work out and how you want it to work out. The more you get into the habit of conceptualizing risk taking, the more comfortable you will feel with taking real-life chances.

Conceptualizing the best that can happen and the worst that can happen puts a risk into focus.

Once you internalize the fact that there is no place on earth where time stands still, or where

you can hide from risk, the idea of risk taking becomes less threatening. You'll understand that successful people continually take informed risks.

In your own life, you often do things you are fearful about. Remember when you tried to break the school's high-jump record, or asked someone whom you really didn't know very well for a date?

While there are no iron-clad certainties where risk is involved, as Henry Ford II is reported to have said:

Nobody can really guarantee the future. The best we can do is size up our chances, calculate the risks involved, estimate our ability to deal with them, and make our plans with confidence.

More Ways to Master Risk Taking

Since risks are in the air we breathe, here are eight guidelines to help you deal with them in an informed, logical manner.

1. Consider the odds, visualize alternatives. When you face a risk, develop the habit of calculating the odds for success. Ask yourself: "Are my chances favorable or not so good?"

When you decide the odds are against you, either bypass the risk entirely, or visualize alternative routes of action that could bring similar rewards.

As a simple illustration, suppose you need a jacket and find one you like on sale for $75. The sale ends today. You have no credit cards, but you do have $30 in your wallet and $20 in your checking account. Your paycheck will arrive tomorrow, but it's drawn on an out-of-state bank and your bank's policy is to wait seven days before crediting such checks to customers' accounts.

Should you write a check for the jacket, hoping that somehow the check won't bounce? No. Your check probably will not clear the bank.

There are other ways to handle your problem. You can ask the manager whether the store has a "layaway" plan. If so, will a $10 deposit hold the jacket until your paycheck is credited to your account? Another alternative is to wait until you save sufficient money to buy a jacket that you like.

Always make a rational assessment of your chances, and, when necessary, visualize alternatives.

2. Plan ahead. F. Lee Bailey, one of America's most prominent lawyers, shares rules he learned as a Navy pilot. In his book, *To Be a Trial Lawyer* (John Wiley & Sons), he says members of his training class who survived to become aviators thoroughly learned the following rules.

Rule 1
An airplane is a wondrous instrument of motion, and if in your thinking and handling of the controls you stay ahead of it, it will take you from place to place safely and very well.

Rule 2
If you get behind in thinking and handling an airplane, it will surely kill you.

Rule 3
If most of the time you are trying hard just to stay even as you control an airplane, at some point it will get ahead of you—now apply Rule 2.

The point, Bailey explains, is that "thinking ahead and anticipating what may happen next are vital elements of success in many human endeavors. Flying is one of them. Trying lawsuits is another."

Risk taking is still another.

3. Take only necessary risks. Always ask yourself: "Is this risk necessary?" You may find that you need not assume it.

A classic example of the unnecessary risk is the act of passing another car on a two-lane hill when the driver can't see over the crest. If chance puts an oncoming vehicle into your path, you pay a severe price for taking an unnecessary gamble.

Avoid taking risks that cannot benefit you.

4. Risk only as much as you can afford to lose. How much you can afford to lose is a murky, subjective question that varies with the individual and with the circumstances.

We're not talking about losing the rent money in a poker game, but about going only as far out on a limb as you can while maintaining rational respect for the consequences.

The biggest danger of risk taking is that you may lose sight of how much you realistically can lose. History is rife with instances of people losing more than they could afford in stock deals and greed-based ventures. ("Invest now and double your money in three months.")

A more personal example of risking unwisely is the case of Adrian A., a young executive who wants a job promotion. Her choice of strategy is to look for another job.

Adrian has two choices. She can try to keep her search quiet, fearing her employer will fire her if word gets back, or she can leak the news about her search, hoping her employer will offer her a better position.

The second choice holds the higher risk; is it more than Adrian can afford to lose?

The probable answer is "yes," the risk is too high. Unless her skills are in short supply, Adrian should have another job offer in her pocket before her boss discovers she's on the market.

Otherwise, if the boss gets wind of her search, becomes annoyed and fires her, Adrian suffers a setback.

While there are plenty of exceptions to every generalization, it's safer to keep quiet about a job hunt when you are employed. To publicize it may cause you to risk more than you can afford to lose.

5. Be sure the reward is worth the risk. A woman in a Midwestern state was arrested for writing $600,000 worth of bad checks. She used the money to buy tickets for the state lottery. She never won a dime.

Most people would say she risked too much for too little. Her action was not "risk-effective."

The size of the reward always should dictate the degree of risk. In the early 1800s, President Thomas Jefferson risked war with France, and conflict with the Congress, by insisting that the United States must have the nearly 830,000 square miles of land between the Mississippi River and the Rocky Mountains, stretching from the Gulf of Mexico to the Canadian border.

Tough talk, courtly diplomacy and $15 million were required to strike the deal that became known as the Louisiana Purchase. Through it, the U.S. took title to land that eventually formed all or parts of 15 states.

Jefferson stuck his neck out, but he was playing for historically high stakes.

When in doubt about whether you should go ahead with an idea, remember: A rational risk does not dwarf the prize.

6. Leave the dares to fools. As a child, you probably heard the taunt, "I dare you to do it." Walk a high ledge, swim a river, climb a tree.

Perhaps as a child you prided yourself on never turning down a dare. You're not a child anymore. And you must learn to recognize a dare when you hear or see one.

A grown-up version of a dare may sound like this: "You would never tell the boss how you really feel about him," or "You haven't got the nerve to tell that professor what a jerk she is."

Dares are a variety of unnecessary risks that fools take. Don't fall for them.

7. Take only smart risks. What is known as the "Icarus complex" dramatically illustrates nonthinking actions.

Icarus is the young man in Greek mythology who was told by his father never to soar higher than his parent. Shrugging off Pop's warning, Icarus strapped on wings of feathers held together by wax. As he neared the sun, the wax melted and he plummeted back to earth with a bone-crunching thud. Goodbye, Icarus.

Those who take Icarian risks seem to do so with consistency. They believe they always are on the verge of making it big—"I've got a fabulous deal cooking" or "My friend is going to get me a job in a film studio, any day now." Somehow their ships never seem to come in.

What's wrong? Are they simply unlucky? More likely, the Icarus crowd live on a diet of constant hope and rare achievements because their style of operating is to make impulse decisions based on few facts.

They never learn that it requires *more than the mere willingness to take a risk* for the risk to pan out.

They got the correct message that those who take risks in life achieve the greatest rewards. What they failed to get was the other part of the message. Additional factors are in the success equation—such as research, effort, judgment, timing, resources and follow-through. And so losers leap without looking, taking dumb risks.

Don't emulate Icarus. Allot the dumb risks to mythological figures.

8. Bypass risks for egotism. Some people turn risks into failures because their motivations stem from an unusually strong desire to show the world who's pulling the strings. Two illustrations of taking risks for egotism are:

- The German dictator whose view of himself and his nation as being invincible led to World War II.
- The American president who believed his power was great enough to cover up Watergate.

And can you recall the tale of Rumpelstiltskin? The big-headed little rascal wagered high stakes (a child) that the heroine of the story could not guess his name. Then he tramped into a nearby forest and began singing his name in verse, mistakenly assuming that no one could overhear him. The self-centered elf lost his bet.

One final example of the folly of taking a risk that stems from being too sure of yourself: A story is told of the Union Army officer who during the Civil War stood on the front lines and said disparagingly of the Confederate marksmen: "Those idiots couldn't hit the side of a ba..."

The Lighter Side of Risk

Do you know the story about the 250-pound, tough-as-nails Army sergeant who opened a valentine signed by all but a few privates in his platoon?

The sergeant, with no sign of being pleased, shouted, "Okay, all you creeps who signed this card—give me 50 push-ups."

All the "creeps" hit the floor and complied with the order. When they finished, the sergeant bellowed in a voice that could cut steel, "Now, all you chicken livers who were afraid to sign, get down and give me 100 push-ups."

A little risk can be an energy saver.

How Do You Rate on Risk Taking?

Here's an activity to help you get a handle on where you stand when it comes to taking a chance. This is a fun test and there are no right or wrong answers.

Check Your R.T.Q. (Risk-Taking Quotient)

Circle the letter in front of the choice you probably would make for each situation.

1. *Dating for major social event:*
   A. You would invite a person you enjoy and feel sure would accept your offer.
   B. There's a real stunner you've always had a crush on. You'd love to ask this person but you're not sure the stunner would accept and you don't know what kind of an evening you'd have. You would invite the stunner.
2. *Buying a car:*
   A. You can afford to buy a two-year-old model that belongs to your friend's father. You know

it was well-maintained and would be a good buy. It is a staid model that doesn't fire you with enthusiasm. You would choose this car.

B. You spot an ad in the newspaper for a flashy four-year-old sports model with 50,000 miles. You look at it and fall in love. It costs $3,000 more than the other car but you might be able to swing it if your parents will loan you some currency. The guy who owns it is moving to another job where he will have a company car. The mechanic you take the car to says it appears to be in good shape. You would choose this car.

3. *Getting a job:*

A. You have been offered a summer job you can do with one hand tied behind your back. It pays $5 an hour. You need the money for next year's tuition and this job would pay just enough to get you through the year with no frills. You would take this job.

B. You have been offered a summer job you are not certain you can handle. You could build your contacts network because the job offers exposure to many people. The pay is minimum wage, but you have the chance to earn a $2,000 bonus for high performance. The bonus would make it possible to have money for fun things, rather than just squeak by on a survival standard of living. You would take this job.

4. *Accepting invitation to weekend party:*

A. You have been invited to a weekend house party with some old friends you know well. You expect the weekend will be pleasant, if bland. You would accept the invitation.

B. On the same weekend, you have been invited to go white-water rafting with a group you could describe as friendly acquaintances. The group is comprised of popular people at your school—it's a group you've secretly wished you could be a part of. The problem is you don't know whether you would have a marvelous time, or would feel out of place. You would accept this invitation.

5. *Choosing a class:*

A. You need a specific course to complete requirements for your major field of study. One class is taught by a professor you know well. You feel confident that if you work hard, you can pull an A. You would choose this class.

B. Another class in the same course is taught by an adjunct professor who is a vice president of a large company. The VP has taught the course several times before and previous students say she's a tough taskmaster but fair—and really knows the material. You would have to work yourself ragged to keep up and might not get as high a grade. On the plus side, you probably would learn more current data and make a good contact. You would choose this class.

6. *Keep or quit your job:*

A. You are 25 years old and unmarried. You have been employed by the same firm for three years and have received several promotions. You like the company and the bosses. With continued regular promotions, you should be making $33,000 annually in another five years. You have just been offered a promotion that will pay $24,000. You would accept the promotion and stay with the company.

B. You are offered a job with a new high technology firm at an annual salary of $31,000. The firm is 2,000 miles away in an area of the country you know little about. The company will pay your moving expenses. The company president says that if all goes well, within five years you could be earning $45,000. You would accept this job offer.

7. *Investing money:*

A. You have managed to save an extra $2,500. You can invest it in a savings institution for a return of 6 percent. You would know exactly how much money you would earn on your investment each year. You would invest in this institution.

B. You can invest your $2,500 in a variable rate mutual fund. It is now paying 9 percent interest but because the rate fluctuates with the economy, it could dip well below 6 percent. You would invest in the mutual fund.

8. *Buying rental property:*

A. You are 25, single, have saved and inherited from a doting aunt a total of $20,000, and need a tax write-off. You have found a house in the suburbs that you could rent to others for enough money to pay the mortgage. It is in a stable neighborhood and in good physical shape. You would buy this property.

B. You have seen another property in an older city neighborhood that a growing number of young professionals say is a "great investment opportunity." Some have already bought, renovated and moved into the houses. The house you've seen needs work but you could do much of it yourself. If the neighborhood continues to be upgraded, the potential rent would be much higher than the suburban property. On the other hand, a few naysayers believe the rising potential of the city neighborhood is temporary. You would buy this property.

9. *Going back to school:*

A. You are 35, married and have two children. You are successful in your field but have gone as far as you can without an advanced degree. You like your job and don't see that working another 25 years or so would be distasteful at the level you now occupy. You would stay as you are.

B. In the same circumstances, with your family supporting any decision you make, you decide to quit work for two years, get your advanced degree and hope that it will bring more money and higher-level jobs. Your spouse would have to support the family while you are in school, plus you would have to borrow by taking a second mortgage on your home. If nothing in the job market changes, the payoff could be terrific—but the market could change. You would go back to school.

10. *Deciding when to say "yes":*

A. You are a new college graduate. You have narrowed potential employers to three companies. The Black Co. is your first choice by far. After that, you rank the Green and White companies equally. You receive an offer from the White Co. You are asked for an immediate decision. You fear you will lose out on the offer if you wait until you hear from the Black Co. You would accept White's offer.

B. Under the same circumstances, you realize you could ask the people at the White Co. for a few more days to consider the offer. You realize you could call the managers at the Black Co., let it be known that you have another offer and ask if Black has come to a decision about you. You would gamble that you can keep the White Co. on the string and "force" an offer from the Black Co.

Scoring: To repeat, there are no right and wrong answers. This quiz merely helps you to recognize your R.T.Q. Here's how to score.

Give yourself one point for each "A" decision. Give yourself two points for each "B" decision.

If you score 10 points, you like to play it safe. You may want to try to boost your risk-taking comfort level a bit so that you do not miss out on good opportunities.

If you score between 13 and 15, you are willing to take chances, to reach out and grab opportunities as you see them.

If you score between 16 and 20, you are a born risk-taker. Be sure your risk taking is rational rather than emotional.

Last Thoughts

You can see why mind-set makes a big difference in success. Accomplished though she is, Sally Ride never could have become America's first woman astronaut if she had suffered from a negative mental attitude or a poor self-image.

Anyone who doubts the value of conceptualization can think about Jack Nicklaus, the highest-earning golfer in the sport's history. Nicklaus uses conceptualization techniques extensively to see himself winning tournaments. He visualizes each shot he makes. He "sees" the ball sailing down the fairway to the target spot. And, like a movie in his mind, he mentally watches as the ball plops into the hole.

What can you win by taking risks? After saving and then rebuilding Chrysler Corporation against all odds, Lee Iacocca became the nation's hottest industrial folk hero.

Our grandparents used to talk about somebody botching a job because "his heart wasn't in it." Whether you choose to call it heart, mind-set, positive self-image or anything else that describes the development of your inner resources, how the world treats you begins with how you approach it.

SECTION THREE

Outside Forces that May Affect Your Future

T*his section identifies potent career shifts taking place in the United* States. Going beyond merely identifying trends, it encourages readers to practice the art of critical analysis in applying trends to themselves.

Trend watching is discussed in three main categories: *labor market* (people), *job market* (jobs) and *workplace changes.* Included are such factors as the coming youth labor shortage, technology and the middle class, the world marketplace, drug testing, comparable worth, telecommuting and the emphasis on being a service-producing economy.

The section concludes with advice for readers whose career years may be riddled with uncertainty.

Trend Watching—What Does It All Mean?

The president of a group of bird watchers once asked a farmer if the bird lovers could roam over his land to pursue their wildlife studies. A little suspicious, the farmer asked for more information. "What exactly is it you want to do?" the farmer questioned.

"We want to watch birds," replied the leader.

Still not satisfied, the farmer tilted his head and asked:

"Watch 'em for what?"

It's the same with trends. How many times have you been admonished to pay attention and stay current with what's happening in the nation and the world? Plenty of times, we bet.

The problem is, you may not always be sure of what you're watching for. In this section, we'll help you to find out. As you read the following sampler of key trends affecting careers, you'll notice that they are divided into three categories:

1. *labor market*

2. *job market*

3. *workplace changes*

For the first several trends listed in each category, we give examples of the types of questions you should ask yourself. Then we give examples of the answers you might come up with. These are only examples. You might think of other questions and answers that we do not list.

Soon you'll get the hang of figuring out ways that various trends could affect you.

At this point, you should practice your new skill. Every place you see "Q. (your question)" and "A. (your answer)," think about how the trend could impact on your life.

Here are selected trends.

Trend Watching in the Labor Market (People)

A Youth Shortage Is Coming

Population statistics show that fewer young people are passing through the labor supply pipeline—one-fourth fewer than in recent years. The trend will last another decade. Some observers say the shrinking pool of young workers signals a bright new era of opportunity for those starting their careers.

Analysis

Q. With one-fourth fewer young workers to compete against, will I find it easier to get a job? Does the youth shortage mean I don't need to become qualified through education and training?

A. Getting the first job or two may or may not be easier for me than for people who started their careers in the 1970s. Everything I read and hear tells me that people with no skills will find jobs scarce. A TV newscast reported that it is becoming more and more difficult for Americans to find high pay for eye-hand-foot skills. Competition is increasing from immigrants. Jobs are being lost to workers overseas. Some workers of the future will be computers. All these trends mean that although there will be fewer young workers to go up against, overall labor may be in plentiful supply.

Q. Does the smaller number of young workers mean I'll get promoted faster than normal?

A. No. I talked to my family and they say promotions depend on many things. Their generation—the baby boom generation born between 1946 and 1964—was huge. By now the older baby boomers have most of the boss jobs. Using simple arithmetic, I figure the boomers will keep clogging management promotion ladders until the year 2010.

Q. Does the shortage of young workers mean I can expect a higher beginning salary?

A. Depending on the job situation, pay scales may be higher for me than they used to be for beginners. But I read in *Career World* magazine that many new jobs are in service industries that pay about $7,000 less a year than jobs in manufacturing. It's obvious I'd better develop skills in demand if I want to bring in the bucks.

Women Shake up the Working World

The tidal wave of women leaving home for a job is the single most important change that has happened in the American labor market. Women now make up 44 percent of the work force; by the year 2000, their share will increase to 47 percent. By the same year, 60 percent of working-age women will be at work. In less than a generation the size of the female labor force has more than doubled. Today the majority of working-age women have jobs. More than half of mothers with children one year old or younger are in the labor force.

Analysis

Q. (For females) Should I plan on working rather than staying home to raise a family?

A. Yes. I have aptitudes, interests and talents that go beyond homemaking. I may change my mind and not work, but then again, my husband could become disabled or die and I would need to support my family. My counselor says a study shows that 20 percent of working women are separated, divorced or widowed, and 25 percent are single. That means nearly half are supporting themselves.

Q. (For males) Would having a working wife—rather than one who is a full-time homemaker—change my life or career?

A. Yes. A working wife obviously would give us two incomes and we could afford more luxuries. If my wife or I were offered a good job in a distant city, we would have a tough decision to make about whether to relocate. If we had children, I might have to take time off from work to share duties such as taking them to the doctor.

Minority Youth Ranks Grow and Grow

Soon one out of five new people in the labor force will be a minority youth. New Americans, mostly Hispanic immigrants, when added to the high-birthrate population of black Americans, will give the U.S. a steadily rising percentage of racial minorities, according to the Kiplinger Washington Editors, Inc. Minority youth has a long history of high unemployment. The youth labor shortage can be a big opportunity to turn that record around *if* more education and training opportunities for inner-city youth become available and are capitalized on.

Analysis

Q. (For minority individuals) Does this trend mean it'll be easier for me to get a good job than it was for my parents?

A. My teacher says yes and no. Yes, in the sense that after 20 years of equal opportunity emphasis, employers are accustomed to seeing minority applicants. Also, everybody has a better chance when there's less competition for jobs. No, if I do not obtain job skills that employers require.

Immigrants Swell U.S. Labor Force

Immigrants will represent the largest share of the increase in the population and the work force since World War I, according to government figures. The United States offers very attractive opportunities to immigrants. International events may again require the U.S. to take in political refugees. While precise estimates are not possible, about 450,000 immigrants (750,000 if illegals are included) are expected to enter the country each year over the next 15 years. This would add 4 to 6.8 million immigrants to the work force by the turn of the century.

Analysis

Q. (your question) ______________________________

____

A. (your answer) ______________________________

____

____

____

____

____

American Workers Face Middle-Age Spread

With the decline of young workers, the average age of the work force will march steadily upwards. By the year 2000, the big group will be in their peak working years, 35-54, making it harder for your generation to win promotions. An aging labor force will be more experienced and thus more productive. At the same time, there will be a growing need for early retraining as some occupations move in and others disappear.

Analysis

Q. (your question) ______________________________

____

A. (your answer) ______________________________

____

____

____

____

____

Workers in "World Shoe" Don't Know What to Do

The nursery rhyme about the old woman in a shoe with too many kids to care for reminds us that our planet is becoming crowded with would-be workers. World population forecasts suggest a massive increase in the labor force is taking place. The explosion of the world population is likely to lead to hot international competition for jobs, especially between the developed and less-developed nations. Will there be enough jobs to go around the world? As with children in the nursery rhyme, will too many workers get broth without bread?

Analysis

Q. (your question) ______________________________

____

A. (your answer) ______________________________

____

____

____

____

Jobs Will Change

Young people will work in industries and occupations markedly different from those in which their parents are working today. Some forecasters believe there won't be enough work to go around as new technologies catch on. Others, looking at population changes, believe our nation won't have enough people to do all the jobs. Some say our factories will nearly disappear and that jobs of the future will be dull and low paying. Others say new industries and opportunities will spring up to replace those lost. It is impossible to know precisely where we are heading, but there's little argument about one aspect: *The nature of work will change.* It is not so much that jobs are becoming high tech, but that technology will alter how most jobs are performed. In the future, a house painter may use a robot for routine spraying. Auto mechanics already consult computers to diagnose car troubles. Bank tellers leave routine transactions to teller machines while they use their own judgment in deciding whether a payroll check is a forgery.

Analysis

Q. (your question)____________________

____

A. (your answer)____________________

____

____

____

____

Trend Watching in the Job Market (Jobs)

Most U.S. Job Growth Is in Service Industries

Jobs for Americans will continue to shift from goods-producing industries (manufacturing, mining, construction and agriculture) to the service-producing sector (transportation, trade, finance, services and government). The Bureau of Labor Statistics predicts that virtually all U.S. job growth between now and the 21st century will be in the service-producing sector, which already accounts for nearly three-quarters of all American employment. The U.S. is not unique. Other major industrial nations are headed toward a service-producing economy too. Service-producing sectors now account for more than 6 out of 10 jobs in France and Japan.

Analysis

Q. Should I avoid a career in manufacturing?

A. Not really. I read a *Business Week* magazine article that says the "battered U.S. manufacturing sector is fighting back" and that a leaner, more efficient industrial base is looking good. What I will do is look for a well-managed company in an industry that appeals to me—*if* I decide manufacturing is where my heart is.

Are Service Jobs Tight With a Buck?

From *Career Opportunities News:* "There is growing concern by economists over the caliber of the nine million new jobs created in the U.S. since 1980. Many knew that higher-paying manufacturing jobs were being reduced and service industry positions were growing. But few realized the relatively low salary levels for most of the new jobs." Nearly 60 percent of new jobs are in a services category that includes hotels, office services and allied health, where the average annual pay is about $14,000. Nearly one-third of new jobs are in retail trade, where the average wage is less than $10,000 annually. This means only one out of 10 new jobs are in the better-paying fields.

Analysis

Q. If I go into a service job in hotels, office services, allied health or retail trade, will I earn a modest salary?

A. Probably yes, if I don't find a way to rise to a management job or start my own company.

The Middle Class: An Endangered Species?

Some observers declare that America is losing its middle class due to several key developments. Foreign imports and new technology may be creating two classes of people—the highly trained, well-paid technical workers at the top, and the moderately trained, low-paid people who have jobs in services at the bottom. Other observers disagree with this premise, pointing out that the income of the middle class has remained stable. They assert there is no solid evidence that the middle class is shrinking. There is probably merit in both views; the middle class may become smaller but not disappear. Another possibility is one of timing. Middle class shrinkage may occur 25 or 30 years from now rather than at the turn of the century.

Analysis

Q. If the people are right who say that "Middle America" is about to become extinct, what can I do to protect myself? I may not rise to top management levels, but I don't want to be a laborer either. Maybe I should go into computers, even though this field is not one that greatly interests me. What should I do?

A. I'll compromise. I'll choose a field that's interesting, but I'll also learn to use a computer. My counselor says many jobs will require computer skills.

Business Goes International

Our economy is becoming more international because nations depend on each other for materials, technology, capital, labor, imports, exports—the full range of economic factors. Jobs go to the nations offering the cheapest workers capable of doing the required task.

Analysis

Q. I want to be a manager. Will I work overseas?

A. After checking out this question in my school media center, I discovered that employers tend to hire citizens of the country in which the work is done. I probably couldn't get hired to work overseas unless I had a special ability. I haven't decided whether to major in international business—I want to interview several graduates of international business programs before I make that decision.

Q. Should I major in a foreign language?

A. I was thinking about it until I found out that the only jobs for which foreign language is the number one qualification are in teaching, translating and interpreting. Instead, I'll minor in a foreign language, or become fluent in one. That way my bilingual ability will be a plus in whatever field I choose. I hear that Japanese, Chinese, Russian or Spanish would be a good choice.

When Robots Apply for Jobs

Robots look nothing like the cuddlesome humanoids of the movies. Typically they are gawky mechanical arms with rotating and clutching devices, doing such routine duties as spray painting or spot welding. The robotics industry in America hasn't moved as quickly as expected, and an increasing share of the robotics market is going to Japanese and some European producers. Robots are expensive. Robots will become more sophisticated. Robots will become widely used as companies seek ways to boost productivity. Estimates vary as to how many human workers robots will replace. One study projects about 4 percent of the blue-collar work force will be replaced by robots by 1995. Others say that industry can't come up with the many billions of dollars required.

Analysis

Q. (your question) ______________________________

____

A. (your answer) ______________________________

____

____

____

____

Talk of a Leisure Society Is Overworked

Despite a lot of talk about an upcoming leisure society where machines do the work and people aren't bothered by blue Mondays, Americans in the decades ahead are likely to be very interested in careers. Work and its rewards appear to be in the human genes. A recent Department of Labor survey reports that most workers, if given a choice for change, would rather work more hours and make more money. A preference for a shorter workweek was expressed by only 6 percent of men and 9 percent of women. Even among higher-paid workers, only about 10 percent of men and 20 percent of women were willing to trade hours of work—and the income linked to them—for additional leisure. George Bernard Shaw observed, "Perpetual holiday is a good working definition of hell." Was he right?

Analysis

Q. (your question) ______________________

____

A. (your answer) ______________________

____

____

____

____

____

High Tech: Fast Growth, Few Jobs

High technology is seen by many career seekers as the wave to catch. But, relatively speaking, there won't be many high-tech jobs. New high-tech industries will account for only a fraction of total U.S. employment by the end of the century. Remember, high tech depends on automation and automation replaces human labor. Those who capture the high-tech wave will have solid training in science or engineering as a base to which management or other skills are added. All the headlines for new jobs—gene broker, laser engineer, local network technician, robotic mining supervisor, hypersonic pilot, moon base ranger—should not hide the fact that we still will need good repairers, clerks, doctors, teachers and other familiar workers.

Analysis

Q. (your question) ______________________

____

A. (your answer) ______________________

____

____

____

____

Union Jobs Lose Popularity

Unions by the year 2000 will be shadows of their earlier selves—they've been losing members steadily as the economy shifts structural gears. Membership dipped by three million between 1980 and 1985; overall employment rose by seven million during the same period. Union membership is now about 18 percent of the work force. Some analysts expect it to drop to 12 percent or less by the 21st century. Although unions won't be invited to as many employment parties as they once were, professional organizations (for lawyers, doctors and so forth) may act like unions if competition diminishes their members' paycheck power.

Analysis

Q. (your question) ______________________

____

A. (your answer) ______________________

____

____

____

____

Job Growth Spurred by Geography

In general, there'll be greater job growth in the South and West and slower gains in the Midwest. For college graduates in particular, a Michigan State University study says the sunniest prospects for new college graduates are in the Southwest and Northeast, and the cloudiest are in the Northwest. (Hot job mecca or no, beware of geographic areas that depend on a single firm or industry for jobs. If the business goes in the tank, you could find yourself living in a ghost town, trying in vain to unload your house for a fair market price.)

Analysis

Q. (your question) ____________________

____

A. (your answer) ____________________

____

____

____

____

____

Prospects for College Grads Vary

When corporate recruiters prowl college campuses, they usually extend a welcoming hand faster to graduates in engineering and business than to graduates in fine arts and social sciences. Job prospects for graduates vary by major. But even in such high-demand fields as engineering, trends change from year to year. Mechanical engineers were hot in 1984, but at the bottom of the wanted list for engineers by 1986. Petroleum engineers were golden before the oil market went to pot, but many of them had a hard time finding jobs by 1986.

Analysis

Q. (your question) ____________________

____

A. (your answer) ____________________

____

____

____

____

____

Small Business Mania Is Everywhere

Entrepreneurship (ahn-trah-prah-NUHR-ship) is for those who put taking risks ahead of taking paychecks. In simple terms, being an entrepreneur means running your own business or being self-employed. The trend is sweeping the country. It is the small independent businesses that are creating most of the new jobs in the economy; at the same time, employment in the largest industrial corporations is falling. Women are flocking to entrepreneurial ventures. Some three million women are self-employed, a 75 percent gain in 10 years. Women-owned firms are the fastest-growing segment of small business.

Analysis

Q. (your question) ____________________

____

A. (your answer) ____________________

____

____

____

____

____

Part-Time Jobs Are Popping Up Everywhere

Nearly four million people now work part time. Short-hours work grew more rapidly than full-time employment over the past two decades, increasing to 17 percent of those employed in 1986. Not everybody is thrilled about the chance to work fewer hours. It's difficult to find a full-time job in a supermarket, for instance. The markets prefer to hire part-timers, partially because they don't have to pay the employee benefits that full-time workers receive. Finding a responsible, high-paying part-time job continues to be a challenge. Those who accomplish it often start out with a 40-hour-week commitment and talk the boss into letting them cut back on time. Probably to pay bills, more people are moonlighting (holding two jobs) than ever before. Many try to fit in a second job with a hobby—an art lover works in a framing shop, a movie buff in a video store.

Analysis

Q. (your question) ______________________

____

A. (your answer) ______________________

____

____

____

____

Temporary Jobs Are With Us Permanently

Workers employed by temporary-help agencies are a rapidly growing area of employment. Their numbers almost doubled from 1982 to 1985; now there are more than 735,000 workers in the temporary-help industry. Those who work as "temps" are likely to be young and to work part time. Many are women and blacks who are concentrated in clerical jobs and industrial help assignments. The largest temporary-help firms have offices across the country and some employees sign up in one city for jobs in another locale to which they'd like to relocate.

Analysis

Q. (your question) ______________________

____

A. (your answer) ______________________

____

____

____

____

Trend Watching in the Workplace

Technology Is Reinventing the Workplace

Are you ready for glasers (nuclear lasers) that rocket an almost infinite number of messages around the world by satellite? Fifth-generation computers with artificial intelligence? New biological tools that grow human insulin in the laboratory? Technological change—often involving the use of microprocessors, information technology, computer-controlled offices and genetic engineering—is on the upswing. All these technological advances won't make the human worker obsolete. But rapid turnover—with some people changing jobs five or six times during their worklives—and the remaking of industries will require workers to adjust more quickly and more often.

Analysis

Q. Will I have to accept change as a constant force in my life?

A. Yes. I can't afford to doze off and get stuck in a rut.

Comparable Worth: The Battle Rages On

Women have depressed wages, earning about $7 for every $10 paid to men. Women's advocates say the gap is due to sex-segregated job classification systems that reward men's work at higher pay rates. The comparable pay concept means equal pay, not for the same job, but for work of comparable value. It means ending systems that pay nurses less than tree trimmers and secretaries less than truck drivers. Comparable worth supporters say pay should be based on the job's worth to the employer as opposed to the job's market rate. Several states have passed comparable worth legislation but limited it to state employees. State employees in Washington scored a big comparable worth victory in court, but it was later overturned in a federal appeals court. The issue is far from being decided. Unions will push it; employers will resist.

Analysis

Q. If comparable worth were to become the law of the land and there were no sex-segregated job classification systems, which occupations would pay the best?

A. Probably those requiring the most demanding education.

Tomorrow's Office Can Be Your Kitchen

The information age allows some people to work at home in new ways. Many are telecommuters who accomplish their work with a personal computer and modem. Telecommuting appeals particularly to people who have child-care problems, physical limitations, limited mobility or aversions to downtown congestion. A big disadvantage to working at home is it can be very lonely—many people need the social interaction that takes place at work. Some home workers worry they'll be passed over for promotion—out of sight, out of mind. About one in thirteen workers labor at home eight or more hours a week, but that figure can be a bit misleading. Mostly they are full-time workers who do the majority of their toiling elsewhere and perform only a small part of their jobs on home grounds. Opinion is divided about how many people will work at home in the future.

Analysis

Q. I don't like the idea of being stuck at home. Would I ever be forced to do my job at home?

A. It's unlikely. My counselor says there will continue to be many more opportunities to work in a centralized place than to work at home.

Q. I want to be a homemaker and work too. I'd like to do my job at home.

A. Perhaps I can. I read an article that says many telecommuters work full time in an office before arranging to do their jobs at home. I might try that approach. I should keep in mind what one of my teachers said—that a great deal of the work done at home is piece work, or paid at a low hourly rate.

Job Sharing and Flextime Gain

In job sharing, two employees share one full-time job. Flextime or flexible scheduling plans offer a two-part work schedule; the main part consists of a "core time" when all employees must be at work. The beginning and end of each workday is a flexible period when they can choose their own arrival and departure times. A survey by the Administrative Management Society shows 17 percent of companies report using job sharing, up from 11 percent in the early '80s. Flextime has grown from 22 percent of companies in the early '80s to 29 percent today. How many people are on flextime?

The U.S. Department of Labor says about one of eight full-time workers is on a flextime schedule. As the number of working parents, part-time workers and semiretired employees increases, more people will press for greater control of their own work schedules.

Analysis

Q. (your question)________________________

A. (your answer)________________________

The Dual-Career Couple Is the Norm

It's two for the money in America. Already 60 percent of all households have two income earners. The figure will jump even higher as more and more women hit the job market running. This trend can give workers more flexibility to make job and career moves, because one breadwinner can pay the bills for a period of time.

Analysis

Q. (your question)________________________

A. (your answer)________________________

Maternity Leave Policies Change

Many U.S. workers don't have the right to take time off to bear children. In all other industrialized countries except South Africa, they do. By the year 2000, it's likely that women no longer will have to choose between job and junior. A 1987 U.S. Supreme Court decision upholding a California law guaranteeing a new mother's job for several months may be the turning point. If a national parental leave policy is not established, the issue will be fought state by state. Most observers think motherhood will win. Why? The pressure of numbers. By the end of the century, nearly half the work force will be female. Moreover, two of every three newcomers to the work force over the next decade will be women; most of them will bear children during their working years. An issue of upmost importance to half the nation's workers cannot be ignored.

Analysis

Q. (your question)________________________

A. (your answer)________________________

Child-Care Issues Grow Up

More and more companies are offering day-care benefits for employees' children—and sometimes for elderly parents who cannot remain alone all day. Companies may reimburse employees for day-care costs, or may provide care centers on the work site. The number of large companies offering day-care benefits has quadrupled in recent years to

2,500. Nearly all large companies may do so by the year 2000, say researchers.

Analysis

Q. (your question) ______________________________

____

A. (your answer) ______________________________

____

____

____

____

Quality of Worklife Movement Is Nice to People

Workers in the late 20th century have higher expectations of job rewards than ever before. This attitude has given rise to the quality-of-worklife movement. QWL means many things to many people but most would agree that it requires the worker to be treated as more of a person and less of a number. The worker's ideas are listened to, the worker may choose to pack a week's hours into four days or a worker may elect to do some of the work at home—to mention just three of many QWL variations. In one definition, the quality of worklife is the pursuit of happiness *and* a job.

Analysis

Q. (your question) ______________________________

____

A. (your answer) ______________________________

____

____

____

____

Appetites Grow for Cafeteria-Style Benefits

More companies will offer employee fringe benefits on the cafeteria plan. This permits employees to use benefits credits as they wish. They can, for instance, choose to take college courses at the expense of retirement benefits, or health insurance over extra vacation days. About one-fifth of the nation's 100 largest companies offer cafeteria-style benefits. In round numbers, employee benefits are worth about one-third of your pay. If, for instance, you earn $20,000 yearly, your benefits in corporations would be about $6,600; thus your total compensation would be valued at $26,600. This is only a rule of thumb; actual cases vary considerably.

Analysis

Q. (your question) ______________________________

____

A. (your answer) ______________________________

____

____

____

____

Companies Get Tough on Drugs

At no time in the past have illegal drugs in the workplace posed so menacing a danger to the American economy. Their presence on the job is diluting the energy, integrity and reliability of the American labor force as competition from foreign enterprise grows more threatening. The epidemic of drug abuse is so tragic that many companies say they no longer can overlook it and are instituting get-tough policies to cope with the problem. Studies show that between 20 percent to 25 percent of employers already screen job applicants for drug use—a figure expected to rise to nearly half of employers by 1990. Most of these employers say they reject individuals from employment if evidence of drug use is found.

Analysis

Q. (your question)________________________

____

A. (your answer)_________________________

____

____

____

____

Lifelong Learning Is a New Reality

If a motto were emblazoned on the family crests of tomorrow's workers, it appropriately could be one suggested by leading careers authority Kenneth B. Hoyt: "Always a commencement, never a graduation." That is, tomorrow will hold lots of beginnings, but workers will never be finished learning. Figuratively speaking, graduation day will never come. Lifelong education/training has been recommended for years. What's new, urgent and real about the idea is the threat of obsolescence caused by technology. Workers who decide they've learned it once and once is enough will find themselves in deep trouble in the job market.

Analysis

Q. (your question)________________________

____

A. (your answer)_________________________

____

____

____

____

A Job Is Not Forever

More and more young professionals and managers are becoming advocates of loyalty to oneself. That's because companies are no longer doing handsprings to encourage corporate loyalty as they strip away layers of bureaucracy. They're firing hundreds of thousands of employees who mistakenly thought that as long as they worked hard and kept their noses clean, their future was safe in the hands of their organizations. Seniority is no longer a guarantee of job security, much less of promotion and advancement. Only diamonds are forever.

Analysis

Q. (your question)________________________

____

A. (your answer)_________________________

____

____

____

____

____

Who Will Win the Rat Race?

Now you have an idea of *what you are watching for* when you watch trends.

After reading this section, a young woman complained to one of us, Dr. Laramore, that trend watching is a lot of trouble and not worth it "since life is a rat race anyway."

"Maybe so," Dr. Laramore replied, "but trend watching helps you figure out which rat to bet on."

Player Pianos, Big Bands and Advice for Tomorrow

Player Piano is a novel written decades ago by Kurt Vonnegut, Jr. He uses the instrument as a metaphor for one vision of America's high-tech, machine-driven future.

The view is not a happy one. Only a thin tier of technical superchiefs are employed to manage society's needs. Everyone other than the well-educated managers and engineers is surplus.

No one starves but happiness is a forgotten human condition. The elite managerial-technical corps grow bored with machines. The others grow bored with make-work.

Player Piano's world is safe, sterile, stultifying—and essentially lacking in career opportunities.

In real life, one camp of experts sees the future with essentially a player-piano view: a superb education for the elite few at the top and not much beyond high school for the masses.

By contrast, another camp of experts says there'll be big bands of live musicians tinkling out tunes in the workplace.

They remind us that America grew from an agricultural society to a mechanical society, and is now becoming a computerized society. The big-band people say that the computerized society will not replace the mechanical society overnight. Probably it will not replace it completely any more than the mechanical society replaced the agricultural society completely.

Many occupations we know today existed 50 years ago—salesperson, lawyer, secretary, to name several. Many occupations we know today are likely to exist 50 years from now. The job duties change, but not the basic function.

The big-band camp argues that change will come only gradually to American workers because—and this is important—*we do not live in a linear world.*

Trends do not unfold in a straight line. We take a step or two forward, then follow with a step or two backward. Cable TV started off with a rush of glowing projections, then slowed because the costs were crushing; birth rates peak and fall; Democrats and Republicans alternate political control. We do not live in a linear world.

There is no argument that change is more rapid than ever before in history, but it's also likely that the great bulk of jobs in the United States will continue to be conventional, although updated. The big bands may slim down to smaller groups, but a player-piano society is not probable during your career.

Now that you know about player pianos and big bands, here's advice for those who want a healthy and harmonious future.

- Master the basic principles of your discipline. Unless you know them well enough to innovate, you may find yourself replaced by a machine. Computers can solve routine problems.
- Keep abreast of changes in your field on a regular basis. Consider making a written record of the changes you think are likely, describing how you think they may affect your career.
- Be ready to make at least one major career change in your working life. Expect that you may have to take sabbaticals (learning vacations) for reeducation several times throughout your lifespan.
- Become a skilled job hunter. In good times and bad, jobs open each year.

* * *

Baron Rothschild was a famous financier. He once observed that only two men in Europe really understood trends in the gold market. One was with the Bank of England. The other was with the Bank of France.

"Unfortunately," Baron Rothschild said, "they disagree."

That's often true of experts; nevertheless, informed views can cause you to focus on points you might otherwise miss. Being informed is a good way to break into tomorrow's most lucrative and rewarding fields. Careers tomorrow is what we look at next.

SECTION FOUR

TOWARD TOMORROW'S CAREERS

In a time when the future arrives faster every day, it's sensible to anticipate how career fields are expected to be affected by change. This section sets forth key occupational directions for selected areas of work. It is an overview for interest reading and is not intended to be a comparative analysis of occupations.

Attention is generous to industries and occupations promising brighter-than-average employment prospects, but note also is taken of those headed for the sunset. Advice is given where appropriate.

Job market remodeling will not come as a surprise tornado, but more as a changing of seasons. This important section offers a basis for readers to intelligently scan career horizons.

CAREERS: LOOKING TO THE FUTURE

This informal rundown highlights interesting points and trends in the job market. After reading it, you'll have a good idea of the big picture in work. The section is not designed to be a comparative text contrasting features of one occupation with another. You learn to do that in later pages describing research techniques.

The job outlook in the United States is relatively bright. The manufacturing sector will continue to struggle, but the service field will be a big breadwinner. While the century's last decade won't be a golden age, *Fortune* magazine predicts that it will be a silver one. That's good news for job seekers who are readying themselves for tomorrow's work.

People holding some of the most visionary of the new occupations will design full-size electric cars that don't depend on Mideast oil, use ultrapowerful computers to figure out how to make cheap, inexhaustible energy from fusion, animate movies by computer, stretch fiber-optic cables to improve communications and revamp the genetic makeup of plants, and, perhaps, animals.

Your generation will have opportunities to do things that our ancestors never envisioned.

Should this exciting news cause you to assume that, in an era of sophisticated technology, all of the fabulous jobs are in technical and scientific fields like computers and superconductors? To nab a hot career, do you have to be, as one student asked, a TechnoJock or a RoboMind? Not at all, and not by a long shot.

There still will be lots of room for people who travel in different, more familiar directions. What the headlines don't say is that more jobs open up because of the need to replace workers who leave or die than because totally new jobs are created.

Rewarding career opportunities will exist in a host of non-technical fields, some of them substantially more rewarding—like chief executive officer—than the garden variety job in high tech.

The average rate of growth for all occupations between now and the 21st century is about 19 percent. As you can see by looking at the inset titled "Projections: 2000," occupations grow at uneven rates; computer programmer may soar more than 69 percent, while welder isn't expected to grow even a full percentage point. Growth potential is only one of the characteristics that should border your career choice, but do keep an eye out for healthy industries that are expected to grow fast enough to create new job openings and expanding opportunities for promotion.

Based on both government and private reports, here are selected trends in the career universe.

AGRICULTURE

Agriculture—sometimes called agribusiness when related industries are counted in—is the nation's largest industry, with more than $1 trillion in assets. It accounts for 20 percent of the gross national product. A couple of million people work in agriculture—altogether a solid industry, but one with planet-size problems fraught with aggressive change.

As farms become larger and larger, it will be nearly impossible for young people to become **farmers** from scratch. More new farmers will become hired hands than farm owners. The farm crisis of the '80s will bottom out, but the long-term jitters come from having exported our crop know-how to South America and other countries, now competitors in the world marketplace. Water shortages and poor land quality add to farmers' increasing concerns.

A Bright Side

Waiting in agricultural laboratories and greenhouses are a cornucopia of new plants and technologies some say will bring a second Green Revolution, with bigger and healthier plants.

Other technological gains, from crop-picking robots to computerized health monitoring of livestock, should boost farm earnings—and thus career opportunities.

A Bumper Crop of Careers

Enrollments have plunged in agricultural colleges nationwide, probably because of evening television's grim stories showing heartbroken farmers losing their land after generations of working the soil. Other reasons for an anti-ag attitude are reported in a survey of California high school students, who see agriculture as being down on the farm, hard work, boring, male, blue collar and insecure. They don't know about well-paying jobs as secure as non-agricultural careers, and haven't gotten the word about the full range of agricultural careers, such as aquaculture, genetic engineering and plant science.

New Opportunities

Larger farms will spur the growth of new farm services to meet their needs—financial counseling, management, consulting services. With the dawn of the biotech farm, animal health-care companies will hire staff to help farmers solve their problems of decline. Computer personnel will specialize in farm systems. **Market advisers** and **crop brokers** will devise marketing strategies. **Agricultural engineers** will automate the farm scene. There are lots of good jobs in agriculture other than watching the corn grow.

Business & Office

It's glad tidings for the broad managerial and professional occupational categories—they're likely to increase faster than average. But for some white-collar workers, office automation is throwing jolts and slowing growth, perhaps to a standstill.

Management Jobs

Global competition and financial pressures to hold down costs are changing the look of American management. Companies no longer can afford to hire lots of report-writing middle managers. They want individuals who can show they've improved the company's products and profits. The buzz word is "value-added managers." A value-added manager in an accounting firm, for example, supervises others *and* brings in new accounts. A valued-added manager in any business makes a *measurable* difference to the bottom line.

Many of tomorrow's best management opportunities will be found in small- to medium-size companies, particularly service firms.

Entrepreneurship will continue to be a popular fast-track choice for young people who tire of waiting for crowded management ranks to open. Business magazines regularly report on surveys of small, hot growth companies. Among favorites: business service firms, such as contract cleaning of buildings, rapid mail delivery, software development, office equipment repair and temporary help.

Look for a need to fill. Hospitals, for example, often can't afford expensive high-tech equipment but are anxious to use it on a shared-time basis. An entrepreneurial company in New Jersey equips trucks with multimillion-dollar medical diagnostic equipment to make the rounds of hospitals.

To maximize your chances in a management job, stick to functions that make money or products, or cut costs; stay away from cost-draining positions like strategic planner. Don't count on lifetime security, especially at companies in mature and declining industries, such as steel and shoes.

Office Workers

Automation is swallowing up many routine clerical jobs, forcing a large number of clerical workers into *upskilling* and *downwaging.* That is, many

Projections: 2000

Education strikes again! Employment in occupations that require the most educational preparation—such as executive, administrator, manager, professional worker and technician—will grow faster than average between now and the year 2000.

The occupations requiring the least education, such as private household worker and laborer, will crawl along, or actually decline—except for the rapidly growing service workers.

The source of the following projections and others in this section, except where noted, is the Bureau of Labor Statistics (BLS), U.S. Department of Labor. BLS actually forecasts three alternative scenarios of growth: high, moderate and low. Here is the moderate version.

Occupation	No. of Persons (in thousands) 1986	2000	Percent change
Total employment	111,623	133,030	19.2
Executive, administrative, and managerial workers	10,583	13,616	28.7
Education administrators	288	325	12.9
Financial managers	638	792	24.1
General managers and top executives	2,383	2,965	24.4
Marketing, advertising, and public relations managers	323	427	32.5
Accountants and auditors	945	1,322	39.8
Personnel, training, and labor relations specialists	230	278	21.2
Professional workers	13,538	17,192	27.0
Electrical and electronics engineers	401	592	47.8
Computer systems analysts	331	582	75.6
Lawyers	527	718	36.3
Teachers, preschool	176	240	36.3
Teachers, kindergarten and elementary	1,527	1,826	19.6
Teachers, secondary school	1,128	1,280	13.4
College and university faculty	754	722	−4.2
Dentists	151	196	29.6
Physicians and surgeons	491	679	38.2
Registered nurses	1,406	2,018	43.6

(continued)

Occupation	No. of Persons (in thousands) 1986	2000	Percent change
Total employment	111,623	133,030	19.2
Technicians and related support workers	3,726	5,151	38.2
Licensed practical nurses	631	869	37.7
Drafters	348	354	1.6
Computer programmers	479	813	69.9
Sales workers	12,606	16,334	29.6
Cashiers	2,165	2,740	26.5
Sales agents, real estate	313	451	43.9
Salespersons, retail	3,579	4,780	33.5
Administrative support workers, including clerical	19,851	22,109	11.4
Switchboard operators	279	330	18.3
Computer operators, except peripheral equipment operators	263	387	47.2
Bookkeeping, accounting, and auditing clerks	2,116	2,208	4.3
Payroll and timekeeping clerks	204	180	−12.0
General office clerks	2,361	2,824	19.6
Receptionists and information clerks	682	964	41.4
Secretaries	3,234	3,658	13.1
Typists and word processors	1,002	862	−13.9
Private household workers	981	955	−2.6
Service workers, except private household workers	16,555	21,962	32.7
Janitors and cleaners, including maids/housekeepers	2,676	3,280	22.6
Waiters and waitresses	1,702	2,454	44.2
Nursing aides, orderlies, and attendants	1,224	1,658	35.4
Hairdressers, hairstylists, and cosmetologists	562	662	17.7
Police patrol officers	349	409	17.4
Guards	794	1,177	48.3

(continued)

Occupation	No. of Persons (in thousands) 1986	2000	Percent change
Total employment	111,623	133,030	19.2
Precision production, craft, and repair workers	13,923	15,590	12.0
Carpenters	1,010	1,192	18.1
Electricians	556	644	15.9
Painters and paperhangers, construction and maintenance	412	502	21.9
Plumbers, pipefitters, and steamfitters	402	471	17.2
Aircraft mechanics and engine specialists	107	129	20.1
Automotive mechanics	748	808	8.0
Machinists	378	373	−1.5
Operators, fabricators, and laborers	16,300	16,724	2.6
Sewing machine operators, garment	633	541	−14.5
Electrical and electronics assemblers	249	116	−53.7
Welders and cutters	287	307	6.7
Bus drivers	478	555	16.2
Truck drivers	2,463	2,968	20.5
Industrial truck and tractor operators	426	283	−33.6
Farming, forestry, and fishing workers	3,556	3,393	−4.6
Gardeners and groundskeepers, except farming	767	1,005	31.1
Farm workers	940	750	−20.3
Farm operators and managers	1,336	1,051	−21.3

are required to learn the use of word processors, computers, electronic spreadsheets and other technical wonders, but their pay does not reflect their increased technical skills. Pools of clerical workers labor in factory-like environments that some call "electronic sweatshops."

Prospects are much happier for **secretaries** who are paraprofessional assistants. Many will have associate or baccalaureate degrees; almost all will have a strong basic education. As middle-management ranks shrink, heavy-duty secretaries with interpersonal skills who can think, organize, manage time, master office technology and, in general, give the boss a hand, will find enthusiastic bidders for their well-paid services.

Shorthand, yes or no? Don't give up on the time-honored skill yet; it's still in demand, but may not be long for the business world. Various companies are bringing out voice-recognition systems. Speech uttered into a small microphone, with brief pauses between words, appears almost instantly on a computer screen, and, when desired, is printed on paper. Although one day soon we will be able to operate computers and generate information simply by talking, it will take years for the technology to become reliable and cheap enough to widely replace traditional dictation by shorthand.

Elsewhere on the office front, **receptionists** will thrive because it's difficult to replace a smiling face with a machine.

Who Are All These People?

If you're uncertain what some of the jobs we mention in this section involve, remember to ask your school counselor, career center technician or librarian for occupational materials that describe the nature of the work. A basic guide is the U.S. Labor Department's *Occupational Outlook Handbook*, which comes out every two years.

Economists

Economists used to meld into academia, but now more than half work for government agencies and business entities bunched in Washington, New York, Chicago and other large cities where they collect, analyze and interpret data on economic issues. Usually economists specialize in such areas as finance, international trade, labor, agriculture or industry. For a profession where you need at least a master's degree, this is not one of the easier ways to hit a six-figure income.

Recently, scores of major companies have erased their economics departments, chiefly because of budget crunches and because economists have a lackluster record of forecasting over the past 15 years.

Banks and corporations that haven't dropped economists are giving them value-added tasks—moving them into "line" positions where they help managers make decisions on everything from loans to marketing costs.

For security, go government; for money, consider becoming a business economist at a major securities firm.

Computer Jobs

Computers are only about 40 years old, but already it's becoming possible for people—not just computer jocks—to operate them simply by talking. Already it's possible for computers to program one another. Already it's possible to be jobless in this young career field.

Does all this mean the demand for computer specialists has peaked? Most industry experts think not, expecting demand for experienced, *skilled* computer specialists to go on indefinitely. Computer-based occupations are still among the fastest growing in the job market, but the problem is that so many people are hopping on a good thing that the rivalry for jobs, especially for beginning programmers, has grown hot and heavy. Graduates with four-year degrees have an edge over those with two-year degrees.

Despite competition, computer software is a good bet in the growth department; sure, there's lots of software in the market now, but finding the right program is increasingly a frustrating grope. Just as a one-size-fits-all garment rarely fits anyone perfectly, off-the-shelf software usually needs nips and tucks to correctly match a company's needs.

The situation offers computer specialists a kaleidoscope of opportunities, from writing new programs to finding and adapting canned ones.

Systems programmers, who help design computer systems that mesh with the rest of the organization, have bright occupational skies, but data-entry jobs are spiraling down, partly because more and more data are being exchanged between computers without re-keying.

Applications programmers, who create software for specific purposes—accounting, inventory control, word-processing, for instance—may hit a wall in growth potential because of increasingly sophisticated programming capabilities of computers, ready-made programs and global competition.

Data-base managers will find pivotal positions at many companies monitoring the creation and flow of facts and figures. Management information system (MIS) managers are finding jobs scarcer than before, but those who can broaden their qualifications from technical whiz to astute business executive can become members of top management as chief information officers.

Data security specialists keep computer data secrets safe, work that will provide good jobs for engineers, mathematicians and systems programmers.

Systems analysts solve information problems, analyzing the way a company uses and stores information, then design methods to help the organization run more smoothly. No one expects a shortage of information problems in the years ahead.

Information brokers—electronic librarians for hire—use home computers to tap into big on-line information services and sell tailored research to clients, such as high-tech companies or real estate firms.

Other jobs in and around computers include selling and servicing them, and training people to use them.

Employers continue to have the upper hand in the entry-level computer job market, so the thing to do is gain experience through internships and part-time paid or volunteer jobs while you're a student. Consider, too, majoring in a wider discipline, such as business, engineering, accounting or a science, then using your computer know-how as a secondary, facilitating skill.

If you really want to do high-level work with computers, consider a master's or a doctorate in computer engineering or computer science.

Artificial Intelligence

More than three decades ago a new idea was introduced to the computer science community under the distinctive label "artificial intelligence." With it came the first attempts at programming computers to mimic human thinking, such as asking questions like a doctor and offering a diagnosis. We already have computers that can plan military strategy—imagine someday having software that can drive the tanks, fly the planes and negotiate the truce.

These are examples of *expert systems,* the first AI discipline to have a major impact on business and industry. An expert system is a computer program that contains detailed knowledge of a particular subject area. It is like pushing a button and requesting, "information please."

Expert systems are now used in a number of commercial functions—to approve credit card charges, do financial planning and design aircraft, for instance. In essence, the AI system tries to recreate the thought processes of experts; **knowledge engineers** help make the transition from an expert's mind to a computer program.

AI is a very small field, one eyed longingly by programmers and management information system managers. The best jobs will go to those able to design and apply expert systems to business needs, and to those with advanced training in computer science.

For years, AI was the stepchild of computer science but universities are beginning to offer AI studies. Examples: At Carnegie-Mellon University, AI is one of four components of a PhD degree in computer science. Master's and PhD programs in artificial intelligence are offered by Massachusetts Institute of Technology; the AI program is interdisciplinary and may be obtained through academic departments other than the computer science department.

The AI outlook is uncertain in the near future. Major AI firms already have folded or laid off people.

The biggest motor driving new interest in the technology is Pentagon spending, and breakthroughs aren't coming fast enough, AI critics say. The plodding progress may slow the flood of federal research money now pouring into the industry. AI backers believe that ultimately researchers will unearth mathematical rules that govern the mind and then it will be only a matter of repeating these rules in a computer program.

At the moment? One AI scientist sums it up: "Anything a five-year-old or an animal can do, artificial intelligence can't."

Associations change with the times, but their future looks favorable into the 21st century. Large-scale human cooperation will always require human coordination. Is now a good time to cheer? Two, four, six, eight: ready, set, associate!

Association Management

Travel to glamorous resorts. Lodge in luxury hotels. Enjoy chateaubriand dining. The expense-account life—once or twice a year, at least—is a hallmark of association management careers.

Nearly a million people are thought to be employed by an estimated 40,000 national, regional, state and local associations. Professional societies and trade associations cover virtually every business and professional interest, from the Flying Chiropractors Association to the Procurers of Painted-Label Sodas.

Associations lobby legislators, provide professional development and educational programs, stage conventions and trade shows and maintain consumer services. Recently, some groups have had to supplement income from members' dues with activities that produce non-dues revenue, such as operating a specialized mail-order book business.

The variety of the association industry's activities requires the skills of many specialists, from **attorneys** and **public relations experts,** to **meeting planners** and **association executives.** The trend to unite similar interests has even spawned a new mini-industry: professional management companies that run associations. A good place to begin an association management career is in a small organization, moving up from one association to another.

The field pays adequately at the bottom, well at the middle and handsomely at the top. You need strong interpersonal skills to deal with association members and survive office politics.

Washington, D.C., is the mecca for association careers, followed by New York City and Chicago. An association job can be found in any of the 50 states, usually in state capitals.

The Law

Verdict: Oversupply. Sentence: Except for top graduates of famous law schools, competition for jobs and clients will be crushing.

Look for special niches created by new technologies or trends: robotics law to deal with damage robots cause, high-tech law to establish ownership rights in breakthrough discoveries and employment law to represent employees in their court challenges of personnel practices employers used to take for granted. Immigration law offers wide-open opportunities.

It's important to track the legal job market trends as you move through law school. Right now recruiters are searching for **attorneys** with expertise in taxes and product liability, but not for those who deal in antitrust and environmental matters. Golden oldies, too, such as real estate and personal injury law, are likely to keep successful lawyers in style.

If you can't find a job right away, you may want to sign on with a legal temporary help service firm. Legal gypsies say working by the day, week or month is a good way to test their interest in a particular firm.

Law firm managements may want permanent employees to bring in new business as well as service existing clients. Among lawyers there's a wall of resistance to sales activities—you'll be wise to accept the idea if you hope to travel the partnership track.

Lots of lawyers who say "no way" to selling legal services decide they'll go into non-legal work in business and return to night school for an MBA. The dual degree, they reason, will add armor to their value in the corporate job market. It's probably a good idea.

The number of **paralegals**—paraprofessionals who assist lawyers with structured, well-defined tasks—is growing like crazy. The hitch is that paralegals find their salaries topping out at about $25,000 and many, discouraged, leave the field.

Human Resource Management

Still called "personnel" by many companies, human resources is a small but interesting segment of business management. An **HR executive** might recommend whether to restructure employee benefits, establish a workers' child-care center, offer parental leaves or require applicants to be tested for drug abuse.

The field has shot up in status since the days when it mainly dealt with hiring and firing. With so many companies merging, buying other companies, closing plants, installing automation and locating facilities in cheaper labor markets overseas, there's plenty of human resource work to do.

Even so, have widespread efforts by large companies to reduce their workforces triggered cutbacks in human resource departments? No. Studies show employment stability in human resources. Companies lean on HR experts as they try to develop leaner organizations and expand training programs to meet technological change, as well as make concerted efforts to operate without violating anti-discrimination laws and employee rights.

Two stars on the human resource scene are the **executives** who know enough about labor and employment law to keep their companies away from multimillion-dollar liability court cases, and **compensation specialists** who help companies control pay expenses, a gigantic slice of business costs.

Graduates are lined up to enter the HR field. Get a jump on the competition by making con-

The Fastest-Growing Occupations to 2000

These are the occupations expected to have the biggest growth spurts between now and the 21st century. They will have the *highest rate of growth,* but, with two exceptions, will not provide the largest actual number of jobs because they are relatively small occupations. The two exceptions are computer systems analyst and computer programmer, both of which are big occupations that have a high rate of growth.

- paralegal
- medical assistant
- physical therapist
- physical therapy assistant
- data processing equipment repairer
- home health aide
- computer systems analyst
- medical record technician
- employment interviewer
- computer programmer
- radiologic technologist
- dental hygienist
- dental assistant
- physician assistant
- office machine servicer
- operation/systems researcher
- occupational therapist
- EDP equipment operator
- data entry keyer, composing
- optometrist

tacts in the industry. Try to line up an internship or enroll in a cooperative education program. Attend meetings of professional societies, such as the Employment Management Association or the American Society for Personnel Administration.

Despite HR's new recognition, it still won't be a major channel for advancement to the chief executive officer's spot. You say you'd be perfectly happy to be a vice president of human resources—fine! You have the potential of pulling in an income of six figures.

You don't have to work inside a corporate human resources department—you may even make more money on the outside, as a **technical recruiter** or **executive search specialist.** Don't overlook a wide range of human resource jobs, including **employment agency counselor, outplacement consultant** and **career counselor.**

Look Out for the Falls!

Some career fields are shrinking. Occupations that are losing jobs include the following.

- electrical/electronic assembler
- electronic semiconductor processor
- railroad conductor, yardmaster
- railroad brake operator
- industrial truck/tractor operator
- chemical equipment controller
- stenographer
- farmer
- statistical clerk
- PBX installer
- telephone central office operator
- telephone directory assistance operator
- typesetter
- shoe worker
- data entry keyer, except composing

Accounting and Auditing

Accounting is a good choice if you're after a first-rate business career. Top graduates, particularly of the most highly acclaimed schools, are hired by big accounting firms, major industrial corporations and government agencies. The next layer of grads find jobs in smaller accounting firms and business companies. Marginal grads—whether defined by grades or personal characteristics—may tire of waiting for a staff accountant's position and settle for a job at the bookkeeper level.

To be among the sought-after graduates, master accounting basics, from auditing to taxes, obtain work-related experience while in school and become joined at the hip with a computer.

You need at least a bachelor's degree in accounting, and, for greater job market clout, a master's in the discipline. After that, aim for certification: Pursue the CPA (certified public accountant) credential for accounting firm employment; the CMA (certified management accountant) for corporate jobs; the CIA (certified internal auditor) for auditing; and CISA (certified information systems auditor) for work with computer systems.

Nearly a million **accountants** and **auditors** mind the money in the American business world and they are likely to multiply as complexities grow in federal, state and local tax laws. Major accounting firms keep the cash flowing by offering management consulting, software programming and help to clients on everything from merger advice to computer shopping.

You could become a high-salaried corporate chief financial officer, but the biggest payoff may be as head of a major accounting firm where you could be looking at annual paychecks as long as a telephone number.

Tax work is eternal. Auditing is assured. And cost accounting in high-tech industries gives practitioners high visibility as they keep track of expenditures for constantly changing products and interact with a variety of executives.

Banking

Once a garrison of stuffy routine, the banking brigade throughout this decade has been fighting a vigorous free-for-all battle for business. By the 21st century, banking, as your parents knew it, will be unrecognizable. The reasons are complex, but brutal global and domestic competition—and unprecedented new mergers, some with department stores and industrial companies—are radically reshaping a business nearly as old as civilization.

Before things began to change, every institution knew its place. Commercial banks offered checking and savings accounts and made personal and business loans. Savings and loan associations focused on home mortgages. Investment banks raised money for corporate stock issues and takeovers. Things are different now and those well-defined boundaries are memories.

Not only will tomorrow's financial landscape look strange to veteran eyes, it may be exceedingly difficult to map. During the '90s, no-holds-barred competition may well crumble the remaining legal walls between commercial banking, investment banking, securities and insurance. Already, commercial banks, desperate for profits, are tailgating investment banks by offering funds for ambitious corporate maneuvers; consumers are buying can openers and making bank deposits in department stores; and investment banks are playing the role of commercial banks by promising huge bridge loans as temporary financing for proposed mergers. And it seems that nearly everybody wants to sell insurance.

That's not all that's changing. Some bankers worry that the United States' worldwide banking clout could go the way of manufacturing. Telecommunication technology now makes it easy for Midwestern business owners to shop overseas for the most favorable loan rates and terms. Four of the world's five largest banks and four of the six largest securities houses are Japanese, says *Fortune* magazine.

Smart, high-energy financial professionals with a compulsion to win will see these shifts as opportunities. They will find the rough-and-tumble marketplace of banking an invigorating challenge and the financial rewards worth putting in the vault. What's more, tomorrow's banking leaders will need able support troops, ranging from **operations staffers** who are computer savvy, to **marketing specialists** who can invent profitable new products. On the decline side, there'll be a dwindling number of slots for **loan officers** and **clerks,** chiefly because of computer programs that determine and process routine credit applications.

Currency traders sell and buy yen, marks, pounds, Swiss francs and other foreign currencies, usually for dollars. Daily trading averages $200 billion in the foreign-exchange market. A wrong move can be disastrous. Highly paid currency traders need not only nerves of steel and good instincts for timing, but also little desire for a private life—one trader carries a small screen with foreign-exchange quotes while he jogs.

Another pressure-packed occupation is **investment banker.** Sharp investment bankers in their 20s work 80 hours a week and earn more money than many corporate chief executives. Some banking analysts say the days when investment bankers live like monarchs in exile are numbered; others say don't bet on it.

What education can make banking your berth? The field is well known for welcoming well-rounded individuals with liberal arts backgrounds, ranging from lapsed philosophers to French majors. But an MBA offers the quickest ascent. Finance, economics, accounting, computer science and marketing courses are important, as are languages for global work and agribusiness for rural communities.

The investment banking field is almost "by invitation only," available to top graduates of a nationally known university, often Harvard or Stanford. Connections never hurt, but brains and deal-making ability are more important in an industry noted for boardroom crises and high-rolling conflicts.

As the lines blur between financial institutions, exciting new career patterns are developing in banking and other money places. Maybe you'll want to cash in.

Insurance

No one says it's easy to juice up income in insurance. Many try and fall by the wayside. But those who succeed in insurance sales or in related actuarial work may be richly rewarded in six figures.

There are many fields of insurance—life, property, health, product and professional liability, for instance. Except for life insurance, rates for coverage lately have risen higher than kites, causing some companies to self-insure. Will the increase in self-insurance put a big dent in career opportunities? Probably not, but there are likely to be fewer good jobs in marketing because even though sales are bounding up, computers are helping a smaller number of insurance sellers handle more business.

Insurance agents work for a single company; **brokers** are independent and handle multiple insurance companies, negotiating the best terms and rates for clients.

Actuaries use math, computers and statistics to figure the business end of insurance and pension programs. They need advanced college degrees plus completion of some exams to achieve professional recognition. Those who pass all the tests are titled fellows of the Society of Actuaries and they stand the best chance of whoopee earnings. Computers and expert systems will reduce the size of the occupation by an unknown degree; chances are you'll have to be one of the best in the field to survive until retirement time.

The insurance field is top heavy with male bosses and bottom heavy with female clerks—but who says policies can't change?

Securities

Most jobs in the stockmarket are in sales. If you can bring in brokerage accounts and sell clients money-making stocks, you will be in the chips as a **broker.** The securities field is growing; federal deregulation and a lively market have led trading firms to expand and other financial organizations, such as banks, to enter the business.

Liberal arts majors flocking to brokerage houses fill trainee spots. Take some business administration, economics and finance courses—the test to become a registered representative is getting tougher and clients are getting wiser.

Representatives with the knack for trading may choose related jobs, all potentially lucrative: **over-the-counter trader, government securities trader** and **option trader,** for instance. **Securities analysts**—members of a tiny but elite occupation—choose securities for brokers to recommend. Analysts' pay can be phenomenal. Supernovas are rumored to earn six or seven figures in good years.

All the years aren't good. To survive, you need a solid personal savings plan to hang in when the inevitable bear claws Wall Street.

Financial Planning

Financial planning is a growth industry populated with investment gurus—investment counselors, bank trust officers, attorneys, insurance agents, accountants and, the newest breed, financial planners.

Financial planners take stock of a client's money situation and suggest strategic investment moves. They do this by gathering data from the client, writing a plan to help the client reach stated goals and either back off and let the client implement the plan, or sell the client securities, insurance, real estate or other financial products.

Planners who earn commissions on the financial products they sell may not be as objective advisers as planners who work only on a fee basis. Straight out of college, you'd be lucky to get $20,000 as a trainee; once established, high five- and six-figure incomes are not unusual.

Financial planners work for banks and other financial institutions, financial planning service firms and on their own.

What's ahead for planners in this largely unregulated industry? Most likely more federal regula-

20 King-Size Occupations

Although other occupations may be faster growing, those listed below offer more job opportunities because they already employ huge numbers of people. Here are the 20 occupations expected to grow most in the *number of job openings* between now and 2000.

- retail salesperson
- waiter/waitress
- registered nurse
- janitor/cleaner
- general manager/top executive
- cashier
- truck driver, light and heavy
- general office clerk
- food counter/fountain worker
- nursing aide/orderly
- secretary
- guard
- accountant/auditor
- computer programmer
- kitchen food preparation worker
- elementary teacher
- receptionist/information clerk
- computer systems analyst
- restaurant cook
- gardener/groundskeeper

tion to protect clients, and more education to deal with increasingly sophisticated financial products.

Planners approach the field from a variety of educational backgrounds in financial service, reflected by the string of initials after their names. A rundown: CFP—certified financial planner, ChFC—chartered financial consultant, CLU—chartered life underwriter, RIA—registered investment adviser, MSFS—master of science in financial services (a university degree, not a professional certification).

Although you can enter the field with a business administration major, an increasing number of specialized financial planning courses and degrees are being offered. Which avenue of entry is best for you depends on your professional goals. Research to get the right answer.

Consulting

Management consultants are business doctors who increasingly diagnose the ills of non-profit entities, like museums and charities, as well as industrial companies.

Consultants face solid prospects, but the glamorous and golden days of generalists and sky-high fees appear to be numbered. Estimates place the number of consultants at 50,000 in several thousand consulting companies. Major accounting firms pounce on about one-third of the business; to walk in their hallways, you need an advanced degree in business administration, or in the discipline in which you plan to consult. Others who rent out their expertise are able to do so by dint of experience and contacts, such as that gained through successful retail or restaurant management.

Accounting and other types of large consulting firms increasingly lay claim to the advice market, which makes it prudent to start your consulting career in a large consulting firm where you'll have back-up in dealing with your first clients.

Specialization is a key to successful consulting. Clients want specialists who can solve specific problems in specific areas, not business philosophers.

In a career field that rises and falls with the economy, that depends on persuasion to effect change, and that requires a high tolerance for travel, the monetary rewards are apt to be attractive, if no longer majestic.

Other Business Fields

Purchasing agents in large industrial firms have better-than-average prospects of lucrative employment. **Mortgage brokers** will find rewards taming monstrous loan applications, both locally and through nationwide computerized loan-search networks. **Corporate fitness directors,** who work to keep employees in good physical shape, will encounter more competition than job openings in corporate America. English majors who master the new micrographics technology will find good jobs in electronic image management. Taking aim at opportunities in the business and office sector could be right on target as a prize career choice.

Communications and Media

Perhaps because television has a special power to influence hearts and minds, and to change the way people view the world, the medium is a career magnet for thousands of bright young people.

Television's immediacy—its quick, visible reporting of events as they happen—makes it a dramatic example of passing messages through mass communications. But professional communicators use many methods and avenues to inform, educate, persuade or entertain. Ideas, information and attitudes also move through journalism, photography, film, radio, audio, video, advertising, public relations, book publishing, magazines and newspapers.

These categories shelter many of the economy's most interesting jobs—the kind that permit you to make money doing what you most like to do. Some put you in the spotlight—a **talk show hostess,** for example, or **news anchor.** Others bring status within a profession—**advertising creative director** or major **advertising account executive.** Still others offer no public recognition, just well-paid obscurity in stimulating environments—**film librarian** or **radio traffic director.**

The next couple of decades will see stunning gains in communication capacity through computers and breakthrough electronic broadcast technology. This growth will create new jobs galore. The problem for you will be establishing a beachhead and beating off the competition. Got the message?

Journalism

Computers and videotex are changing the tools of writing in the sense that you can use a personal computer/word processor that corrects spelling, electronically erases typos and allows you to pull information to your screen instantly from libraries, newspapers and other data bases. Videotex technology—electronic print on a television screen or monitor, often two-way and interactive—started out with a bang, suffered financial setbacks from lack of demand, and now is beginning a slow renewal. When videotex becomes well established, many will find good opportunities in such information services as gardening advice, sports information or dating bureaus. The often-predicted death of print journalism is unlikely in your lifetime.

Television

Networks. Advertising income isn't keeping pace with rising costs, and videocassettes and cable television are pulling network audiences away. That's why networks have become cost-conscious and will keep staffs lean. The networks' prime time isn't over, but now it's shared among aggressive competitors.

Individual stations. Advertising revenues are somewhat better here, but stations, too, will resist a hiring binge when taking on new employees.

Cable television. The best prospects probably are in business administration and marketing areas.

For all electronic media, major on-air personalities and producers of hit shows collect lots of money for their efforts.

Television career advice hasn't changed channels: It's still important to know about all the places offering you employment. Keep your portfolio (work samples) current, luggage in good repair, and be ready to relocate often enough to snap up advancement opportunities. If you don't find yourself in stiff competition for a job opening, there must be something wrong with it.

CONSTRUCTION

The construction industry is heading into new times when many traditional ways of working and doing business will undergo substantial change.

Commercial. Almost everywhere in the country, there are far more big buildings than needed. It will take years for demand to catch up to the overbuilt office market. Some industry analysts predict that more than a million jobs in commercial construction will be lost until a new wave of commercial building perks up the job market. Commercial construction that is being built is centering on less expensive, low-rise suburban office buildings and office parks in growth areas. Large developers will overwhelm some small developers as the competition heats up.

Residential. Houses cost too much for many people and the number of young house buyers is not likely to grow until the second or third decade of the new century. The residential construction job market certainly is not a disaster—but it's not a feast either, compared to the residential building boom of the '70s and fairly good demand of the '80s.

Heavy Construction. Companies building sidewalks, dams, energy plants and other huge, complex structures have had a jackhammer headache in recent years. Oil income is down and oil-rich countries have cut back on major improvements; much of the Third World is so busy wrestling with suffocating debts that they are not buying much king-sized construction either. Fighting back, heavy construction companies are trying to create work by providing financing or investing in projects—the "build/own/operate" formula. Demand for construction workers and engineers on heavy projects, both in the U.S. and overseas, will be modest until world conditions change.

A Sunnier View

The outlook is bright for construction workers who can remodel and rehabilitate office buildings, including the updating of heating, air-conditioning and elevator systems.

The job market will be bustling, too, for rehabilitation, renewal and conversion workers in the residential market. Because new housing is so costly, older housing will be spruced up and redesigned into multiple units to shelter a large number of people.

Architects

Fewer **architects** will design tomorrow's world. Because computers are automating the production of architectural drawings, specifications, cost estimates and schedules, some analysts expect as many as four-fifths of the nation's 95,000 architects to be beating the bushes for jobs by the year 2000. Other experts disagree, insisting that architects are not being replaced by computers but are using them to do more perfect work. CAD (computer-aided design) is the hottest topic at architectural schools today.

In any case, the walls of tradition are crumbling as architects move into alternative settings. Some are abandoning the "design only" role and entering into the entrepreneurial aspects of buildings owners, developers, financiers, contractors and even realtors.

Other architects are becoming **facilities managers,** or administrators of real estate departments in large corporations. Many work in government agencies.

Job prospects are bleak for graduates of two- and four-year architectural technology programs, except in rural offices where one or two architects do all the design work and are assisted by architectural technicians.

Architecture has been described as "frozen music." From the days of Ictinus, the designer of the ancient Greek Parthenon, the field has attracted creative people who want to build cathedrals and homes, castles and shopping centers. Aim for architecture in its classic design sense only if you have outstanding talent, and if you don't starve easily.

Building Trades

Construction employment in the year 2000 will include familiar trades—**carpenters, pipe fitters, cement finishers, electricians** and so forth—but new opportunities will exist for workers who can handle computerized equipment in such tasks as earth-moving, materials-handling and erection work. Supervisors who can increase productivity by eliminating wasteful delays will be sought after.

On balance, construction journeyworkers will find good prospects in the decade ahead if they are ready to relocate from time to time, following the trail blazed by builders and remodeling firms. If you like to work with your hands, work outdoors, be part of a team, and work quickly and finish the job without someone looking over your shoulder, consider the construction trades.

Some trades are nearly indestructible. Even when construction sinks, plumbers float.

Always a Money Maker for Some

With an overbuilt office market, low population growth and fewer households forming, construction will slow. But some people have always made a great deal of money in building and development activities—rain or shine. Smart **builders** study the market and demographic trends before acting, obtain access to reliable financial resources, keep their political contacts in good working order and take well-reasoned risks to reach for giant rewards.

Consumer and Home Economics

Although diverse in nature, careers in this cluster gather 'round the family. The occupations focus on the improvement of family living and the family's consumer practices.

Other than teaching, most of the jobs are in business—research and testing of products, promotion of products and services, or representing companies to consumers. Technically, selling is not included in this job group, but, in real life, sales skills often are vital.

Home Economics

Think of the **home economist** as a "person of a thousand faces" and you've got the picture. As a home economics graduate, you could be a **radio journalist** working on consumer information shows...a **home economics instructor** at the high school or college level...a **fashion expert** who chooses next year's clothing for a department store...a **researcher** cooking up a leaner strain of beef...a **corporate home economist** responsible for testing new home appliances...a **director of a retirement center**...a **dietitian** counseling patients on weight loss...a **manager** running high-stakes cookoff promotions. All these and more are jobs in the home economics family.

Interior Designers

Interior design is typically overcrowded and even more so when construction is in a slump. Don't confuse designers with decorators. Anyone can hang out a shingle that says "decorator," but the basic requirement for an **interior designer** is a certificate or diploma from a three-year professional school, or a bachelor's degree with a major in interior design. As the population ages, designers should find good career angles in planning interior spaces for the elderly and others who want small living quarters. Many designers struggle financially, but big names can warm their pockets with six-digit earnings.

Fashion Work

Fashion designers study in vocational schools that offer two- and three-year programs, or in college and university programs leading to a bachelor's degree. To become a household word, you probably will have to live in a garment center, such as New York or Los Angeles.

Fashion merchandisers work across the country, often starting out as trainees after graduation; a sure sense for what's going to sell is the most valuable talent.

Fashion models need more than a perfect face atop a lithe body; the ability to "sell" the merchandise while whirling under hot studio lights or floating down runways is a basic requirement. Unfortunately, the field attracts shady promoters, so learn as much as you can about the workings of the industry and use common sense in your dealings.

Child and Elder Care

In pay, the vast majority of child-care jobs are views from the cellar. **Directors of child-care centers** do better—they earn salaries comparable to teachers. At the other end of the age scale, new ventures in elder care are appearing, sometimes sponsored by corporations as employee benefits. Recently, home economics education has emphasized gerontology, the study and problems of the aging.

Wrap-up on Home Ec/ Consumer Jobs

Future projections don't help much because graduates of home economics programs—and others in this cluster—follow pathways in many industries. Prospects are much dimmer for **home lighting consultants,** for instance, than for **dietitians.** There will be more jobs for **preschool teachers** than for **models. Independent retirement planners** have less security than **housing managers.**

The most that can be said is that concerns for the family and home will continue to churn up attractive career positions for tens of thousands of people.

Environment and Natural Resources

In recent years we've seen what devastation can result from technological failure—the fiery end of *Challenger,* the Chernobyl nuclear plant disaster and the fatal chemical leak at a Union Carbide plant in India are gruesome illustrations.

Beyond industrial failure, air and water toxicity creates anxiety—Love Canal, radon, asbestos, a hole in the ozone layer, oil spills, ocean pollution—all environmental threats that practically guarantee environmental protection activities will persist and may even expand in the decades ahead.

Many environmental protection specialists have advanced degrees in the life sciences (such as botany, zoology, microbiology, biochemistry, biophysics), and most work for government agencies.

Natural resources management, including marine science, embraces wildly diverse careers. As a **soils conservationist,** you might teach farmers and government employees how to make the best and most efficient use of soil. Or you might specialize in the conservation of other renewable resources: wildlife, forestry, fisheries, zoos and aquariums.

Many young adults see environment and natural resources careers as consisting of "freedom jobs"—and head for the Great Outdoors. It's easy to understand their yearning because the work can be enormously gratifying. As a generalization, the pay for professional-level positions is moderately good, often on a government pay schedule or comparable to it. As a certainty, the competition for such jobs as **park ranger** is grizzly.

Forestry

If you want to manage, develop and protect forest lands, about one-third of the nation's land space, it's over the river and through the woods to a four-year collegiate school of forestry. Whether you work for private industry or government, the job market is always tight.

Environmental Engineering

The ever-growing mountains of materials we discard can no longer be ignored. The waste disposal problem—particularly hazardous waste—touches on several disciplines, including civil, mechanical and chemical engineering. The **environmental engineer** deals with all these areas, plus has expertise in soil mechanics and hydrogeology (groundwater).

Hydrology

Water is almost sure to replace energy as the nation's next natural resource crisis. Nearly every part of the U.S. faces serious water troubles, either a shortage, pollution or leaky pipes. Experts who have been warning there will be no creek to be up are being taken more seriously. Enter **hydrologists,** scientists who study the distribution, circulation and physical properties of water. Other than government agencies, hydrologists work for utilities, mining companies and industrial corporations. The water peril is real—people who can help solve it will be sought after.

Ocean Engineering

Oceanography is a field whose future always seems to look brighter than its present. Since the '60s, people have been talking about great opportunities exploring earth's last frontier but a bountiful job market has yet to spring from the sea. **Ocean engineers** explore and use the ocean, and although a mainstay of employment—oil exploration—has substantially dried up, the search for mineral deposits and ocean nutrients continues to attract pioneers to the field.

The Good Earth Careers

Environmental and natural resources careers have come into prominence only within the last two decades. Many people who entered the field in the late '60s, early '70s, will be retiring in the '90s. You may be one of those who fill the empty shoes.

FINE ARTS AND HUMANITIES

Fine arts celebrate aesthetic communication, functioning as media for profound expression of thoughts and feelings. Not all arts are highbrow. Many offer entertainment and a break from daily routine. In whatever realm, art contributes to the quality of life. Humanities encompass the social and moral values of a culture, enriching our existence as human beings.

Job families often included in this cluster are visual and performing arts, writing, religion, language, history and museum management.

The statistical generalities for fine arts and humanities are somber: Many who cherish their hours in these pursuits cannot earn a living through their work. Fortunately, the job market has infinite exceptions and there will always be tremendous opportunities for people of superior talent or even genius who are in the right place at the right time.

Two tips: If you find yourself irresistibly drawn to an insecure occupation—singer, free-lance photographer, sculptor, art critic, and the like—thoroughly learn the ropes of *marketing* your talent. And prepare for a back-up occupation that pays the bills.

Acting

"Actors are like troubadors going through the country looking for castles. There's no job security. When you're hot, as I am now, there's a fad factor. But by the time this (Broadway show) ends, no one will remember, and you go back to square one," says giant talent James Earl Jones in a statement appearing in *Parade* magazine.

Jones well captured the insecurity of acting. Most **actors** and **actresses** are unemployed. More than 75 percent of those serious enough about the profession to join a union, Actors Equity, are out of work each year.

Formal training is the way to whiz in show biz: Study voice, stage movement and acting in a college drama program, or in a conservatory. Of the nation's three dozen or so acting conservatories, some are attached to universities, such as the Yale School of Drama, or the Professional Actor Training Program at the University of Washington. Others are separate entities, such as the Julliard School in New York City. A conservatory is studio-intensive compared to a regular college program that is liberal arts-oriented.

Although expansion in the movie and television industry is expected to result in tens of thousands of new jobs for actors, musicians and other artists, the odds still are that the show will go on without you.

Filmmaking

Who are the people who make movies? Aside from **producers, directors, screenwriters,** and **film editors,** there are **casting directors, camera operators, unit managers** and scores of other behind-the-screens specialists. Filmmaking reaches from feature movies, television shows and video productions to documentaries, commercials and industrial/educational films.

There are three basic ways of preparing for film life: college study, on-job training and independent filmmaking. The college route is good because students get a chance to taste the kind of work they'll be doing, make important contacts and shoot film for their portfolios. You can get into filmmaking without going through a college film program; the key is finding a friend who will open doors for you to be hired as a messenger, mailroom clerk, assistant or other entry-level worker. Think about how you will make your entrance.

Museum Jobs

Competition for jobs in the nation's 5,500 or so museums is fierce and pay for all but directors of the best-known is on a scale nearly as antique as the items displayed. But the work can be soul-satisfying for those with advanced degrees in related disciplines—art history, anthropology, folklife studies or zoology, for instance.

Large museums divide job categories into six specialties: **curator, educator, registrar, conservator, exhibit designer** and **museum director.**

If you enter the field through a museum training graduate program, be sure the one you choose is affiliated with a museum, has a faculty experienced in museum work and offers an internship experience of at least six months.

Music

The sound and style of tomorrow's music will change but demand for its people will continue at a modest tempo. Among music lovers with relatively reliable careers are **music teachers, record company publicists, recording engineers, music arrangers** and **disc jockeys.**

That's for opening bars in the scope of music opportunities; the industry contains at least 100 separate occupations, ranging from **symphony conductor** and **rock concert impresario,** to **opera singer** and **music video performer.**

Within the music industry there's much argument about how electronic music will affect jobs. Machines may drum some live musicians offstage and out of the studio, but automation is creating a few new jobs for people who can combine music, computers and sound technology.

The staff of the Kiplinger Washington Letter agree. In *The New American Boom* (Kiplinger Washington Editors Inc.), they say: "Live performance will remain a vital part of the American scene, but make no mistake about this: Electronic renditions of the arts, played in the home, will be the entertainment boom field of the next several decades."

The standard advice to musicians who need back-up help is this: Get a teacher's certificate after obtaining a four-year degree in music education.

Unless you're a performing star or recording company executive, the music field is not known for lush paychecks. Your chances of reaching the top in music are about the same as winning a state lottery.

Visual Arts

Yes, you can earn a living in fine arts, but for most people, it continues to be a brave career choice.

Gifted **painters** and **sculptors** must find a support base—family, mate, patron, part-time job—until sales of their work enable them to be financially self-sufficient. Few artists ever reach financial independence. What it boils down to is talent—natural major talent honed by ambition, perseverance, endless hard work and self-discipline.

Many artists pursue fine arts as a part-time career, or combine their artistic training with a related study: arts administration, stage design, museum work or teaching. An art history PhD, for instance, might enjoy a luminous art-wrapped career as a combination college professor, art author, museum researcher, curator and gallery director.

The field of graphic art, also called commercial art or design, offers steadier paychecks. **Editorial artists** illustrate magazines, album covers, posters and other publications. **Illustrators** paint or draw pictures for books, magazines, advertisements and film. **Fashion illustrators, cartoonists, animators** and **medical illustrators** all find work in specialized markets. In an information age, jobs for graphic artists will increase faster than average.

Even artists can't escape computers: Computerized business graphics is coming of age. CAD (computer-aided design) technology is used in advertising, audiovisual presentations, business statistics and corporate publications.

Regardless of computers, the big money in art will always depend on a touch of genius and savvy marketing, whether the work is museum quality—or the next Garfield.

Take Out "Employability Insurance"

The vast majority of people who immerse themselves in the arts during their student years do not go on to support themselves as artists, but work at other jobs—often whatever they can find. Why not hedge your bets by gaining a practical marketable job skill?

High-Flying High-Tech Jobs

Most career writings about high-tech jobs focus on gee-whiz technology and a new wave of work. This is misleading. Why? Because most of the glamorous new fields—lasers, fiber optics sensors, superconducting devices—employ few people. They make great headlines but few jobs. And even some of the newest fields—such as artificial intelligence—have already suffered personnel layoffs.

The plain fact is that fast-growing high-tech industries do not need as many human hands as the older industries. By definition, automation means transferring to machines tasks performed by humans.

The significance of high tech in the job market is not the relatively small number of jobs it will create but how it will alter existing occupations.

But suppose you want to head for a high-tech occupation—such as engineer, scientist, math specialist, technician or computer specialist. What are the possibilities? Here's a random sampling of job titles.

- applications programmer
- CAD/CAM specialist (computer aided design/ computer aided manufacturing)
- graphics programmer
- human factors specialist
- MIS specialist (management information systems)
- process controller
- systems programmer
- quality assurance specialist
- security specialist
- genetic engineer
- robotics engineer
- systems analyst
- bioprocess engineer
- knowledge engineer
- telecommunications network analyst

Salary is an important reason to consider a high-tech career. Payment tends to outpace inflation and there's lots of opportunity for overtime in jobs that require work at a customer's place of business—computer installation, for instance.

Technical careers authority Steven S. Ross, a journalism professor at Columbia University, has compiled this capsule compensation chart for high-tech workers. The scale is meant only as a generalized guide.

Occupation	Education	Low-High
Scientist	BS, MS, PhD	$25-80,000
Engineer	BS, MS	$25-60,000
Programmer	BS	$18-50,000

(continued)

Occupation	Education	Low-High
Engineering technologist	BS, BSET	$18-35,000
Technician	AAS, AOS, BS, BA	$14-25,000
Technician	on-job training	$12-25,000

Key: BA=bachelor of arts degree; BS=bachelor of science degree; BSET=bachelor of science in engineering technology; MS=master of science; PhD=doctorate; AAS=associate in applied science; AOS=associate in occupational studies.

Want a reading list? Try these.

- *High-Tech Careers* by Joyce Lain Kennedy and Steven S. Ross (40 pages; $4.50; available only from Sun Features Inc., Box 368V, Cardiff, CA 92007).
- *The High-Tech Career Book* by Betsy A. Collard (William Kaufman, Los Altos, CA).
- *Careers in High Tech* by Connie Winkler (Arco/Simon & Schuster, Old Tappan, NJ).
- *Succeeding in High Tech* by Marlene Shigekawa (John Wiley & Sons, Somerset, NJ).

Health Care

Prospects for a strong job market in health care are robust, considering that as the nation's population ages, it will need large doses of health care. But stunning and sweeping changes are occurring in American health care and the careers associated with it. Some changes are positive, others are seen as harmful to patients and health workers.

Many of the changes are spawned by new technologies—genetic engineering, computers, robotics, lasers and optics—but most center on money problems.

Health care costs skyrocketed until the early '80s when Medicare and other insurance programs put a lid on them by adopting prospective payment plans that pay a flat fee for treatment regardless of how much the hospital spends on a patient. Hospitals began losing money, laying off staff and sending patients home quicker and sicker. When the carte blanche era ended for health care, the hospital industry—where the majority of health workers are employed—caught a cold that, in some cases, has gone into pneumonia.

A number of hospitals are closing; others are changing over to nursing homes; still others are competing for funds and staff with health facilities that have lower overhead: surgery, urgent-care and birthing centers, for example.

Overall hospital usage may fall as much as 50 percent in the next decade. For-profit hospital chains are proliferating across the country, swallowing many independent and non-profit hospitals. Some of these chains will become "supermeds," new health-care corporations dispensing health services across the board: hospitals, health maintenance organizations, health insurance, walk-in clinics, pharmacies, dental clinics and mental illness treatment centers, as well as home computer services for remote diagnostics and consultation.

Industry analysts say we won't adopt the type of national health system (socialized medicine) seen in Great Britain, but it seems certain that American health care will become more impersonal, more bureaucratic and filled with increasing numbers of salaried, rather than independent, practitioners. Goodbye, Dr. Welby.

How Automation is Affecting Health Jobs

Computers are being used to monitor critical care patients so that a single nurse can watch over as many patients as two or more nurses could monitor a few years ago.

Automated delivery systems that allow robot carts to deliver food and supplies, and pick up refuse and dirty dishes, are likely to displace some unskilled workers at many hospitals.

In the artificial intelligence area, computer expert systems will help physicians—and individuals on their own—to diagnose various ailments. Computers also will store treatment "protocols"—prescribed routines for various illnesses that physicians and other health professionals will be required to follow.

With bureaucracy and technology merging, more and more medical treatment will be "by the book ...oops, computer."

Opportunity Calls

Within the next 20 years, there'll be about 16 million Americans 65 and older, including a couple of hundred thousand who are age 100 and older. Our aging population paints a bright future for nursing homes and geriatric-care services and the people who can make them work, including orthopedists and arthritis specialists, who will be kept busy treating ailments of older Americans.

Hospital and health facility marketing specialists who can bring in the business, and cost-containment personnel, who can keep the institutions solvent, will find lots of takers in their bids for jobs in the health care industry.

Government paperwork has generated increased demand for people to handle medical records.

There's much talk, if little action, about the need for multicompetent technicians who can wear at least two allied health hats, such as X-ray technology and respiratory therapy.

Many **pharmacists, physical therapists** and **occupational therapists** are bailing out of hospitals for better-paying work in industry, outside service enterprises or independent practice.

Medicine

The surplus of **doctors** will continue for at least another 15 years. Some health industry analysts believe that independent practitioners will become relatively rare and that by the early 21st century, a majority of American doctors will be on salary, rather than self-employed. Other experts disagree, but many expect a continued growth in group practices.

Nursing

In contrast to an oversupply of physicians, a monster shortage of **registered nurses** is shaping up. Projections of shortfall by the year 2000 range from 350,000 to 600,000 RNs—chiefly in hospitals. Nursing, a field that needs a high level of altruism and idealism, has been left in the dust by a rush to loftier and better-paying careers. Many registered nurses who stay in nursing are fleeing hospitals for less stressful and higher-paying jobs in other health care settings.

Hospital nursing executives expect demand for **licensed practical nurses** to remain the same or even decline. They do not see a shortage of LPNs. If you enter an LPN program, look on it as a stepping stone and make plans to later upgrade to registered nurse status.

Give nursing a close look; the shortage condition means there will be some very attractive opportunities because they'll welcome you with open arms.

Dentistry

An oversupply of **dentists** will last until the early 2000s. Their jobs are changing. Drill-and-fill dentistry is a practice of the past. Dental technology increasingly is able to prevent tooth decay and gum disease, which allows dentistry to shift focus to prevention, diagnosis and aesthetics. Time-release fluoride pellets, tooth decay vaccines, genetically-engineered tooth enamel and other wondrous new products are on the horizon, all of which may contribute to a growing demand for orthodontics and cosmetic dental work.

Veterinary Science

Veterinarians, too, are abundant, both for companion and farm animals. Women make up half the enrollment at veterinary colleges. Owners of small-animal practices usually earn more than owners of food-animal or large-animal practices, but a vet with a race horse practice can look forward to riding high.

Other Health Practitioners

Chiropractors will encounter competition in establishing a practice as graduates continue to pour out of chiropractic colleges. There's much optimism about prospects for **podiatrists** because of increased interest in jogging, and older people have more foot problems. The outlook is encouraging for **optometrists,** too. Half of Americans have eye deficiencies and one-third of optometrists are pushing retirement age.

More Than 200 Allied Health Occupations

Many of the more than 200 occupations that assist, facilitate and complement the work of physicians and other medical specialists are new. They emerged only within the last 25 years in response to the rapid advancements in health care technologies. What are the most promising allied health jobs today?

Here are the views of 2,500 educators who train students for health care occupations. Their perspectives on selected occupations are gathered regularly by an arm of the American Medical Association, the Committee on Allied Health Education and Accreditation.

Most attractive
- perfusionist
- physician assistant
- occupational therapist
- ophthalmic medical assistant
- medical record administrator
- medical record technician
- radiation therapy technologist

Very attractive
- EEG technologist
- diagnostic medical sonographer
- respiratory therapist

Attractive
- nuclear medicine technologist
- respiratory therapy technician
- histotechnologist
- medical assistant

Moderately attractive
- cytotechnologist
- emergency medical technician
- radiographer
- surgical technologist
- specialist in blood banking
- medical laboratory technician
- medical technologist

200 Ways to Put Your Talent to Work in the Health Field is a booklet that briefly describes what various allied health workers do and where to get more information about allied health occupations. For a copy, enclose a long, self-addressed envelope stamped with two ounces of first-class postage with your request to the National Health Council, 34th Fl., 622 Third Ave., New York, NY 10017.

Health Is a Good Choice

It's hard to think about the career potential in the health care industry without getting carried away. We really are entering a golden age of health with new technologies to defeat diseases from cancer to central nervous system disability. Speaking about the health team has become a cliché, but it's true: It takes many specialists working together to pull off the miracles in medicine. If you want to be a maker of miracles for patients, obtain the best health-related education you can; if you want to run the business operation, adding business courses to your studies will ready you for an age when many hospitals worry about keeping their doors open.

HOSPITALITY AND RECREATION

This is a fun group of jobs for which some forecasters expect great things in the coming two decades. Hospitality means tourism in its broadest definition—travel, lodging, food. Recreation encompasses the activities that entertain tourists. Jobs range from **airline travel club manager** to **bartender,** from **golf course superintendent** to **baseball umpire.** A leading reason why the hospitality and recreation industries may be headed for a prosperous period is that baby boomers are maturing, have more jingle in their jean pockets and see travel and leisure pursuits as a right, rather than a privilege.

Travel

Automation in ticket sales and travel planning may squeeze travel agency-related jobs in the years ahead. Although skies are sunny now, the travel industry is only as good as the economy; a downturn brings storm warnings.

The technical complexity of the equipment and the business leaves little room for beginners to sprout wings on the job—you need airline experience or formal training. You can take a four-year degree program in travel, but an intensive few months in a vo-tech travel program is the route most **travel agents** choose.

If it becomes commonplace to buy tickets by telephone or computer, smart travel agents will survive by emphasizing counseling rather than order-taking. They'll function more as travel planners, comparison-shoppers and consumer advocates, helping clients to sort out the bewildering number of travel options. They'll establish larger firms and scout for more commercial accounts, even going so far as to locate personnel in large corporate offices.

Travel agents earn little and change jobs frequently. The real money is in business accounts, tours and ownership of a large profitable agency.

Lodging Industry

Hotels and motels are concerned that a smaller number of young people in the population may spell labor shortages in the next decade or so. This could be a strategic time to enter the field.

Find room in the inns one of two ways: formal education or work your way up the ranks. You can study for an associate, bachelor's or master's degree in hotel administration. Some hotel corporations offer management training programs only to college graduates, while others will consider high-school graduates.

Banquet sales is a good break-in area which, once you begin to earn commissions, can result in high earnings. A successful **banquet booker** might become an **assistant manager** and finally a **general manager.** Promotion opportunities are best in major chains, rather than in small companies, because you can transfer to other locations as positions open up. Ambitious people in the hospitality field should plan on relocating and on making a total commitment where hours are concerned. Hotel management is very demanding.

Pay ranges from barely adequate to above average, but don't forget that besides salary and other normal fringe benefits, many hotel executives have part or all of their room and board and other incidental living expenses paid for by their employers since they frequently live in the establishments for the convenience of their employers.

Food Service

The giant food service industry creates employment for six million people and gobbles more than 40 percent of household food budgets. Americans like to eat out and the steep rise in the number of two-income households allows them to pay for it. After putting in a hard day at work, people are too wiped out to hassle with kitchen chores.

The restaurant industry, like travel, is at the mercy of the economy.

Food service management offers a variety of attractive possibilities. Managerial jobs exist in restaurants, cafeterias, hotels, country clubs, fast-food places, airlines, steamships, catering companies and corporate kitchens.

There's a full menu of ways to prepare. You can attend a two-year community college or vo-tech institute for an associate degree in food service management that qualifies you for the technical aspects of food management. A four-year program with a major in food service prepares you for a management position.

To accommodate the national feeding frenzy, America needs **chefs,** plain and gourmet. You can learn on the job, including in the armed forces, or through a three-year apprenticeship program.

A third option is to attend a school. It may be a culinary arts program in a vo-tech school or community college. Many hopefuls attend a *toque blanch* school, so named for the tall white hats worn by chefs. The toque blanch schools—such as the Culinary Institute of America at Hyde Park, N.Y., the California Culinary Academy in San Francisco, or the Washburne Trade School in Chicago—prepare you to handle 50 diners, each requiring a different combination of dishes served in sequence and concurrent with their table companions' varied choices. Other students enroll in *cordon bleu* schools that lead to careers in small-scale catering, teaching, writing about food, preparing food for photography, writing cookbooks, or cooking in a very small restaurant.

Earnings vary as much as the difference between Tex-Mex cooking and French cuisine. Entry salaries are modest, but superstar chefs who handle multimillion dollar budgets earn in the six-figure bracket.

Sports

Sports! You love them, but you know you're not pro-athlete material. Still, you keep wondering: Isn't there a place for me? Maybe, if you have the right training. Sporting work settings for non-athletes include fitness facilities, resorts, sporting goods suppliers, sports-medicine facilities and media.

You might be a **team information director/publicist,** a **physical education teacher** or **coach,** an **athletic trainer,** a **sports event promoter,** or a **sports broadcaster,** to mention several possibilities.

To prepare for work in the world of sports, talk with your school counselor about vo-tech and college programs that will make you a strong contender to finish first in the career of your choice.

Suppose you *are* qualified to become a pro athlete? Even if you're snatched up before you can say "NFL," the mammoth money bins where pro athletes keep their salaries may be less full in future years. Pro pay is leveling off and may even take a hit. The smartest, most successful athletes plan and prepare as hard for life after play as they train for glory on the field.

More Careers in Leisure Land

Club management differs from association management in its recreational focus and facilities management. **Managers** of the nation's private clubs—country, university, yacht, luncheon and fraternal—earn handsome incomes when fringes are counted in.

With the exception of the Disney operations, the kiddy theme parks are slowing down, offering fewer career opportunities. The reason is there aren't enough young children to entertain.

Believe it: Love Boat jobs are hard to land. Cruise director positions are so scarce that some **cruise directors** break in as shipboard entertainers.

Is a Downturn Ahead?

Recent changes in the tax laws eliminate some tax deductions for business meals and entertainment. In anticipation of tax changes, anxious lobbyists for hospitality industries said the sky would fall—that business would drop and people would lose their jobs. Business did fall off a hair, but so far the lobbyists' dire predictions have not come true. Executives are still buying expense-account meals and companies are still buying season tickets for professional sports. At this point, there's no panic in the streets, but it may be too early to assess the damage. A delayed reaction to spending money could set in when companies pay their first tax bills under the new law.

In the long view, tax law is not a factor that should sway your career decision. What Congress taketh away, Congress can giveth back—when the public hue and cry is loud enough.

Manufacture and Repair

By 2000, fewer production workers will be manning fewer plants in manufacturing America. Automation will see to that. But the demand for engineers, technicians, salespeople and upper-level managers may increase.

New, smaller flexible manufacturing plants will employ a fairly small number of highly skilled operatives to supervise and service the equipment. The changeover will be hard on unskilled, unschooled workers.

During much of the '80s we were warned that U.S. manufacturing had bought the big factory in the sky. The obituary was a misprint. What really is happening, according to the latest analysis, is a change in the *mix* of what we make.

Old, weakened industries will continue to falter: basic iron and steel, apparel, textiles, leather, shoes and tobacco, for example. Their losses are due to the inability of American goods to compete on price and quality in a global market.

By contrast, employment is growing in other manufacturing sectors, some of which are high tech, some not. More jobs are anticipated in printing and publishing, communications equipment, computers, pharmaceuticals, medical instruments, plastics and fabricated metals, to pinpoint a few promising industries.

Scientists and engineers are included here, although many of these professionals actually work in other career clusters, from agriculture to transportation.

Whatever we make, we may have to repair, which is why many occupations, from home appliance repairer to boiler repairer, fit into this group.

Factory-Focused Technology

In non-chemical manufacturing, a trio of core disciplines dominate: mechanical, electrical and industrial engineering. Most of the other areas are subspecialties or combinations of the three core disciplines.

Mechanical engineers are sought after for all things mechanical, such as engines and motors. Industrial plants and production lines fall within the purview of mechanical engineering. BSMEs (bachelor of science in mechanical engineering) are substituting sophisticated computer software for pencils and calculators. Knowledge of automated systems is vital for career durability.

Electrical engineers in this group are not the people who design microchips, but the BSEEs (bachelor of science in electrical engineering) who design power plant distribution systems, communication systems and plan installation of energy-using equipment.

Industrial engineers also emphasize high-quality, low-cost production in manufacturing. BSIEs (bachelor of science in industrial engineering) work in the services sector as well as in manufacturing jobs; in the latter they perform the same function as manufacturing engineers.

Manufacturing engineers, who have a BSMfgE (bachelor of science in manufacturing engineering) are experts in high quality production know-how on the factory floor. The changeover to automated production is just starting to roll, and it will be years before the machines are everywhere. The outlook for MfgEs is generally promising.

Robotics engineers are one type of manufacturing engineer. They may design or modify robots and other automated manufacturing devices to handle specific tasks. A wait-and-see attitude is your best posture before committing to robotic engineering; American robot production may stall because of cutbacks in investment and research, plus stiff competition from abroad. If you're interested in robotics, keep a watch on the business news until you must declare one engineering discipline or another.

The duties of **robotics repairers,** who handle robot service and maintenance, can overlap with those of **robotics technicians,** who assist engineers by setting up and programming new automation.

Computer-aided design (CAD) systems, basically the graphic arts equivalent of word processors for drafters, have brightened the job market for **CAD operators;** CAD training requires a drafting or design background, but not computer literacy.

CIM (computer-integrated manufacturing) managers are emerging from engineering or manufacturing departments to wed automation to production.

Communications

Soon we can reach out to touch someone anywhere, instantly and with visuals and foreign language translation! Freed from most of the shackles of government regulation and charged by the growth in microprocessors and high-capacity networks, the communications industry is becoming gigantic.

One of the problems in identifying opportunities may stem from terminology. The distinctions between broadcasting (television, radio and so forth) and telecommunications (the transmission of voice or data over telephone links) have blurred. That's why the broader term "communications" is replacing "telecommunications."

The most employable people in communications have degrees in electrical engineering or computer science. Business majors are good bets and good jobs should be available for those who can market and sell.

Fiber Optics

Fiber optics is less doing more. It is a new transmission technology, using light to convey data through hair-thin glass fibers that are replacing copper cable in many communications systems.

Beyond carrying telephone messages and data more efficiently from city to city than can copper wire or microwaves, fiber optic systems are beginning to move inside certain equipment such as super-fast computers and civilian aircraft. One category of fiber optics work is filled by professionals—

usually those who hold undergraduate or graduate degrees in physics or electrical engineering with a specialization in optics. Another category is handled by craft workers who install and maintain fiber optic systems.

Superconductors

Scientists have long known that certain materials conduct electricity with no resistance when they are cooled to temperatures too cold to be practical. Now, research continues to raise the mercury and lower the cost hurdles on the superconductor scene. Scientists say it's only a matter of time until they break the room-temperature barrier, an achievement that promises nothing short of astounding change the world over.

Imagine: Trains that fly above their rails at aviation speeds, ultrapowerful computers, cheap energy from fusion—all these Utopian technologies and products once only dreamed of are suddenly coming into focus.

Discoveries by physicists in several nations only within the past year or so are being lauded as a gigantic leap in both electrical and electronic technology, impacting virtually everything affected by energy. Scientists are comparing superconductivity developments to the rapid emergence of electronic computing 40 years ago. Some say it will dwarf the change spawned by transistors.

The race among scientists around the world to push superconducting materials has just begun. Projections range from three to 10 years before the new high-temperature materials can be engineered into useful products, and perhaps 10 to 20 years before electric utilities can take full advantage of the revolutionary new superconductors.

In any scientific discovery, scientists—in this case, **physicists**—are the advance guard. They are followed by engineers and engineering technicians as the technology is scaled up from the laboratory to field applications and factory floors.

Although **electric and electronic engineers** will play a pivotal role in applying the technology, other technical personnel will join in, depending on the application. **Computer scientists** will develop new computers, **automotive engineers** will design electric cars, **civil engineers** will design roadbeds for flying trains.

Superconducting, which has been termed the "new billion-dollar" business, will not be the source of a lot of new jobs; instead, the industry will affect the *content* of many jobs.

Plastics

The plastics job market looks good. One reason for optimism is the development of superplastics—materials chemically engineered to possess an infinite variety of properties that can be used to make almost anything—from waterproof diaper covers to forever plastic caskets. Some industry insiders insist the day of the polymer has only begun.

Many employers prefer a specialization in polymers—bachelor's, master's or doctoral degree, but some hire **electrical, chemical** and **mechanical engineers,** and a variety of **chemists.**

Ceramics

Advanced ceramics is turning up amazing discoveries that point to an exciting career field of the '90s—in fact, one of the best. Imagine ceramic knives that never need sharpening, artificial bones stronger than metal and ceramic engines for cars that use less fuel, give greater power and require no cooling or lubrication.

Because the essence of ceramics is sand—cheap and plentiful, and remade with high temperature chemistry—some observers see the technology as a catalyst for a new "stone age" industrial revolution. At the center of the breakthrough in ceramics technology are **ceramic engineers,** who use math and physics to sculpt careers.

Jobs are available in refractories (which produce materials that can stand superhigh heat), defense

Emerging Careers for the Next Century

How can you tell if you're looking at a genuine budding career or somebody's flight of fancy? Dr. S. Norman Feingold describes a five-point formula for identifying an emerging occupation.

1. It has become increasingly distinguishable in recent years.
2. It has developed from changing needs in existing areas, such as the latest in medical care, personal services, business.
3. It has become possible because of technology or environmental change, such as home computers, solar science, satellites.
4. It shows growth in numbers of people employed and attending new education and training programs.
5. It requires more than two months' training.

Here are 30 new occupations compiled by Dr. Feingold and co-author Norma Reno Miller in *Emerging Careers: New Occupations for the Year 2000 and Beyond* (Garrett Park Press, Garrett Park, MD 20896).

Most of these occupations exist, although others have yet to come on-line.

1. artificial intelligence technician
2. aquaculturist
3. automotive fuel cell battery technician
4. benefits analyst
5. bionic electron technician
6. computational linguist
7. computer microprocessor
8. cryonics technician
9. dialysis technologist
10. electronic mail technician
11. fiber optic technician
12. fusion engineer
13. hazardous waste technician
14. horticulture therapy assistant
15. image consultant
16. information broker
17. information center manager
18. job developer
19. leisure consultant
20. materials utilization specialist
21. medical diagnostic imaging technician
22. myotherapist
23. relocation counselor
24. retirement counselor
25. robot technician
26. shyness consultant
27. software club director
28. space mechanic
29. underwater archaeologist
30. water quality specialist

Others, including Edward Cornish, have anticipated occupations in the future that don't exist now: manager of robot housepainting crews, real estate developer on the moon, holographic inspection specialist. If you want to read further about jobs in the future, Cornish's book, *Careers Tomorrow: The Outlook for Work in a Changing World,* is available from the World Future Society, 4916 St. Elmo Ave., Bethesda, MD 20814.

Even more about robot farms, gene machines and other career futures is discussed in Adrian Paradis' *Planning Your Career of Tomorrow* (VGM Career Books/NTC Publishing Group).

contracting, electronics, fiber optics, and an impressive spread of other employers. The automotive industry may loom as a field of opportunity if the ceramic engines develop as expected.

Biotechnology

Biotechnology uses living organisms to make or modify products and improve plants or animals. *Genetic engineering,* in which the genetic material of one organism can be added to another to create such things as a self-fertilizing corn crop or a frost-resistant strawberry, is the best known sector of biotechnology.

Other sectors are *monoclonal antibody technology,* in which antibodies are made by cloning them from a single cell; and *bioprocessing,* the activities necessary to bring a product from the laboratory to the marketplace.

Exciting applications exist for the products of biotechnology—human health care, plant and animal agriculture and energy and environmental management. Balanced against this promise are biotech critics who worry about scientific foul-ups in the environment.

The big pay-offs in biotechnology have yet to materialize. Many biotech companies are a decade old and still do not have a product on the market. The most profitable segment of the industry today is the medical diagnostics market.

If you decide to try biotechnology—whether by aiming to be one of the few who is hired in a tiny field, or by waiting for the predictions of a boom to come true—you can prepare in almost any area of science, and at any level. Research positions go only to PhDs, but much of the work can be done by holders of undergraduate degrees. Once the biotech ball really starts rolling, marketing and sales jobs will open, and for these, an academic background in science and business is advised. One caution: Because of automation, biotech production will create fewer jobs than did the chemical production of past years.

Science Disciplines

The formula for **chemist** employment is simple: It's replacement jobs for chemists who leave the lab. The chemical work force has suffered a long-term slide and the field will inch along slowly in new job creation.

The small **physicist** job market, also creeping along, is tough to call because so many physicists work in research and development. Demand for physicists depends on R&D expenditures, which go up and down. The superconductor industry should open a few new avenues of employment to PhD physicists.

Most jobs for **geologists** and **geophysicists** are in or related to the petroleum industry, which lately has been in the doldrums because of low prices. Forecasters expect job opportunities to pick up in the middle '90s. Many openings will arise to replace geologists and geophysicists who retire each year.

Employment prospects for **biological scientists** will be best for those with advanced degrees who can do research in genetic, cellular and biochemical areas of biology.

The job market odds for **mathematics graduates** are best in applied math and related work. Math may be a more marketable undergraduate major than chemistry or biology. Many math majors are doing graduate work in computer science or computer engineering.

Engineering Disciplines

All engineering disciplines are heavily influenced by electronics and will continue to be so for the foreseeable future.

Electrical engineering is likely to remain in strong demand, especially for the computer area.

Materials will grow rapidly, including **ceramic engineering, metallurgical engineering, material science** and **plastic engineering.** The search for new, strong, lightweight materials for use in consumer products and building materials is the stimulus.

Energy saving is a growing field—**mechanical engineers** will be the chief benefactors of this movement.

Civil engineering could grow rapidly if we tackle the nation's decaying bridges, leaking sewer systems, worn-out roads and other infrastructure projects. Signs of this happening are not yet apparent.

This generalized outline does not reflect the fact that engineering is a cyclical profession, dependent on the state of the economy and political moods. Even so, the booms and busts tend not to be very deep.

Engineering experts do not agree on the outlook for the profession. Some professional engineering groups insist that engineering is in a depression and that, in fact, the profession may be a goner. Other engineering analysts say that far from being dead, an engineering shortage is in the making.

Which view is correct? It's the new college graduates in some engineering disciplines principally in demand by defense contractors who are in short supply. But 45-year-old engineers working on a product that has been cancelled are in a tough job market because they are not always able to compete with younger engineers who are paid less.

In some cases, the difference in outlook is almost like traditional management-labor union disputes. Industry wants a competitive labor market to avoid runaway wages, educational institutions want to keep their classes filled, and experienced engineers want to earn as much as possible without always looking over their shoulders at new graduates.

A shortage of engineers may or may not develop but there probably won't be a shortage problem. Job descriptions traditionally are elastic; when there aren't enough engineers, technicians do more work. Academic standards are relaxed.

The strength of science and engineering is fundamental to this country's quality of life. If engineering declines as an attractive career choice, we're all in trouble.

Technologists, Technicians and Repairers

Engineers may be assisted by technicians, who are graduates of one- or two-year technical programs, and by technologists, graduates of four-year technical programs.

Engineering technologists are nearest to engineers in training, but they have fewer theory and math courses than do engineers. The gap between engineers and engineering technologists is not large in slow-moving fields; it is in cutting-edge technology where skill differences are the greatest. Some graduates of four-year engineering technology programs go on to get an MBA with a goal of running their own operations, constructing houses or working in high-tech companies.

Engineering technicians perform simple and complex lab tests and maintain high-tech equipment ranging from satellite dishes to factory robots.

Other technicians and repairers who learn their skills in vocational-technical programs or associate degree programs—and who stay abreast of changing technology—will do well in the job market. Many use their know-how to open their own repair businesses.

Among those with better-than-average job prospects are **air-conditioning/refrigeration/heating mechanics, biomedical equipment technicians,** and **business machine service technicians.**

Among those with slow job growth prospects are **drafters** and **electric/gas appliance repairers.**

Television technicians and **vending machine technicians** face average growth. Once again: Think electronics!

A Glance Ahead

If the economy doesn't change much (no war, no depression), job opportunities for scientists will slowly improve and the numbers of young people competing for the jobs will slowly decrease, according to the Commission on Professionals in Science and Technology.

PhD scientist jobs at universities will open as older faculty retire, and the call for scientists in industry will increase.

Despite a somewhat brighter job future than scientists enjoyed in the '70s and '80s, remember that the hard sciences are not for everyone. Academia is usually a low-pay proposition, and industry can be a pressure cooker with the notable rewards of your innovations going to your employer. Math prowess is essential; can you really say fractions are your friends?

The job market for newly graduated engineers through the end of the century is likely to be comfortable—or better.

Because many engineers spend their careers managing others in research labs, engineering projects, departments or entire companies, advanced education may be desirable. What kind? An MBA will give you more cards to play than will a master of science in engineering management, but the latter will give you a better hand in technical management.

A generalist degree, the MBA teaches you basic principles of management that can be applied almost anywhere, from cosmetics manufacturing to aerospace contracting. A wise career strategy is to qualify for as broad a universe of jobs as possible, and an MBA gives you a wide and well-recognized credential.

By contrast, your true interests may be focused on depth rather than breadth. Graduate programs in engineering management—also called engineering administration and management science—provide specific training for managing technical people and technology.

Hourly-wage plant workers are finding out that the disposable employee is a fact of corporate life. In addition to layoffs and terminations, a growing number of such workers are being forced into a "contingent" pool of workers. In this arrangement, to cut costs, companies dismiss workers, then subcontract the work to smaller companies. The smaller companies hire the fired workers at half the pay and no benefits.

A shift toward automated design and assembly is not killing off manufacturing, but certainly is causing a significant shift in the occupational mix within industries. It's thumbs up for salaried, white-collar workers, those requiring the most training. It's a problem for hourly-wage factory workers.

Marketing and Distribution

The marketing function goes far beyond sales activities. It includes *everything* that must be done to move goods/services from producer to customer. Marketing encompasses the price at which the products are sold, the way they are promoted, the places where they are stored and the manner in which they will be delivered.

Targeted Marketing Comes Into Its Own

Mass marketing uses mass media to urge all of us to buy the same consumer goods—soap, autos, food—and has done so for the better part of a century. In the '50s, a soup company reached half of all American households just by sponsoring a popular television show. Things are no longer so simple. The business of courting an increasingly diverse population of customers is changing in complex ways. Fragmentation and regionalization of markets is the dominant trend.

That is, mass marketing of many national products is being replaced by pinpoint targeting of markets. Products, promotion, advertising and sales strategies are being tailored to fit different age, ethnic and economic groups, and different regions of the country, even neighborhoods. The reason marketing strategies are being redefined is that markets themselves are breaking up along regional and population lines—ethnic, teenage, suburban, yuppie and older markets, for instance. A single product or message about it that appeals to one group may flop with others.

To illustrate, the previously mentioned soup company used to sell the same cheese soup in every state. Market research suggested sales would rise in states like Texas and California if the soup were changed to reflect a preference for Mexican flavors. Now the company sells spicy nacho cheese soup in areas where Mexican flavors go over big and requires the regional marketing staff to find ways to promote the regionalized flavor on a regionalized basis.

For national television and national magazines, targeting or regionalizaton is bad news. For local television/radio stations and newspapers, it's good news. For young marketers, regionalization is a career blessing, transforming regional marketers from troops carrying out headquarters' orders to nearly autonomous managers who take decision-making responsibility early in their careers. Regional marketers still spend plenty of time calling on retailers, but increasingly they also have their own advertising budgets, make media deals, sponsor area sports events and arrange for sales promotions and cooperative programs with retailers.

Localized marketing is a boon for young people who excel at concocting competitive strategies, and who wish to see quickly the results of their efforts measured in rising sales.

Another dominant trend important to your career planning is the growing reliance on marketing through technology. Electronic data bases and selection systems are becoming the lifeblood of the business. Don't choose marketing as a solo undergraduate major; instead pair it with information science. At the graduate level in marketing, don't leave school without knowing how to make a computer sing.

Advertising

Tens of thousands of advertising specialists work in corporate advertising departments or in media concerns, but it's "Madison Avenue"—the advertising agency sector—that most people think of when they think of a career in advertising.

Madison Avenue has undergone unprecedented upheaval in the past few years, largely as a result of new austerity in company advertising budgets. "Much of the frivolity that ad agencies were known for—the opulence, the private boats and airplanes whisking clients down for golf games in the islands—is gone," explains the head honcho of a famous advertising agency.

Four trends could influence your future prospects in advertising.

1. Leaner advertising budgets are bringing a no-frills lifestyle to Madison Avenue. Many agencies are giving fewer bonuses, smaller raises and lower salary offers to potential new employees. Mergers and layoffs have wiped out some jobs. You no longer can count on high pay to offset low security.
2. Mega-agencies with worldwide offices are servicing giant multinational corporations. Some creative people, who prefer advertising's traditional free-wheeling atmosphere, find the new bureaucratic environments stifling.
3. Talented specialists and strong managers may find the most attractive opportunities in smaller, independent agencies that carve out sales market niches by offering highly personalized service.
4. Tomorrow's advertising aces will fill themselves in on the whole marketing picture, including such consumer promotions as coupons, sweepstakes and discounts. Advertising agencies are beefing up profits by serving the client's total marketing needs, not just providing print and broadcast ads.

Creative geniuses are splendidly rewarded, but the breathtaking money goes to account executives who handle a large national account, then take it along when they open their own advertising agencies.

Public Relations

A **public relations specialist** is no longer the person called in at the last minute to share the blame, but one who anticipates issues and shares those anticipations with top management.

In moving from apologist to futurist, public relations specialists need hard evidence to support insights, which means learning to use electronic data bases. That, plus the necessity to maneuver through the maze of emerging electronic media, points to course work that promotes a high degree of computer and electronic communication literacy.

Because PR specialists are paid to generate favorable public opinion for employer organizations to many publics, success in the field requires much more than a generalized desire to work with people. Public relations requires considerable knowledge of communications and media, and writing ability is extremely helpful. Having the abilities to think clearly and devise strategies is essential for the top jobs. Nearly all PR professionals are college graduates.

In college, take your degree in communications, public relations or journalism with a PR emphasis—or in liberal arts with a major in English and plenty of information science and computer courses.

Sales Promotion

To score in sales promotion, you need a fast flow of ideas, strong communication skills and a way with people. The trend toward targeted marketing is causing growth in sales promotion opportunities.

Activities in sales promotion include couponing, premiums, contests, sweepstakes, point-of-sale materials and videos, sampling, demonstrations, trade and sports promotions, collateral materials such as product flyers, and anything else that will pull the consumer to purchase the product or service.

A sales promotion is inviting a high school football team to a fast-food hamburger place after a big game for a free feed. Spectators at the game are given coupons good for a free soda with the purchase of a hamburger. The spectators pour in to see the team. And, as an added public relations touch, the newspaper photographs the team chowing down.

Market Research

Increasingly electronic, market research is a systematic and objective gathering of information to solve marketing problems. It's how producers of goods/services avoid groping in the business dark. Let's say a pet food maker wants to introduce a new health food for cats. Who will buy the greatest quantities of it? Will it sell best in health food or pet supply stores? Should it be packaged in red or blue paper? Market research personnel try to answer such questions, identifying opportunities and reducing risks. Computer skills are mandatory. Expect artificial intelligence expert systems to make inroads on demand for market research managers who design research projects.

Sales

If you're a sales natural—a person who never met a stranger—a career in sales can be bountiful in both self-actualization and material rewards. There's not much argument that sales is one of the most lucrative roads to the bank. And most sales jobs do not require a college education. What can you sell? Look in telephone yellow page directories—for starters! Many industrial products are listed only in obscure trade catalogs, print and electronic.

Jobs in technical sales, often in high-tech fields, are among the best paying and are the ones that most new sales-minded college graduates hope to land. The products are for resale—goods for biosensors, components for satellites, membranes for mining, liquid crystals for computers, materials for seeing-eye robots and a world of other industrial innovations or staples.

A handful of colleges offer industrial distribution as a major; the program may be located in schools of engineering, business or education. Other people enter the technical sales field from management engineering, industrial technology, engineering technology, industrial engineering or another engineering discipline related to the products being sold. The prevalent job title is **sales engineer.**

As a rule, earnings for industrial products salespeople are higher than for those in consumer product sales.

Retailing

Seismic change is shaking traditional retailing. Competition is everywhere.

More people will shop at warehouse clubs that lack frills and don't take credit cards, but offer members prices 8 percent to 15 percent above wholesale, compared with typical markups of 35 percent for discount stores and at least 50 percent at department stores.

A growing number of customers enjoys shopping in the comfort of their own homes, by catalog, direct mail or cable video programming.

Chain stores are setting up shop in small towns, threatening local merchants.

Big department stores are merging and acquiring smaller ones.

Retail companies are cutting back, expecting buyers to purchase for several departments and **merchandise managers** to supervise several buyers. Retailing experts say the streamlining is permanent, not temporary efforts to save a few dollars.

With earthquake-sized changes lurking everywhere, why consider retailing? While mid-level management and some clerical jobs may shrink, openings for creative marketing and merchandising specialists will grow. Retailing needs leading-edge ideas to navigate changing markets and population trends.

Another reason to put retailing in your future is that you can move up fast. Retailing has always offered responsibility at an early age—some department store presidents are in their 30s. Studies confirm that top retail executives in general tend to be much younger and have less graduate training than do their counterparts in other industries.

By making electronic comparisons of products, **retail buyers** are using computers to purchase goods. By contrast, automobile sales representatives are using computers to sell cars.

Computer systems that can do much of the sales job are beginning to turn up in auto dealers' showrooms. The systems can greet customers, compare features of competing models, add up the cost of options and work out the amount of monthly payments. Some systems even write up an order and phone it to the factory. **Automobile marketing managers** say the systems assist, not replace sales personnel. Honk if you believe that.

Media has popularized the idea of electronic shopping in malls and at home for nearly a decade, but so far it's been more vision than reality. Shopping is a social experience for many people, and the mall marketers are going to do their best to make shopping fun with lunchtime concerts, dancing bears, celebrity guest speakers, even meeting rooms available for customer use.

Direct Marketing

Direct-marketing managers have long used direct mail to woo customers and now their sales efforts include alternatives, such as video cassettes in which sales messages are transmitted in a promotional package for playing on VCRs.

Anticipate technology in the early 21st century which could cause us to dismiss video cassettes and even disks, in favor of "chip storage," a bit of plastic the size of a credit card that carries incredible amounts of information for sound or visual display on a video screen.

Direct marketing managers also use catalogs, telemarketing, direct-response television ads, door-to-door sales, home merchandising parties and multi-level marketing techniques.

Fund Raising

Fund raising, a form of direct marketing, helps make the world a better place. **Fund raisers** for non-profit and charitable organizations use the same direct-mail and telemarketing techniques employed by *People* magazine and the May Company. Universities, museums, symphonies, animal rights organizations, research foundations, health facilities and other groups all survive because of contributions.

Fund raisers are becoming a more educated group—4 out of 10 have at least one master's degree. That's good. They'll need all the preparation they can get to market worthy causes in the '90s. Large corporate contributions may be topping out after a steady two-decade climb, leaving a gap that hopefully will be filled by medium-sized and small companies. Corporate chiefs are becoming more concerned with fierce business competition, and less with social concerns.

Fund raising, an honorable profession, is occasionally sullied by crooks. Legitimate fund raisers are adequately paid and the work can be enormously satisfying.

Food Plus Retailing

Get ready for future shock in the supermarket, say food merchandisers.

Machines will grow everywhere. A video shopping terminal will display items from frying pans to furniture that customers can order and pay for through the machine with a credit card. A coupon-dispensing terminal will hand out coupons directly to customers, and a store directory terminal will tell them where products are in the store. A nutrition and recipe inquiry terminal will answer customer's questions about food values and provide recipes. A wine inquiry terminal will offer information on type, price and wine brands.

By 2000, shopper convenience may equate with the days earlier in the century when your great grandmothers called Joe the Butcher and had everything delivered.

Food marketing is a ripe idea for tomorrow's careers. Study in a two-year community college program in food marketing or distributive education, or in a baccalaureate program in food marketing.

Selling to the New America

A wave of recent immigration is radically remaking the map of the American consumer marketplace. Marketing specialists have long known about seniors, yuppies and female careerists. The new purchasing powerhouse is immigrants—most of them from Asia and Latin America. Asians and Hispanics now account for nearly 10 percent of the American population and in the next century, they and their children—together with black Americans—will constitute a majority of American consumers.

A lightning-struck career field, marketing crackles with new challenge in new markets and new technologies. Concerning the latter, the savviest marketers will use technology, but not tie their whole professional life to it. The danger is in allowing the computer to crowd out people as crucial sources of information.

Personal Services

Personal services, a cluster of occupations that require extensive person-to-person contact, does not undergo much technological pushing and shoving. The technological change that does happen is not expected to greatly influence or limit job openings in personal service industries.

Be Your Own Boss

Personal services includes many great opportunities for the self-employed or would-be entrepreneurs to develop prosperous businesses. Compared to industrial enterprises, start-up capital requirements are small, and the services market is spreading. The increasing numbers of singles, families headed by a single parent, working couples and the elderly illuminate a need for services that these groups, for reasons of time or energy, can't provide for themselves.

The businesses range from clothing alterations, therapeutic massage and bodyguard services, to family counseling, color consulting and shopping chores. First, learn the business so you can judge whether future employees are productive workers, then take courses in small business management. Here are several examples of personal service businesses.

Car Detailers. Road-weary cars get a new lease on life at car appearance centers, where a team of cleaners lavish meticulous attention on metal beasts. Polishing and waxing, engine cleaning, carpet and upholstery shampooing, vinyl top cleaning and dyeing, deodorizing and other tender treatments are offered to satisfy auto addicts.

Janitorial Business. Organizing an army of men and women with mops and brooms is a dirty business but one in which some people clean up. Commercial cleaning contracts are the prizes in the market.

School Reunion Services. For a fee, these firms locate school alums, issue invitations to reunions, hire the halls, plan the refreshments and handle the finances.

Super Helpers. Resourceful and enterprising people help busy executives, overworked homemakers, the elderly, the disabled and others whose "circuits are overloaded." Super helpers do anything legitimate, often on an hourly rate basis. They may organize business files, pay bills, arrange for movers, conduct garage sales, pick up mail, clean garages and shepherd children to the dentist.

Pet Groomers. This business is hard, dirty work, but many people in it think it's the cat's meow. Groomers work in their own shops, sometimes home-based, and occasionally pick up and deliver pampered pets.

Looking Good Businesses. Cosmetology and barbering are popular choices; the highest financial rewards go to those who open their own establishments. Because of volume, owning several salons catering to the low end of the business—cut-rate haircuts and styling—can be very profitable. The most glamorous facet of physical self-improvement revolves around expensive health spas and antiaging salons.

Make a Wise Choice

Many personal service opportunities—like party planning and color consulting—are not of sufficient interest to enough people to count on a stable income. The timeless businesses, such as window cleaning service, clothing alterations and beauty care, tend to be more reliable income producers.

Public Service

The unifying theme of this occupational cluster is services to people. Activities are not oriented toward making a profit; instead, they focus on providing the support systems that lubricate society's engine. Jobs are found in non-profit organizations and government agencies—national, regional, state, county and municipal.

Teaching

Computers teach many subjects, but they cannot provide the interpersonal learning experiences offered only by schools and human **teachers.** A computer cannot recruit students for a debate team or organize a field trip to a museum, and it cannot listen sympathetically and offer constructive advice when a student can't get his or her mind around a difficult subject.

Neither can a computer reach out and engage a student's interest. For that, human beings are needed. Teachers will continue to provide leadership, guiding students in the right direction and counseling them in cloudy moments.

Which is not to say that technology will not change the complexion of education. Video tapes, cassettes and disks make it possible to give first-rate lectures in living color on almost any subject, from history to Spanish, science to driver's education. Students can watch reruns of visual presentations when they want to be sure they fully understand the material.

Technology will enable individual learning assignments to be made, carried out, evaluated and recorded. Because technology will save teachers many hours of clerical work, more of their time can be devoted to meeting the human needs of individual pupils. With technology, teachers will be more—not less—important.

Education is one of the most certain job markets to predict because it's tied to birth rates. Demographers differ somewhat on particulars, but here's the outlook according to the Center for Educational Statistics, U.S. Department of Education. The baby boomlet that began in 1977 is causing an expansion in the number of elementary-school teaching jobs that will continue at least through the late '90s. As the boomlet kids grow, demand will pick up for secondary-school teachers in the early '90s and by the mid '90s, prospects should improve for college professors.

Among unpredictable factors are political decisions, such as the influx of immigrants and the number of children they'll have, and the depth of such societal trends as the movement toward lifelong learning.

A massive teacher shortage is facing the nation, according to the National Education Association, the American Federation of Teachers and the Rand Corporation. But studies by the U.S. Department of Labor and by private consultant C. Emily Feistritzer insist that there is no national teacher shortage at present, and that one is not likely in the foreseeable future. The opinion gap is chiefly due to who is considered a qualified teacher.

The public tends to think of teaching as a homogeneous profession, when, in fact, it is a collection of professionals with expertise in different fields. Thus, while many areas of teaching are expected to be roughly balanced in supply and demand, there are shortages in some geographic areas of teachers of math, science, special education and engineering, and a surplus of teachers of elementary grades (despite the increase in jobs), home economics, social science, health education and art.

Teachers face problems that would make many tough managers hide in their offices. Constant disciplining, underprepared students, an avalanche of paper work and too few supplies are just some of the complaints voiced by teachers. Even when they do an award-winning job, they rarely get a merit pay increase.

Discussions of educational reform always include paying teachers more and recognizing the value of outstanding teachers—developments long overdue.

Counseling

Two-thirds of **counselors** are in educational services. In school settings, counselors are concerned with expanding the number of opportunities for students and with encouraging them to make good choices. A Maryland high school guidance counselor says, "Since I know you are in the 'process of becoming,' I work with your expectations because I want you to stretch to your potential."

The job market and pay for counselors in education roughly parallel those of teachers. But when budgets are tight, counselors may be laid off to retain a full staff of teachers. School counseling currently is a slow-growth field with the bulk of openings brought about by replacement needs.

Most counselors in education work in high schools, but some are employed in elementary schools, as well as in colleges and universities. The work of school counselors is mosaic in scope. Some tasks aid students with improved decision making, long-range planning and setting academic and career goals. Other counseling tasks focus on personal student concerns, ranging from poor study habits, personal values and religion, to parental neglect, sexual behavior and substance abuse. Interested? As a school counselor, you'll be helping students cope with a litany of problems; don't expect short days.

College counselors (counselors who work in colleges) lend concerned ears to a wide spectrum of issues as they try to help students in two- and four-year colleges and universities deal with personal, social, educational and career problems and concerns. **College career planning and placement counselors** specialize in a host of career development activities.

Other kinds of counseling professionals are found in the public service sector, including **rehabilitation counselors, mental health counselors, employment counselors, drug abuse counselors** and **prison counselors.**

Depending on the area of counseling that interests you, obtain a master's degree in guidance and counseling, student personnel services, rehabilitation counseling, counseling psychology, psychology, or a related field. Most states require public school counselors to have both counseling and teaching certificates; state departments of education can provide specific information. Many counselors are certified or licensed, reflecting a trend toward rising professional standards.

Technology affects counseling only in that it provides more efficient tools. The helping professional, not a machine, serves as the facilitator of change to improve the human condition.

Library Science

Librarians—finders and disseminators of information—are no longer stuck in the stacks, but have the chance to be part of the dramatic technological change sweeping through progressive libraries everywhere.

Of the nation's estimated 100,000 libraries, about one-half are thought to be computerized in some substantial sense, which means librarians increasingly must know how to use a computer. But their professional judgment and knowledge will also be needed for years to come.

Austere government budgets are keeping the lid on hiring librarians for public and school libraries. Librarian ranks will grow slowly throughout the remainder of the century, with most job openings created by those who retire or leave the field.

A master's degree in library science (MLS) is necessary to obtain an entry-level professional position in most public, school and special libraries. State requirements for school libraries vary widely, but most require that school librarians be certified as teachers; not all states require a degree in library science.

Public librarians work in a kaleidoscope of settings. **Children's librarians,** knowledge professionals for small fry, handle an encyclopedic range of duties, from conducting story hours to finding the right book for a child. **Acquisitions librarians** choose books, periodicals, films and other library materials. **Reference librarians** directly provide people with access to the information they need and want.

Media specialists, as librarians who work in school settings are often called, teach students how to use the school library or media center. They often work closely with classroom teachers in curriculum development. Sometimes they are saddled with the additional role of keeper of the study hall.

Academic librarians cooperate with faculty members at colleges and universities to ensure the library has reference materials for courses offered.

Special librarians work in information centers, or in libraries maintained by corporations and government agencies. When the focus is on a particular field, such as law or medicine, an advanced degree in the appropriate subject specialization (as well as an MLS) is highly desirable.

To find out more about the many worlds of library science—from children's outreach services, prisons and urban administration offices, to corporate information management, school media centers and historical archives, check library career literature available at—you know where.

Social Work

Social workers provide the caulk that keeps many unfortunates from falling through society's cracks. In dealing with trouble spots in a community, social workers often counsel or refer clients to samaritans and helping agencies.

You can work in a government agency doing casework with a bachelor's degree in social work, but if you want professional clout and supervisory positions, obtain a master's degree in social work.

After a half decade of decline, enrollments in schools of social work are rising once more. Why the upturn? One reason may be that in some sections of the country, jobs have become more plentiful as substantial numbers of the nation's social workers retire. Social work educators suggest that renewed interest in the field may be a response to the emergence of AIDS, the growing population of the elderly and a rise in the number of homeless people.

Whatever the reasons for social work school enrollments going up, remember that the job market for social workers is controlled by funding. Social workers flourish when government budgets are fat and tax laws are favorable to non-profit organizations. When the opposite is true, social workers face tight job markets.

Prospects are favorable for social work graduates in the '90s, particularly in Sun Belt states and rural areas. Geriatric care is a growing specialty—the elderly face complex problems in retirement, health care, finances and housing. As a new wave of immigrants sweeps into the country, many will need social services to help make the transition to productive citizenship. Demand should expand for social workers in outpatient health facilities, including health maintenance organizations.

Social workers now provide the bulk of psychotherapy services in the United States, according to the National Association of Social Workers; social work services usually are less expensive than psychotherapy offered by psychologists and psychiatrists.

Social workers earn moderate incomes. Those who advance to executive positions in large organizations or government agencies usually earn in the mid-five figures.

Government Jobs

Government service reflects the job market in microcosm, employing people from **accountants** to **warehouse workers.** Hot hiring prospects for federal jobs in the late '80s include **computer specialists, systems analysts, customs investigators, corrections officers, food inspectors, pharmacists, mathematicians, engineers, tax agents, secretaries, nurses, physical therapists, auditors, border patrol officers** and **air traffic controllers.**

The size of the state and local government labor force varies widely. Typical jobs include **law enforcement officers, firefighters, teachers, secretaries, computer programmers, civil engineers, city managers, urban planners** and **garbage collectors.**

Many people enter government because they seek security. Taxpayer revolts and recessions combined to deny that security to thousands and thousands of government employees in the early '80s as RIF (reduction in force) orders flew right and left. That's why many people are surprised to learn that in the mid '80s, public employment at all levels began an upward trend that is expected to continue as the population increases, particularly in the South and the West.

About 17 million people work for federal, state and local governments; replacement needs alone will create several million job vacancies each year. Most opportunities will occur at state and local levels, but the federal government is no slouch—it hires up to 1,000 people a day. The government job market isn't booming, but with numbers like that, it qualifies as a big bang.

Money? Generalizing about the pay policies of thousands of different employers is perilous, but many analysts agree that roughly speaking, high-skill occupations are relatively underpaid in the public sector, and low-skill occupations are overpaid relative to comparable work in the private sector.

Why Go Government?

You won't rake in the money, but you'll probably be able to live a comfortable middle-class life. Government work more and more resembles jobs in the private sector in the sense of requiring longer hours, offering less security and pressuring you to produce. Many public jobs can result in high excitement (negotiating arms agreements), pleasant benefits (serving as a flight attendant on *Air Force One*) and seeing the world (teaching in a foreign land). Closer to home, how would you feel as a firefighter who rescues a child from a blazing inferno? Or maybe you just like the give-and-take of the political scene at City Hall.

Transportation

Occupations in the transportation cluster involve moving humans, creatures and objects from one place to another, by land or sea, by air, space or pipeline.

The much touted "coming revolution" in transportation featuring people capsules, tube trains, sky lounges and other futuristic vehicles is not quite ready to swing around the corner. Researchers *are* hard at work on hypersonic planes and computer-guided cars, but American transportation will look much the same at the beginning of the new century as it does today.

Autos and trucks will continue to clog the highways, creating gridlocks and commuter rage. Airplanes will dot the skies, stressing airports and traffic systems. Railroads will chug along with bulk cargo shipments and fewer and fewer passengers. Mass transit systems will have their wheels to the wall in the absence of massive federal government funding. Space transportation? Literally, it is up in the air as bureaucrats debate what to do next.

All these problems create employment opportunities. The transportation job market is rolling along toward employment of four and a half million workers in 2000, but will not be uniformly merry in all types of transportation services. Here's a quick look.

Air Transportation

Major airlines are becoming bigger and fewer in a rash of buyouts and mergers. Most of the majors have negotiated two-tier wage scales that, for a few years, pay new workers lower salaries than previously hired ones. Labor costs are being slashed as a survival strategy to compete with newer, low-cost, non-union carriers.

Despite the restructuring since the 1978 deregulation of the industry, air transportation remains the kind of career field that dreams are made of—travel, time off, good pay.

By the turn of the century, most major airlines will retire more than 60 percent of their current pilots, according to a study by the Future Aviation Professionals of America, a private firm specializing in airline career information. From now through the late '90s, FAPA forecasts the hiring of between 42,000 and 52,000 **pilots,** 50,000 **aviation maintenance technicians/mechanics** and 100,000 **flight attendants.**

Observation: Airlines carry about 90 percent of all non-auto intercity transportation. The top five airlines—United, American, Texas Air, Delta and Northwest—control about 85 percent of passenger traffic. In the years following deregulation, the number of airlines nearly quadrupled, but much of what went up came down. In all, more than 160 smaller airlines have folded their wings since 1978. As a flight crew member, if your airline closes its doors, you lose your rung on the seniority ladder; if you find employment with another airline, you have to start at the bottom of its seniority ladder. While you're young, it's okay to take a chance on a new or financially risky airline to build up flying time and experience. By your late 20s, you should seek career employment with an airline that has a history of stability.

Air traffic controller is one of the highest paid occupations open to high school graduates who have at least three years' general work experience. These traffic cops of the skyways prevent mid-air collisions of aircraft. There aren't enough of them to handle increasingly crowded skies. The Federal Aviation Administration will have to re-hire some of the workers fired during an illegal 1981 strike, or train thousands of new controllers, a process that takes about five years. Don't even think about this work unless you can do two things at once.

Trucking

Q. How can you make six figures yearly as a truck driver?

A. You can earn more than $100,000 annually by buying a tractor-trailer and leasing your rig and services to a nationwide moving company. But learn to sing "On the Road Again" with gusto, because you'll be away from home weeks at a time.

Not quite three million truck drivers are on the go over U.S. streets, roads and highways. Behind the wheels are local truck drivers, driver-sales workers, private mail drivers, long-distance drivers and special drivers, such as the wheelers for dealers who haul massive triple-deckers laden with shiny new cars.

This occupation often carries the union label—lots of truck drivers belong to the Teamsters or to unions associated with the industry in which they work. The union influence is seen in the high earnings of many truckers. There's not much upward mobility, though—truck drivers rarely advance to terminal manager or trucking company executive. Some do buy their own trucks and equipment and become entrepreneurs.

Can truck-driving schools really help you get behind the wheel of a big rig? Yes, but be sure to talk with some of the school's graduates to see how satisfied they are with the school and its placement help (section 14 has more advice on dealing with a vo-tech school).

Transportation Engineering

By choosing transportation engineering as a career, you turn right onto a careerway where opportunity lights are bright green. Anyone who's ever been trapped on an expressway or busy road during the rush hour knows why the nation needs specialists to keep the traffic crush moving. Transportation engineers who work for government agencies, and most do, earn civil service pay at the professional level. Private transportation consultants can earn substantially more—up to six figures. Titles vary—**traffic engineer, director of traffic planning and highway safety,** and **transportation safety engineer** are typical. By any name, transportation engineers keep us in motion. They plan, design, operate and manage such facilities as roads, transit systems, airports and highway systems. Most major in civil engineering, although some study electrical, systems or other fields of engineering. Many need only a bachelor's degree; others pursue graduate study in transportation to get a master's degree.

Space: The Big Frontier

The race to space is not a thing of the past, although it may be oriented more toward the future than the present.

Temporarily sluggish, the American aerospace industry continues to plan for tomorrow. The NASA space station—a planned giant orbiting station resembling an interplanetary Tinkertoy—is moving ahead, but it's obvious the program is taking tentative first steps in a marathon walk that may be completed in the mid to late '90s. Preparation for a Mars-vicinity manned flight is in the offing, too, but the scientific community continues to debate the usefulness of manned launches. The real disagreement is over allocation of federal spending; until the argument is settled, the non-military, non-commercial side of space will have to pull in its belt.

The federal government has pulled out of the commercial satellite launching business, opening up the arena to private industry. Both small entrepreneurs and aerospace giants trying to fill the void will find stiff competition from Japan, China, the Soviet Union and Europe.

Other business pursuits—the manufacture of pharmaceuticals and semiconductor components, for instance—have suffered rocky times. NASA costs and policies have diluted corporate interest. No large commercial concern has stepped forward offering to share the expense of space station development.

Despite the turtle-like progress of the past several years, most forecasts of America's space future are optimistic. Tomorrow's spacefarers will have occupational specialties not unlike those recognized in the 20th century, ranging from engineering and science to medicine and education.

Will there be a colony in space within your lifetime? Space planners say future missions to Mars will carry prefabricated buildings and greenhouse modules with solar panels to establish a permanent base that will be energy self-sufficient. Huge layers of ice beneath Mars' surface will supply water for drinking and agricultural use. Because the planet's atmosphere is mostly carbon dioxide—needed for plant growth—space analysts think that a human colony will become self-sustaining. What do you think? Place your bets.

Now that you've had an introductory look at what's in the career universe, let's return the spotlight to *you.* Begin with the following section.

SECTION FIVE

EVERYONE CAN HELP

N*o career exploration exists in isolation. None of us could find our way* without the knowledge and kindnesses of others. This section shows who can help you toward career success and how. It explains the role of career tests and test-givers, and it shares a simple, but effective technique to maximize your chances of long-term success.

Weave a Tapestry of Contacts

Contacts have been a critical component of success since the dawn of civilization. They will be no less important in the 21st century.

"Who you know" has always, does now, and will forever make a huge difference in how high you rise, although contacts are no substitute for competence.

Making contacts is not dependent upon your family's socioeconomic status. Any number of special people may be willing to wave your banner once you reach out and hand it to them. Some of these special people are

- parents
- teachers
- relatives
- friends
- friends' parents
- neighbors
- clergy
- merchants
- co-workers
- school leaders
- scouting, youth leaders
- coaches
- team members
- employers
- doctors, dentists
- real estate, insurance agents
- bankers
- friends' friends

These special people and their contacts form your personal network.

Networking is seeking out acquaintances, advice-givers, potential mentors and friends, and systematically building on these relationships.

Your first reaction may be that you're too shy to reach out. Fight shyness by recognizing that networking is a legitimate, proven technique in career development. Make just one contact. It will lead to another and another and another. Soon you'll have a network.

Many contacts will be introduced to you by a third person at parties, meetings and other gatherings. Consider having cards printed with your name, address and telephone number. When you are introduced to a business person, chat a few minutes, then offer your card and ask for your new contact's card in return:

"I enjoyed meeting you. I'd like to give you my card (pause)—and perhaps I could have yours? Thank you."

Exchanging cards with a business person helps you establish yourself as an equal.

Your savvy makes a favorable impression on your new acquaintance, and you open the possibility of a future relationship.

Even when there's no third person to introduce you, it's okay to talk to strangers, assuming you exercise good judgment and avoid suspicious people.

Don't ignore the person in the seat next to you when you're traveling a long distance by bus, train or air. Speaking to a stranger is acceptable behavior under these circumstances. Find out who the person is, what he or she does for a living, and all the relevant job facts you always wanted to know.

A young man in Michigan uses an advanced method to keep track of everyone he meets. He records names and details in a home computer. His entire personal network is available on a green screen.

Creating a *personal contacts log* in a computer may not be practical for you, but you can build the same resource with index cards. When you meet an individual who might be of help to you in the future, add that person's name to your personal contacts log. Here's a simple format to use:

Personal Contacts Log

Name: ______________________________ Phone No: ______________

Address: ______________________________

When & Where Last Seen: ______________________________

____

____

Comments: ______________________________

____

____

Referred by: ______________________________

A tapestry is a beautiful fabric picture that looks more or less the same on both sides. During the career exploration portion of your life, most of the networking you initiate will flow one way: to your advantage. Generally speaking, adults enjoy lending a hand to young people. As you become established in a career, however, your networking must become dual-sided, like a tapestry. The following segment explains.

Pumping Life Into Your Network

At the outset of a career search, your networking returns much more than you give. It's all take, take, take. But as you establish yourself on a campus or in a job, your network will not survive if you don't share the wealth.

In their book, *Working and Liking It* (Random House/Ballantine Books), career consultants Richard Germann and Diane Blumenson discuss the concept that benefits must flow two ways.

The authors note that a network of contacts is a human resource and information exchange system—one that allows you to tap into a vast reservoir of knowledge about practically everybody and everything.

Reciprocity in networking, they explain, is a concept to guide you securely throughout your career.

Networking provides the visibility you need to choose a career, land a job and get ahead in your life.

Need Help? This Beats Calling 911

When you begin to weave your tapestry of contacts, take a few minutes to analyze the types of help you need and from whom. Draw a line down the center of a sheet of paper. On the left side write the kind of help you need; on the right side jot down the people who are your prime candidates to offer each type of help. Glance at this example:

Help Resources

1. Emotional support	*Family:* Discuss my interests, values, aptitudes and abilities; ask family for job ideas that match my traits. *Friends:* Share with them some of my anxieties about beginning my career exploration and decision making. Find out how my friends feel about their career challenges.
2. Need help with interviewing skills	*Family and school counselors:* Practice interviews and ask them to critique, telling me what I do wrong. Use a tape recorder and listen to myself.
3. Get to know more about careers that I am vaguely interested in.	*Family:* Get the names of some of their friends and associates who are working in jobs of interest and arrange to spend the day at their workplaces learning more about what they really do. *Friends and their parents:* Collect names from them to widen my network of contacts. *Neighbors:* Do I know someone who is working in the jobs that interest me? Do they know someone who is? *Former employers:* (You can usually count on them if you did a good job when on their payrolls.) Have I covered all bases with those for whom I worked, including my babysitting jobs?

How often should you ask for help? Don't be chintzy with your requests. As a leading business publisher, Malcolm S. Forbes, says, "The smart ones ask when they don't know. And, sometimes, when they do."

Will a Career-Planning Course Help?

Besides high schools and colleges, a number of public and private organizations offer career-planning help in seminars, workshops and formal courses.

How good are they? That's like asking how good is a mathematics course. The quality varies all over the lot.

To our tastes, some of the courses seem more like a sensitivity-training experience than an exercise in career planning. Other programs, laden with technical flow-charts and formulas, invite napping.

Aim for a well-balanced course that seems to offer a blend of inspiration and introspection with occupational information and job-market reality.

Some high schools provide inadequate courses in careers; they are little more than four-week units paired with driver education. Others offer full-blown courses, often in night school programs.

You're more likely to find a comprehensive career-planning course in a community college, or in the continuing education division of a four-year college or university. A call to the institution's admissions office should put you on the trail of available offerings.

If you are more troubled about your future than your friends seem to be, perhaps you should consider paying for a commercial life/work planning program. A number of private firms hold group sessions, but find out about the costs up front; most programs total more than a thousand dollars.

You can find private counselors and life/work planning consultants in telephone directories under "vocational guidance" or "careers and vocational counseling."

Ask, too, at such non-profit organizations as public library education and job information services, Y's, adult education centers and community organizations.

You can acquire as much information from books as a counselor can impart, but some people can't learn that way. Others need hand holding. Still others gain needed confidence through counseling.

Do whatever works for you.

Tests also can help you. Let's look at them now.

HERE'S THE STORY ON CAREER TESTS

Name your price! I'll pay anything you ask if you'll give my son a test to reveal what he should do with his life.

—Anxious father to school counselor

This type of call comes regularly from parents who would pay thousands of dollars for tests that lead their offspring to the good life with job satisfaction, high pay, a bright future and work security.

Unfortunately, the magic-bullet test is a myth. It is a misperception. It is a figure of imagination. The reason is not complicated:

Career development is a process, not a test.
We repeat:
Career development is a process, not a test.

It's not surprising that vast numbers of people believe otherwise. Popular magazines print test after test to measure your assertiveness, your managerial ability, your marriage relationship and your diet habits. And if that's not enough, pop questionnaires reveal your personality traits and your potential longevity on this planet. Still other clever exams supposedly divulge your attractiveness to the opposite sex, and evaluate whether you are ready for an adult relationship.

These tests usually include a scoring standard that lets you know whether you are okay, need help or are a hopeless case. People love these harmless evaluations, which is fine unless you naively believe 100 percent in the results.

In school settings, counselors often use tests. There are too many students to spend hours and hours interviewing each one, drawing out interests, aptitudes and personality traits. Tests are the practical substitute for lengthy interviewing. They provide counselors with foundation facts about what's right for you.

When administering tests, experienced counselors always explain that career development is a process in which tests are but one component. The problem is that even when a counselor spells it out, a listener may choose to hear a different story.

To illustrate, a counselor did everything except shout through a bullhorn in emphasizing to a student that the career interest survey she was taking was exactly that—merely an indication of her general interests. Even so, the young woman later told her father she had taken a test at school that showed she should be a meat cutter.

How amazing, her father thought, that a test could be so specific. Intrigued, he called for enlightenment. When the father was accurately informed about the nature of the test, he learned that his daughter's interests indeed did appear to include the possibility of meat cutting, but the results also pointed toward 50 other possible occupations.

The young woman closed her ears to a simple truth:

Tests are a sample of behavior. They give valuable clues about oneself and about relevant career options. That's their maximum contribution to your future success.

How, you may ask, do some private testing organizations get away with advertising their instruments as miraculous bridges over rivers of indecision? The answer is that the value of the help is in the mind of the receiver.

Many career seekers who have shelled out as much as $2,000 for a test battery, with a little interpretive counseling thrown in, rave about how the experience set them on the pathway of a promising career.

Maybe it did. In reality, what probably occurred is that the tests erased some self-doubts and supplied the missing incentive to do additional research.

Another reason costly tests often work is that the "expensive-must-be-good" syndrome is in play. When you pay lots of dollars for a benefit, aren't you inclined to rate it above a similar benefit you could have obtained for a few dollars? We are. It's human nature.

Tests can open windows of understanding, but it is important to remember that career development is a process of which tests are but one part.

The Career Tests You're Most Likely to Meet

Now that you have an idea of what tests can and can't do, here's a cram course on evaluations you are most likely to encounter:

Interests

These tests identify your preferences. They help you discover what you *want* to do. You are asked to rate various activities as to whether you "like," "dislike" or "feel indifferent" about them.

A profile of your answers is compared with profiles of people working in various occupations. If you like independent work, you'll receive a list of occupations that require independent performance, such as chemist or writer.

On the other hand, if you want to be near theater, shopping, sports events and other resources in urban areas, your job possibility list will not include park ranger or agricultural equipment dealer.

There are no right or wrong answers, and interest surveys are not a measure of your intelligence. They are limited to suggesting what you want to do.

Aptitude

These instruments do not measure whether you want to do the work, but whether you *can* do the work.

Aptitude tests predict "potential for doing." More precisely, these tests help you discover hidden talent. A hidden talent is an aptitude. An aptitude is a readiness to acquire a given skill, or to master a particular subject.

An aptitude is not an ability. An ability is a skill. When you have acquired an ability or a skill, it means you have developed a level of expertise in a given activity. You can do a thing well.

An aptitude or hidden talent is a promise; an ability or skill is its fulfillment.

You may have an aptitude for voice and music, but if you fail to develop it, you'll never make a skilled singer.

Again, a profile of your answers is compared with profiles of people working in various career fields. If you score high in mathematical aptitude, for instance, you'll receive a list of occupations in which that aptitude is important, such as telecommunications equipment designer and insurance actuary.

Conversely, if test results show a weakness in spatial relationships (how parts of an object relate to each other in three dimensions), your job possibility list will not include civil engineer or drafter.

Because aptitude tests are not intelligence tests, you are sometimes asked to demonstrate an aptitude by doing a work sample; you can't simply claim to have finger dexterity, you must demonstrate it.

Personality

These tests look at whether you have the *right temperament* for the work. Questions ask how much you enjoy various activities (somewhat like interest tests), how you make decisions, how you think, how you view the world and how you deal with other people.

Your personality type is compared with the personality profiles of people who work in various occupations, and once again you're given a list of occupations that could be a good match.

Assume that your dominant personality type is social. You like to work with people—informing, enlightening, training and curing them. Your list of possibilities could include psychologist, professor, industrial trainer and nurse.

It would not, however, include microwave oven repairer or space station transmitter engineer.

Selected Career Tests

While there are hundreds, perhaps thousands, of career tests on the market, here are some of the best known.

Test	Description	Publisher	Audience
JOB-O	A general career interest inventory that provides one with an interesting game-like format to match educational aspirations and job interests with 120 major job titles.	CFKR Career Materials P. O. Box 437 Meadow Vista, CA 95722	12-16 yrs.
COPS (Career Occupational Preference System)	An interest-inventory test developed to measure job activity preferences leading to 14 career clusters.	EDITS P. O. Box 7234 San Diego, CA 92107	14-adult (A variation—COPS-P—is for the college-bound adult.)
CAPS (Career Ability Placement)	A multi-dimensional test measuring aptitudes and abilities keyed to entry requirements for many jobs.	EDITS P. O. Box 7234 San Diego, CA 92107	14-adult

(continued)

Test	Description	Publisher	Audience
SDS (Self-Directed Search)	A survey of aptitudes and interests. Comes with an occupations-finder guide which lists jobs for each of six work styles: realistic, investigative, artistic, social, enterprising, conventional.	Psychological Assessment Resources Box 998 Odessa, FL 33556	14-adult
Strong-Campbell Interest Inventory	Compares interests with those of people successfully employed in a wide variety of occupations. Uses same work themes as SDS.	Consulting Psychologist Press 577 College Ave. Palo Alto, CA 94306	14-adult
Myers-Briggs Type Indicator	Measures personality types and interests based on Jung's theory of 16 types. Booklet provides career implications.	Consulting Psychologist Press 577 College Ave. Palo Alto, CA 94306	14-adult
Harrington-O'Shea Career Decision Making System	A comprehensive measure of career interests that combines abilities and values with extensive interpretive information.	AGS Inc. Publishers' Building Circle Pines, MN 55014	14-adult

TYPES OF QUESTIONS IN CAREER TESTS

To help you understand the differences in the types of career tests you may take, here are brief examples for each.

Interest Surveys

Make an *X* under **L** for the activities you would like to do. Make an *X* under **D** for the things you would dislike doing or to which you would be indifferent.

Realistic	**L**	**D**
Fix electrical things.	_____	_____
Take woodworking course.	_____	_____

Investigative	**L**	**D**
Read scientific books, magazines.	_____	_____
Take chemistry course.	_____	_____

Artistic		
Attend plays.	_____	_____
Take art course.	_____	_____

Social		
Go to parties.	_____	_____
Attend religious services.	_____	_____

Enterprising		
Sell something.	_____	_____
Give talks.	_____	_____

Conventional		
Keep your desk and room neat.	_____	_____
File letters, reports, records.	_____	_____

Aptitude Tests

Look over the following sample questions. These questions are just a sampling of four subtests typically found within aptitude tests.

1. MECHANICAL REASONING (MR)

This test is a measure of Mechanical Reasoning. Following are questions about mechanical facts and principals. Place a heavy black mark in the box corresponding to the best answer. Practice on the following examples.

Example 1:

Which person is carrying the heavier load?

- [] A
- [] B
- [] No difference

Example 2:

In which direction will the submarine move if the control fins are turned in the direction of the arrow?

- [] Dive
- [] Surface
- [] No difference

In Example 1, you should have darkened the space next to the letter **A**. **A** carries the heavier load since the bricks are closer to **A** than to **B**. In example 2 the correct answer is **surface**. The submarine will surface since the flow of water adds buoyancy by pushing up beneath the fins.

2. SPATIAL RELATIONS (SR)

This is a test of Spatial Relations. Following are patterns which can be folded into figures. You are to choose which figure can be correctly made by folding the pattern and then darken the answer space above it. Only one of the four figures is correct for each pattern shown. Practice on these examples.

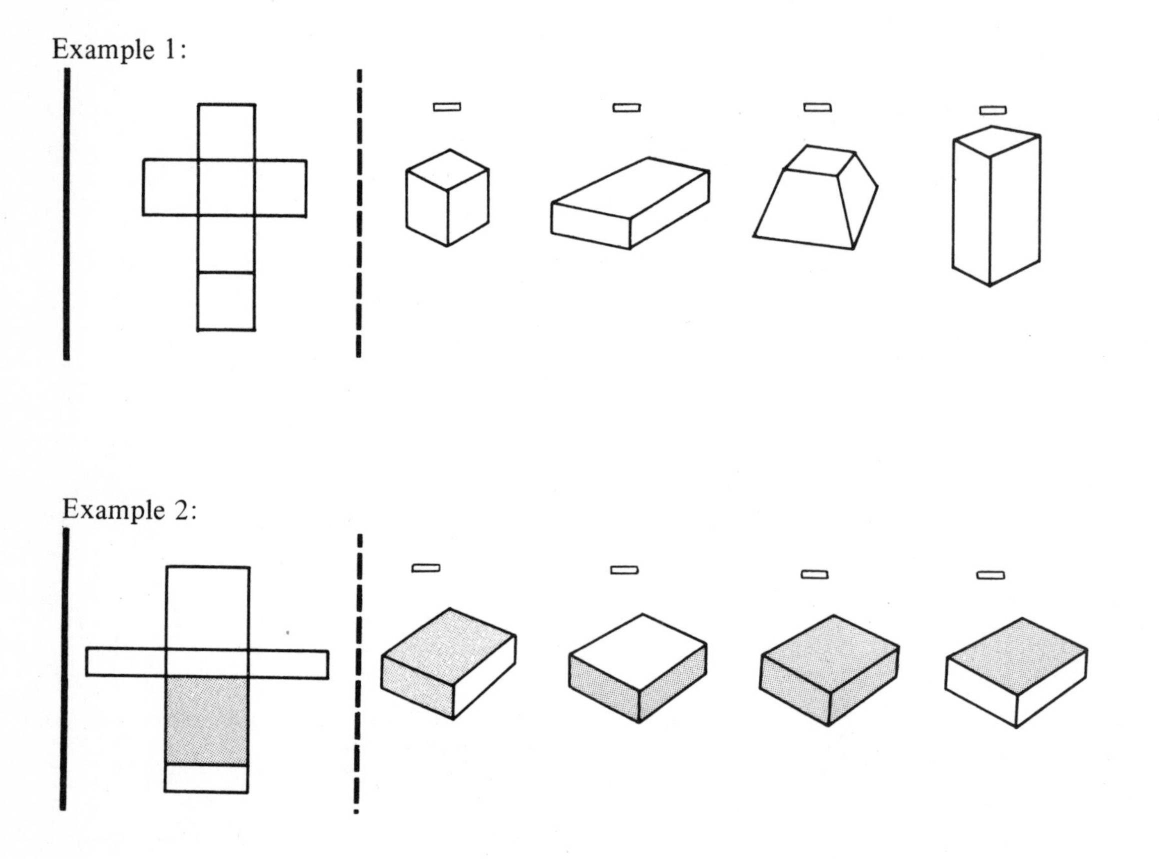

In Example 1, the first figure, the cube is correct. You should have darkened the answer space above the first figure. In Example 2, all of the figures are correct in shape, but only one of them is shaded correctly. The last figure is correct.

Remember the surfaces you are shown in the pattern must always be the outside of the folded figure.

3. VERBAL REASONING (VR)

This is a test of Verbal Reasoning. Following are sets of facts and conclusions. In many cases from reading the facts you can determine which conclusions are true and which are false. If the conclusion is True darken the space under the letter **T**. If it is **False** darken the space under the letter **F**. If the facts don't provide enough information to determine if a conclusion is true or false, darken the space under the letter **U** for **Uncertain**.

Read the facts in the example below. The facts state that everyone on the farm is related to Sue. Kim lives on the farm. Therefore Kim is related to Sue. The space under the letter **T**, **True**, has been marked for the first conclusion.

The facts also state that Sue has only one child, a boy. Therefore Kim cannot be Sue's daughter. The second conclusion is marked **F** for **False**.

Since from the facts it is not clear whether Sue lives on the farm, the third conclusion has been marked **U** for **Uncertain**.

Now practice on the remaining conclusions.

Example:

FACTS

Everyone on the farm is related to Sue.
Sue's only child is a boy.
Kim lives on the farm.
Jack is Sue's husband.

T	F	U	CONCLUSIONS
▮	▯	▯	Kim is Sue's relative.
▯	▮	▯	Kim is Sue's daughter.
▯	▯	▮	Sue lives on the farm.
▯	▯	▯	Sue has a son.
▯	▯	▯	Jack lives on the farm.

You should have marked **T** and **U** for the fourth and fifth conclusions. If you have any questions you should ask now.

4. NUMERICAL ABILITY (NA)

This is a test of Numerical Ability. Below are two sample problems. To the right of each problem are five possible answers. Work each problem and then darken the space next to the correct answer. Only one answer is correct for each problem.

Example 1:

ADD

	▭ 15
14	▭ 16
+ 11	▭ 25
	▭ 26
	▭ 27

Example 2:

MULTIPLY

	▭ 34
11	▭ 40
x 4	▭ 43
	▭ 46
	▭ Not given

In Example 1, the correct answer is 25. You should have darkened the answer space to the left of 25.

In Example 2, the correct answer is 44. Since 44 is not among the given answers, you should have darkened the space next to **Not given**.

(Reproduced with permission by EdITS, copyright 1976.)

Personality Surveys

Which answer comes closest to telling how you usually feel or act? Circle *A* or *B*.

Does following a schedule
A. appeal to you, or
B. cramp you?

Are you inclined to
A. value sentiment more than logic, or
B. value logic more than sentiment?

Which word in each pair appeals to you more?

A. firm-minded	B. warmhearted
A. hearty	B. quiet
A. thinking	B. feeling
A. speak	B. write

(Reprinted from the *Myers-Briggs Type Indicator,* Form F, with permission of the publisher.)

Interested in Taking Career Tests? Here's How

Most tests can be taken by making arrangements with high school guidance departments, college counseling centers, public employment service offices and private counseling firms. The tests may be free, cost a modest amount, or, in the case of private counseling firms, cost from $25 to several hundred dollars.

Most tests cannot be ordered individually. When you cannot find a place that offers the test you want, contact the test publisher for a referral.

Doing It Your Way

Because you're going to be seeking out people for your contacts network, you'll be the recipient of many suggestions.

A downside to all of this advice may occur when the guidance of people who count (parents, teachers, friends, and so forth) is on a collision course with your idea of your own best future.

They may be right when they say you'll wind up as a mud-wrestler if you drop out of school, or that you won't get a job with a major in French unless you want to teach, interpret or translate.

Pay attention when key people talk: There's a difference between having faith in your ability to make decisions and in being stubborn.

However, the final decision must be your own. You may think you're not an authority on anything, but you are—you are your own best authority on knowing what you want for yourself.

SECTION SIX

You and Only You: On the Road to Awareness

In this section the focus is on self-awareness. You learn how to use identity inventories to bring forth the real you. To create these identity inventories, you'll use a variety of activities designed to sharpen your perceptions.

You'll complete a separate identity inventory for each of these considerations:

- your interests
- your aptitudes and skills
- your academic abilities
- your personal values
- your work values
- your personality traits
- your lifestyle preferences

At the end of the section, you'll put everything together in a brief summary, revealing your identity snapshot.

What Do You Like to Do Best?

We succeed at what we like to do. That's a fact.

Your interests are your like-to-do's. Discover them. Here are three activities devoted to revealing your interests.

The Terrific Ten

Quickly write down 10 things you like to do most. Anything goes. Your likes can be related to leisure, work, hobbies or whatever. Here's an example:

swimming
reading
watching films
running
science
math puzzles
talking with friends
collecting coins
my own paper delivery business
studying World War II aircraft

Don't spend a lot of time constructing your list. Just write what pops into your head. Next to each item that you jot down, write the codes that apply. The codes are:

1. Place an *X* next to those things you have done within the last three weeks.
2. Place an *A* next to those things you like to do alone.
3. Place a *P* next to those things you prefer to do with other people.
4. Place a *$* next to those that cost $10 or more each time you do them.
5. Place an *O* next to those you would like to be a part of your occupation.
6. Place an *L* next to those you would like to be a part of your leisure.
7. Place a *C* next to those you would like your life's companion to have on his or her list.
8. Place an *R* next to those you think you'll be able to do after you retire.

Go back over your list and describe the setting where you could most likely do each of these things. This could include the mountains, a city, the suburbs, a coast, the country, a small town, and so forth.

Terrific Ten Summary

I like:	Code	Setting

The Terrific Ten activity doesn't have a scoring guide and it doesn't offer magic answers. What it does do is direct your thoughts to those activities you would do with a song in your heart, to how much they cost, and to whether you would like them to be a part of your job or a part of your leisure.

The Executive Summary

The process of reviewing your past to find leads to your future is called the *diary approach.*

A complete diary approach takes weeks and as many as 100 pages of writing. At some point in your life, you may need to experience the whole process.

For now, let's do a quick wrap-up, which we call an *executive summary.*

First, glance at the following list of words that describe activities and functions other people say they enjoy doing. After you have the general idea, reach into your own history and fill out the executive summary form that follows. We've filled in examples to get you started on the executive summary form.

Examples of Activities/Functions

accept challenge
adapt/modify
administer
advise
analyze
appraise
approve
assemble
assign duties
assist/help
audit

be free
brainstorm
budget
build
build morale
build team

calculate
care for
catalog
change
classify
coach
collect
communicate
compare
compile
compute
conceive ideas
conduct
consolidate
construct
consult
contract
control
coordinate
correct
counsel
create
critique
cross cultural
cut costs

data
delegate
demonstrate
design
develop
direct
discover
distribute
do artwork
do physical work
do precision work
draft correspondence
draw up standards

edit
efficiency
empathize
enjoy others
entertain
entrepreneur
establish priorities
estimate
evaluate
examine
exchange information
execute
expedite

figure
finance
forecast

gather information
give information
guide

handle detail
handle objects
help people

identify needs
implement
improve
increase productivity
influence
inform
initiate
innovate
inspect
inspire
install
instruct
integrate
interpret
interview
invent
investigate

judge
justify

layout
lead

(continued)

liaison
liberate
listen
lobby

make consensus
make decisions
make policy
manage
market
mentor
moderate
monitor
motivate

negotiate

observe
operate machines
optimize
organize
overhaul
own

people
perform
persuade
plan
policy
present
preside
procure
program
project
promote
protect
provide treatment
publicize
publish
purchase

raise funds
read/speak languages
realize ideas
recruit
repair
report
research

resolve conflict
review
risk

schedule
select
sell
service
set objectives
solve problems
speak
staff up
strategy
supervise
support
survey
synthesize
systematize

teach
teamwork
tend
things

think
train
translate
travel
treat

unify
use tools

value
verbalize
volunteer

work independently
work outdoors
work well with others (teamwork)
work with children, etc.
write features/ads
write instructions
write proposals
write reports
write—

Executive Summary

Activities	Things I Like	Things I Dislike
School Subjects		
1. history	gather info.	review
2.		
3.		
Hobbies		
1. collect stamps	examine	budget
2.		
3.		
Extra-Class Activities		
1. yearbook	write	edit
2.		
3.		

Activities	Things I Like	Things I Dislike
Work Experience		
1. movie usher	assist/help	monitor
2.		
3.		
Community Activities		
1. church youth	speak	draw up standards
2.		
3.		

(In identifying your likes and dislikes, you are not limited to the sample functions and activities just given. Write any aspect of an activity that turns you on or off.)

Although your interests are going to change as you mature, certain preferences are bedrock. If, for instance, you're a nature lover who enjoys nothing more than hiking the overland trails, it's improbable that at age 35 you'll turn into a hot-house flower.

From the insights gathered in the Terrific Ten and executive summary activities, fill out the identity inventory of your interests.

Identity Inventory:
MY INTERESTS

Interests I would like to pursue in my career

1. ______
2. ______
3. ______
4. ______
5. ______
6. ______
7. ______
8. ______
9. ______
10. ______

SUMMARY: (Top three interests)

1. ______
2. ______
3. ______

What Can You Do Best?

We tend to succeed at things we like, and common sense tells us that if we can't carry a tune in a basket, we can't sing grand opera.

In choosing a future that works for us, we also need to know what we can do well—our aptitudes and our marketable skills.

What's the difference between aptitudes and skills?

An aptitude is a promise and a skill is that promise fulfilled.

An aptitude is the bud; the skill is the rose. You may have an aptitude or a talent for drawing, but until it's polished and perfected, you can't say you have a skill in art.

For brevity, we'll discuss only skills. We'll count on you to remember that while you may be on your way to acquiring certain skills, for some of them, you're not quite there yet.

Concerning skills, here's a statement that may knock you off your chair:

Do you know you possess more than two dozen marketable skills?

Astounding? It's true. And after you finish this section, you'll be able to name quite a few of them.

Skills up Close

All skills are not created equal. Some you can do like a champ, others moderately well and still others only by hanging from your fingertips.

Skills have differing values in the marketplace, too. A computer scientist who creates artificial intelligence products worth millions of dollars is more handsomely rewarded than a mathematics teacher who should go down in history for preventing hundreds of students from being mathematically illiterate.

When you contemplate the acquisition of skills, you'll find they come in three varieties:

1. *Formally-acquired skills* are those that come to you as a result of taking classes or reading books. Examples include learning to use a wordprocessor, ballet dancing and car repairing.

2. *Informally-acquired skills* are the ones you learn by trying, failing and trying again until you master them. You also gain these skills by watching another perform them, then giving it a go. Examples: riding a bike, roller skating or running a photocopy machine.

3. *Natural skills* (talents) are those you were born with. They're in the genes. Examples: sing-

Marketable Skills: What They Are

abstract reasoning
accounting
acting
adjusting/adapting
administrating
analyzing
answering telephone
applying knowledge
arbitrating
assembling
assessing
athletics

baking
balancing checkbooks
bookkeeping
budgeting
buying

camping
carpentry
charting
checking
classifying
cleaning
clerical
collaborating
collecting
color analysis
comparing
competing
compiling data
completing
computer programming
concentrating
conceptualizing
controlling
cooking
cooperating
coordinating
coping
copying
counting
creating
cutting hair

dancing
debating
defending
defining
delegating
developing rapport
diagnosing
diplomacy/tact
directing
disproving
dressing
driving

economy/thrift
editing
electrical skills
enforcing

equipment operation
evaluating people/
situations
expanding
experimenting

finger dexterity
first-aid skills
following directions
following through

gardening
generating
getting along with others
good manners
guiding

handling detail
handling tools
healing/curing
homemaking
human relations
hypothesizing

identifying
illustrating
imagining
implementing
improvising
influencing others
initiating
integrating
interior design/decorating
interpersonal relationships
interpreting
interviewing
inventing

judging

leading
listening

managing money
managing people
manicuring
manual coordination
mathematics
mechanical repair
memorizing
mentoring
modeling
modifying/adapting
motivating

navigating
negotiating

observing
organizing
overseeing

painting
parenting
persisting
photographing
physical coordination
planning
playing musical instrument
plumbing
policy making
precision working
predicting
preparing
presenting
problem solving
promoting
proofreading
public speaking
purchasing
putting on makeup

questioning
quick learning

reading
recognizing
recombining ideas
recommending
recruiting
reducing
reevaluating
renovating houses
researching
responding
risk taking

scheduling
self-actualizing
selling
serving others
sewing
shaping materials
singing
sorting
speaking
speaking foreign language
speed with accuracy
spelling
summarizing
supervising
supporting others
systematizing

teaching
technical comprehension
tending
testing/screening
time management
training
transcribing
traveling
troubleshooting
tutoring
typing

unifying

verbalizing
visualizing in three
dimensions

wallpapering
word processing
working in teams
writing

---

ing, a knack with children or animals, throwing a ball.

A skill formally acquired by one person may be informally acquired by another; it might be a natural skill for a third individual.

Except when it comes to credentials and professional licensure (such as acquiring a medical degree before attempting brain surgery), it's not all that important how you acquire skills.

What counts is that you can say "I can do that," and know how to evaluate how well you can do it.

As a warm-up, look over the extensive list of skills on these two pages. For more inspiration, look again at the examples of activities and functions people like to do that appeared earlier in this section.

A rich variety of other exercises follows, all designed to help you mentally shake hands with your skills.

A Test of Skills

In each of the following categories, check the statement that best describes your skills in this field.

Scientific

_____1. I can follow directions to measure things accurately either in volume or size, if directions are simple.

_____2. I can follow detailed instructions to do scientific experiments and have good ability to accomplish detailed observations of experiments and write down accurate accounts of these observations.

_____3. I understand scientific principles and have successfully performed scientific experiments. I am curious about scientific articles, and if asked, I could explain detailed scientific ideas.

Mechanical

_____1. I can use a screwdriver and pliers to take apart or put together simple things.

_____2. I can make some repairs and understand the workings of mechanical objects and simple machines, plumbing and electrical devices. I have used power tools.

_____3. I usually figure out what is wrong with a machine, plumbing or electrical device, and am challenged to do so. I understand the principles of these devices and how they work. Friends come to me for a variety of mechanical difficulties.

Clerical

_____1. I can file and I know how to use a dictionary. If instructions are available, I can run a photocopy machine. I can type simple materials, although I may not use standard typing procedures.

_____2. I can type a business letter accurately and am well organized. I can figure out the details of an office quickly. I can follow directions. I occasionally find ways to streamline the procedures I am asked to accomplish.

_____3. I am a rapid and accurate typist and can take shorthand or use a dictating machine. Not only am I well organized, but I have the ability to supervise others. I can operate most office equipment. I can organize an efficient office. I can compose letters and write reports with a minimum of direction.

Computational

_____1. I can do basic math functions (adding, subtracting, dividing and multiplication). I can make change and usually manage to balance my checkbook.

_____2. Numbers come fairly easy to me. I understand decimals and can compute percentages and interest. I know how to read graphs and tables.

_____3. I understand and can compute statistics. I can use advanced mathematics functions and prepare written and oral reports using mathematical equations and principles. I know how to prepare budgets. I understand the basic function of computers, golf and racing handicaps and the stock market page.

Sales

_____1. I have difficulty trying to sell materials. If necessary, I allow people to look at merchandise, make a decision and then I complete the sale.

_____2. I can comfortably point out assets of a given product for sales purposes. I am friendly and find talking to people easy.

_____3. I am very persuasive. It's easy for me to convince someone to endorse any idea or product. People enjoy my company and persuading someone to make a decision is a fascinating challenge.

Social Service

_____1. I dislike listening to other people's problems. I generally am at a loss about what to do if someone asks me for help with a personal problem.

_____2. I get along well with people. Many of my friends ask me to help them with their problems. At times I assist people in making decisions or in finding resources to help them.

_____3. Helping people discover solutions to their problems is easy and satisfying for me. I spend a lot of time helping people with their problems. I can refer people seeking help to appropriate agencies. If I am presented with a problem, I try to find a solution or a service that helps with the problem.

Verbal

_____1. I can talk with friends, but talking before large groups frightens me. I can write a simple sentence, but writing a report is difficult. I do not read a great deal and often I do not understand what I read.

_____2. I can talk to small groups on a familiar subject. I can read and understand most materials if they are not extremely technical or difficult. I can write or present an oral report using a variety of sentence structures.

_____3. I am effective when speaking to large groups. My vocabulary is large and I use it well both in speaking and in writing. I can skillfully prepare extensive written materials and I am an excellent reader.

Art

_____1. I can dance simple steps, or play a musical instrument in an elementary way, or draw something if I can copy it, or originate a very simple design.

_____2. I can dance to most musical rhythms, or I have sung or played a musical instrument in a group or alone, or I have drawn or painted something that has been on display.

_____3. I can easily pick up a new dance step or routine; I have danced either in a group or alone in a performance, or I have had extensive musical training either vocally or instrumentally.

Now that you've tested your skills in eight areas, let's get the results on paper. Fill in the following chart—and remember it well for future reference.

SKILLS

Career Field	I can do these well	I can do these OK	I can't do these well
Scientific			
Mechanical			
Clerical			
Computational			
Sales			
Social Service			
Verbal			
Art			

Although these immediate pages focus on what you do well, here's a preview of how all the parts will fit together by the end of this section. Check over the eight categories again and, this time, decide how much you like each one. Fill in this chart, too.

INTEREST

Career Field	Turns me off	Some interest	Really interesting
Scientific			
Mechanical			
Clerical			
Computa- tional			
Sales			
Social Service			
Verbal			
Art			

You've already guessed that if you have both a high skill and interest in the same field, the merger is a sign that you may have hit on a happy choice.

Suppose your skills and interest coincide in the scientific, computational and mechanical categories. This suggests that engineering is a lively option for you.

High ratings in mechanical, verbal and art categories are a clue to look at architecture, printing, landscape architecture and interior design.

Match-ups in clerical, sales and verbal categories point to sales manager, travel agent, retail buyer or personnel counselor.

One more illustration: If you ranked high in computational, clerical and sales categories, don't overlook such options as store manager, computer programmer, computer sales representative, certified public accountant or mathematics teacher.

Clearly, these informal self-help guides are like all tests—fallible. But they do help move you off point zero.

Behind Yesterday's Hills: New Skills

This activity is another based on the diary approach. On the theory that history is the best predictor of the future, we want you to take a backward look at your life for inklings of skills you'll use in the future.

Write at least two accomplishments for various life segments, starting at age seven. Seek help in the memory department from your family.

What is an accomplishment? It's anything you did that you think was wonderful. It's anything you have felt proud of doing and enjoyed. It's anything that was satisfying and meaningful.

Perhaps you were the spelling champ in the third grade or maybe you resisted enormous peer pressure to do drugs in the tenth grade.

It's possible you brought home an A in Spanish, even though you have a tinny ear for languages. Were you the features editor for your school paper? Did you earn the money to buy your own car? Even if the high spot of your life last year was to organize your class notes into neat files, that's an accomplishment.

Accomplishments need not be network news, just important to you personally.

Once you begin rolling down memory lane, you'll be surprised at how many accomplishments you have to your credit.

That's the easy part. The hard part is that for the activity to be of major value, you must analyze the skills used to make every accomplishment happen.

If you were a school newspaper features editor, you probably used these skills: planning page layouts, decision making, instructing writers, writing, editing, proofreading, researching, persuading people to be interviewed, and more.

Splitting accomplishments into skills is a challenging task. It's not the sort of thing you do every day, so it may take awhile to get into the swing of it. Don't be discouraged if you're stymied. It happens to us, too, and we've been doing it for a long time.

When you're stuck, just take your time and review the examples of activities and functions again, and the list of marketable skills listed earlier in this section. Inspiration will strike.

Now here's a format for your convenience, but you'll probably want to expand it on sheets of blank paper.

Yesterday's Hills and New Skills Format

Life Segments	Accomplishments	Skills
5-9 years old		
10-12 years old		
13-15 years old		
16-18 years old		
19-21 years old		
22-25 years old		

Skills From Data, People and Things

Another way to part the curtain of uncertainty surrounding your future is to look for skills you can market by using the data, people and things concept.

- *Data* are information, ideas, statistics and facts.
- *People*—all ages, both genders, every ethnic and racial group and social class.
- *Things* means tools, machines, equipment and materials.

All jobs involve all three categories of data, people and things, but most jobs emphasize one over the other. The researcher works with data; the nurse with people and the engineer with things.

When you get within striking distance of making a career choice, you'll want to keep these broad divisions in mind, but in this section we use the concept as a treasure chest from which to pull skills you may have.

DATA:
words • symbols • knowledge • facts • information • numbers • ideas • charts • graphs • designs • blueprints • statistics • opinions • theories • techniques • budgets • evaluation measures • tests • drawings • flow charts • surveys • costs • work assignments • objectives • goals • policies • procedures • recommendations • memoranda • curriculum • monitor systems • stock-figures • handbooks • guidelines • literature • historical documents • catalogs • reports • regulations • briefs • future plans

What skills can you use in working with data? In the list below, circle those that most appeal to you. Underline those you have used.

examining • comparing • calculating • computing • gathering • compiling • classifying • filing • analyzing • collating • observing • investigating • composing • reporting • presenting • organizing • writing • reading • copying • creating • transcribing • coordinating • combining • synthesizing • interpreting

---

PEOPLE:
children • young adults • older people • Asians • Hispanics • blacks • whites • men • women • highly educated • deprived • retarded • handicapped • gifted • college students • professional • trades • emotionally disturbed • powerful • influential • social • extroverted • introverted • sick • middle-aged • ex-prisoners • abused • religious • residents of underdeveloped nations • people of different cultures • political • alcoholics, drug abusers • normal • wealthy • middle-class • poor • deviants • rigid • flexible • free spirits • conformists • high achievers • ambitious • laid-back • high-pressured • risk takers • carefree • task-oriented

What skills can you use in working with people? Circle those that most appeal to you. Underline those you have used.

attending to • serving • taking instruction from • supervising • communicating • instructing • caring for • persuading • managing • training • teaching • entertaining • motivating • coaching • consulting • coordinating • treating • leading • facilitating • criticizing • counseling • advising • negotiating • confronting • informing • empathizing • problem-solving • supporting

---

THINGS:
electrical sockets • lamps • word processors • photocopy machines • computers • stoves • brooms • vacuum sweepers • ovens • pots • paper • chain saws • pliers • screwdrivers • lawn mowers • power tools • heavy equipment • fork-lift trucks • cars • bicycles • motor bikes • telephones • gauges • controls • hair dryers • laser equipment • microwave ovens • furnaces • air conditioners • nuclear reactors • gasoline motors • electric motors • transformers • gas turbines • cleaning equipment • cameras • showers • spinning wheels • building supplies • dental equipment • airplanes

What skills can you use in working with things? Circle those that most appeal to you. Underline those you have used.

moving • pushing • carrying • feeding • loading • running • emptying • stacking • flying • starting • delivering • adjusting • monitoring • manipulating • cutting • guiding • assembling • operating • controlling • regulating • setting • overseeing • adapting • designing • demonstrating • repairing • keyboarding • painting • calibrating • selling

Summarize the skills you prefer to use in each category on the following form:

Skills Summary	Data	People	Things
Skills I prefer to use in working with:			

Now that you've pulled together marketable skills, you have—or can easily develop—information for the identity inventory of your aptitudes and skills.

Identity Inventory:

MY APTITUDES & SKILLS

What I may be able to do in the future with training and experience—or can do now—that will help my career.

1. ______________________
2. ______________________
3. ______________________
4. ______________________
5. ______________________
6. ______________________
7. ______________________
8. ______________________
9. ______________________
10. ______________________
11. ______________________
12. ______________________
13. ______________________
14. ______________________
15. ______________________
16. ______________________
17. ______________________
18. ______________________
19. ______________________
20. ______________________
21. ______________________
22. ______________________
23. ______________________
24. ______________________

SUMMARY: (Five job skills that I have right now.)

1. ______________________
2. ______________________
3. ______________________
4. ______________________
5. ______________________

Skill Secrets From School Records

Your educational track record is established in black and white. By bringing your grades to the fore now, you'll clearly see how they reflect both skills and interests.

And you'll have to face up to the possibility that your academic talents aren't up to your aspirations. When you're panting to be a veterinarian but are going down the tubes in chemistry, you'll have to bring your grades up or choose another career.

If reports of your grades seem to have been eaten by the family dog, obtain a transcript from your guidance counselor or registrar.

Working with the transcript, fill in the identity inventory of your academic abilities.

Identity Inventory:

MY ACADEMIC ABILITIES

My most important educational experience:

____

____

Job-related courses I liked and did well in:	Knowledge & skills gained in this course:
__________	__________
__________	__________
__________	__________
__________	__________
__________	__________
__________	__________
__________	__________

General courses I liked and did well in:	Knowledge & skills gained in this course:
__________	__________
__________	__________
__________	__________
__________	__________
__________	__________
__________	__________
__________	__________

∞

WHAT ARE YOUR PERSONAL VALUES?

No matter how many frills are added, the concept of personal values is simply a matter of what is and what isn't important to you.

Taking pen to paper for two no-nonsense activities will help to sort out your personal priorities, always an important consideration in a career choice.

What Counts Most

Rank the following considerations. Place the number **1** before the item most important to you, the number **2** before the item that is next in importance and so on.

_______ Satisfying and successful career
_______ Job security
_______ Good family relationships
_______ A world without discrimination
_______ International fame
_______ Pleasure
_______ Strong religious faith
_______ Lovely home in a beautiful setting
_______ Self-knowledge
_______ Ability or position to influence world affairs
_______ Satisfying love relationship
_______ The right to do what I want
_______ Excitement
_______ Ability to stimulate and/or influence the minds of others
_______ Enough money to live comfortably
_______ Sense of accomplishment
_______ A world in which humans and nature are in balance
_______ Love and understanding of friends

Feel free to talk over your ranking with family and friends. Consider what you would accept as a substitute—a trade-off—for each value; suppose job security is a high-ranking value but you would consider unusual opportunity as a substitute. These are lively discussion topics and new doors of understanding may open. There are no right or wrong answers. After doing this exercise, summarize what's important to you on the values identity inventory.

Identity Inventory:

MY PERSONAL LIFE VALUES

Value (Order of importance)	*Trade-off* (What I would accept as a substitute)
1. ____________________	1. ____________________
2. ____________________	2. ____________________
3. ____________________	3. ____________________
4. ____________________	4. ____________________
5. ____________________	5. ____________________

SUMMARY: (Top two values, which are "must have's")

1. ____
2. ____

∞

How Do You Really Feel About Work?

Now that you have a better idea of where you stand on personal values, shift gears and determine how you feel about work values.

Which of the following statements most accurately reflects your heart-of-heart feelings about work?

Nothing is really work unless you would rather be doing something else. (Sir James Barrie)

By working faithfully eight hours a day, you may eventually get to be a boss and work 12 hours a day. (Robert Frost)

If you first don't succeed, try, try again. Then quit. There's no use being a damn fool about it. (W. C. Fields)

As motivational expert Denis Waitley has said, "Attitude is a choice you make." Note your attitudes about work on the following evaluation form. It may be interesting to ask family members and friends to try this activity, too, and compare your response with theirs.

Work Values Evaluation

I would prefer (Select A or B)

_____ A. Work for organization
_____ B. Self-employment

_____ A. Structured environment: well defined duties and responsibilities
_____ B. Unstructured work: room for creativity and initiative

_____ A. Short hours: maximum eight hours per day
_____ B. Long hours and weekend work usual

_____ A. Similar duties every day
_____ B. Variety of duties every day

_____ A. Fast pace, high pressure
_____ B. Slow pace, low pressure

_____ A. Work indoors in pleasant environment
_____ B. Work outdoors in all weather and conditions

_____ A. Work for large business
_____ B. Work for small business

_____ A. High prestige and status
_____ B. Low prestige and status

_____ A. Work opportunities after 65
_____ B. Early retirement

_____ A. Work alone
_____ B. Work with other people

_____ A. Close supervision
_____ B. No supervision.

_____ A. High level of responsibility: make key decisions
_____ B. Low level of responsibility: no critical decisions

_____ A. Guaranteed regular hours
_____ B. Possible overtime

_____ A. Challenges and risks in work
_____ B. Work offers security

_____ A. Visible end products: specific achievable goals
_____ B. Can't see results of work, long-range goals

_____ A. Work in specific geographical area
_____ B. Willing to relocate anywhere

_____ A. Live close to work

_____ B. Live half hour or more from work

_____ A. Little or no travel

_____ B. Frequent travel

_____ A. Few opportunities for advancement and professional development

_____ B. Many opportunities for advancement and professional development

_____ A. Little work with machines

_____ B. Close work with machines

Now that you know you want a job in which you're not required to work more than two hours a day, that will pay $200,000 a year and that guarantees lifetime security, what more is there to say? Say it anyway and say it on your identity inventory for work values.

Identity Inventory:

MY WORK VALUES

Values (Order of importance)	*Trade-off* (What I would accept as a substitute)
1. ______________	1. ______________
2. ______________	2. ______________
3. ______________	3. ______________
4. ______________	4. ______________
5. ______________	5. ______________
6. ______________	6. ______________
7. ______________	7. ______________

SUMMARY: (Top three values, which are "must have's")

1. ______________
2. ______________
3. ______________

∞

YOUR PERSONALITY: WHICH TYPE ARE YOU?

What do Madonna, Willie Nelson, Lionel Ritchie, Tina Turner, Bruce Springsteen, Prince, and Michael Jackson have in common?

None of them is an ISTP or an ISFP. (You'll understand once you study the charts on the following pages. Although it sounds like alphabet soup, this is not a joke.)

You probably know about every music star mentioned above. But can you identify Carl Jung (pronounced *yoong*)? He was a Swiss psychologist who developed a theory about personality that could help you choose a career.

Jung said there are 16 basic personality types. While his brilliant work opened the door, it was embellished by two women before it became a practical tool for everyone.

SENSING TYPES

INTROVERTS	1. **ISTJ (INTROVERT, SENSING, THINKING, JUDGING)** Serious, quiet, earn success by concentration and thoroughness. Practical, orderly, matter-of-fact, logical, realistic and dependable. See to it that everything is well organized. Take responsibility. Make up their own minds as to what should be accomplished and work toward it steadily, regardless of protests or distractions.	2. **ISFJ (INTROVERT, SENSING, FEELING, JUDGING** Quiet, friendly, responsible and conscientious. Work devotedly to meet their obligations and serve their friends and school. Thorough, painstaking, accurate. May need time to master technical subjects, as their interests are usually not technical. Patient with detail and routine. Loyal, considerate, concerned with how other people feel.
	5. **ISTP (INTROVERT, SENSING, THINKING, PERCEPTIVE)** Cool onlookers—quiet, reserved, observing and analyzing life with detached curiosity and unexpected flashes of original humor. Usually interested in impersonal principles, cause and effect, how and why mechanical things work. Exert themselves no more than they think necessary, because any waste of energy would be inefficient.	6. **ISFP (INTROVERT, SENSING, FEELING, PERCEPTIVE)** Retiring, quietly friendly, sensitive, kind, modest about their abilities. Shun disagreements, do not force their opinions or values on others. Usually do not care to lead but are often loyal followers. Often relaxed about getting things done, because they enjoy the present moment and do not want to spoil it by undue haste or exertion.
EXTROVERTS	9. **ESTP (EXTROVERT, SENSING, THINKING, PERCEPTIVE)** Matter-of-fact, do not worry or hurry, enjoy whatever comes along. Tend to like mechanical things and sports, with friends on the side. May be a bit blunt or insensitive. Can do math or science when they see the need. Dislike long explanations. Are best with real things that can be worked, handled, taken apart or put together.	10. **ESFP (EXTROVERT, SENSING, FEELING, PERCEPTIVE)** Outgoing, easygoing, accepting, friendly, fond of a good time. Like sports and making things. Know what's going on and join in eagerly. Find remembering facts easier than mastering theories. Are best in situations that need sound common sense and practical ability with people as well as with things.
	13. **ESTJ (EXTROVERT, SENSING, THINKING, JUDGING)** Practical, realistic, matter-of-fact, with a natural head for business or mechanics. Not interested in subjects they see no use for, but can apply themselves when necessary. Like to organize and run activities. May make good administrators, especially if they remember to consider others' feelings and points of view.	14. **ESFJ (EXTROVERT, SENSING, FEELING, JUDGING)** Warm-hearted, talkative, popular, conscientious, born cooperators, active committee members. Always doing something nice for someone. Work best with encouragement and praise. Little interest in abstract thinking or technical subjects. Main interest is in things that directly and visibly affect people's lives.

INTROVERTS

3. **INFJ (INTROVERT, INTUITIVE, FEELING, JUDGING)**
Succeed by perseverance, originality and desire to do whatever is needed or wanted. Put their best efforts into their work. Quietly forceful, conscientious, concerned for others. Respected for their firm principles. Likely to be honored and followed for their clear convictions as to how best to serve the common good.

4. **INTJ (INTROVERT, INTUITIVE, THINKING, JUDGING)**
Usually have original minds and great drive when they choose to use them. In fields that appeal to them, they have a fine power to organize a job and carry it through with or without help. Skeptical, critical, independent, determined, often stubborn. Must learn to yield less important points in order to win the most important.

7. **INFP (INTROVERT, INTUITIVE, FEELING, PERCEPTIVE)**
Full of enthusiasms and loyalties, but seldom talk of these until they know you well. Care about learning, ideas, language, and independent projects of their own. Tend to undertake too much, then somehow get it done. Friendly, but often too absorbed in what they are doing to be sociable. Little concerned with possessions or physical surroundings.

8. **INTP (INTROVERT, INTUITIVE, THINKING, PERCEPTIVE)**
Quiet, reserved, brilliant in exams, especially in theoretical or scientific subjects. Logical to the point of hair-splitting. Usually interested mainly in ideas, with little liking for parties or small talk. Need to have sharply defined interests. Tend to choose careers where some strong interest can be used and useful.

EXTROVERTS

11. **ENFP (EXTROVERT, INTUITIVE, FEELING, PERCEPTIVE)**
Warmly enthusiastic, high-spirited, ingenious, imaginative. Able to do almost anything that interests them. Quick with a solution for any difficulty and ready to help anyone with a problem. Often rely on their ability to improvise instead of preparing in advance. Can usually find compelling reasons for whatever they want.

12. **ENTP (EXTROVERT, INTUITIVE, THINKING, PERCEPTIVE)**
Quick, ingenious, good at many things. Stimulating company, alert and outspoken. May argue for fun on either side of a question. Resourceful in solving new and challenging problems, but may neglect routine assignments. Often turn to one new interest after another. Skillful in finding logical reasons for what they want.

15. **ENFJ (EXTROVERT, INTUITIVE, FEELING, JUDGING)**
Responsive and responsible. Generally feel real concern for what others think or want, and try to handle things with due regard for other people's feelings. Can present a proposal or lead a group discussion with ease and tact. Sociable, popular, active in school affairs, but put time enough on their studies to do good work.

16. **ENTJ (EXTROVERT, INTUITIVE, THINKING, JUDGING)**
Hearty, frank, able in studies, leaders in activities. Usually good in anything that requires reasoning and intelligent talk, such as public speaking. Are usually well-informed and keep adding to their fund of knowledge. May sometimes be more positive and confident than experience in an area warrants.

In the early 1940s, Katharine Briggs and her daughter, Isabel Briggs Myers, questioned people whose personality types they already had identified.

They asked these people about their attitudes, behavior and responses to particular concepts and situations. From their research, the women designed a testing instrument—a questionnaire now known as the *Myers-Briggs Type Indicator,* or MBTI, for short.

The MBTI takes about 30 minutes to complete. It is designed to identify your natural bias in four areas:

1. *extroversion or introversion (E or I)*
2. *sensing or intuition (S or N)*
3. *thinking or feeling (T or F)*
4. *judging or perception (J or P)*

Once you identify your type, you are given clues to possible career options.

If you want to take the MBTI, published by the Consulting Psychologist Press, ask about it at your school counseling center or at a private counseling service.

In the meantime, by reading the descriptions of each of the 16 personality types on the preceding two pages, you can make an educated guess as to which type you are.

Your Working Style

Have you found your personality type? If so, reflect on these typical working styles associated with each characteristic.

Extroverts
like variety and action
tend to be faster than average
dislike complicated procedures
are often good at greeting people
are often impatient with long, slow jobs
often don't mind interruptions
often act quickly, sometimes without thinking
like to have people around
communicate freely

Introverts
like quiet for concentration
tend to be careful with details
dislike sweeping statements
don't like interruptions
work contentedly alone
may have problems communicating

Sensing Types
dislike new problems
like established way of doing things
enjoy using skills already learned more than learning new ones
work along steadily with realistic idea of how long it will take
reach a conclusion step by step
are patient with routine details
are impatient with complicated details
are seldom inspired and rarely trust inspiration
seldom make errors of fact

Intuitive Types
like solving new problems
dislike doing the same things over and over again
like learning a new skill and using it
put two and two together quickly
are impatient with routine details
follow their inspirations—good or bad
often get their facts a bit wrong

Thinking Types
are relatively unemotional and uninterested in people's feelings
may hurt people's feelings without knowing it
like analysis and putting things into logical order
can get along without harmony
tend to decide impersonally, sometimes ignoring people's wishes
need to be treated fairly
are able to reprimand people or fire them when necessary
tend to relate well only to other thinking types
may seem hardhearted

Feeling Types
tend to be very aware of other people's feelings
like harmony; efficiency may be badly disturbed by office feuds

often let decisions be influenced by
their own or other people's likes and dislikes
need occasional praise
dislike telling people unpleasant things
relate well to most people
tend to be sympathetic

Judging Types
are best when they can plan their work
and follow the plan
like to get things settled and wrapped up
may decide things too quickly
may dislike to interrupt the project
they are working on for one more urgent
may not notice new things that need to be done
want only the essentials needed
to get on with a job
tend to be satisfied once they reach a
judgment on a thing, situation or person

Perceptive Types
tend to be good at adapting to changing situations
don't mind leaving things open for alterations
may have trouble making decisions
may start too many projects and
have difficulty finishing them
may postpone unpleasant jobs
want to know all about a new job
tend to be curious and welcome new
light on a thing, situation, or person

Occupations and Types

Some of the career choices that seem to be associated with each personality type follow.

Caution: Do not consider only these examples. Each activity and example in this section is selected to help you expand your options—not to limit them.

Later on we'll discuss the best time and the best way to narrow your choices.

1. **ISTJ** (introvert, sensing, thinking, judging)
accountant
auditor
bank officer
business executive
cashier
computer programmer
financial planner
insurance agent
lawyer
purchasing agent
traffic analyst

2. **ISFJ** (introvert, sensing, feeling, judging)
accountant
anesthesiologist
animal caretaker
bartender
cook
counselor
librarian
nurse
pharmacist
psychologist
secretary
social worker
waiter/waitress

3. **INFJ** (introvert, intuitive, feeling, judging)
air traffic controller
chemist
clergyperson
composer
dentist
mathematician
nurse
pilot
writer

4. **INTJ** (introvert, intuitive, thinking, judging)
accountant
chemist
engineer
geologist
lawyer
mathematics teacher
psychologist
surveyor

5. **ISTP** (introvert, sensing, thinking, perceptive)
antique dealer
appliance repairer
art historian

automobile mechanic
bricklayer
cabinetmaker
electrical engineer
furrier
gem cutter
jeweler
pilot
printing press operator
tool designer

6. **ISFP** (introvert, sensing, feeling, perceptive)
accountant
animal keeper
biologist
cook
counselor
environmentalist
food inspector
forester
nurse
oceanographer
teacher
truck driver
wildlife worker

7. **INFP** (introvert, intuitive, feeling, perceptive)
clergyperson
dietitian
historian
journalist
library assistant
medical librarian
music teacher
public relations writer
translator

8. **INTP** (introvert, intuitive, thinking, perceptive)
actuary
architect
artist
credit analyst
financial planner
lawyer
pilot
systems analyst

9. **ESTP** (extrovert, sensing, thinking, perceptive)
accountant
announcer
automobile mechanic
coach
disc jockey
landscape architect
locksmith
machinist
pilot
secretary
travel agent
welder

10. **ESFP** (extrovert, sensing, feeling, perceptive)
actor
advertising manager
announcer
clergyperson
dancer
disc jockey
employment interviewer
model
photographer
police worker
public relations worker
secretary
truck driver

11. **ENFP** (extrovert, intuitive, feeling, perceptive)
actor
college professor
editorial writer
foreign service officer
lawyer
newspaper reporter
teacher

12. **ENTP** (extrovert, intuitive, thinking, perceptive)
architect
clothes designer

fashion artist
job analyst
landscape architect
lawyer
physician
political scientist

13. **ESTJ** (extrovert, sensing, thinking, judging)
bank teller
claim adjuster
curator
economist
lawyer
loan officer
office manager
school principal
urban planner

14. **ESFJ** (extrovert, sensing, feeling, judging)
account clerk
athletic director
bartender
clergyperson
cosmetologist
counselor
guide
manager
occupational therapist
secretary
teacher
veterinarian
waiter/waitress

15. **ENFJ** (extrovert, intuitive, feeling, judging)
actor
advertising manager
clergyperson
counselor
graphic designer
lawyer
teacher
urban planner

16. **ENTJ** (extrovert, intuitive, thinking, judging)
auditor
buyer
city manager
funeral director
hotel manager
store manager
teacher

You'll notice that some careers appear in several personality types. A lawyer, for instance, appears often because of various specialties; a trial lawyer probably would be an extrovert, whereas a patent lawyer might be an introvert. A public relations writer may be an introvert, while a public relations worker who deals with media is likely to be an extrovert. These examples are for general information only. For greater detail on the MBTI, see a career counselor.

A Second Opinion

Here's another activity to help you come face to face with your personality traits. After finishing this activity, compare it with your MBTI outcome.

How well do they correspond? It may be enlightening to discuss your personality traits with those who know you well. Do they agree with your self-assessment? Others may have observations you'll want to consider, even to the point of changing some perceptions about yourself.

(This may be superfluous advice, but don't listen to anyone who, when asked to describe your personality, says your traits qualify you for the primate-of-the-year award. This is serious business.)

Concerning the following activity, note that each characteristic in the left column has a corresponding opposite in the right column. Mark the circle that best describes you.

In the first example, if you see yourself as more tactful than thoughtless, you mark either circle 5, circle 6 or circle 7, depending on how tactful you think you are. Circle 7 means very, very tactful. If you see yourself as more thoughtless than tactful, mark circle 1, circle 2 or circle 3. Circle 1 means very, very thoughtless. What if you are sometimes thoughtless and sometimes tactful? Mark circle 4.

There are no right or wrong answers; this exercise is designed to enhance your self-awareness.

Personality Profile

	1	2	3	4	5	6	7	
Thoughtless	○	○	○	○	○	○	○	Tactful
A loner	○	○	○	○	○	○	○	Friendly
Awkward	○	○	○	○	○	○	○	Poised
Stubborn	○	○	○	○	○	○	○	Ready to cooperate
A goof-off	○	○	○	○	○	○	○	Dependable
A dreamer	○	○	○	○	○	○	○	Realistic
Cranky	○	○	○	○	○	○	○	Agreeable
Easily upset	○	○	○	○	○	○	○	Unshakable
Messy	○	○	○	○	○	○	○	Neat
Unsure of yourself	○	○	○	○	○	○	○	Confident
Easily hurt	○	○	○	○	○	○	○	Thick-skinned
Not to be trusted	○	○	○	○	○	○	○	Loyal
Calm	○	○	○	○	○	○	○	Quick to anger
Sad and worried	○	○	○	○	○	○	○	Cheerful
Childish	○	○	○	○	○	○	○	Mature
Cautious	○	○	○	○	○	○	○	Adventuresome
Mean	○	○	○	○	○	○	○	Considerate
Critical	○	○	○	○	○	○	○	Tolerant
Impatient	○	○	○	○	○	○	○	Patient

	1	2	3	4	5	6	7	
Rude	○	○	○	○	○	○	○	Respectful
Bossy	○	○	○	○	○	○	○	Democratic
Stingy	○	○	○	○	○	○	○	Generous
Ashamed	○	○	○	○	○	○	○	Proud
Secretive	○	○	○	○	○	○	○	Open
Dishonest	○	○	○	○	○	○	○	Honest
Impulsive	○	○	○	○	○	○	○	Thoughtful
Flighty	○	○	○	○	○	○	○	Serious
Phony	○	○	○	○	○	○	○	Real
Not understanding	○	○	○	○	○	○	○	Understanding
Dependent	○	○	○	○	○	○	○	Independent
Slow to forgive	○	○	○	○	○	○	○	Forgiving
A quitter	○	○	○	○	○	○	○	You keep trying
Quiet	○	○	○	○	○	○	○	Energetic
Rebellious	○	○	○	○	○	○	○	Accepting
Easily influenced	○	○	○	○	○	○	○	Able to think for yourself
A pessimist	○	○	○	○	○	○	○	An optimist
Easily bored	○	○	○	○	○	○	○	Usually interested

Now that you've looked into a mirror of your personality, you probably will be more alert to potential clashes and matches as you consider various career fields. It doesn't take a sage to figure out that if you're easily upset, you shouldn't take a job in which you'd be responsible for customer complaints, or that if you are a person with great patience, you have the personality to consider elementary teaching as a career.

Enough reflecting—it's time to record.

Now you're prepared to fill in the identity inventory for personality traits. No one will smirk when you put on paper the fact that you are brave, honest, highly intelligent, gifted with a marvelous sense of humor, caring, sensitive, compassionate, cooperative, cheerful, calm, relaxed, competitive, persistent, confident, disciplined, positive, hardworking, thorough, enthusiastic, goal-oriented, sociable, creative, and attractive—all in all, the most appealing person in America.

Identity Inventory:

MY PERSONALITY TRAITS

Evaluations by myself and others suggest that I have the following characteristics:

1. ______
2. ______
3. ______
4. ______
5. ______
6. ______
7. ______
8. ______
9. ______
10. ______
11. ______
12. ______

SUMMARY: My five most dominant traits are:

1. ______
2. ______
3. ______
4. ______
5. ______

LIFESTYLE: FIGURING OUT WHAT YOU WANT

Maybe you still aren't 100 percent sure whether you want to share the sky with eagles or the ground with prairie chickens, but by now you do have an insider's knowledge of yourself.

Use this enlightenment to anticipate your preferred lifestyle. When people gripe about their jobs being dismal or their lives uninspiring, look for a lifestyle that is incompatible with their values.

What is lifestyle, exactly? The answer is profound, yet simple: It's how you live your entire life.

Lifestyle includes where you reside geographically—North, South, East or West. It includes whether you live in a small town, large city, farm, military base or convent. It includes whether you live in a rental apartment, condominium, detached family dwelling, houseboat or estate with guarded gates.

No matter where you live, that area and residence color your life. Your days living near the ocean or in the mountains will be quite different from your days in the desert or the flat Midwest.

Lifestyle also includes leisure-time pursuits. If fishing every other day is your idea of heaven and you live in New York City, the odds are you will not be completely satisfied with your lifestyle.

Your lifestyle includes the kind of car you drive, the amount of traveling you do and the kinds of vacations you take. It includes the types of friends you have.

What decides lifestyle? In most major ways, your decisions set the stage. Contributing factors are your education, marital status and family responsibilities.

Beyond that, the chief determiner of how your lifestyle shapes up is your career, and, increasingly, in an age of two-income families, the career of your spouse.

Unless you inherit for a living, your career determines whether you can pay for the lifestyle you want and whether you have enough time from your job to enjoy it.

Your Own Crystal Ball

There's no time like the present to pick up a tablet of paper, find a quiet corner and jot down your visions of what a lifestyle should be. Be sure to include your values and try to project yourself into the future. These headings can serve as a guide:

Residence. Where do I want to live? (Describe in detail the geographical location, the kind of apartment or house and your surroundings.)

Work Values. What kinds of things do I want to do on the job? (Include a description of the physical location of your workplace and the kinds of people you want to work with. Example: I want to work where I can be outside a great deal and work mostly by myself.)

Friends. What kinds of people do I want to be associating with socially?

Family Life. What do I want my family to be like? This includes marriage, children, and so forth.

Recreation and Cultural. Which cultural resources do I want to be available? libraries? theater? museums? (Don't just jot things down; describe in detail where you want to go and how often.)

Hobbies. Which hobbies do I want to participate in?

Education. How much education do I want?

Finances. How much money do I want to make?

Scenarios

As the saying goes: "Just when you've got it together, somebody moves it."

So it is with lifestyles. Unforeseen changes may dramatically alter your wish list.

Here are a number of wished-for lifestyes. After each is a statement of what happened in real life. For each case history, ask yourself how you would cope in the situation.

What would pull you through—education, skills, reserves of personal strength?

This activity makes great after-dinner discussion at the family dining table.

Debbie. Debbie wants to live in a small town, where she will be close to nature and away from the pressures of a big city. She wants to work outdoors most of the time. She would like to raise animals. She wants to ride and show horses as a hobby. She wants to get married and have four children, she thinks. She would like her husband to share her interest in animals.

Debbie also likes camping and would like her family to share her interests. She enjoys the company of a few friends, but does not care for large gatherings or parties. She wants to be active behind the scenes in some community activities. Debbie wants secure careers for herself and her husband, but her needs are simple and most of her leisure pursuits are simple.

She figures that extra income can be made by breeding horses. Because Debbie wants to spend time with her children when they are young, she would like a career that could be interrupted or continued on a part-time basis.

Real life: Debbie went to a dude ranch on vacation, met Joe and married him. Joe, an investment banker, was offered a Wall Street position too good to turn down. The newlyweds moved to New York City. Two years after their marriage, Joe decided he did not want children.

How would you cope with this unforeseen change?

Peter. Peter wants a job that will utilize his creative ability and isn't routine. He would like some travel in his job. The idea of working from 9 to 5 sounds awful to Peter. He would prefer to have a job where he can perform a task at a time of his choosing. He wouldn't mind having several projects to work on at the same time.

The atmosphere of Peter's work environment must be modern and neat. He also wants a nice house. Peter wants his wife to work, too. He hopes both he and his wife will have professional careers so their circle of friends will be stimulating. He believes that a suburb would best suit his needs.

Real life: Peter became an insurance broker. He married a librarian who worked for two years before she became pregnant and quit her job. She told Peter she felt she should stay home with their child for several years at least. Peter has to choose between scrimping and lowering their lifestyle, or accepting a higher-paying but rigid job.

How would you cope with this unforeseen change?

Cheryl. Cheryl loves the ocean and water sports. She loves to boat, water ski and surf. She hates cold weather. She wants to own a boat and a house with a view of the ocean.

All these things are expensive, so she knows that she will need a career that pays well but will allow enough time for her to enjoy leisure pursuits. She wouldn't mind working in the city if she can enjoy a home on the beach. She would also like access to tennis courts. She would eventually like a family, but has no desire to marry soon. She likes structure, so she wants a job where she knows what to expect.

Real life: Cheryl graduated from high school but decided against further education or training. She was in a hurry to get to the sun and fun. Cheryl moved to Maui, Hawaii, from her native Ohio, knowing no one in her new state.

Cheryl was lucky and quickly found evening work as a waitress at a resort hotel, a job that left her days free for the beach.

After three years, Cheryl became weary of her life. She decided she'd had it with living on an island without good friends. She was tired of her job, and of the people she met on the beach—they didn't seem to think the same way about things as she did.

Cheryl was debating whether she should return to Ohio where she knew people and where the values of the community were those she had grown up with when she was fired from her job.

How would you cope with this unforeseen change?

John. John never missed a police show on TV. From the time he was 12, he talked about going into police work when he grew up.

John's father, a doctor, wanted him to become a doctor, too, or at least a lawyer. He believed John would outgrow his early passion.

To please his father, John enrolled in a college and began to prepare for a life as a professional and the good-life rewards it would bring. But John never stopped saying he wanted to be a detective.

Real life: John hated book work and dropped out of college after one miserable year. During the ensuing shouting match with his father, John kept trying to explain that he just wasn't a student.

He preferred action, being out and around all day—not being behind a desk or around a bunch of sick people.

John never married and his dream came true. He became a fine police officer and was on his way to becoming a detective when he was shot in the line of duty. Afterwards, John was destined to spend the remainder of his life in a wheelchair.

The police chief personally offered John a desk job in personnel. John was grateful. Then it hit him: John would never be promoted in the personnel department until he returned to college and obtained his sheepskin. What an ironic twist of fate, John thought, being forced back to the very schooling he'd escaped a decade earlier.

How would you cope with this unforeseen change?

∞

Fairy Tales and Reality

You've been a good sport, sticking with us through both your wish list and the harsh doses of reality that sometimes happen in real life. For that kindness, we have a special treat for you.

Here's a fantasy capsule of Snow White's lifestyle. We admit we carried her life a bit further than the Brothers Grimm intended.

The Lifestyle of Snow White

Age	Residence	Major Activities	People Close to Snow White
15	luxurious castle	being tutored playing with dukes and duchesses	father governess
20	small cottage	feeding dwarfs cleaning cottage buying apples from queens dressed as witches	Happy Sleepy Grumpy Sneezy Dopey Doc Bashful
30	castle	raising young princess redecorating castle giving parties	husband princess
60	small cottage on castle grounds	watching TV playing bingo baby-sitting young princes and princesses	daughter grandkids

Don't give out yet. There's only one more identity inventory to complete—it's on lifestyle preferences.

Identity Inventory:
MY LIFESTYLE PREFERENCES

First choice If I could design my life, I would prefer:	**Trade-off** What I would accept as a substitute, at least temporarily:
Urban, rural area ______	______
Part of country ______	______
Have extra leisure time ______ (yes, no)	______
Working indoors, outdoors ______	______
Working days, evenings, nights ______	______
Working weekends, off week days ______ (yes, no)	______
Not working weekends ______ (yes, no)	______
To run my own business ______ (yes, no)	______
To leave my work at the office ______ (yes, no)	______
To carry my work in my head ______ (yes, no)	______
Other preferences:	
______	______
______	______
______	______
______	______
______	______
______	______
______	______
______	______
______	______

∞

IDENTITY SNAPSHOT

—A Summary of Myself—

Interests:

Aptitudes/Skills:

Academic Abilities:

Personal Values:

Work Values:

Personality Traits:

Lifestyle Preferences:

(Note: Do not include physical characteristics, including disabilities, on your identity snapshot. These considerations are discussed in section 7 of the *Career Book.*)

The Wrap-Up

Casey Stengel was one of baseball's greatest and most colorful characters. He was also a good judge of baseball talent.

Out on the coaching line one day he pointed to a player and asked, "See that fella over there?"

His companion nodded and prompted, "What about him?" "He's 20 years old. In 10 years he's got a chance to be a star. Now that other fella over there, he's 20 years old. In 10 years he's got a chance to be 30."

Having persevered through all seven of your identity inventories, we're betting that in a decade you will be more than 10 years older.

We can't know whether you'll be a star—or an eagle—but it's a certainty that you are much better acquainted with yourself than ever before.

And surprise—you're not half-bad!

Just one more activity and you can wrap up this section.

Using all the data on your seven identity inventories, summarize it on your identity snapshot to the left. Choose only the most relevant, most important items.

All this thinking, writing and boiling down helps organize and fix the information in your mind.

SECTION SEVEN

YOUR CAREER AWARENESS

W*hen you want your dreams to come true, wake up!*
Waking up is what awareness means. This section and the one that follows tell you how to develop awareness as a skill and use it to make intelligent choices about your career path.

Unlike totalitarian countries, this nation offers freedom of career choice. Without it, your personal dignity as a unique individual is denied. Because stereotypes, biases and other misperceptions limit your chances to be a successful career-climber, it's important to understand how you may acquire slanted viewpoints. This section recommends methods of pushing aside self-limiting images.

We let you in on many ways to acquire career information you need, and conclude with a list of 700 job ideas.

Awareness: A Life Force

Awareness is knowing that Sherlock Holmes is not a new housing development.

Humor aside, awareness means you take note of the change when your best friend's braces are removed, when the trees begin to bud, when your family pet grays and grows old.

You recognize these things because you sense, feel, observe and understand what's going on. You stay awake, tune in, are in touch with the world.

For your career growth, awareness means you perceive job-related facts and impressions and realize what they mean. You actively gather and store information you can use later.

We sometimes take for granted our awareness and knowledge about a subject. Let's use aviation as an example.

Boarding an airplane is routine today, so much so that you probably give little thought to the wonder of jet travel. But during a visit to the Smithsonian Institution's National Air and Space Museum in Washington, D.C., you quickly become very aware of how far people have soared in only a few years.

You see the *Spirit of St. Louis,* the silvery monoplane in which Charles Lindbergh spanned the Atlantic in a single gulp of determined flying. Nearby, *Friendship 7* stands, the dark plexiglass spacecraft piloted by John Glenn, the first American in orbit.

A brief 35 years separates the heroic feats of these men. Imagine: Propeller blades became rocket launchers in one-third of a century! Your awareness can be electrifying as you realize that scheduled commuter flights between planets may begin within your lifetime and as you consider how such progress may affect your personal career plans. In this case, your awareness can lead to an expansion of career options in a variety of ways. To name a few imaginative choices, maybe you can become

- a space flight instructor
- a shuttle reservation agent
- an importer of outerspace goods.

Awareness is a skill you can sharpen every day if you're alert to what's happening around you. Lack of awareness can mean missed opportunities.

By any measure, awareness is a powerful force in life.

You Are Unique

Gee, Son, people will really wonder about you if you become a ballet dancer.

Now that you've lost a hand, you'll need to change from the automobile design curriculum, won't you?

My little girl doesn't need to know about careers. She's a beauty and when she grows up, she'll marry a fine man who will be attracted to her accomplishments and she will lead a country-club life.

Should a 50-year-old be admitted to medical school?

You're quite short. Most managers are taller than average. Why don't you consider accounting?

Our career center has a pamphlet on opportunities for Jewish youth in retailing but no publication about auto mechanics.

City kids aren't likely to be happy as forest rangers. Blacks aren't either.

The drop-out rate for Hispanics in high school is so high that we try to get them into a trades program.

In the harsh glare of print, statements of this nature are laughable—if not uncommon.

Perhaps you've run into such bias yourself. You may already know that dogeared stereotyping clamps a lid on your freedom.

If not, think about it. Is it really going to matter 500 years from today if you of the hairy legs adore leaping about the stage in tights? And where is it written that you, who could rival any Miss America contestant, should not ride around in a police cruiser keeping the peace?

What does matter is that you believe in yourself as a unique human being who will have the liberty to live up to your personal capacity. Stereotyping steals your freedom of choice.

∞

The Greek God Days Are Fading

Before a variety of laws benefiting physically disabled people were enacted, you didn't stand much chance of being employed at many American corporations unless you were a Greek god or reasonable facsimile.

Now secretaries who are blind type dictation using a braille dictionary; company supervisors learn basic sign language to communicate with deaf technicians; and people with cerebral palsy operate computers.

If you have a characteristic that has traditionally limited career choices, don't assume you need a list of good jobs for the physically disabled. That's an outdated notion.

You choose a career the same way persons who do not have disabilities do. Only you have to be resourceful enough to figure out a way the occupation can be adapted to your special needs. It will not be possible in every instance, but in many cases, you will have other strong skills that may compensate for your limitation.

Having a disability does *not* prevent you from perfecting other job skills that can crown your career with success. You can show ingenuity in solving problems, demonstrate careful planning, show perseverance, and other positive attributes.

Your challenge will be to get managers and supervisors to think of a disability as only a single characteristic and not as something that is all-embracing. You want them to focus on abilities plural, not disability singular. This is how it is explained by Rami Rabby, a New York City-based management consultant.

Rabby says that "Once you think of my blindness as only one part of the body that happens not to work as well as it might on the same level as any other kind of limitation that anybody has, then you're beginning to look at it in the kind of perspective that I think the industry should."

To illustrate, Rabby once presented a training program on disability and employment at a major bank that does a lot of overseas business. After Rabby explained that emotional perceptions are to blame for blocking the entrance of disabled people into mainstream society, a vice president said, "All this stuff in the seminar is interesting, but in the final analysis, I feel sorry for you because you're blind."

In his response, Rabby countered her emotionalism with logic: "I understand that you do and that is the problem. There is no reason that you should feel any more sorry for me because I'm blind than I should feel sorry for you (in dealing with job-related international banking) because you don't happen to know Hebrew, French and Spanish, as I do. Because in the practical situation of employment, the two are absolutely identical."

A manager, after all, plans, organizes, coordinates and controls. Which is the more restrictive in a supervisory job—a lack of vision or a lack of organizing ability? Is it easier for a person to learn dictation skills or interpersonal skills? Is it reasonable to assume that one cannot think because one cannot see?

As Rabby explains, disabled applicants must try to make interviewers grasp the whole package they offer, not zero in on a single feature. Blindness, for instance, must *not* be perceived as the central aspect of a candidate. If the interviewer starts out asking "How are you going to do this job?", give a factual, brief answer, but immediately move the conversation to your technical qualifications and experience or education.

The principle is the same as for any job seeker: Deal briefly with shortcomings and refocus on your strengths.

While American industry has a long way to go before debunking the Greek-god hiring standard once and for all, progress is being made.

It's ironic that it existed in the first place. In ancient legends, Hephaestus—the Greek god of crafts—used his strong arms over the fires of his smithy to create world-class works. Hephaestus was lame.

Getting On With Success—No Matter What

Arthur Godfrey was a famous radio and television personality. Author Robert Metz tells the story about Godfrey's frustrating efforts to be a patriot. During World War II Godfrey tried to join the Navy. He was turned down time after time.

Finally Godfrey asked for help from President Franklin D. Roosevelt, who called and asked why Godfrey was being rejected. An officer told President Roosevelt that the Navy couldn't give Godfrey a commission because of leg injuries he suffered in an automobile accident.

When Godfrey told the story many years later, he said F.D.R. asked, "Can he walk?" "Yes, he can walk," the Navy officer replied.

"Then give him the commission," F.D.R. roared. "I can't walk and I'm the Commander in Chief!"

This anecdote illustrates preconceptions that hinder disabled persons in the job market. The Foundation for Science and the Handicapped has done much to dispel the myth that the disabled cannot participate as valuable members of the work force, as the following sampling of disabled high-performers illustrates. It is drawn from numerous profiles in the foundation's publication, *Able Scientists—Disabled Persons,* available for $12.95 from the foundation at 154 Juliet Court, Clarendon Hills, Ill. 60514.

- Odette L. Shotwell, PhD (postpolio), is an organic chemist at the Northern Regional Research Center, U.S. Department of Agriculture in Peoria, Ill., where she heads a department of eight specialists.
- Lawrence Wos, PhD (blind), directs a research program in automated reasoning in the mathematics and computer science division at the Argonne National Laboratory near Chicago.
- Cynthia Dusel-Bacon, BA (arm amputee), is a geologist in the United States Geological Service and uses a specially adapted microscope to study geological characteristics of rock slices.
- Donald L. Ballantyne, PhD (deaf), is a world authority in transplantation biology at New York University School of Medicine.
- R. Kent Jones, BS (multiple sclerosis), a civil engineer with the Metropolitan Sanitary District of Greater Chicago, supervises the activities of his section from his wheelchair.
- Anne B. Swanson, PhD (brittle bones), is associate professor of chemistry at Edgewood College in Madison, Wisc. Dr. Swanson uses an elevated platform to compensate for her short stature.

These individuals decided they would have a career, no matter what. They decided that in spite of barriers to openness and accessibility in the job market, they wanted the same things most of us want out of life—including using our abilities to the fullest, participating in the workplace and being judged on how well we do with what we have.

You never know when one of the crowd will make Commander in Chief.

Freedom Starts in Your Mind

If you are your own "jailer," you'll have to accept the limitations inherent in considering only those careers traditional to your sex, race, cultural background and disability.

The next activity reveals how you feel about all this.

Type Casting

Close your eyes and see a pilot. Envision the pilot in full uniform walking out to the plane. Now the pilot is sitting behind the controls of the plane.

Do you see a woman? Probably not; based on the reactions of thousands of students who did this exercise, you most likely see a man.

All of us suffer from occupational stereotypes that not only are sex related, but personality and image related as well.

Imagine that you are a Hollywood casting director. After each of the following occupations, jot down your impression of how you would cast each role. Consider appearance, personality, age, gender, racial or ethnic group.

accountant: ______________________________

____

____

heavy equipment operator: ______________________________

____

____

nurse: ______________________________

____

____

stockbroker: ______________________________

____

____

chef: ______________________________

____

____

sporting goods store manager: ______________________________

____

____

civil engineer: ______________________________

____

____

surgeon: ______________________________

____

____

flight attendant: ______________________________

____

____

secretary: ______________________________

____

____

insurance broker: ______________________________

____

____

professional wrestler: ______________________________

____

____

When you can't see yourself in a role you've described, you probably won't consider the occupation for yourself. In your mind, it's not "you."

If you can't match yourself with the image you hold of a career field, your mind is closed about a particular occupation and you are prematurely limiting your choices. Open your mind. Let in fresh air.

The Stork Doesn't Bring Stereotypes

As you surmised from the last activity, you too are not without stereotypical notions. Where do they come from? Certainly not heaven. Several possibilities are

- newspapers, magazines, books
- television, radio
- knowing a person in the field of your stereotype
- your parents and friends

Sometimes wrong perceptions of an occupation become so widespread that it's humorous. In *Powermom* by Hester Mundis, the author gives her hilarious version of a "career guide."

Of airline pilots, she says it's a good choice because you travel extensively on the job, but bad because you never get to watch the movie. A stereotype.

As a retail buyer, you buy beautiful clothes with other people's money, but you can't afford the same clothing for yourself. Another stereotype.

Photographers, Mundis explains, can make money attending gala social functions just by taking pictures, but the downside is your friends expect you to take pictures for free. Still another stereotype.

When you're surrounded by stereotypes, what's the answer? Take direct fact-finding action. Make an appointment to spend a day with someone in the career field in question. Watch, observe. Compare the factual information you acquire with your previous perception.

If we were to shadow Hester Mundis' examples, we'd find that pilots often are stranded in faraway places and must return to home base as passengers, in which case they can watch any movie shown.

Buyers may be given big discounts on beautiful clothing for their own wardrobes.

Photographers need only insist to friends that photography is their living and they do it only on a professional basis.

Hester Mundis was joking, of course, but you can see how stereotypes, like rumors, get into the culture.

By now you know that the stork doesn't bring stereotypes; misinformation does. The only cure is to get the correct facts.

Myth: Women Want Only a Job, Not a Career

The American job market is still a predominantly masculine forum. "One quarter of all employed women are crowded into just 22 of the 500 occupations distinguished by the U.S. census," according to Dr. Barbara F. Reskin, a University of Michigan sociologist.

This bunching up into nursing, teaching, librarianship and other traditional women's fields is called *occupational segregation.* Its consequences: low pay. The ratio of earnings for women is 70 cents for every dollar earned by men.

Still, women are branching out. They are climbing new career mountains and establishing marks that won't soon be erased.

The next time you hear that women aren't interested in the world beyond husband, home and family, help stamp out that myth by referring to these examples of top U.S. businesses run by women. They are drawn from a recent *Savvy* magazine survey of women in leadership positions.

HIGH PERFORMANCE WOMEN

EXECUTIVE	COMPANY NAME	EMPLOYEES	INDUSTRY
Estée Lauder, chairman	**Estée Lauder,** New York, NY	10,000	cosmetics
Katharine Graham, chairman	**The Washington Post Co.,** Washington, D.C.	7,000	publishing, broadcasting
Mary Wells Lawrence, chairman	**Wells, Rich, Greene,** New York, NY	900	advertising
Mary C. Crowley, president, ceo	**Home Interiors & Gifts,** Dallas, TX	40,000	home furnishings
Helen K. Copley, chairman, ceo	**The Copley Press,** La Jolla, CA	4,000	publishing
Colombe M. Nicholas, president	**Christian Dior—New York,** New York, NY	20	product licensing
Donna Wolf Steigerwaldt, chairman, ceo	**Jockey International,** Kenosha, WI	3,200	apparel manufacturing
Diane Von Furstenberg, chairman	**Diane Von Furstenberg,** New York, NY	30	furnishings, fashion
Mary Kay Ash, chairman	**Mary Kay Cosmetics,** Dallas, TX	1,200	cosmetics
Charlotte Beers, managing partner, ceo	**Tatham-Laird & Kudner,** Chicago, IL	350	advertising
Leona J. Lewis, chairman **Lana Jane Lewis-Brent,** president, ceo	**Sunshine-Jr. Stores,** Panama City, FL	2,200	supermarkets, convenience stores
Beatrice Coleman, president	**Maidenform,** New York, NY	4,000	lingerie, sleepwear
June Collier, president, ceo	**National Industries,** Montgomery, AL	3,000	wiring assemblies
Lillian Katz, chairman	**Lillian Vernon,** Mount Vernon, NY	1,500	mail order
Bonita Wrather, chairman	**The Wrather Corporation,** Beverly Hills, CA	2,500	oil & gas, real estate
Gertrude R. Crain, chairman	**Crain Communications,** Chicago, IL	960	publishing
Dorothy Stimson Bullitt, chairman emeritus **Priscilla Collins,** chairman **Harriet Bullit Rice,** chairman	**King Broadcasting Co.,** Seattle, WA	400	radio, television cable stations

(continued)

EXECUTIVE	COMPANY NAME	EMPLOYEES	INDUSTRY
Paula Kent Meehan, founder	**Redken Laboratories,** Canoga Park, CA	1,000	hair products, cosmetics
Judy Thompson, president, ceo	**Thompson Tractor,** Birmingham, AL	486	heavy equipment
Helen Jo Whitsell, chairman	**Copeland Lumber Yards,** Portland, OR	600	building materials
Ellen Sigal, ceo	**Sigal/Zuckerman,** Washington, D.C.	25	building development
June Morris, president	**Morris Travel,** Salt Lake City, UT	350	travel agency
Sandra L. Kurtzig, president,	**ASK Computer Systems,** Los Altos, CA	456	computer systems
Lynn Wilson, president, ceo	**Creative Environs of Lynn Wilson,** Coral Gables, FL	35	architectural design firm
Marjorie E. Bowstrom, chairman, ceo	**Zollner Corp.,** Fort Wayne, IN	1,600	pistons

This list of examples should dent arguments based on stereotypes of women. If you want to go for total demolition of beliefs not supported by facts, begin to keep files on outstanding women.

Among those you might find are Sally Ride, former astronaut; Dianne Feinstein, Mayor of San Francisco; Dr. Mary Betty Stevens, leading arthritis physician; Betty Vetter, national expert on science and technology careers; Sandra Day O'Conner, Supreme Court Justice; Madeleine Kunin, Governor of Vermont and Margaret Heckler, Ambassador to Ireland.

One last stereotype to explode: Women can't handle budgets. When she served as Secretary of the U.S. Department of Health and Human Services, Margaret Heckler oversaw an annual budget of $318 billion, the third-largest budget in the world. Only the budgets of the United States government and the Soviet Union are larger.

Use the Right Job Titles

Use language that helps smash stereotyping. It's in your best interests to say letter carrier, not mailman; repairer, not repairman; advertising lay-out planner not advertising lay-out man.

A foreman is a supervisor and a new car salesman is a new car sales associate. A poetess is a poet.

Why should you strive to use sex-neutral language?

Sexist communication labels either females or males into roles solely on the basis of sex. Nonsexist communication does not prelabel. It does not assert that male is the norm (repairman) and that female is something less than the norm.

An old saying suggests, "Tell me a people's language and I'll tell you the values of that people."

In addition to the fact that sexist communication indicates that one is behind the times and has a patriarchal view of the job market, we urge you to think in sex-neutral job titles because doing so keeps your mind open to opportunities. Watch your thoughts, warns writer Frank Outlaw. Thoughts become words, then actions, then habits, then character, then destiny.

Sexist job titles do not encourage you to think about being all you can be.

Ethnic and Racial Stereotyping and Other Antiquities

"Bathe regularly and become dentists," Greek immigrants once were advised.

The Greeks arriving in the New World in 1908 were told they could prosper by fixing the bad teeth Americans develop from eating too much candy.

The dispenser of the advice, Seraphim G. Canoutas, a lawyer, included the information in *The Immigrant's Guide in America,* a manual that spewed tips on everything from immigration formalities at Ellis Island to a list of more than 5,000 Greek-owned businesses in the U.S. and Canada, most of them florist shops, shoeshine parlors and restaurants.

It was teeth repair, however, that the lawyer thought offered the most dazzling possibilities: "In no other country in the world are as many sweets consumed as in America. This excessive indulgence, especially among women, results in the ruin of their teeth. Dentists, therefore, have become plentiful and make more money than candy store owners."

Frankly, we haven't the slightest idea whether dentistry became a stereotype for Greeks, but Canoutas' advice is an example of how publications and media can foster narrow occupational perceptions.

Years ago, many people incorrectly thought most Irish became cops, most Jews became retailers, most blacks became teachers and most Asians became medical laboratory workers.

All that's old hat. Today's professionals who are responsible for portraying workers in media, film and advertising have, for the most part, become sensitive to the wrongness of stereotyping and try to avoid it.

If you're a member of an ethnic group or a racial minority, avoid stereotyping yourself. Push aside limiting images as you exercise your full freedom of choice in deciding who you are going to be in life.

The Best Life—How to Find It

You may have a general idea of the kind of life you would like to have. You may already have some information about several career areas.

That's not enough.

It is only the beginning.

To be rewarded with a blockbuster career, you must become a comparison shopper looking at all possibilities within your awareness range.

You may not have thought about it in quite this way but the lifestyle you want can be fulfilled by more than one career pattern. Perhaps two dozen occupations have your name on them. If you like people and faraway places, for instance, you might like to be a travel agent or a tour guide or an airline reservation agent or a corporate travel department manager or a trade association convention manager—or maybe you'll see a recruiting poster and join the Navy.

The point is that you have to scout far and wide before you can answer such key questions as these:

What are the jobs?

Where are they?

What do I have to do to get them?

A logical way to begin is to write down all the career fields that look good. Before you settle down to serious selecting—before you narrow your sights to a handful of outstanding prospects—you first must be aware of all the wonderful things in the world from which you can choose.

There's so much, in fact, that the array of opportunities can be dumbfounding. Not only is the sheer volume of ways to earn a living nearly overwhelming, but they cram a constantly changing careerscape.

The classic way to deal with a mass of unwieldy information is to break it into several small stacks.

In career development, groups of related occupations are often called *career clusters* or *job families.* Career clusters are formed in several different ways.

- Some occupations share a cluster because they are part of the same industry—both physicians and respiratory therapists are in the health cluster.
- Other occupations are kindred because they require a certain kind of training, such as apprenticeship (plumbers and electricians).
- Still other occupations are clustered because they involve similar activities, such as working with people. Sales engineers and technical manufacturer's representatives work with customers in similar ways.
- The common bond for some groups of occupations is a shared interest, such as in the environment or in music.
- A particular skill is the glue that holds together other groups of occupations. Mechanical ability is an example.
- A new clustering system, known as *worker traits,* combines both interests and skills. This clustering system is fast gaining popularity. Artists and sculptors illustrate this concept.

As you can imagine, a job can be slotted into several career clusters, depending on how it is viewed. For example, clerical occupations are found in all clusters.

There are two main reasons why it's important to understand how the cluster concept works.

1. If you discover an occupation you like, you may spot one you like even more by exploring the cluster. A young man interested in the work of a marine geophysicist should scan the entire environment-and-natural-resources cluster. Other options in marine science, such as hydrologist or marine meteorologist, might be more attractive to a specific individual.
2. If you have an avid desire to enter a particular field but fail to qualify for some reason, you may come upon a satisfying related opportunity by exploring alternatives within a cluster. A young woman whose eyesight does not meet vision requirements to become a pilot might choose to become a marketing specialist for an airline rather than exclude aviation as a career area.

Career clusters are a technique to help you shop for the best work niche in life.

Clearly, if comparison shopping is good for your pocketbook, it's even better for your career.

Clusters related to industries and broad functions are found at the end of this section.

Make a Future File

Career information is more usable if you organize it in a file. Because it deals with your future, let's call it a *future file.*

You can use notebooks—say, one notebook per career field. If you don't want to use notebooks, use file folders. Keep copies of articles and notes on interviews you conduct. If you have a microcomputer, you can create an electronic future file.

The way you keep your file is far less important than the care with which you do research, take notes and organize your findings.

Organizing is in itself a technique that will enhance your career awareness.

Samples of forms you can use to summarize the information in your future file appear next. The forms show you how to organize information you gather. Examples of how the forms might be filled out follow.

EXPLORATION INTERVIEW REPORT

Name: ______________________

Title: ______________________

Organization: ______________________

Address: ______________________

Date of Interview: ______________________

Key information obtained: ______________________

____

____

____

(Don't forget to add this name to your contacts log described in section 5.)

EXPLORATION INTERVIEW REPORT

Name: Chris Littlejohn

Title: Employee Benefits Administrator

Organization: Sun Up Clothing Company

Address: 1234 Horizon Parkway, Poway CA 92888

Date of Interview: July 6

Key information obtained: Littlejohn is very happy in his work. Says most benefits people like the field. He says that if I am not mathematically talented but prefer English, I might want to consider becoming a communications specialist in benefits, because after the plan is designed and implemented, employees must be made aware of programs.

Career Field/Occupation

____

EXPLORATION SUMMARY

After exploring this option, am I interested in it as a potential career choice?

Yes ☐ Maybe ☐ No ☐

Likes	Dislikes

Nature of Work

Working Conditions

Employment

Training

Other Qualifications

Advancement

Earnings

Job Outlook

Related Jobs

Sources of More Information

Career Field/Occupation

EMPLOYEE BENEFITS MANAGER (also called employee benefits administrator)

EXPLORATION SUMMARY

After exploring this option, am I interested in it as a potential career choice?

Yes ☐ Maybe ☐ No ☐

	Likes	Dislikes
Nature of Work	Handling employee fringe benefits such as insurance & retirement funds. Satisfaction from helping people by protecting them from injury, sickness, old age.	Probably need more math and finance courses.
Working Conditions	Pleasant office, environment	Would like to get out of office more often.
Employment	Jobs are available in most kinds of industries and companies; jobs are located throughout the United States so I could probably live wherever I want.	Jobs are in cities. I'm not sure but I might like to live in a more rural area.
Training	At least a college education.	
Other Qualifications	Need analytical ability, good judgment, organizational skills, personality to deal with people.	Must understand accounting, economics, finance; too technical for my liking.
Advancement	Can become top compensation & benefits executive.	Is a position that rarely leads to top corporate management.
Earnings	Often between $25,000 and $40,000 + bonus of 10% to 20%. Pays well.	
Job Outlook	Expanding field.	

(continued)

Related Jobs

Personnel jobs, insurance work,
investment and financial services, banking

Sources of More Information

1. International Foundation of Employee
Benefit Plans,
Box 69
Brookfield, Wisc. 53005

2. Employee Benefit News, a trade journal.

WHAT'S YOUR N.A.C.Q.—NEW AGE CAREER QUOTIENT?

A flood of new occupations came with the 20th century. The latest official tally shows 20,000 separate job titles, and many have a befuddling number of variations.

People who do essentially the same work may be called "engineering technicians" at one company, "engineering and science technicians" at another and "electronics technicians" at still another.

Many newer titles—such as computer graphics technician—that may become commonplace in the 21st century are not yet included in the official record.

Whatever the number of job titles, there are men and women working as bonsai culturists and cosmetologists, wedding brokers and well drillers, humor awareness therapy consultants, speech writers and bodyguards, ultrasonic hand solderers, video game arcade managers, banjo musicians, and thousands more.

Of this multitude of occupations, how many job titles can you name? Time yourself for two minutes and list as many occupations as possible.

1. ____ 2. ____
3. ____ 4. ____
5. ____ 6. ____
7. ____ 8. ____
9. ____ 10. ____
11. ____ 12. ____
13. ____ 14. ____
15. ____ 16. ____
17. ____ 18. ____
19. ____ 20. ____
21. ____ 22. ____
23. ____ 24. ____
25. ____ 26. ____
27. ____ 28. ____
29. ____ 30. ____
31. ____ 32. ____
33. ____ 34. ____
35. ____ 36. ____
37. ____ 38. ____
39. ____ 40. ____

How many titles did you jot down? If you listed 25, you have average awareness of the world of work. And you want to be more than average, right?

You Won't Know Unless You Ask

Chances are, you need to beef up your career knowledge.

The technique: Ask questions in a structured interview.

Select people who work in your favorite jobs—or jobs you want to know more about. Use a tape recorder, if possible. Locate interviewees through teachers, friends, relatives, neighbors, bankers, physicians, merchants and graduates of your school. You also can call employers and professional associations to locate other people who work in jobs you like. Some school counselors maintain a list of resource people.

Don't be frightened because you fear interviewing is an imposition. Most people really like to talk about their jobs, and it's flattering to be asked for advice. Tell prospective interviewees that you are a student doing a career study. Although the career study is not homework assigned by a teacher, nevertheless it is a career study and you are making a truthful statement.

You might want to ease into interviewing by practicing first on family members. Here's a list of questions to ask.

1. What type of formal training have you had?
2. What fields have you worked in over the years?
3. What other training or experiences have you had that were helpful to you?
4. What other occupations did you consider before deciding on this one?
5. Will you describe briefly an average day's activities?
6. What do you like best about your present position?
7. What do you dislike most about your present position?
8. What are the main problems or frustrations you encounter in your work?
9. What activities other than your job are you involved with that are a source of satisfaction to you?
10. What kinds of training or experiences would be helpful to the person entering your field now?
11. What advice do you have for someone considering your field today?
12. Are there related fields I should explore?
13. Do you think that your past mistakes help you to make better decisions?
14. What interests do you have? Did they help you decide what job you wanted?
15. What school subjects do you use in your work and how? What subjects do you recommend someone taking in school that would help in your job?
16. How has your particular job changed over the past 10 or 20 years? What do you think the job will be like in another 10 years?
17. Are your personal hobbies very different from your job or are they similar?
18. How does this job support your way of living in terms of income, knowledge, working hours and leisure time?
19. Why is this job important to you?
20. Do you know of any common characteristics a person should possess to be successful in your field of work?

You also can use this technique to interview someone who lives far away. Send a thoughtful letter that includes the questions you want answered, a blank audio cassette tape and return postage. It works!

Before You Ask, Prepare

Time is a non-renewable resource. Treat it with respect, especially when it belongs to someone else.

An ounce of preparation is worth a pound of dumb questions you could have learned answers to by reading. Spend an hour in the library's business reference section checking on an individual, organization or career field.

Even if you're not a whiz at library research, librarians usually enjoy lending a hand to sincere knowledge-seekers. You may be surprised at how much advance information you can uncover. Before an interview write out your questions.

Your show of respect for the interviewee's time will keep the door open for other young people coming behind you. In addition, making a good impression on someone who can become a valuable professional contact in a field that you may someday want to enter is like having money in the bank.

An Update on Informational Interviewing

Informational interviewing means asking someone for data you genuinely need. It is not a synonym for job interviewing; you are not asking to be hired.

During the last decade, many job-seekers thought informational interviewing, along with networking, was the "secret of the job search." Although millions of individuals probably found the technique invaluable in their career decision-making process, others abused it.

Too many job hunters used informational interviewing like a trick or gimmick. As a result, business people today tend to be skeptical if you ask for such an interview.

Advice: Never mention the term *informational interview.* Instead, clearly announce yourself as a student. Say that you're still in the dark about what to do with your post-graduation life.

You want to keep it simple and state, as earlier suggested, "I am doing a career study."

Alternatively, you can say, "I am researching my future career"; "I am gathering information to use in making my career decisions"; "I have read a great deal about this career field but I need the kind of personal interpretation that only someone in your position can supply to a young person."

Ask your prospective interviewee for 15 minutes and keep the meeting within that limit unless you clearly are invited to stay longer.

As a term, *informational interview* is shopworn but the technique itself remains vital and effective. Use it correctly—the same way a reporter collects facts and feelings for an article.

How to Get Career Research Interviews

Telephoning

Step 1. Find out the name of the individual you wish to interview. Simply ask the receptionist at the company's office for the name of the person holding the position.

I wish to write a letter to the marketing manager. Can you spell the manager's name, please? It's Marye Lee Ferarri, you say?

That's F-e-r-a-r-r-i. Thank you very much.

(Slight pause). Oh yes, while I have you on the phone, what is Ms. Ferarri's secretary's name, please? Ms. Fields—F-i-e-l-d-s? Got it. Thanks again.

Step 2. The following week, call back and introduce yourself to the marketing manager's secretary. It helps to keep a smile on your face even when talking on the phone.

Good afternoon, Ms. Fields. My name is Rolf Preisendorfer.

Step 3. Explain your reason for calling. Keep it simple but persuasive.

I am a student researching my future career. I am not looking for a job. It would mean a lot to me if I could speak for a few minutes to someone who is successful in marketing, a field that interests me very much. Do you think you could help me out by arranging a short 15-minute appointment with Ms. Ferarri sometime within the next two weeks? I could come early in the morning or late in the afternoon. It won't take long and I'll have my questions ready in advance. Could you set up an appointment?

Step 4. Chances are the secretary won't give you an answer on the spot. He or she will want to check with the boss, and probably ask you to call back. But if the answer sounds like a rejection, don't give up. Try for a future time.

Oh, Ms. Ferarri will be out of the country for the next two weeks? In that case, I'11 check back with you in a month, Ms. Fields. Thank you for talking with me. Obviously you understand what it's like to need advice.

Step 5. If you are turned down flat, ask the secretary to suggest another marketing manager who would be willing to speak with you. Try to make the secretary an ally. If you are granted an interview, be sure to write a thank-you note to the secretary, as well as to the manager.

Writing

Arranging a career research interview by mail is basically the same as arranging one by telephone. You must obtain the name (and its correct spelling) of the person you wish to reach. Your letter must state the purpose of the appointment you seek, and it must close by saying you will follow up by telephoning to find out when an appointment would be convenient. Keep your letter to one page.

Career research interviewing gives your career direction. Two other gains are possible. You can acquire poise to use in future job interviews and you may meet an individual who one day will be in a position to support your upward climb.

Newspapers Are Goldmines

Your daily newspaper is another source of career information.

Look for two types of advertisements: classified help-wanted ads, which are concise requests for applicants, and larger career opportunity ads, which are more complete requests for applicants.

The classified ads are grouped together in one section. The display ads may be grouped in one section, or they may be spread throughout the paper, particularly in the business, sports and features sections.

As you look through, clip the ads that immediately make your eyes light up. Put these standouts in your future file. Wait several weeks, then call or write to request an interview with the employer, saying that you are a young person researching your future career. The reason to wait several weeks is that until the job is filled, the employer will be busy interviewing applicants.

News articles and features often give information that relates to jobs. For instance, look for announcements of new business managers, store openings and coming events such as fairs and concerts.

Here's the program: Each day for one week, choose a newspaper article that contains some career information. Read the article carefully to see how many of the blanks on the following form you can fill in using only information from the article.

Career Awareness Capsule (from news articles)

Job title ____________________

Personal qualities needed ____________________

Skills needed ____________________

Education needed ____________________

Salary range ____________________

Disadvantages of job ____________________

Advantages of job ____________________

Career outlook (are jobs available; does the future look bright or dim?)

____

Job duties ____________________

Lifestyle ____________________

Rarely will you fill in every blank from a single article, but the exercise will snap up your career awareness.

You'll never read the newspaper the same way again. You'll be alert to picking up career information—not only from newspapers, but also from magazines and other print materials.

Free Help From the Yellow Pages

Step 1. Whenever you have a spare three minutes, sit down with the thickest telephone yellow pages directory you can find. The only other tools you need are a felt-tip pen or pencil, a tablet of paper, and your identity inventories from section 6. Go through the directory, A to Z, circling each classification that appeals to you.

Ask yourself only one question: "Does this subject interest me?" If the answer is "no," move on. If the answer is "yes" or "not sure," write the heading on your tablet.

Trust your immediate reactions; don't linger over the heading, weighing one factor against another. Be quick about it.

By the time you finish scanning the telephone directory, you may have listed hundreds of headings.

Step 2. Reduce the number of headings on your list to the 30 you like best.

Step 3. For each of the 30 headings, ask yourself: "What in my education, training or experience validates my interest in this particular field?"

There are exceptions, but if you are genuinely interested in a subject, you probably have read about it, studied it, worked or played at it.

Step 4. By now you have trimmed your list of interesting headings to 15 or so. The next question to ask yourself is: "In view of my requirements, such as lifestyle desires, travel and earnings potential, which fields should I consider?"

If you can't answer this question for certain of your choices, or perhaps most of them, do more research. Turn to section 8, "Your Career, Your Research."

Step 5. By now your list should be a manageable size, and you will treat the yellow pages directory headings like career headings. Rank the headings, putting the most appealing at the top.

Ten Interesting Career Fields/Occupations

1. ______________________________
2. ______________________________
3. ______________________________
4. ______________________________
5. ______________________________
6. ______________________________
7. ______________________________
8. ______________________________
9. ______________________________
10. ______________________________

Step 6. Turn back to the yellow pages directory and find a list of companies that have the kinds of jobs you chose. After doing enough research to show you have respect for your interviewee's time, set up appointments with people at the firms who can give you more information. Start with your first choice.

The object of the yellow pages directory exploration is to broaden your horizons: You will discover entire career fields you may otherwise have overlooked.

Extend Your Vision

Are you aware of the art masterpiece *American Gothic*? The Grant Wood painting portrays a couple in front of their Iowa farmhouse. The dour husband, his hand rigidly clasping a pitchfork, stands next to his persimmon-faced wife.

The painting might never have come to be if the American artist had not extended his vision. You see, in his youth Grant Wood didn't focus on the fact that he had options. He thought he must paint like a Frenchman.

After spending years in France, copying the charming landscapes that Renoir and Monet and others had already made famous, Wood decided it was time to look back across the Atlantic to his homeland in Iowa.

At age 35, he described his decision to a journalist: "I think at last I've learned something about myself. I think you've got to paint—like you have to write—what you know."

You can benefit from Wood's observation. Choosing a careeer makes you a chooser. Like writers and artists, choosers do best with what they know.

You can know a lot about careers with a minimum of effort. You've already gained sophistication in using newspapers and yellow pages directories to boost your career awareness.

Now take a look at other possibilities.

Libraries

In addition to general-interest media, many of America's libraries have career centers filled with guidance publications and occupational literature. These centers can open exciting new vistas to you. Read all about it in section 8 and treat yourself to a library visit soon.

Television

Television shows that depict careers rarely are accurate, but at least they contain some information.

"General Hospital" brings viewers into the world of medical and allied health workers.

"Falcon Crest" makes viewers aware of the work of a winery owner.

"Miami Vice" communicates the flavor of work involved with law enforcement.

As you watch such TV programs, be aware of more than the plot. Think about the characters' job responsibilities and personal qualities. What about the skills needed for employment and the training necessary?

Are there clues to the quality of family life made possible by the job and the availability of leisure time?

If you have sufficient interest, the next step is to find real-life people in the job and begin a series of interviews.

Cultural and Sports Events

Use museums, art galleries, theatrical productions and ball parks for more than cultural enrichment and recreation. Try to talk to the people who make the events happen; ask what they do, how they like their jobs and how they live their lives.

If you're an opera buff, for example, ask the stage-door guard if you may speak with the stage manager. Explain that you are a student exploring your future career and that you would like to check on the various jobs involved with producing an opera. Depending on your manner and appearance, the stage manager may allow you backstage. If not, you lose nothing by trying.

If you have the opportunity, talk with people working in the jobs of stagehand, hairdresser, make-up artist, musician, singer, lighting technician, sound technician and photographer.

At the ball park, interview an usher. Why? You may realize that somebody manages the usher corps for the ball park; somebody manages the usher corps managers for many establishments, and somebody must own the company that hires the ushers and their managers.

Movies and More

When you watch a film, notice the credits of who did what. Try to think of the variety of occupations that were required to make the motion picture.

Use the same thought process when you dine out: Make a game of naming all the people who provide you with a restaurant meal. Examples: agriculture specialist, fertilizer manufacturer, farm equipment sales representative, farmer, truck driver, cook, server and cashier.

Who makes a zoo function? In a fire station, who responds to an emergency? Who built the zoo enclosures or fire station?

Extend the same who-does-it reasoning to products. Who works to make possible the tapes and discs you buy? cosmetics? jewelry? school supplies? books? furniture? cars? Think about it.

Person-in-the-Street Interviews

Anyone who imparts information has the potential to increase your awareness.

(Use common sense, of course. Stay away from suspicious-looking people. Never put yourself in a position where your safety may be in jeopardy.)

A dialogue with a letter carrier may reveal that permanent postal employees enjoy super job security—they cannot be laid off.

Speaking with a young physician might bring forth the competitive dimension: Increasing numbers of doctors make it more difficult for newcomers to launch careers.

No matter that you have no desire to enter a given field. Let's suppose that retailing doesn't ring your register. By talking with retail clerks, you may zero in on a previously unrecognized factor, such as the satisfaction of owning your own shop, or the physical demands of standing all day. You'll perhaps remember such factors when considering other careers.

With a bit of practice you'll soon see careers everywhere you look.

700 Job Ideas

This career awareness section is painted with a broad brush. In a general way, we discuss how to acquire career information and apply it to yourself.

(The finer points of career research are revealed in section 8.)

If your career awareness is still dim, stoke your creative fires by reviewing the following 700 job ideas, 50 for each of 14 occupational clusters. Remember, an occupation can be slotted into more than one career cluster. A copywriter, for instance, could be placed in *Communication and Media* or in *Marketing and Distribution.*

A number of the job titles will seem puzzling or unclear. That's because many of them reflect new ways to earn a living in an information age.

Here's our recommendation when you come across an interesting but unfamiliar title: View your uncertainty as an opportunity to practice research skills. Make it a point of pride to find out what the job entails.

One immediate reward for uncovering what lies behind a mystery job title is a feeling of accomplishment. (*Translation:* Don't write to us for an explanation of a particular job title—in effect, asking us to do your homework for you; that's not what this book is about.)

Clusters: Job Ideas at a Glance

Agriculture (including Agribusiness)

agricultural attache (foreign service)
agricultural broker
agricultural cooperative manager
agricultural economist
agricultural engineer
agricultural journalist
agricultural produce commission agent
agricultural research chemist
agricultural sales representative
agriculture instructor
agronomist
arborist
beekeeper
botanist
commodity broker
county extension agent
crop insurance specialist
dairy technologist
entomologist
farm appraiser
farm broadcaster
farm machine operator
farm manager
farm products advertising manager
farm realtor
feed research aide
floral designer
florist
food technologist
4-H Club staff member

fruitgrower
grain buyer
grain farmer
greenhouse superintendent
horticulturalist
hydroponics horticulturalist
irrigation engineer
landscape architect
landscape contractor
meat inspector
milk processing plant manager
ornamental horticulturalist
plant geneticist
plant nursery owner
plant propagator
rancher
silviculturist
soil scientist
veterinarian
vineyard manager

Business and Office

accountant
actuary
administrative assistant
applications programmer
collection company representative
company treasurer
computer liaison specialist
computer operator
computer security specialist
computer tape librarian
corporate attorney
corporate fitness director
credit officer
data base manager
data communications programmer
data processing auditor
data processing customer support specialist
data processing training specialist
documentation specialist
electronic mail supervisor
employment interviewer
financial analyst
foreign exchange trader
human factors engineer
human resources director
immigration attorney
information scientist
information systems consultant
insurance sales agent
internal auditor
investment counselor
job retraining specialist
legal secretary
loan officer
management consultant
management information systems manager
messenger service owner
operations officer
paralegal assistant
personnel recruiter
real estate appraiser
secretary
software attorney
statistician
systems analyst
systems programmer
technical services manager
telephone answering service supervisor
title examiner
word processing specialist

Communication and Media

art director
book editor
cable television station manager
camera operator
columnist
commentator
commercials producer
computer conference network director
copywriter
critic
educational television consortium coordinator
electronic communications technician
electronic news editor
foreign language teacher
humorist
interpreter
journalism professor
media director
microwave engineer
newspaper editor
newspaper syndicate executive
newswriter
photographic laboratory technician
photojournalist
phototypesetter
printing company supervisor
proofreader
radar systems engineer

radio station manager
recording engineer
satellite-instruction educational facilitator
screenwriter
sign painting company owner
singing messenger service owner
space payload preparation specialist
special events director
technical writer
telecommunications equipment designer
telecommunications installation engineer
telecommunications manager
teleconferencing design engineer
teletext editor
television announcer
television news anchorperson
television news editor
television reporter
translator
transmitter operator
video manager
video-taping service owner

Construction

architect
architectural drafter
boatbuilder
bricklayer
building contractor
building inspector
building materials purchasing agent
building trades instructor
building trades union leader
cabinetmaker
carpenter
cement mason
civil engineer
combination welder
construction apprentice program administrator
construction association executive director
construction engineering professor
construction estimator
construction expediter
construction manager
construction painter
construction project manager
custom home builder
demolition specialist
electrician
equipment subcontractor
excavator
facilities planner
furnace installer
general contractor
glazier
heating/air-conditioning contractor
heavy equipment operator
insulation installer
land developer
lather
marine architect
pipe fitter
plasterer
plumber
roofing contractor
sandblaster
sheet metal worker
solar heating installer
stonemason
structural steel worker
subdivision marketing manager
surveyor
television cable installer
tile setter

Consumer and Home Economics

adult education instructor
advertising agency stylist
better business bureau manager
business home economist
cafeteria food operations manager
cake decorator
child care service owner
child development specialist
children's institution director
community fund-raising coordinator
consultant dietitian
consumer information specialist
consumer protection government agent
cooking instructor
credit counselor
customer service representative
educational toy maker
fashion coordinator
fashion designer
fashion model
federal food inspector
food chemist
food editor
food photography stylist

food service supervisor
food technologist
furniture refinisher
gerontologist
home economics instructor
home furnishings editor
home lighting consultant
homemaker rehabilitation specialist
housing manager
interior decorator
interior designer
nutritionist
pattern designer
picture framer
preschool teacher
product information manager
public information director
research dietitian
residence director
retirement planner
television consumer advocate
test kitchen researcher
upholstery company owner
wine maker
women's magazine beauty editor

Environment and Natural Resources (including Marine Science)

air pollution control specialist
aquaculturist
astronomer
biogas conversion tester
chemical engineer
chemical oceanographer
conservation officer
conservation organization executive director
energy utilization manager
environmental analyst
environmental epidemiologist
environmental physicist
exterminator
fisher
forester
forestry technician
geodesist
geothermal geologist
groundwater protection specialist
hydroelectric systems engineer
hydrologist
ichthyologist
industrial hygienist
land reclamation specialist
marine animal trainer
marine biologist
metallurgical engineer
meteorologist
microbiologist
mine manager
minerals economist
noise pollution engineer
ocean engineer
oil company executive
petroleum engineer
photovoltaic energy researcher
pollution control engineer
recycling director
refinery manager
resource recovery engineer
safety engineer
seismologist
solar energy engineer
timber buyer
toxicologist
volcanologist
wastewater treatment plant supervisor
water pollution control inspector
wind energy systems engineer
wood technologist

Fine Arts and Humanities

actor
animator
anthropologist
archaeologist
archivist
art appraiser
art dealer
art director
art teacher
art therapist
calligrapher
cartoonist
choral director
choreographer
cinematographer
comedian
costumer
creative writing teacher
dancer
film director
film editor
genealogist
historian

illustrator
industrial designer
industrial filmmaker
jewelry designer
lighting designer
make-up artist
mathematician
motion picture producer
muralist
museum curator
music composer
music conductor
musical instrument maker
musician
philologist
philosophy professor
photographer
playwright
religious education director
scene designer
sculptor
singer
sociologist
special effects technician
stage director
stage manager
textile designer

Health

anesthesiologist
animal health technician
audiometrist
biochemist
biological photographer
biomedical engineer
cardiologist
cardiovascular perfusionist
child abuse therapist
chiropractor
computerized tomography (CT) technician
dental hygienist
dentist
dialysis technician
electroencephalographic (EEG) technician
emergency medical technician
genetic biologist
geriatric specialist
health physicist
hospital administrator
licensed practical nurse
medical assistant
medical illustrator
medical laboratory technician
medical records administrator
medical social worker
mobile medical clinic director
nuclear magnetic resonance (NMR) technician
nuclear medicine technologist
nurse-midwife
nurse practitioner
occupational therapist
oncologist
ophthalmologist
optometrist
oral surgeon
orthoptist
osteopathic physician
pediatrician
pharmacist
physical therapist
podiatrist
positron emission tomography (PET) technician
psychiatrist
psychologist
radiologic technologist
recreational therapist
registered nurse
respiratory therapist
sonographer

Hospitality and Recreation

airline travel club manager
athletic director
athletic trainer
banquet manager
bartender
botanical gardens public relations director
camp director
caterer
catering sales manager
clown
convention manager
corporate travel manager
country club manager
cruise director
dude ranch operator
executive chef
food and beverage director
golf course superintendent
health spa manager
hotel controller
hotel/motel manager
industrial recreation program director

jockey
laserist (light show)
lifeguard
nursing home activities director
physical fitness instructor
professional athlete
pro sports scout
puppeteer
pyrotechnician
recreation director
recreation establishment manager
reservation agent
resident manager
resort vice president, sales and marketing
restaurant manager
show animal trainer
sports coach
sports equipment supplier
stunt performer
theme park manager
tour guide
travel agency owner
travel school president
travel wholesale tour packager
umpire
video dating service director
yacht rental agent
youth program director

Manufacture and Repair

aeronautical drafter
air-conditioning mechanic
anodizer
biomedical equipment repairer
bookbinder
business machine servicer
CAD/CAM (computer aided design/manufacture)
camera repairer
ceramic engineer
chemical engineer
computer games manufacturer
computer graphics simulation technician
computer service technician
cost control manager
cost estimator
digital design engineer
director of product engineering
electrical engineer
electronics engineer
farm equipment mechanic
fiber optics researcher
food and drug inspector
home-based skate board builder
industrial engineer
instrument repairer
knowledge engineer (artificial intelligence)
laser technician
magnetics manufacturing technician
manufacturing engineer
manufacturer's service representative
materials manager
mechanical drafter
mechanical engineer
model maker
numerical-control operator
package engineer
petroleum engineer
planning and scheduling manager
plant engineer
quality control supervisor
refrigeration mechanic
robotic line supervisor
roboticist
systems engineer
tool-and-die maker
tool designer
vice president, manufacturing
vice president, research and development
watch repairer
welding engineer

Marketing and Distribution

advertising manager
air freight manager
antiques dealer
auctioneer
branch store coordinator
clothing manufacturer's representative
college recruiter
commodities broker
computer memory products representative
computer software distributor
contract administrator
direct mail entrepreneur
expediter
fashion merchandiser

fitness equipment retailer
import-export agent
inventory control supervisor
laser equipment sales engineer
mail-order wholesaler
marketing consultant
marketing information systems manager
marketing research analyst
material handler
media buyer
medical imaging equipment distributor
memorial consultant
merchandise displayer
microcomputer sales engineer
microwave component sales manager
mobile radio/paging device sales engineer
multi-level marketer
new product development manager
package designer
package research specialist
physical distribution manager
product demonstrator
public relations representative
real estate sales agent
retail buyer
retail store manager
robotics sales engineer
sales manager
securities sales agent
semi-conductor sales
strategic marketing engineer representative
telecommunications equipment sales representative
telephone long-distance carrier sales representative
television time sales representative
vice president, marketing
warehouse manager

Personal Services

alteration tailor
astrologer
attendant to physically disabled
barber
beauty salon chain owner
biofeedback technician
blade-sharpening service owner
bodyguard
career adviser
carpet cleaning contractor
chauffeur
color consultant
companion
cosmetics representative
cosmetologist
cosmetology instructor
custom tailor
day-care director
delegate guide
domestic cook
dressmaker
electrologist
embalmer
escort for the blind
family and marriage counselor
funeral director
graphologist
hair stylist
home attendant
housekeeping service owner
house-sitting service owner
hypnotherapist
laundry plant supervisor
limousine service operator
manicurist
massage therapist
party planner
personal pilot
personal shopper
pet animal trainer
pet-grooming shop owner
reducing salon manager
shoe-repair shop manager
shoe-shine stand owner
social secretary
tattoo artist
tax preparer
taxi driver
wedding consultant
window-cleaning service owner

Public Service

administrative officer
bailiff
blood bank donor recruiter
border guard
CIA intelligence specialist
city manager
college alumni director
coroner
correction officer
cultural affairs officer
customs inspector
deputy attorney general

detective
economic development coordinator
education lobbyist
equal opportunity representative
faculty adviser, college or university
federal aid coordinator
financial aid officer
fire protection engineer
foreign service officer
foreign student adviser
harbor pilot
Internal Revenue Service agent
judge
labor standards director
law enforcement community relations specialist
license inspector
mail carrier
military recruiter
police officer
port authority manager
postmaster
psychiatric social worker
public defender
public works commissioner
public works inspector
reference librarian
school guidance counselor
school principal
secondary school teacher
sheriff
special education director
state governor
substance abuse counselor
urban planner
U.S. senator
volunteer services coordinator
welfare director
young adult librarian

Transportation

aircraft company president
aircraft mechanic
Air Force officer
air traffic assistant
air traffic controller
airline pilot
airport ground equipment supervisor
airport manager
ambulance service contractor
automobile design engineer
automobile electronics repairer
automobile manufacture chief executive officer
barge captain
bicycle mechanic
bus driver
bus line operations manager
command module pilot
contract carrier operations manager
corporate airplane pilot
cruise ship captain
diesel mechanic
electronic flight control engineer
express-delivery service contractor
flight attendant
flight school director
flight test engineer
helicopter pilot
hot-air balloon operator
hydrofoil boat pilot
hypertechnology engineer (aerospace research)
independent trucking contractor
launch station operations manager
local truck driver
locomotive engineer
long-distance truck driver
motor home rental agent
motor vehicle dispatcher
motorboat mechanic
motorcycle mechanic
passenger service representative
passenger train dispatcher
rapid transit manager
satellite launch preparation specialist
service station manager
space mission specialist
taxi garage manager
terminal operations manager
traffic engineer
traffic safety administrator
wind tunnel model designer

Career Awareness: Make It Work for You

Careers are like colors: If you haven't seen a rainbow, you might think your choices are limited to black and white.

For more shades of discovery, turn to the following section. In it, we tell you how to find out anything you want to know about any occupation.

SECTION EIGHT

YOUR CAREER, YOUR RESEARCH

Information is power. Without factual information about careers and the job market, you are without power, flying in a sandstorm.

While most of you require career market research to see where you might find a home for your goals, others will be stimulated in their career search by the "shopper effect"—wanting something you find while browsing in the marketplace.

This section deals with the quality of the market research you need and how to get it.

What Career Information Really Means

Having increased your career awareness (read section 7 if you haven't done so) and compiled future files of possible careers, you're ready for graduate work in the finer points of career market research.

First, let's be clear about the importance of such career characteristics as

- what's involved in the work
- the places of work
- the size of the occupation
- the training to enter the field
- career ladders
- personal qualifications
- earnings
- working conditions
- future prospects

What's Involved in the Work

The need to know what a job is all about seems obvious. After all, you know whether a particular occupation requires you to shuffle electronics in a bank, sit at a computer work station in an engineering office, or seat people in a restaurant. But if a specific career is a serious contender for your affections, it's time to go beyond the basic outline and get to the nuts and bolts.

Here's a consumer checklist of questions you'll want answers to before making a commitment.

1. Exactly what tasks might I do on the job?
2. What would a typical day or month be like?
3. What is the product or service?
4. Would I chiefly work with data, people or things?
5. Would I travel? Where and how often?
6. Would I sit all day? Stand? Get outside the office?
7. How closely would I be supervised?
8. How would my tasks relate to co-workers?
9. What distasteful things would I have to do?
10. Is there any danger to my health or physical safety?

The Places of Work

While schools and campuses tend to be alike in appearance, work sites are as different as night and day.

You might be working on the 95th floor of a 100-story office building, or deep in the earth in a mine shaft. You might be working at a construction site, a factory, a restaurant, a store, or in a ship, a plane, even a space station.

The place where you work also is dictated by your employer—private industry, government agency or non-profit organization.

Do beautiful surroundings count with you? The most glamorous offices are those connected with executive headquarters of large corporations, banks, utilities and well-endowed foundations. At the opposite end of the luxury scale are the offices of small, struggling companies, charities and low-level government offices.

Another aspect is where the work is located—in cities or rural areas. For career mobility, learn whether the occupation is available only in a few places or is found in most states.

The greater the number of places where you can find employment, the greater your control over your career and lifestyle.

Here are questions to consider.

1. Do I have ample opportunity to relocate to any number of states if I choose?

2. Are the jobs available in the geographic areas I prefer?

3. If the job is available only in government agencies, am I cut out to be a civil servant?

4. If the job is available only in large corporations, am I able to function in a bureaucracy?

5. If the job is available only in marginally profitable businesses, can I tolerate the instability?

6. Are the companies where I might work respected as good corporate citizens and fair employers?

The Size of an Occupation

The size of an occupation is a clue to how many job openings it will have year after year.

Because a small career field has a rocketing rate of growth, don't assume there'll be tons of job openings. On the other hand, because a huge, sleepy career field has modest growth, don't assume job openings will be scarce.

For example: Assume an occupation of 5,000 people and a growth rate of 35 percent annually. That's 1,750 job openings each year.

Now assume an occupation of 500,000 people and a growth rate of 10 percent annually. That's 50,000 job openings a year.

The ideal combination is a fairly large occupation that is showing rapid growth.

Among the questions to answer are

1. How large is the occupation?

2. Does it have a fast, average, or slow rate of growth?

3. How many job openings are expected annually?

4. Is there a high personnel turnover because the work is poorly paid or dull or unattractive in some other way?

The Training to Enter the Field

If you're in school now, be certain not to overlook the high school and college courses useful or necessary to prepare for the career you have in mind.

You can get ready for jobs in many ways, including enrollment in college programs, vo-tech schools, home study courses, government training programs, military services training, apprenticeships and more.

The amount of training you have usually determines the kinds of jobs available to you. In many cases, it is also a major factor in how fast you're promoted to higher-level positions.

For some occupations you'll have to be certified or get a license. Doctors, nurses, school teachers, barbers, cosmetologists, electricians and plumbers are examples of those who must be licensed to practice or do business. If you are considering an occupation that requires state licensing, be certain that you check the requirements for it in the state in which you plan to work. After you invest heavily in an education, you don't want surprises.

Here are appropriate training questions:

1. How much education or training is required to qualify in the job market and to meet legal certification or licensing requirements?

2. How long does it take?

3. What does it include?

4. How much does it cost?

5. Where can I get a list of accredited schools?

6. What kind of high school or college program is required? What subjects should or must be chosen?

7. Is there more than one way to prepare? If so, what are the alternatives?

8. Is it possible that instead of formal training, I could learn on the job?

Career Ladders

Career ladders often are described in career information so that you can get a pretty good idea of how far you can advance. Some occupations have very short career ladders. A laser technician, for example, will not advance beyond the position of supervising technician—without going back to college for an engineering degree.

If you are an ambitious person and the occupation you're considering does not lead upward, chuck it and look for something with greater advancement potential.

Try these career ladder questions:

1. What proportion of workers are promoted?
2. What are the upward steps?
3. How long would it normally take to receive my first promotion? My second?
4. How high could I rise in the field?
5. How long would it take to reach the top?
6. Would I need additional education?
7. Would I need another type of work experience?
8. What are the related occupations to which I could move?
9. Is this a field that might permit me to start my own business?

Personal Qualifications

Look for information in your career research that helps you know whether the occupation fits in with your unique personal characteristics. For a particular job, you may need to use specific skills and talents.

For example, an occupation could require that you motivate others, work under close supervision, work in a highly competitive atmosphere, enjoy solving problems, work as part of a team or use creative talents.

There's only one question for this category: Is this occupation compatible with me as revealed in my identity inventory for personality traits (section 6)?

Earnings

When you are researching a career in depth, you'll probably come across the average earnings for an occupation. Sometimes, instead of average earnings, the figures are expressed as median earnings, which means that half of the people in the career earn more and half earn less.

Although income figures give you an inkling of the relative ranking of jobs by earnings, don't bronze the figures. At best, they are statistical compilations. Look at earnings figures as hints of what you might be paid.

Your paycheck will depend on many things: your experience and ability, the industry you work in, and the section of the country where you live.

Differing pay scales among companies, unionization, seniority and quality of performance are other factors that explain why often there is a vast spread in the earnings of people in the same occupation.

Another factor in the size of your paycheck is your ability to negotiate a salary equivalent to your value; some people are persuasive and fairly rewarded, while others never bother to learn negotiating skills and are underpaid.

When you're looking at what an occupation typically pays, don't overlook the dollar value of employee benefits. These include such items as health insurance, paid vacation, retirement funds, social security and sick leave.

In big round numbers, employment "bennies" (benefits) are worth about one-third of your salary; the national annual average is in the $7,600-per-person neighborhood.

Some jobs offer special "perks" (perquisites) that can save you a bundle. Flight attendants may receive reduced airline fares, sales supervisors may receive cars and hotel employees may receive uniforms.

When self-employment is your tycoonish aim, forget about average earnings. There are too many variables. If you can scratch out a living after six months in your own business, count your blessings. You may be a millionaire before age 30 or you may be in Chapter 13 (bankruptcy) by 25.

Young entrepreneurs tend to ignore benefits, too. As one young electronics company head whose business is run out of his garage says:

"Health insurance? That's the last thing on my mind. The meter doesn't tick when you're sick."

Questions to help evaluate pay scales include these.

1. What is the base annual salary for the job at the entry, mid-, and top-level?

2. Are bonuses given for superior performance?

3. Does a sales job pay salary plus commission or only commission? (High-performance salespeople often prefer commission only because they can earn astronomical incomes. It's safer for beginners to ask for salary plus commission.)

4. Does the job pay overtime? (Overtime is a feature of clerical and craft jobs.)

5. Does the occupation typically offer an expense account?

6. What employee benefits are usual with this occupation?

7. How much money could I reasonably expect to earn in this occupation after five years? Is this my idea of "good money"?

8. Are raises based on merit, or on rigid pay scales determined largely by seniority? Is this the way I want to work?

9. Have others in this field gone on to open their own businesses and have they prospered?

10. Does this occupation leave time for me to moonlight and earn a second income, if I choose? Does the occupation pay so little that I probably would have to have a second job to accumulate any savings?

Working Conditions

By checking out working conditions, you make sure that when an occupation calls to you, it's with a smile. How well you like the way things are on the job is a big part of career satisfaction.

Considerations discussed in this category are somewhat related to those in the category of "places to work." Here's an analogy to something familiar. "Places to work" are like houses or apartments for living. "Working conditions" are everything that affects the way you live in a building.

There are several aspects of working conditions to consider:

Overtime work. When overtime is required, you must give up some of your free time and be flexible in your personal life. Could you cancel a vacation at the last minute if necessary to finish a crash project and meet a deadline? The trade-off for overtime is more money and/or promotion.

Shift work. People who work nights—such as nurses or auto repossessors—have their days free for shopping, hunting, fishing, gardening or education. They can also spend their days looking for a better job. A downside is that an individual's biological clock may rebel at night-owl hours.

Environment. Work settings vary from clean air-conditioned offices to dirty, greasy or poorly ventilated establishments that bear remarkable resemblance to municipal land fills.

Variable settings are a fact even within the same occupation. Take sludge professionals, as an example. Sludge is the slushy, revolting mass left over after water and sewage treatments. While you may be an up-and-coming environmental engineer working in a cushy office punching a pristine computer keyboard most of the time, every now and then you might have to take field trips to collect sludge for testing and review. The samples may drop on your carpet and stain it forever.

One more illustration: When you work in a bureaucracy, space is usually at a premium. So plan on being a cubicle creature surrounded by a few inches of space and portable partitions that never offer total privacy.

Outdoor work. Breathing in fresh air is terrific except on smog-alert days and when it snows, rains, hails, sleets, blows or overheats.

Hazards. Some jobs are downright dangerous. You could fall, burn or cut yourself in a kitchen, tumble from a roof during construction, inhale a cancerous substance in manufacturing or chemical plants or suffer heaven knows what as a stunt performer in a film. Some people like leaping from airplanes to fight forest fires, but others prefer seeing it on television. Which type are you?

Physical demands. If you really like working out, you can find a job that requires standing, stooping, crawling or heavy lifting. Be sure you have the physical strength and stamina required before seeking one of these jobs. Also think ahead 10 or 20 years. Does a physically demanding job offer less strenuous options for older workers?

These questions can help you realize what working conditions are really like in a given career field.

1. What do people in the job say they like most about their work? The least?
2. Are the hours regular or irregular? Long or short? Does the work involve a part-time or flex-time schedule? Would you work evenings, weekends or holidays?
3. How much vacation is usual for the industry?
4. Is the work steady or seasonal?
5. Would the job become harder as you get older?
6. Is the work hazardous?
7. Is the occupation one that would eventually depress you or lift your spirits?

Future Prospects

"How's the job market?" is the question of questions.

If surgeons are in oversupply, would you really want to spend 13 or more years training with the real possibility that you'll be underemployed?

Do you want to spend six months in manicuring school when every manicurist in your area has had difficulty keeping busy three days a week?

Is it realistic to invest your time and money in becoming a PhD archaeologist when the job market is nearly non-existent?

Is it smart to spend years and years getting ready to be a professor of English literature if jobs are few and far between?

These are the kinds of reasons why you must get facts straight about the job market for any career field you are considering. Wishful guessing doesn't count.

When you check on job prospects, here are a few tips to keep in mind.

- Because there's a shortage in an occupation one year doesn't mean it will continue forever. Demand may be cyclical. To illustrate, in some years, engineers are in short supply. The word gets around and soon students are pouring into engineering schools. When the economy takes a dip, the market is stuffed full of engineers. During the energy crunch of the '70s, petroleum engineers were the hottest things on two legs; now the demand for their services is moderate.
- Think of your own life cycles in relationship to job outlook. Age discrimination is illegal but alive and well in America.

Again focusing on engineers, the ones who stick to the technical side and do not switch to management roles can expect job troubles (if they're ever unemployed) once they're past their 50th birthdays, and sometimes sooner.

Professional athletes are yet another and even more dramatic example of short-career people. If age will impact on your job future, what could you do as a second career? Think about it now.

• Revolutionary technology is a fact of the Information Age you can't ignore. In a time of robotics, fiber optics, artificial intelligence, laser marvels, space and ocean exploration—whirlwind scientific and technological change—another question you must deal with is whether choosing a particular occupation would paint you into a corner. Ask yourself: "Will I develop skills in this career that I can transfer elsewhere if my job becomes obsolete?"

• When you hear that demand is going through the roof in certain fields—such as immigration law or computer programming—realize that the demand is for *experienced* people. Neophytes have an uphill battle. Getting that first job can be a killer! Anticipate how you are going to overcome the no-experience barrier. The answer usually is to make friends in the field while you are a student, and to obtain experience as a student intern.

• Remember that because you learn that a job is in great demand, there's no guarantee that it's in demand where you live. College towns often are teaming with jobless graduates who never moved away, but who could find employment if they would relocate to another community. Competition is almost always greater in warm places than cold, except skiing country.

• Any occupation that depends on government action is subject to immediate change. When the government mandated mainstream education for the disabled, demand for special education teachers shot up. The opposite is true too. When the programs of the Great Society were cut back, workers at community agencies across the land lost their jobs.

• Swings in the economy have a dramatic effect on your future prospects. Here's an overview of recession winners and losers.

Because an industry's kitty of jobs is closely related to demand for its output, enterprises providing necessity goods or services usually offer more job security than those dealing with luxury goods.

Capital goods are items bought by companies to manufacture products, such as tools for assembly lines. Consumer goods are finished products used by people like you and us; an example is running shoes. Makers of capital goods are more vulnerable to downturns than are those that supply consumer goods.

Durable goods mean things that last for a number of years, such as refrigerators and automobiles. Nondurable goods are often used within a year, such as margarine or facial tissues. In tough times, jobs are less secure in durable goods industries, because people tend to put off purchases of big-ticket items.

Even in hard times, some industries buck the trend and do well. Those with a silver-lining track record in past recessions include enterprises that help customers make do with what they have.

Who are these recession winners? Here's a sampling: home- and auto-repair companies and the firms that serve them. When people can't buy a new house or car, they fix up the old one. Do-it-yourself projects for clothes and home furnishings prosper, too. Other businesses that thrive sell things that help people forget economic troubles or cheer up, such as movies, cosmetics and beer.

Losers in a recession include industries concerned with houses, autos, furniture, carpeting, home appliances and other costly products that can be ignored until the economy heals.

Most of us are security-minded. Even people who are champion risk takers prefer to gamble at times of their choosing.

In searching for a citadel strong enough to keep the wolf away from your doors, your choice of employer is important—how well is the organization managed and how strong is its position in an industry?

Even job function affects the stability of your employment; the larger the department, the weaker your security. In recent recessions, the people who really took it on the chin were the middle managers. Top management decided they could run their businesses with fewer managerial go-betweens.

Middle managers who survived the cutbacks often were those who knew how to boost profits or reduce costs for their companies.

Where you live is another factor in job security. The Midwest and Northeast have been taking the hardest punches in recent recessions, while growth areas, such as Phoenix and other Sun Belt locales, have been faring much better.

Recession job jitters can clobber workers with the fewest skills; young women and men who offer little more than willing hands may find no takers.

"Last-in, first-out" (LIFO) is a common condition in recessions. It means there is security in seniority and that the most recently hired workers are the first to go when there are reductions in staff. Being "lifo'd" has been particularly hurtful to women and minorities.

Because any young person is subject to being lifo'd, it's wise to devise a back-up plan to use while the skies clear. Here are several plans others have employed.

Rita J., a laid-off trade show manager with office skills, worked for a temporary help agency until she turned up a job in her field.

Harold B., a furloughed pilot, expanded his part-time real estate sales business into a full-time venture while waiting to be recalled to work.

Irene P., a civil service employee who was fired when her agency's budget was cut, found a temporary appointment in another agency while waiting for a permanent job in the merit system.

At this point in your life, you probably haven't idea one about an appropriate back-up plan; you're having lots of trouble coming up with a primary plan! Even so, we confidently suggest that your circuits will not become overloaded if you spend a little time here and there thinking about the perfect back-up plan for you.

To recap, here are questions that should be on your mind as you evaluate a potential career.

1. Do I have a reasonable chance to find a job in this field?

2. Will I be able to work as long as my health is good? If not, what could I do in advance to prepare for a second career?

3. Have I done enough research to know that technology isn't likely to cut my career short if I choose this field?

4. Does this field offer adequate opportunities to develop transferable skills?

5. Am I willing to live where the best jobs in this field are located? Where is that?

6. Does this occupation depend on government action for its ups and downs?

7. Is this occupation strongly affected by swings in the economy?

8. If I should be lifo'd, do I have an alternate plan? What is it?

The Keys to Gathering Career Market Research

Now that you know *what* you're supposed to find out, the question is, *how?*

Chances are, you've met more than one dead end trying to track down intelligence on careers that may be right for you. That's not surprising. A lot of this information is tedious or tough to get. Read with us and you'll become a master sleuth in no time.

To paraphrase the great 19th-century British Prime Minister Benjamin Disraeli:

The most successful person in life usually is the person who has the best information.

As you move from career awareness (section 7) to digging for in-depth, specific information for a few favored careers, think about original sources and secondary sources of research data.

Original sources include people doing the work in the fields you like and their employers.

Secondary sources are printed materials, electronic texts and everything else pertinent to the fields.

Always go after the secondary sources first; use original sources to validate or disprove what you think you've learned. You get the most from interviews when you know the right questions to ask.

We'll look at secondary sources of career information before examining techniques of field interviewing, bearing these two considerations in mind.

The Material Must Be Objective

Pamphlets, books, films and other career information can be biased or incorrect. Company recruiters want their organizations to attract the cream of job candidates so you'll never see recruitment literature that says a company is anything other than wonderful.

All educational institutions—from private vocational schools to well-known universities—need students. They need business. The job opportunities flowing from a given course of study may be overstated; beware of the phrase "unlimited opportunities." There are no such things; all opportunities are finite.

As a generalization, labor unions and professional societies tend to think there are too many people in their fields, while educational institutions tend to think there are too few. Viewpoints frequently benefit those who hold them, which is another way of warning you to watch out for vested interests.

Finally, determine the age of the career material. Anything older than three years is questionable. Anything older than five years is suspect. The working world is moving *that fast!*

Answers to the following questions will help you assess secondary information:

1. Is the material objective?
2. Does the material describe the important abilities and personality traits needed?
3. Does it mention the drawbacks as well as the good points?
4. Does it present realistic salary data—not just the higher ranges?
5. Does it suggest that you will become rich and famous if you choose this career?
6. Is the material older than three years? five years?

Create Your Own Super Future Files

You learned in section 7 to create future files in building career awareness. Now it's time to use the same concept and create super future files, in which you save every scrap of information on the field you're researching. You will be uncovering data too important to misplace.

As we mentioned earlier, the very experience of researching, filing and retrieving information can help you come to a well-reasoned career decision.

The Career Hunter's Guide to the Library

For career seekers, a library is more exciting than a candy store is for 10-year-olds.

Well-equipped public and school libraries have almost everything you need to get started in your research. If they don't have an item you want, they can borrow it from another library through the interlibrary loan system.

We're talking beyond books. Libraries collect and lend films, videos, records, artwork and pamphlets and help you to use on-site computerized guidance systems.

While libraries have always been sources for career information, many are establishing special career centers. If you haven't checked out your library lately, here are a few examples of what you could find.

- The Education and Job Information Center at the Brooklyn, N.Y., central library offers career counseling, free resume-writing assistance, career seminars and more.
- The Oklahoma state library department offers suggestions to all librarians on aiding the jobless and on starting a business at home.
- The Lorain, Ohio, public library operates a job information center. Among its services are distribution of several booklists on career development, counseling on resume writing, and literature on job interviewing.
- About 250 people consult the Hemstead, N.Y., library's job information center each month to receive career counseling, educational and occupational information and data about jobs listed in a state-operated job bank.

Many libraries that haven't established education and job centers because they are strapped for funds have reorganized the materials they own into career sections.

Try Library "Cousins"—School Career Centers

Career centers have sprung up over the past two decades in high schools and colleges. They offer resources similar to those described in contemporary libraries. The centers may be extensions of the school libraries or separate entities.

In both libraries and career centers, ask the librarian or career technician for help before starting an exhaustive search. These specialists will be very familiar with materials and show you how to get down to serious digging for information.

Here Are the Meatiest Resources

While no rundown on career materials can be complete in a single section, here are the categories and resources we consider to be basic or unusually valuable.

Government References

The *Occupational Outlook Handbook* is issued every two years by the U.S. Department of Labor's Bureau of Labor Statistics. It is the ancestor of all collections of occupational information. Although other publishers may rehash and repackage the book, only the federal government has the money and the resources to gather the original data and evaluate it. A minimum of 35 economist-writers and their editors work on the reference.

The OOH is a superb accomplishment that should be supported and expanded. A downside is that two years often pass between gathering information and printing the book. For instance, the 1988-89 edition relies on '86 and '87 statistics.

The presentation is cautious and bland, never bluntly warning readers to avoid a given occupation that seems headed for oblivion. But OOH is a topnotch starting place and you should never begin a career search without looking through it.

With each government budget cut, the *Occupational Outlook Handbook* becomes thinner and describes in detail fewer occupations. Included for each occupation is information on what the job is like, working conditions, personal qualifications, training and educational requirements, chances for advancement, job prospects to 2000, earnings, related occupations and where to find additional information.

The *Dictionary of Occupational Titles* is published by the U.S. Department of Labor. It is the nation's most comprehensive list of jobs. The reference is complex for student use, but if you need to know how to spell a job title, it's an authoritative place to look. Last revised in 1977, the date of its next edition is uncertain.

The *U.S. Industrial Outlook* is published by the U.S. Department of Commerce. It appears each January with forecasts for specific industries. The reference is an easy way to check that you're not planning to enter a declining industry.

In addition, don't overlook free career briefs provided by a dozen or so states. California, for instance, has hundreds of free guides in its series.

Specialized Career Books

Thousands of books are available that deal with specific career topics, such as *Opportunities in Film* by Jan Bone (VGM Career Books/NTC Publishing Group); *Choosing a Career in Business* by Stephen A. Stumpf (Simon & Schuster/Fireside); *Exploring Careers Using Foreign Languages* by E.W. Edwards (The Rosen Publishing Group); *Your Career in Public Relations* by Bob Weinstein (VGM Career Books/NTC Publishing Group); and *Creative Careers: Real Jobs in Glamour Fields* by Gary Blake and Robert W. Bly (The Wiley Press).

A librarian can help you discover career books that relate to your interest by checking in a major reference titled *Subject Guide to Books in Print* (R.R. Bowker Co.).

Sometimes you will want to buy and keep a particular book. If you cannot find the book in a store near you, you may want to order it directly from the publisher. While you can order titles through traditional bookstores, many discount bookstores will not take special orders. Publishers' addresses are listed in several references available in libraries and bookstores.

You can write to the publisher, asking the prepaid price, including postage and handling charges, or, if you are in a hurry and know the book's price, take a chance and add $2.00 to your order to cover shipping costs.

A growing number of publishers maintain toll-free telephone numbers. You can call the number to learn the exact mail-order price of the book. To determine whether a publisher has a toll-free number, call 800-555-1212. (In some areas, you must dial "1" before dialing the information number.) If there is no toll-free number and you want the book as soon as possible, you might want to spend a few dollars on a long-distance call.

Other Career Books

Beyond specialized career books, career concepts are enmeshed in most biographies and in some works of fiction.

After reading Dan Rather's *The Camera Never Blinks,* you understand how the author rose from being a local television reporter to a famous network anchor. You know what it feels like to be a part of the basketball world after reading *Giant Steps* by Kareem Abdul-Jabbar. You empathize with new kids on old blocks after reading the experiences of American Airlines' first woman pilot in *Take-Off* by Bonnie Tiburzi.

Are you an animal lover? After finishing James Herriot's *All Creatures Great and Small,* you have clues as to whether being a small town veterinarian is for you.

Thinking of finance or banking fields where you shift stacks of dollar bills around? Don't miss a rare dramatic look at how high-powered business deals really get made—a vision provided by Hope

Lampert in her book, *Behind Closed Doors: Wheeling and Dealing in the Banking World* (Atheneum Publishers).

Other career books offer a wealth of information on career exploration, planning and development.

Because you'll find information everywhere, learn your way around the many sections of your library or career center.

Many libraries are converting from card catalogs to COM (computer output microform) catalogs. Some libraries print copies of the catalog on microform or paper, while others have installed computer terminals that display the on-line catalog.

First look for the subject of your interest—say "Robotics"—and then you'll want to travel further afield. Although subject headings may vary in individual libraries, a sampling of headings for books on careers and job hunting follows:

Affirmative action
Applications
Apprenticeship
Careers
Civil service
Discrimination
Earnings
Employers
Employment
Employment opportunities
Employment tests
Equal employment
Executives
Grooming
High technology
Image
Job hunting
Job satisfaction
Jobs
Jobseekers
Management
Pay
Personal development
Professional development
Professions
Recruiting
Vocational training
Work

Career Briefs

Career briefs are short articles on specific occupations or industries. The following companies are representative of career brief publishers.

Chronicle Guidance Publications Inc. (P.O. Box 1190, Moravia, NY 13118) publishes a set of some 600 briefs covering a wide range of occupations. The briefs are written in straightforward language and always include a helpful list of additional aids. This is a strong resource.

Vocational Biographies (P.O. Box 31, Sauk Centre, MN 56378) issues books of briefs based on an interview with one person in a given field. An advantage: It covers unusual occupations, such as puppeteer and music video producer. Merely glancing at job titles in the index is stimulating. A disadvantage: The material offers a single perspective.

Career Magazines

Career World (General Learning Corp., 60 Revere Drive, Northbrook, IL 60062) is both the pioneer and premier career magazine for high school and college students. Issued nine times per year (September through May), the magazine is available in schools and libraries. The format is colorful, easy to read. For subscription rates, call the toll-free number 800-323-5471. In Illinois, the number is 312-564-4070.

Business Week's Careers (McGraw-Hill Inc., 1221 Avenue of the Americas, New York, N.Y. 10020) is distributed free through college placement centers, and through some graduate and undergraduate departments. Published six times a year. *Graduating Engineer* (McGraw-Hill Inc.) spotlights careers in engineering fields and is issued four times yearly. If you're not in a college where you can receive free copies, query the publisher for current subscription rates.

Occupational Outlook Quarterly (published by the U.S. Department of Labor; sold by the Superintendent of Documents, Washington, D.C. 20402) comes out four times a year and contains high-quality, in-depth career articles. Write to the Superintendent of Documents for subscription rates.

Other Magazines

Specialized career magazines are basic for research. Additionally, the motivated researcher will find that reading general interest and specialized magazines focused on other topics also can save countless hours of frustration and many false starts down rewardless roads.

Some periodicals, such as *Working Woman, Black Collegian* and *Careers & The Handicapped,* aim toward specific groups.

In *High Technology,* you might be inspired to explore engineering after reading about the space station that will be launched as a joint venture of government and industry.

Changing Times' annual survey of job openings for college grads will tell you which employers are hiring and for what jobs. This survey, issued each spring, previews the employment outlook for various fields.

Business Week is a basic tool for keeping up with trends that directly affect career choices.

To move from outsider to insider in an industry the trade press functions as a perfect conveyor belt. This category of magazines comprises trade journals and professional magazines, like these:

Construction Week

Datamation

Nurse Practitioner

Human Resource Management

Journal of Marketing

Telecommunications

Supermarket News

Chances are that your library or career center subscribes to very few trade magazines; you'll probably have to ante up for the publications you want, but the returns are enormous. You'll know the hot new trends in an industry, see ads for special training opportunities, and learn the jargon so that you speak like a native when you interview for a job. By regularly reading the help-wanted ads, you can anticipate the job market and determine what you must do to become a prime candidate.

A simple way to identify the right trade journals is merely to ask people in the field what they read. A librarian can help you find the appropriate publications by checking under the subject index in *Ulrich's International Periodicals Directory* (R.R. Bowker Co.).

Indexes

Other notable references useful in ferreting out magazine articles of particular interest include:

Readers' Guide to Periodical Literature

Magazine Index

Business Periodicals Index

Subject indexes help you find articles in specific fields, such as finance or science. Examples are:

Art Index

Education Index

Agricultural & Biological Index

The Social Science Index

Newsletters

As television news covers the state of the world in two minutes, so newsletters digest key happenings in industry and in the world.

Some newsletters are narrowly focused, such as *P.C. Letter, The Insider's Guide to the Personal Computer Industry.* Others give advance tips on a wide range of pertinent subjects; an example is the highly regarded *Kiplinger Washington Letter,* which reports on what's happening—or about to happen—in government, industry and the business world.

Because newsletters tend to be considerably more expensive than magazines, libraries are more likely to subscribe to a broadly focused publication than to a narrow one.

You may discover an appropriate newsletter by looking in such references as *The Newsletter Yearbook Directory* or *Oxbridge's Directory of Newsletters.*

Directories

One of the richest mines of information is *The Encyclopedia of Associations* (Gale Research Co.). Here you'll find 18,000 organizations whose sole reason for existing is to promote their special interests.

There are associations for virtually every subject you can imagine: The American Association for Career Education, the Flying Funeral Directors of America, National Association of College Stores, Chinese Institute of Engineers, and the Maltese Falcon Society. The directory is updated yearly.

After finding the associations that fit your interest, it's often possible to obtain free or inexpensive career materials from them. If your library or career center hasn't acquired the booklets and pamphlets published by organizations of interest to you, write a letter along these lines:

Dear Association Executive:

Please send me a copy of the free career literature that your organization publishes. In addition, please include a bibliography of the career materials you offer that are available for a charge.

Sincerely,

Your name,
address

After receiving the initial material, you may have questions, or you may want to get in touch with the association's members in your area who could become a part of your contacts network. To follow up, you can address your letter to the association's education director, public relations director or membership director.

Other Directories

At least 5,000 directories identify numerous topics, ranging from convention meeting dates to employers of engineers to newspapers.

And if you can believe it, the easiest source to find which of these information motherlodes you need is called—what else?—the *Directory of Directories* (Information Research Enterprises).

Here are a dozen or sc examples of available resources:

- *The Directory of Conventions* (Herman Publishers). Every day of the year a convention or conference is held somewhere in the nation. If you want to become a sports doctor, a venture capitalist, or a psychologist, wouldn't it be great to attend a meeting of the American Academy of Sports Physicians, the National Association of Small Business Investment Companies, or the American Psychological Association?

Job interviewing often takes place at these meetings and even if you're still a student, you may meet a manager this year who will hire you another year. Always ask about special student rates because these meetings can be costly to attend.

- *Peterson's Engineering, Science & Computer Jobs* (Peterson's Guides). This annual directory surveys and reports on more than 600 companies that hire technical employees.
- *Editor & Publisher Yearbook* (The Editor and Publisher Co. Inc.). Another annual, this one lists 1,700 daily newspapers.
- *The Washington Information Directory* (Washington Researchers). This is a reference to the right person or publication in Washington's maze of agencies. It is a comprehensive guide to government and non-government sources of information located in Washington, D.C.

Directories that are useful in job hunts include these:

- *College Placement Annual* (College Placement Council), a listing of employers hiring new graduates and the types of entry-level positions they wish to fill.
- *Standard & Poor's Register of Corporations, Directors and Executives* (Standard & Poor), three volumes. The first volume lists the names of company executives and directors. The second volume lists the names of companies and describes what they do. The third volume is an index telling you the name of each company and where to find information about it in the other two volumes.
- *Thomas Register of American Manufacturers* (Thomas). This book tells you who makes what across the country, including manufacturers' names and addresses. For most states there also is a state directory of manufacturers published by Manufacturers' News Inc.
- *The Corporate 1000* (Monitor Publishing). A directory with listings for the top thousand corporations in the U.S. Included are names, titles and direct-dial telephone numbers for key executives; address and main telephone number of corporate headquarters; a description of each corporation and a listing of its major subsidiaries, plus the product lines for each company.
- *The Facts on File Directory of Major Public Corporations* (Facts on File). This directory gives essential personnel and financial data on 6,300 publicly-owned companies that transact the major share of America's business.
- *The Almanac of American Employers* by Jack W. Plunkett (Contemporary Books Inc.) provides profiles of salaries, benefits, financial stability and advancement opportunities in America's 500 largest corporations.
- *How to Get a Job in Lcs Angeles* by Thomas M. Camden and Freda Greene (Surrey Books) gives details on the 1,500 major employers in L.A. Similar books are available for the cities of Chicago, Dallas, Fort Worth, Boston and the San Francisco Bay area.
- State and city chambers of commerce publish local directories of businesses.
- *Everybody's Business* by Moskowitz, Katz and Levering (Harper & Row) is an irreverent guide to 800 or so of the largest firms in the U.S. It's a good book for seeing beyond the public relations releases.
- *Knowing Where to Look* by Lois Horowitz (Writer's Digest Books) is the ultimate guide to research. Horowitz, the reference librarian's reference librarian, gives a crash course in investigatory techniques.

Vertical Files

Most libraries and career centers maintain vertical files on career topics. These are file folders stuffed with career briefs, career literature from associations, bibliographies and articles from newspapers and magazines. Some libraries may include articles on individual companies or employers.

Bibliographies

Libraries and career centers often compile bibliographies, but only of the materials in their collections. For instance, a library might have available a bibliography on careers in music, or on careers in health. Ask if one exists for your field.

Racks and Bulletin Boards

As you roam about a library or career center, glance around and you'll probably see racks containing pamphlets that relate to careers, as well as wall posters announcing current training or job opportunities.

The announcement publications are varied and appeal to a broad range of interests. You may trip over the very piece of information you need to move your career plan forward.

Data Bases

Lois Horowitz, author of *Knowing Where to Look*, says computers are the Great Research Machines, and that their use will grow when we better know how to use them, and when their prices drop. While some schools and libraries will do data base searches on your behalf, you may have to pick up the tab.

To understand how technology is moving to put a wealth of information at your fingertips, here's a little background.

A data base is a computerized library, a collection of information organized for a specific purpose. A data bank is a collection of data bases.

How does a data base come into being? Generally, researchers at a firm or government agency collect scads of information. They scan and digest countless publications, newswires and other data sources. They pack all the information into large computers, index and cross-reference it. Then they rent it out, charging between $15 and $300 per on-line hour.

There are several varieties of data bases. One type is *reference* only. It offers bibliographic information, providing citations to books, magazines and other publications.

The second type is *full-text*, in which the complete text of news stories, articles and other material pops right up on the computer screen.

The third version is *videotext* or *source* data bases, in which you can call forth such data as stock market quotes, airline schedules, newspapers, catalog shopping and educational games.

Maggie III in Colorado Springs, Colo., is billed as the most advanced public-access library computer system in the world. Operated by the Pikes Peak Library District, it runs 24 hours a day and can be contacted from a home computer or any of the district's branch libraries. Researchers have telephoned Maggie from as far away as Australia and Paris.

The cost effectiveness of using data base searches for career information may improve dramatically over the next decade, but for now, the Great Research Machine remains out of reach for most of us.

Computer Guidance Systems

Some libraries and career centers (and other facilities too) help people search for careers through computer guidance systems.

Essentially, the computer approach works like this: You sit at a microcomputer, or terminal, and use the keyboard to run through a program that results in the listing of possible career fields.

When you ask the computer for information about a particular field, the machine feeds back such data as a survey of various opportunities in the field, what the work is like, the names of schools offering the necessary courses, and the salary range. The computer may also indicate local employers who are interested in hiring people in the field. This is the basic music to computer guidance; the words change with each computer system.

An example of the best in life/work planning is Career Design Software, a program based on the work of leading career authority, John C. Crystal (Crystal-Barkley Corp., 111 E. 31st St., New York, N.Y. 10016). The Crystal software strikes more than the single chord of job choice; it offers an entire keyboard of discovery pointing you toward a recognition of what you want to do with your life.

Career Design Software and some other computer guidance systems take into account your personal values, lifestyle preferences and self-evaluation factors, but most do not.

Although there are quite a few private companies marketing computer guidance systems, the largest and most familiar program is operated by state governments. It is called CIDS, which stands for the statewide Career Information Delivery Systems.

How many facts you can obtain from CIDS varies. Depending on the state in which you live, you may find data for national, state and local occupations. Sometimes the information comes to you through computers, sometimes through more traditional means such as microfiche and printed material. All of the data, however, are stored in a computer.

CIDS operate in more than 9 out of 10 states and the information is free to users (your tax dollars pay for the service).

In addition to libraries, CIDS are in high schools, community colleges, public four-year colleges, vocational-technical institutes, public employment service offices, vocational rehabilitation centers, and community organizations.

If you're interested in booting up a CIDS computer or using a private computer guidance system, ask a guidance or career counselor for details.

This book isn't the appropriate place to go into all the bits and bytes of computer guidance, but we do have one tip:

Don't make a career decision based only on what a computer tells you without researching on your own. Computer guidance is a starting place, not a finish line.

BE A LIBRARY REGULAR

Become comfortable in libraries and career centers. The information you need is there, mountains of it. You now know where and how to find it.

Even if the data you're hunting aren't immediately available, you probably can uncover the organizations or individuals to contact for publications or answers.

Why is becoming library-smart so important? As University of California pharmaceutical chemist George Kenyon quips:

A couple of months in the laboratory can frequently save a couple of hours in the library.

The analogy fits career research well, except that the time frame is quite different. It's closer to this idea:

A couple of decades in the job market can frequently save a couple of months in the library.

BEYOND THE LIBRARY: ORIGINAL RESEARCH TO THE RESCUE

After unearthing career information from media and recording it in your super future files, you're ready to move to primary sources and interview people and their bosses at work in the field you're considering.

Refresh your memory by turning back to the career awareness discussion (section 7) and rereading the techniques for obtaining interviews and conducting them.

In case you've forgotten the difference between career awareness and the original research you're about to do, it's a matter of volume and details.

In career awareness interviews, you scan the world of work and become aware of many career options. You are cruising, doing brief interviews with many people. You are screening out options that seem to clash with your preferences.

Now, after weeding out all but the most attractive options, you get down to brass tacks. Now you are considering just a few fields, maybe only one. You are getting ready to set goals and make decisions.

For each finalist field on which you are gathering information, you'll want to dig, dig, dig. You need not only chapter and verse, but paragraph and period. And the way you are going to get it is to validate your extensive media research with person-to-person interviews in depth.

The moment has arrived—go out and interview! This is no time to suffer an attack of shyness. As we said earlier, try not to get yourself in a tizzy about the possibility of being turned down.

If it happens, simply try someone else. Being refused an interview is of no consequence. Most people will give you an appointment. They understand that your career search is not a trivial matter.

Youth Work Clubs Are Valuable Resources

On an imaginary spectrum of career exploration, you find at one end the activity of data gathering; at the other, working in student jobs. Somewhere in the middle is a group of top-notch organizations that let you sample occupations in various ways.

Collectively, these groups are called *youth work clubs.*

Their purpose is to help you meet and learn from people who already are in the career fields you are thinking of entering. Most of the groups aim at high school students. If an organization seems right for you, find out how you can join—or start—a chapter.

Community-Based Clubs

Aspira of America provides educational assistance to the Hispanic community in high schools and colleges through Aspira Leadership Club. (*Aspira* is the Spanish word for aspire.) The clubs offer career information programs, and, in some instances, internships. (Aspira of America, 1112 16th St. N.W., Washington, D.C. 20036)

Exploring is the coed, high school division of the *Boy Scouts of America.* The program, the largest of its kind in the nation, is established in a series of "posts"—places where you can find out what the work world is really like. Each post has different divisions, such as law and criminal justice, computer science, commercial art, and business management. (Boy Scouts of America, 1325 Walnut Hill Lane, Irving, TX 75038)

The Boys Clubs of America emphasize youth employment and offer a self-directed job search program. (Boys Clubs of America, 771 First Ave., New York, NY 10017)

Horizon, the *Camp Fire* career program, encourages members to pursue volunteer work as a way to explore work interests and skills. Participants assess their talents and values relative to work, obtain basic employment information, and focus on career preparation requirements, plus they provide valuable services. (Camp Fire Inc., 4601 Madison Ave., Kansas City, MO 64112)

Dreams to Reality is the career program of the *Girl Scouts of the U.S.A.* The program encourages girls to explore a wide variety of careers, strengthen decision-making skills, and evaluate experiences as they relate to personal life and career choices. (Girl Scouts of the U.S.A., 830 Third Ave., New York, NY 10022)

The *Girls Clubs of America* offer programs in career awareness and education, goal setting, budgeting, and business management. On-job training opportunities may be available. (Girls Clubs of America Inc., 205 Lexington Ave., New York, NY 10016)

Junior Achievement Inc. operates four distinct programs aimed at three different age groups: At the high school level, students participate in applied economics courses and in the JA program, in which they learn by running their own companies. Business basics instruction is presented to elementary students and a business economics course to junior high students. (Junior Achievement Inc., 45 Clubhouse Dr., Colorado Springs, CO 80906)

JETS is the popular name for the *Junior Engineering Technical Society,* an organization with student chapters for those considering engineering or applied science as a career. Students explore technology through project work and activities. JETS is funded by engineering societies, engineering schools and corporations. (Junior Engineering Technical Society, Suite 405, 1420 King St., Alexandria, VA 22314)

The *National 4-H Council* programs offer training in automotive skills, business management, economics, career planning and management, and other fields. (National 4-H Council, 7100 Connecticut Ave., Chevy Chase, MD 20815)

Vocational Education Clubs

Distributive Education Clubs of America students take marketing, merchandising and management courses, along with related student jobs, in high school or a two-year college. (Distributive Education Clubs of America, 1908 Association Drive, Reston, VA 22091)

Future Business Leaders of America—Phi Beta Lambda is the organization for students preparing for careers in business. Future Business Leaders of America is the division for high school students, while Phi Beta Lambda is for postsecondary students enrolled in business, office or teacher education programs. (Future Business Leaders of America—Phi Beta Lambda, 1908 Association Drive, Reston, VA 22091)

Future Farmers of America supplements training opportunities for students preparing for careers in farming and agribusiness. (Future Farmers of America, 5632 Mt. Vernon Memorial Highway, Alexandria, VA 22309)

Future Homemakers of America is a club for students in home economics and consumer homemaking courses. One program stresses career preparation with recognition that workers also fill roles as homemakers and community leaders. (Future Homemakers of America Inc., 1910 Association Drive, Reston, VA 22091)

The *Office Education Association* is for high school and postsecondary vocational office education students. The organization offers competitions, awards and economic-awareness programs. (Office Education Association, 5454 Cleveland Ave., Columbus, OH 43229)

Vocational Industrial Clubs of America is the group for trade, industrial, technical, and health occupations students in high school and postsecondary institutions. Members join clubs in their own occupational area; their activities are a part of the curriculum. A Skills Olympics is held each year to recognize outstanding achievements. (National VICA, P.O. Box 3000, Leesburg, VA 22075)

How Youth Clubs Help

Because youth club activities permit you to test the waters of your career interest, sometimes you discover that a decision you made was wrong.

One would-be lawyer—after talking to judges and attorneys lined up through his Boy Scouts Explorer post—found that he wasn't cut out for the law and switched to an Explorer journalism division. Out of school now, he is writing broadcast commercials and loving every word of it.

"Without Exploring," he says, "I would have wasted thousands of my parents' dollars and years of my time in school before finding out that what I really like to do is write."

After completing this section, you are well equipped for career sleuthing. Not bad for one who, until picking up this book, didn't know clusters from career mobility.

∞

SECTION NINE

YOUR GOALS

S*etting and reaching goals helps you focus on the best place for you to* be in life. Without goals, it's easy to become distracted in your journey toward success. Knowing the difference between striving for goals and drifting along often separates winners from near misses.

This section supplies a variety of thought-provoking activities to help you understand the nature of goals, objectives, reality testing and how to handle disappointment when things don't work out.

Goals Along Life's Winding Road

What! No star, and you are going out to sea? Marching, and you have no music? Traveling, and you have no book?

This astonishment at impetuosity is taken from the French.

For young men and women puzzling over their careers, the American version could be: *What! No goals and you are trying to pick a career?* Without goals, you can't predict where you're going.

From the beginning of time, successful people have realized that if you don't know where you're going, you won't wind up any place you recognize. Yes, you might stumble into good fortune, maybe win a state lottery. But you can't count on luck or serendipity pulling you through.

Zig Ziglar, a major-league motivational speaker, agrees. In his book, *See You at the Top,* Ziglar notes that while it is safer not to set goals and risk being embarrassed in front of friends, it would also be safer for a ship to stay in port or a plane to stay on the ground. But the ship would collect barnacles and become a bucket of bolts in the harbor, and the plane would rust and fall apart on the ground.

A worthwhile but realistic goal is one that makes you reach and stretch, and one that you have at least a 50-50 chance of achieving. Is there really any point of wanting to be a top athlete when you lack coordination, or to becoming the U.S. President when you prefer reading a book to meeting people?

It is not, however, unrealistic to have riches as a goal, visualizing how you will put those little green slave dollars to work supporting you. And it's reasonable to set a high and noble goal, such as deciding you want to play a recognizable role in conquering cancer. Once you fully decide to commit yourself to unlocking your potential, to being all you can be, you begin to grow. Sometimes the whole becomes larger than the parts, an effect seen in people who believe they have a calling and are able to do seemingly miraculous things.

Goals express your belief in yourself. Gather together your star, music and book.

Believe.

Values Translate To Goals

Have you ever heard friends whine the don't-wanna litany? "I don't wanna do this and I don't wanna do that." It can be exasperating, particularly when they never say what they *do* want.

Logic asks: How can you get what you want if you don't know what you want?

Valuable Goals

Work you've already done will give you a head start on this discovery. Turn back to section 6 and review your identity inventory for values.

Write the five most important values on the left side of the chart at the top of the next page. In the right column, write a goal that reflects each value. There are two examples to start you off.

Goals and Objectives: The Difference

Although you may hear the words used interchangeably, goals are not objectives.

Businesses set goals and identify the steps necessary to reach the goals. Objectives are the steps.

Values Checklist

Value	Goal
Having personal freedom on the job.	Owning my own business.
Helping others.	Finding an attractive career in which I can be of service to others.
1.	1.
2.	2.
3.	3.
4.	4.
5.	5.

In Memory Of—

A great way to find out what you want from life is to write your own obituary. Limit your accomplishments and personal factors to 150 words. Style it on the order of newspaper obituaries. In anticipating your own mortality, you'll zero in on goals that are really meaningful to you.

P.S. You were 98 when you passed away peacefully in your sleep.

∞

An objective can be measured so you'll know when you've accomplished it.

Goals are broad and involve long-range periods. Objectives are concrete, specific accomplishments necessary to achieve goals; they usually involve a shorter time period.

Many successful people use the basic goals-objectives method to climb to success. Let's look at an example of using goals and objectives to get what you want.

Pete's Goals

Pete is a junior and Sara is a very attractive sophomore. All the young men want to date Sara. Pete would like to date her himself. He has one problem. He doesn't have a fancy car. He can use the family station wagon—but who wants to pick up a date (one you want to impress) with a station wagon that has rips in the seat covers and dog hair everywhere?

Pete would really like to buy a car, but to do so, he figures he needs $2,800. He found out he can get the perfect car for that price. The guy who will sell it to him will let him have it for $400 down and he can pay the balance by the month.

Pete has $500 in a savings account. He's been saving it for college. At present, he doesn't have a job and his parents don't want him to use his college savings for a car.

Pete has a real flair for landscaping and, by using his dad's riding lawn mower, he opened "Pete's Lawn Service." He placed neighborhood ads suggesting clients could save money by contracting for the season. Evidently, his advertisement was impressive because within a week he had eight clients.

Pete talked his parents into a plan whereby he would borrow the money from his savings account, buy the car, and then pay back the money to the savings account and also make monthly payments on the car from his lawn service earnings.

Sure enough, Pete got a date with Sara and she was impressed with his car. Interestingly enough, Sara was less impressive. He's decided that she is rather shallow. But Pete's wildly enthusiastic about his business, which is "blooming."

Pete thinks that horticulture is a possible career option and plans to research colleges that offer it as a major. He's also decided to talk to some people working in the field.

You can see that Pete had a goal and how he was motivated to reach it. Pete achieved his goal by having specific objectives. Write Pete's goal and the objectives to reach it. Also point out what new goals and objectives Pete has set for himself.

Pete's goal:

____

Pete's objectives leading to his goal:

____

____

____

Pete's new goal:

____

Possible objectives leading to this goal:

____

____

____

Get Specific

The more specific you are in stating a goal and the objectives for reaching it, the better your chance for success. Goals such as "I want to be happy" are too vague.

Break your goals into small, more immediate steps—ones that you can measure. What are some specific things that would make you happy? Looking better? Having more friends?

Then objectives might be: 1. Lose 10 pounds by July 1, and 2. make a point to talk with five people this week whom you think you would like to know better.

Winners Reach Their Goals

Setting goals is no guarantee that you'll reach them. To continue the self-improvement example, here's another goal and the well-planned objectives that would lead to its achievement:

Goal: To lose 20 pounds by June 1 so I won't look like a sausage in my bathing suit.

Objective: Visit my doctor by March 1; get a diet recommendation that is both safe and effective.

Objective: Tell my family of my plan and give them a list of the kind of food I will need and ask for their support. I want to start no later than March 15.

Objective: Stick to my diet and tell all of my friends the day I begin so they will support my effort and not encourage me to cheat on the diet.

Objective: Weigh myself every three days and keep a record of my weight loss.

Your Turn at the Goal Post

Practice is the best way to become an expert goal setter and objective chooser. Try this:

For each time period listed below, write one goal. Be sure to consider whether the goal is realistic and whether the objectives leading to the goal are measurable. (If you are 4 feet tall, a goal to be a basketball star is unrealistic.)

Bear in mind that you should have a 50-50 chance of reaching your goal and that it should be challenging.

Today's goal:

____

Objectives to reach it: ____________________

____

____

This week's goal:

____

Objectives to reach it: ____________________

____

____

This year's goal:

____

Objectives to reach it: ____________________

____

____

The goal to reach by the time I am 30:

____

Objectives to reach it: ____________________

____

____

Choose Your Goals Wisely

When you consider goal ideas, you'll probably want to consider two types of goals: short- and long-range goals. Short-range goals are those to be achieved in the immediate future, the next day or the next couple of weeks.

Long-range goals are those you plan to reach in the future, within the next few months or in more than a year.

The biggest difference between winners who reach their goals and those who don't is in goal selection. Goal-reachers aim neither impossibly high nor uninspiringly low. They think carefully about the kinds of goals they set and calculate the risks involved in reaching them.

Reality Testing: Facing Facts About Your Goals

Do you recognize anyone in this cast of dreamers?

- Marsha, a lead dancer in the sophomore follies, who, not recognizing the big difference between school shows and tapping her heart out on Broadway, has a goal of becoming a musical comedy superstar.
- Rolf, a determined premed student whose C grades in organic chemistry, biology and math make

---

Make Your Own Reality Test

It's easy to look at others and see why they are headed for disappointment. But are you as objective about your own goals? Will they survive reality testing? Try this checklist and see:

	Yes	No	Not Sure (Need more facts)
1. *Do I have the intellectual capacity to achieve my goal?* (To verify, ask your counselor to profile a successful student in your goal area. This should include SAT or ACT scores, preparatory courses and grades and other academic measures. After reviewing the profile, ask yourself, "In the light of this information, what is it in my academic background that could lead me to succeed at this career goal?")	______	______	______
2. *Do I have the necessary physical characteristics to reach my goal?* (Speed won't compensate for height in pro basketball if you're under 6 feet; motivation won't make up for lack of talent in entertainment; determination won't make it magically possible for a blind person to become an air traffic controller. Decide which physical characteristics are required for your goal. If there are shortcomings, maybe you can find ways to compensate. And maybe not.)	______	______	______
3. *Do I have the financial backing to reach my goal?* (Think ahead. Brainstorm for ways to find the money you'll need.)	______	______	______
4. *Do I have the energy to achieve my goal?* (Are you in good health? Will your stamina get you through a career of stress-filled days, if that's the kind of goal you select? For example, high stress jobs include practical nurse, public relations specialist and city manager, among many others.)	______	______	______
5. *Do I have the commitment to reach my goal?* (Are you willing to postpone things you want now to achieve your long-range goals? A college junior, for instance, may be impatient living on nickles and dimes and tempted to drop out of school and take a job that seems, at the time, to pay a fortune. Another example: Can you wait to marry until you and your spouse can have your own place?)	______	______	______

him an unlikely candidate for an American medical school, refuses to admit that, academically speaking, he is overmatched by many other premed students.

• Dyan, a pretty chubby-faced young woman, has targeted magazine modeling as her goal, mistakenly believing that her winning personality can compensate for a lack of the definitive facial bone structure needed for photography.

• Tim, a young man whose drawings everyone admires, insists that he will become an architect although his technical aptitude is slight. He knows that automation is drastically reducing the job market for architects but feels he will be an exception, succeeding where many others will fail.

• Joe, a foreign student whose family sacrificed to send him to the U.S. to become an engineer, stubbornly insists on pursuing this goal although counselors have told him there is ample evidence that people with comparable academic records have consistently failed or done poorly when admitted to an engineering program. Joe fears failure could result in disgrace for his entire family.

How to Handle Disappointment

Even though you've planned your goals well and reality-tested them, there's no assurance that everything will work out.

Losing a job you really want is an example of a missed goal. You're disappointed and that's understandable.

Disappointment is a fact of life and a recent study at the Institute for Social Research at the University of Michigan shows that only one-third of Americans feel pretty sure their life will work out the way they want it.

When things don't work out as you expect, here are several ways to deal with your disappointment.

• Admit disappointment to yourself rather than pretending it doesn't hurt; this acknowledgment helps get grieving out of the way.

• Have a sense of perspective on the loss, realizing that there are alternative ways to satisfy your yearnings. Your challenge is to find them. There are countless examples of disappointments that turn out to be blessings in disguise—you probably can think of several in your own life.

• Analyze what went wrong and determine whether any action on your part (better planning, more attention to details, less indulgence in mere wishful thinking) could have changed the outcome. If so, learn by your mistakes and look at your disappointment as a learning experience—as an opportunity for growth.

For your bulletin board: As Thomas Edison said, "When down in the mouth, remember Jonah. He came out all right."

Realizing Your Potential

When you find that you need straight answers for life's winding road, review your goals and objectives, making sure that they are clearly defined and you have at least a 50-50 chance of achieving them.

SECTION TEN

Your Decisions

As a decision-maker, you take responsibility for your own success or failure. That can be frightening. There can also be fantastic rewards. Controlling your own destiny puts the sunshine and music into reaching for your goals.

This section explains why taking control of your life by making your own decisions is the most rewarding road to follow. There are activities to help you rate your decision-making ability. We offer a seven-step formula for decision making and explain the importance of making flexible, responsible decisions.

Can You Trust the Experts?

Decisions are unpredictable things. Something you decide can turn out to be right or wrong, good or bad, wise or stupid, beneficial or tragic.

Even experts don't always make the right calls. They, who are supposed to be capable of coming up with reliable decisions because of their vast fund of knowledge about whatever it is they are expert in, have been known to make choices that eventually prove to be monumental foul-ups.

In their fascinating book, *The Experts Speak* (Pantheon Books), Christopher Cerf and Victor Navasky cite examples of the most astounding miscalculations, egregious prognostications and just plain boo-boos. Among their treasures are these gems:

- *No one knows more about this mountain [Mount St. Helens] than Harry. And it don't dare blow up on him. This [gol-danged] mountain won't blow.*

—Harry Truman (83-year-old owner of a lodge near Washington State's Mount St. Helens), commenting on predictions that the long-dormant volcano was about to erupt, 1980. Harry made a decision not to evacuate. A few days later, Mount St. Helens erupted, killing, among others, Harry Truman and his 16 cats.

- *God himself could not sink this ship.*

—*Titanic* deckhand, responding to a passenger's question, "Is this ship really unsinkable?" Southampton, England, April 10, 1912. The deckhand had decided to believe and repeat assurances from the ship's designers. At 20 minutes to midnight on April 14, 1912, the Titanic struck an iceberg and sank, drowning 1,500 of her passengers and crew.

- *For [heaven's] sake go down to reception and get rid of a lunatic who's down there. He says he's got a machine for seeing by wireless! Watch him—he may have a razor on him.*

—Editor of the *Daily Express,* London, deciding not to see and interview John Logie Baird (the inventor of television), 1925.

- *The horse is here to stay, but the automobile is only a novelty—a fad.*

—President of the Michigan Savings Bank, advising Horace Rackham (Henry Ford's lawyer) not to invest in the Ford Motor Company, 1903. Rackham made his own decision. He disregarded his banker's advice and bought $5,000 worth of Ford stock. When he sold his shares several years later, they were worth $12.5 million. We have no record of what the banker said when he realized he missed an opportunity to invest and earn millions of dollars himself.

- *The Hawaiian Islands are over-protected; the entire Japanese fleet and air force could not seriously threaten Oahu [Pearl Harbor].*

—Captain William T. Pulleston (former Chief of U.S. Naval Intelligence), August 1941. Apparently the U.S. government decided Pulleston was correct. At 7:55 A.M. on December 7, 1941, Japanese carrier-based planes attacked Pearl Harbor, destroying or severely damaging 188 aircraft and 8 of the Pacific fleet's 9 battleships.

History is spotted with such blue-ribbon bloopers. We encourage using experts to *help* make decisions, but, remember, the ultimate responsibility for making decisions that affect your life is yours.

Where Do You Stand on Decisions?

Decisions, decisions. In your younger days, many of them were made for you. Now it's time to seize the freedom you've always wanted by drawing your own conclusions.

You cleverly realize that many of the choices you make today will define your life tomorrow. Knowing that, you'll be careful about choosing, won't you?

A favorite friend of ours wasn't. At 34, the young man is starting over, a veteran of five wasted years on ski slopes, a victim of embezzlement of his company, and a subsequent filer of bankruptcy.

As the honors graduate of the school of hard knocks said:

> *I wish I had taken my choices more seriously. When I knew it was time to make my own decisions, I did. But I went off half-cocked. I had the* power *to make decisions, but not the practice to make the right ones.*
>
> *When people tried to warn me to watch out for this or that, or not to make a rash decision, I thought to myself, "I'm no dummy, I can think for myself."*
>
> *What I hadn't anticipated when I made so many foolish decisions is that there are a lot of people in the world who spend a lot of time figuring out how to get the best of you. I know that now. I found out the hard way.*

Facing adulthood is an appropriate time to take stock of your personal style of handling weighty decisions.

Are you one who clutches, panics, agonizes endlessly and secretly hopes someone else will take the torturous decision off your hands? Or do you rush into the first thing that pops into your head on the theory that God takes care of fools, drunks and you?

Either approach hurts your chances to succeed in life. One of the reasons people do things they later regret bitterly is that they have not learned how to make good decisions. You were not born knowing how to choose well. You learn by trial and error.

Here's an illustration. If your mother always chooses the clothes you wear, you have had few opportunities to look like a horror show and suffer endless teasing from friends. If you select your own clothing, you have learned through criticism to be careful about the way you dress—you have learned lessons in being responsible for your own actions.

It's not a happy thought, but most people learn to make good decisions by making mistakes. It's what happens later that counts.

Losers view failure as an excuse to quit, while winners view failure as the chance to learn not to do something the same way again.

Some of us learn faster than others who go through life never understanding why the things they do often end badly.

Here are two activities to help you see a true picture of yourself in relation to making decisions.

Are You Satisfied With Your Past?

How do you feel about decisions you have made? List three decisions you made that turned out well:

Decision	Age When Made	What Happened?
Example: Said "no" to drug pusher.	14	Boosted self-esteem and respect
		from friends. Drugs never messed
		up life.
1.		

(continued)

Decision	Age When Made	What Happened?
2.		
3.		

List three of your decisions that you now regret:

Decision	Age When Made	What Happened?
Example: Dropped out of school.	16	Couldn't get a decent job; talked
		parents into letting me go back to
		school at 18. Lost two years.
1.		
2.		
3.		

∞

Who Makes Your Decisions?

You may not realize how much control of your life you give to others. The next activity helps you see to what extent your friends exert their will over your decisions.

Decision-Making Checkup

Type of Decision	Amount of Control Friends Exert		
	None	Some	A Lot
1. What classes or major I take			
2. What books I read			
3. What I will do after graduation			
4. Whether and where I will go to college, graduate school			
5. Whom I will date			
6. Who my friends are			
7. What grades I get			
8. How I treat others my age			
9. What songs I like			
10. What I would like to be			
11. Whether I smoke, drink, do drugs			
12. Whether I get a part-time job			
13. How I treat my teachers, professors, parents			
14. What clothes I buy			
15. What politicians I support			
16. What my hobbies are			
17. Whether I cheat on a test			
18. Whether I get married after graduation			
19. Whether I go to class			
20. Whether I finish school			

The Art of Choosing

Decision making can be sliced up into orderly stages. Our formula uses seven steps.

Once you get them down pat, and practice a bit, the steps tend to merge into a continuous process.

Our seven-step formula simplifies all decisions, whether you're deciding something important, such as your choice of career, or something minor, such as the meal you order for dinner.

Here's how it works.

1. Define the Problem

The precise nature of a problem is not always self-evident. Sometimes you need family and friends to help blow away the fog.

As an example, suppose you're feeling unsure, restless and frustrated without knowing exactly why. After listening to you for awhile, others—who can be more objective about you than you yourself are—may pick up clues and offer a suggestion: "It sounds as though you need to change your major."

You're astonished! It's true! The revelation hits like thunder. Now that you mull it over, your classes have seemed incredibly boring and you aren't quite sure to what end your education is leading. Once you know the problem, you can decide what to do about it.

2. Identify Options

At first reaction, you may think of few or no options. Seek advice. In addition to home-based consultants (family and friends), pull in information from other sources, too.

If you're eyeing another major that seems promising, ask people who are already enrolled in that major what they think about it both as a discipline, and as the basis for a future career or foundation for graduate study.

3. Anticipate Probable Outcomes

If you recall our earlier discussion of expert predictions, you know that everybody's crystal ball is cracked from time to time. Nevertheless, you should make an educated guess about how each option might turn out.

Let's switch your major from English to engineering. While your immediate job prospects will be immensely better as a new technical graduate than as a graduate in liberal arts, some of your credits may not count toward graduation. This means you'll have to go to school longer. Are you prepared to extend your studies?

Some people hate to make decisons because they fear they'll make errors. The way to put this fear in perspective is to make a good guess about the outcomes of each option. "What is the worst thing that could happen?" "What is the best thing that could happen?"

4. Make a Values Impact Statement

People make choices because they value one thing more than another.

Looking back at the discussions on values in previous sections, you'll recall that your values include how you feel about yourself; how you feel about others; your moral, ethical and religious beliefs; your emotional needs and your motivations. When making a decision you must weigh all these values.

When you act in conflict with your values, you usually pay not only the piper, but also the rhythm section and maybe the whole orchestra.

Often you can eliminate a number of your options because you can't live with the consequences. Engineering is a good idea—for somebody else. You just don't want to go to school long enough to get an engineering degree.

If it's an important decision, it's not a bad idea to write a brief statement about how your values relate to each option.

5. Review Your Goals

Analyze whether a decision you're about to make fits with the goals you've set.

Suppose you hanker to become a world-wide travel tour operator (ah, Rome, Venice, Paris... dream on). This is another reason to reject engineering as a major. It's out of synch with your goal.

Before finalizing a decision, ask yourself two key questions:

1. Does this decision support my aspirations?
2. Is it realistic or am I kidding myself about my chances to pull it off?

6. Make a Decision

Ready, aim, decide. If you're still shaky and can't bring yourself to decide something, chances are you can break the mental logjam by acquiring more information.

Without adequate information, it's easy to make damaging decisions; with enough relevant facts about the subject in question, you stack the cards in your favor.

Decide! Write it out: After reflecting on this problem, my decision is: ______________________

7. Write an Action Plan

Once you make a decision, writing a plan to implement it will help cut the ropes of lethargy and send your decision ballooning upward. It need not be an elaborate plan; one paragraph will do.

Let's say you finally decide to drop English, become a world-wide tour operator and switch to a travel and tourism major. Your plan might read like this:

Decide to end English major. Will switch to travel and tourism major. Will locate schools with appropriate curriculum within 10 days. Within three months will decide which university to transfer to. Will also launch career research immediately.

Apply the Technique

Now let's see what you've learned about those rascal decisions hanging over your head. Think of two problems that are causing you to lose sleep and work your way through the seven-step process:

1. Define the problem.
2. Identify options.
3. Anticipate probable outcomes.
4. Make a values impact statement.
5. Review your goals.
6. Make a decision.
7. Write an action plan.

Use the forms on the next two pages:

Problem One

Step 1.

Step 2.

Step 3.

Step 4.

Step 5.

Step 6.

Step 7.

Problem Two

Step 1.

Step 2.

Step 3.

Step 4.

Step 5.

Step 6.

Step 7.

∞

An Age for Decisions

"How can I make decisions now that will affect me for life?" you ask. "Aren't I too young? What if I change my mind?"

Good questions. But remember, you choose the kinds of people you want for friends. You select subjects to study. You determine whether joining clubs or teams is right for you. You choose the college you wish to attend. You elect whether or not to find part-time work. These and other decisions are invaluable reinforcement of your decision-making skills. No decision is irrevocable if you consciously try to make decisions that allow flexibility in the future.

Here are a few examples of flexible decisions.

1. Taking math through 12th grade calculus is a flexible decision. It permits you to choose either a technical or non-technical major in college. Should you ultimately choose a non-technical major, you've lost nothing and gained a head start on understanding an increasingly complex world.

2. Enrolling in a communications program rather than in a traditional journalism curriculum is a flexible decision. Journalism prepares you to work in media; communications includes such courses as speech, sales, public relations and advertising. The 360-degree approach gives you basic skills to move back and forth among media, public relations and advertising, should the winds of the job market so require.

3. A flexible decision for a music major would be to add to a skills repertoire by using electives to study such subjects as business and psychology. If you can't support yourself as a performer, you could become a music therapist, concert promoter, recording manager or other specialist in the music careers cluster.

These are a few examples of inflexible decisions.

1. Unless you want to design the software that runs computers, a computer science major is an inflexible choice. It does not prepare you for many different opportunities. You would have many more options by majoring in accounting, finance, marketing or another foundation discipline. You would take only enough computer science courses to have a sophisticated understanding of how to use computers as tools.

2. A major in driver-and-safety education is too narrowly focused. During tight budget times in some states, driver education is one of the first things school systems do away with. The same concept applies to other closed-end majors, such as black studies. If you want to go into education, think of something with a wide scope, such as a major in a specific academic subject (social studies, for instance), followed by a master's degree in secondary school curriculum and instruction.

3. Another decision that could prove to be inflexible is to begin your career in a non-profit organization, rather than a profit-making private business. Business employers tend to look at people who work in non-profit organizations and government agencies as slow-moving and unable to make a commitment to the bottom line in business—making money. As a rule, you can move from a profit-making business to a non-profit organization much more easily than you can make the opposite move.

What's the best way to prepare so that you can more easily go with the flow of jobs? The answer is clear: Acquire solid foundation knowledge that lets you add on new knowledge as needed. Try not to specialize too soon.

If you acquire a broad background in language, math and science, you can move ahead making decisions with confidence.

A Dozen Suggestions for Choosing a Career

When you're still in a quandary about which road to take, check your tentative decisions against this timeless list of good advice from Dr. Robert Hoppock, the father of modern career information evaluation. Here's what Dr. Hoppock recommends:

- Choose an occupation because you like the work, not solely because of the rewards in money or prestige.
- Choose an occupation that will use the abilities you possess.
- Choose an occupation in which there is likely to be an active demand for workers when you are ready to go to work.
- Do not choose an occupation just because a friend or someone else you admire chose it.
- Avoid occupations that require abilities you do not possess.
- Do not confuse interest and ability.
- Before making a final choice of occupation, find out what are *all* the things you might have to do in it. Find out which of these will take most of your time.
- Do not expect to find a job in which you will never have to do anything you dislike.
- Do not stay permanently in a job in which you dislike most of the things you have to do.
- Beware of biased information from recruiters and other sources.
- Take all the advice that is offered, then act on your own judgment.
- Remember Robert Louis Stevenson's counsel, "To know what you prefer, instead of humbly saying 'Amen' to what the world tells you you ought to prefer, is to have kept your soul alive."

(Source: *Career World*)

SECTION ELEVEN

STUDENT JOBS ARE GOOD FOR YOU

W*ork activities—both paid and volunteer—are vital to your healthy* career development.

This section challenges the notion that student jobs threaten academic achievement, or that they rob you of "only-young-once" good times.

It examines the array of benefits generated by part-time employment, summer jobs and internships.

In addition, it explains how to construct a beginning resume, how to find student jobs, and how to star in an employment interview even though it's your first time out.

The section concludes with tips on making the most of the student jobs you land. It tells how to start off on a good note, how to polish selected skills, and why it's a good idea to keep a log of your achievements.

(In section 16, which is geared to helping you succeed on your first full-time job, we give you accelerated information. For now, though, be sure you master the basics of making good on a job.)

Need a Job? Get Experience. Need Experience? Get a Job.

Whether you are a new graduate of college or high school, you may stumble over the no-experience objection.

This is what typically happens: You hear that the job market is good and you're excited over your prospects. But as you get serious in your job hunt, you become disheartened because the majority of positions seem to require experience.

The no-experience dilemma is a vicious cycle: If you have no experience, you can't get a job, and if you can't get a job, how can you get experience?

We hear frequently about the problem from your point of view:

I am a recent college graduate who is very interested in a career in the computer field. But employers want experience. How do you get experience when you have been going to school most of your life? It's all so puzzling.

I am a college dropout trying to make it in advertising or public relations. All I want is a job where I can learn, but without experience or a degree, or both, no one will give me a chance. It's unfair.

I graduated from high school and applied for a job as a cashier at a drug store. I thought I was all set, but the manager said that the only thing he could offer me was a part-time job. The reason he gave was that I had no experience. He said that if I had had part-time experience while I was in school, I could have been given the full-time job. Isn't that ridiculous?

Puzzling, unfair or ridiculous? Maybe. But have you heard the joke that asks where an 800-pound gorilla sleeps? The answer is, "Wherever it likes."

That's the way it is with employers. Because they control the jobs you want, they hire whomever they like, and the people they usually like best have experience.

The reasoning isn't too hard to understand. Experience is proof you can do the work. When you have no experience, how can you document your claim that although you can't do the job immediately, you soon can?

The market is minimal for those who think they are very interested in work they know little about or simply want to learn at the employer's expense.

Few employers are anxious to risk hundreds or thousands of dollars training a beginner who, after finding out what the work is really like, may bow out.

Moreover, it's a matter of psychology. Employers are far more interested in their own profit pictures than in people who are out merely to improve themselves.

The voice of experience says, "I made the effort to gain the skills that will benefit your organization."

Breaking the no-experience barrier is just one of the reasons why obtaining paid or unpaid student jobs is so important to your career climb.

Student Jobs: What Else Is in Them for You?

In sports, exhibition games help players shape up before the real season begins. So it is with student jobs. The practice you get by working during summers and after school provides opportunities to learn some moves to repeat and some moves to avoid when you enter the full-time job market.

Try to find jobs that relate to a career you think you would like to pursue. When you observe others who work in the field, you gain clues to the satisfactions and frustrations of the work, as well as to the kinds of people who choose it. You make contacts who may one day advance your career.

Moreover, you will learn that the work world

expects you to have not only technical competence in handling a particular job, but also a general understanding of how to behave in business and an ability to work smoothly with others. The result may be that you decide to switch some remaining school courses to more precisely focus on your specific career goals.

When a job in your chosen field isn't available, it's still well worth your time to juggle fast-food orders or take tickets in a movie theater. You may be pleasantly surprised at all the good things that can happen to you.

- You gain independence. As you do your job well, you acquire a sense of responsibility and begin to feel more self-reliant. The independence of having a job and earning some of your own money is a great feeling.
- You gain a new dimension in personality and become a more interesting person. Your self-confidence gets a boost. You'll do things that open new horizons, giving you new subjects to talk about to friends.
- You gain new friends. Shared experience on the job is a good basis for getting to know someone.
- You gain experience with supervisor relationships, in learning how to cooperate with co-workers, and in polishing skills for serving clients and customers. These are skills you can take anywhere.

Whether you work for someone else, are self-employed or do a volunteer stint, student jobs are a conveyor belt to your future. They can carry you from the sandlot league to the ranks of promising young starters.

After-School Jobs: The Naysayers

Much debate has taken place during the past few years about whether working has a negative effect on a student's education, family life and behavior.

If someone throws a roadblock your way on this account, it's useful to be informed about the issue.

The criticisms fall into five main groups: overextension, inappropriate rewards, negative outcomes, wasted youth and family status. What follows is a closer look at each criticism and a response.

Overextension

Criticism: Exhausted students doze in class, skip homework and fail to keep their grades up.

Response: Certainly students can overextend and that's why students and family should jointly consider how much work is too much.

The majority of high school and college students hold part-time or summer jobs. During the school year, most students who work are on the job 10 to 20 hours a week. A job requiring more hours should be questioned.

The number of hours worked should be evaluated on an individual basis. For some students, five hours a week are too many, while others, highly organized and competent, can handle 20 hours with ease.

Another factor is the time of day you work. Working three hours in the afternoon from 2:30 until 5:30 is less taxing than working on school nights from 8:00 to 11:00.

Still another consideration is time off for school studies. Arrange in advance with an employer your right to take leave from work the day before midterm and final exams.

One more tip: Until you are settled into your first year at college or your first year in a new school, don't take a job at all unless it's a matter of financial survival. Spend your time learning the campus ropes.

As for academic problems, no study proves that working per se causes grades to drop on a group basis. What may happen to cause such assertions by some teachers is that students who are less academically able or are not interested in school simply prefer to work longer hours.

A countercharge by other teachers and counselors holds that students who work up to 10 hours a week tend to be better students because they learn to budget their time more efficiently and, consequently, may apply this skill to their study time.

Keep in mind, too, that a major study of the effects jobs have on students made for the National Center for Educational Statistics (NCES) shows that those who worked and those who didn't both averaged less than an hour of homework a day, a fraction of their TV-viewing time.

Criticism: Busy students cut back on extracurricular activities, sapping enjoyment of school and thus moving school away from the center of their world.

Response: The NCES research indicates that working does not seem to drastically affect extracurricular student activities.

Criticism: Exhausted and busy students spend less time with family, do fewer chores around the house, and sleep when home, causing a change in family relationships and structure.

Response: Exhausted students probably do sack out at home. If so, a time analysis study would indicate whether the problem really is the job or something else, like too much social life.

Inappropriate Rewards

Criticism: Student earnings are wasted on material concerns, such as trendy clothing, cars and rock concert tickets.

Response: Some students are saving their pay for college expenses or are helping their families. But the bulk of spending does go toward things students want to buy.

Isn't the freedom to spend your earnings the way you wish one of the rewards of working?

What's more, blowing money on 10 cases of purple bubble gum while a student may help you to learn how to minimize frivolous expenditures as an adult.

Criticism: What students learn in low-level jobs is not skill- and training-oriented.

Response: Every experience teaches something, even grass-cutting.

Jobs that offer considerable interaction with others, such as fast-food service, retail and telephone sales, help you learn how to communicate and how to persuade.

In particular, a major survey among fast-food workers conducted by the National Institute for Work & Learning shows that thousands of young people feel they have gleaned such valuable skills and work habits as how to take direction; how to work in a disciplined setting; how to cooperate with others; and understanding why it's necessary to come to work on time. Another plus: They learned how to operate electronic equipment.

Any job will teach you something, even if it's only that a particular field doesn't agree with you.

Negative Outcomes

Criticism: Students' jobs tend to place them in adolescent ghettos with little opportunity to learn from adults. In this ghetto, they find the workplace to be a school for petty crime as they give away goods to friends, take things from employers, call in sick when they aren't, and work while drunk or stoned.

Response: Young people usually prefer to be with others in their age range whether they are working or playing. Petty crime is a societal issue, not an employment issue.

Criticism: Rather than create healthy attitudes for work, the low-level jobs breed cynicism as students begin to believe that hard work gets you nowhere.

Response: Thoughtful employers, teachers and parents help students understand that a long journey begins one step at a time, that all of us must "pay our dues," that all honest work has value, and that you get out of a work/learning experience what you put into it. The drone jobs will communicate another fact to students: The best jobs are achieved by people who learn to work *smart* as well as hard.

Wasted Youth

Criticism: Because students have the remainder of their lives to work, holding a job robs them of a precious time period.

Response: A student who maintains a proper balance between an after-school job and classroom studies gains a head start on students who do not work.

A California study suggests that a job imparts consumer sense in money management, and an increased sense of responsibility. Both young men and women reported that their jobs encouraged their willingness to stick to a task and take pleasure in getting it done.

Another study issued by the National Center for Research in Vocational Education quotes a senior as saying, "A job teaches something high school can't—survival in today's business world."

In summary, no one argues for all work—no play. On the contrary, in the NCES research, the study director writes that "high school students seem to have an abundance of time at their disposal—so much that even a fairly strong commitment to work does not seriously impinge on other activities."

The youth-robbing argument lacks substance.

Family Status

Criticism: Some parents resist allowing their children to hold after-school jobs because they fear it will appear they need the money. They think junior's working reflects unfavorably on their image as providers.

Response: It is selfish to place status ahead of a young person's career welfare.

"Gee, All I Ever Did Was Baby-sit"

To explain how any job can teach you something or look good on your resume, let's take baby-sitting, the most pedestrian of all youth jobs.

Here's how to show baby-sitting as solid work experience on your resume.

Work Experience

1986-88 Extensive experience in child-sitting for numerous customers. Demonstrated:

- *Supervisory ability.* Often responsible for welfare of two or more children. A customer described me as "competent in handling disagreements, good in human relations." (Mrs. John Apple, address on request.)
- *Sense of responsibility.* No child ever injured while in my care.
- *Good work attitudes.* Never late for job. Another customer said, "You show a mature attitude." (Mrs. Robert White, address on request.)

The essential idea is to translate aspects of any student job into characteristics all employers want.

Even if an employer doesn't take your interpretation of your accomplishments as seriously as you would like—and some won't—the employer will be impressed that you rate your abilities high enough to make such a strong presentation.

It certainly beats a blah "Gee, all I ever did was baby-sit."

HERE'S A SHORT LIST OF STUDENT JOBS

For an idea of the kinds of paid jobs students often obtain, glance over this sampling:

- *Banks and insurance offices*
  clerical worker
  janitorial worker
  mail department messenger
  word-processing operator
- *Restaurant and fast-food shops*
  counter worker
  dining room attendant
  janitorial worker
  kitchen helper
  waiter and waitress
- *Retail stores (department, drug, food and hardware)*
  cashier
  counter attendant
  delivery helper
  janitorial worker
  messenger
  packer and wrapper
  sales worker
  stock clerk
- *Community recreation centers*
  cashier
  clerical worker
  concession stand worker
  crafts instructor
  groundskeeper
  recreation leader
- *Resorts and camps*
  beach attendant
  camp counselor
  clerical worker
  crafts instructor
  dining room attendant
  lifeguard
  sales worker
  trip leader
- *Construction companies*
  carpenter's helper
  clerk
  handyperson
  laborer
  painter's helper
- *Campus jobs*
  cashier
  clerk-typist
  data-processing assistant
  dormitory assistant
  food worker
  research assistant
  science lab assistant
  tutor
  word-processing operator
- *Manufacturing companies*
  assembler (assembles parts for firm's products)
  clerk
  handyperson
  janitorial worker
  laborer
  shipping room and stockroom helper
- *Miscellaneous*
  amusement park worker
  auto agency rental clerk
  car washer
  gas station attendant
  landscape maintenance worker
  library clerk
  newspaper delivery worker
  private postal-service delivery worker
  receptionist
  security guard
  taxi driver
  toll collector

Extensive lists of student jobs appear in a variety of books, such as *Summer Jobs* (Peterson's Guides), and the *Summer Employment Directory of the United States* (Writer's Digest Books).

Internships Are Calls to Audition

You can test an interest in a field—and its interest in you—without making a long-term commitment. How? By obtaining an internship.

Internships are work experiences that offer definite objectives for learning. They are usually short-term work arrangements and may be part- or full-time, paid or unpaid. An internship arrangement with an employer can last up to a year, but most are for three to six months.

Your school counselor may help you locate such work, and you'll find additional internship resources listed in section 12.

What the Laws Say About Your Working

Let's banish a myth: "You must be 16 to get a job."

In fact, in many states, you can be as young as 14 and work in some jobs outside of school hours and during school vacations.

There are two kinds of laws for minors in the job market—those made by the federal government (Fair Labor Standards Act) and those made by the state in which you live. When both the federal and state laws apply, the tougher law must be observed.

What the federal law basically says is that persons who are 14 years old and older can work in certain non-farm jobs that are not dangerous. Under the federal law, the child labor provisions do not apply to anyone aged 18 and over.

The federal law does not require work permits. The vast majority of states, however, do require employers to obtain employment certification (work permits) for employees under 18.

Even 12-year-olds can work in some cases: delivering newspapers, baby-sitting, doing chores. They can work on farms, too, as long as the employment is not detrimental to their health or education.

To find out about particulars of the federal law, you can call a compliance officer at a local office of the Wage and Hour Division, listed in phone directories under U.S. government, Department of Labor, Employment Standards Administration.

Particulars about your state's laws regarding the employment of minors can be obtained from your counselor, librarian or state department of labor.

When You Need to Move Off the Dime, Try Volunteering

Do you recall the story of Buridan's ass—the animal that starved to death because it was standing halfway between two bales of hay and couldn't decide which one to eat?

When you are stuck between equally attractive job alternatives, you need something that forces a decision to move to one or the other, and that something could be a volunteer job.

Most career fields offer related volunteer jobs you can use to acquire experience, make contacts and build up your resume.

A teaching hopeful might try being a volunteer in a recreation program. A would-be veterinarian might clean cages in animal shelters to learn the necessary skill of handling animals. A future forester could volunteer at a botanical garden.

A psychology major at a large state university says she tutors a boy in his home because she gets only theory in class and wants to validate her interest in counseling psychology.

Since volunteering is a 50/50 deal—you're getting but you're also giving—carefully evaluate the organization in which you may invest your time from the viewpoint of what it can do for you in return. What follows are checkpoints you can use to be sure you're receiving maximum career exploration as well as the satisfaction of helping others.

- Does the organization's training consist merely of an explanation of the group's goals, or does it actually train you for specific jobs? What skills will you develop?
- Will you be in a visible position where you'll meet other people, or isolated in a back office?
- Will your volunteer hours be recorded, along with your job description, so you can refer to them on your resume?
- If you find you've made a mistake in choosing an organization, quit. Analyze your reasons for leaving so you'll avoid poor choices the next time.

When you can't obtain a referral to volunteer jobs at high school or college, try a volunteer center (also called voluntary action center). Some 380 volunteer centers across the nation screen and refer applicants to agencies that need volunteers.

Look in a telephone directory under "Volunteer Center of (name of city)." If you can't locate a center and need a referral, or if you want more general tips on volunteer jobs, write to: VOLUNTEER—The National Center, Suite 500, 1111 N. 19th St., Arlington, VA 22209.

Job Search News: First Edition

Just as champion tennis players and skiers begin mastering their techniques at a young age, you are wise to learn the basics of an effective job search early in life.

First, look at job hunting in the right perspective. It's a skill you acquire. In a way, it's like learning to drive a car. You learn what is expected of you, think about it and practice.

Your presentations will become more sophisticated as you progress in a career, but your basic strategy and tactics will not change. Job search verities really are eternal.

Next we're going to show you how to put down on paper a convincing argument about why an employer should hire you. If you don't, who will?

A Practical Guide to a First-Rate Resume

Employers do not hire people to take up space. They hire people who help them earn a profit. When there is no profit, there is no business.

Even non-profit employers who are not supposed to make money—government agencies, community hospitals, schools—cannot allow their costs of operating to exceed the funds they have available. Their employees must produce enough to justify the organization's existence.

You must convince employers you will become an asset, not a liability.

To do this, frame your presentation in such a way that employers will answer *yes* to each of these three main questions:

1. Can this applicant do the job?
2. Does this applicant have a positive work attitude?
3. Does this applicant get along well with others?

In your case, since you are short on experience, what employers are really looking for are signs of promise, of potential, of the ability (if not experience) to do the job.

Beyond that, employers want employees who are dependable, enthusiastic and hard working. They want your presentation to clearly communicate that your personality will fit in well with co-workers.

Rarely do employers want to hire only breathing bodies. They want specific people to do specific jobs.

Your challenge is to convince employers that you have the specific qualifications to do the specific jobs.

One of the tools you need to do this is called a resume (REH-zoo-may).

Why You Need a Resume

A resume most often is a piece of paper. (Sometimes it's stored in a computer, but more about that later.) It serves as a calling card, a self-advertisement. It tells the employer that you have the ability—based on your skills—to do the job you seek. It tells the employer you have positive work attitudes. It tells the employer you have positive personality traits.

Strictly speaking, a resume is a series of written statements that highlight your previous education, paid and unpaid work experiences, and other pertinent background.

Most resumes are washouts. They do not interest anyone. That's because they are filled with trivia, or because they are a bare-bones, boring history of an applicant's background.

A famous salesperson talked about "selling the sizzle, not the steak." He meant that people are not interested in buying a slab of meat. What they are interested in is buying the good taste of the meat, the nourishment of the meat, and the satisfaction derived from eating it.

That's why the resumes that employers actually read dwell on accomplishments. They accent abilities. They describe qualifications. They zero in on skills. All of these factors combine to focus on meeting employers' specific needs.

You list your education and work experience merely to prove that what you say about your accomplishments, abilities, qualifications and skills is true.

It may surprise you to know that on the average employers spend a mere 30 seconds scanning each resume. If this seems insensitive, particularly after you slaved over every word, what would you do if you had a stack of 300 or 400 resumes on your desk in answer to a single help-wanted ad?

You must train yourself to write the kind of resume that—at a glance—tells an employer why it is to his or her advantage to invest time in talking with wonderful you.

Employers aren't focused on what they can do for you. They are focused on what you can do for them.

So when in doubt about what to put in or what to leave out of your resume, apply this two-question test:

1. *Does this information add anything to my objective of being hired for this job?* If not, leave it out.
2. *Does this information say (or suggest) what I can do for the employer?* Again, if not, leave it out.

As we prepare the work sheets and later the finished document, never lose sight of the *concept* of what your resume should say.

In every statement, your resume will in some way tell employers you have the ability to do the job, possess positive work attitudes, and can get along with others.

Overall, your resume will convince employers that they can benefit by interviewing you.

Start With Work Sheets

Begin drafting a resume by putting together a personal evaluation of your qualifications. Use four work sheets, one each for *education, paid work, unpaid work* and *outside interests.*

On each work sheet, make a conscious effort to list accomplishments, abilities and skills—not just the dry facts of your life to date.

You've already compiled a large percentage of the information you need on your identity inventories in section 6.

Look back and transfer the appropriate data from your identity inventories for academic abilities, aptitudes and skills, work values, interests and personality traits.

Step 1: Educational Work Sheet

(Use your identity inventory for academic abilities here.)

Focus on the school or training program which did the most to prepare you for the job you seek, as you fill out a work sheet like the one that follows.

Stress the most important educational institution. If you are a high school graduate, don't mention your elementary school years. If you are a vocational school or college graduate, skip details of your high school experiences.

Write all the separate courses you took. Put a check mark beside those which are useful in jobs. Zero-in on the courses related to the job you have in mind; give as many details about each as you can concerning what you learned, skills you acquired and your accomplishments.

Tip: As you write down the details about your knowledge, skills and accomplishments, make a strong effort to come up with concrete examples that can be measured in some way.

Simply claiming that you are a hard worker (or have another particular strength) is not enough. You need proof to back up your claims.

Here's an example: If someone says, "I am a good dancer," you may think the person is just bragging. But if someone *shows* you how well he or she can dance, you believe the person. The claim now has *credibility.*

In looking for a job, you rarely have the chance to show what you can do, except when you must demonstrate skills like operating a word processor.

That's why you need concrete examples of your strengths that can be measured in some way. The examples give credibility to your claims of being a strong applicant.

How can you give concrete examples that can be measured? In four basic ways. You can use

1. *Numbers*—"Waited on about 100 customers on a typical day." "Missed only one day of work last year."

2. *Percentages*—"Waited on more customers than 90 percent of my co-workers." "Missed fewer days of work than 95 percent of my co-workers."

3. *Amounts*—"Saved my employer $50 a month by suggesting a way to cut photocopy costs." "Increased sales on paper route by $200 per month."

4. *Supreme statements*—"My employer said I was the hardest-working counter clerk she had ever hired." "Was the only student ever twice elected secretary of the Young Tycoons Club at Dover College."

Using concrete examples in your resume highlights your qualifications in a way that does not seem like bragging.

Before filling in your educational work sheet, glance at the sample for Carrie on pages 222–3. Carrie graduated from high school and hopes to become a secretary in a recording company.

Educational Work Sheet

Name of school/training program: ____________________

Address & telephone: ____________________

Year(s) graduated or attended; credential received, if any: ____________________

Class rank: ____________________

Teachers who will give references: ____________________

____

____

Summary of courses: check (✓) those related to the job you have in mind.

____

____

____

Details on these job-related courses:

Course: ____________________

____

What I learned: ____________________

____

____

Skills acquired: ____________________

____

Accomplishments: ____________________

____

Course: ____________________

____

What I learned: ____________________

____

____

Skills acquired: ____________________

____

Accomplishments: ____________________

____

Course: ____________________

____

What I learned: ____________________

____

____

Skills acquired: ____________________

____

Accomplishments: ____________________

____

Carrie's Educational Work Sheet

Name of school/training program: Richard Montgomery High School

Address & telephone: 2700 Monroe St., Caldonia, Utah 78904 725/870-9999

Year(s) graduated or attended; credential received, if any: 1988, diploma

Class rank: Upper one-third in business subjects

Teachers who will give references: Robert Red, English teacher; Roberta Hope, business teacher; Claire Voyant, coach; Ted Tiger, home room teacher

Summary of courses: check (✓) those related to the job you have in mind.

English I, II, III, IV ✓ Typing I, II ✓ Word processing I, II ✓

Accounting I, II ✓ Office procedures I, II ✓ History I, II, III

Shorthand I, II ✓ Art I Physical education

Details on these job-related courses:

Course: Shorthand

What I learned: Learned theory, brief forms, taking dictation and transcription

Skills acquired: Can take shorthand accurately at 80 words per minute

Accomplishments: Took shorthand faster than three-fourths of class

Course: Typing and word processing

What I learned: Learned keyboard touch typing, accuracy, speed, letter styles, tabulation, special functions of word processing

Skills acquired: Can type accurately 70 words per minute, can use contemporary office equipment.

Accomplishments: Received certificate of accomplishment for typing proficiency; two certificates were awarded among three typing classes

(continued)

Course: Office procedures

What I learned: Learned variety of office machines: dictating equipment, photocopier

Skills acquired: Techniques of answering telephones, filing and office systems, equipment operation

Accomplishments: Was selected by teacher to aid fellow students on word processor

Step 2: Paid-Work Work Sheet

(Use your identity inventories for aptitudes and skills, work values, and personality traits here.)

Fill out a work sheet like the one shown for each paid job you have held—from newspaper carrier to store manager. Baby-sitting jobs can be grouped on a single work sheet.

Once again, look for accomplishments, abilities, and skills. Back these up with concrete examples.

Study the summary for Dan on page 224 before beginning your work sheet. Dan is a college graduate who hopes to find employment as a department store management trainee.

Paid-Work Work Sheet

Employer's name, address, phone: ________

Supervisor's name: ________

Dates employed: ________

Starting, ending pay: ________

Nature of job: ________

List of duties: ________

Skills learned: ________

Accomplishments; give concrete examples of each: ________

Dan's Paid-Work Work Sheet

Employer's name, address, phone: Exmoor Flagship Service Station, 3881 Market St., New Madrid, R.I. 78888 314/876-5647

Supervisor's name: Wes Pumps

Dates employed: Sept., 1986 to present

Starting, ending pay: $3.75 per hour/$4.25 per hour

Nature of job: Service station attendant

List of duties: Pump gas, collect cash payments, fill out credit card sales slips, wipe windows, check engine oil & water, jockey cars

Skills learned: Handle customers, handle cash, keep records of sales transactions, responsibly handle valuable property, give favorable image of employer

Accomplishments; give concrete examples of each:
Superior worker – supervisor kept me on when two other part-time workers were laid off due to shortened station hours; supervisor said I was fast learner, hard worker.

(Note: In real life, Dan's work sheet would also describe an earlier job as a sales supervisor at Woolwow Corp. For brevity, the details are omitted here, but are shown on Dan's resume.)

Step 3: Unpaid-Work Work Sheet

(Use your identity inventories for aptitudes and skills, work values, and personality traits here.)

Fill out a work sheet, like the following one, for each unpaid job you've ever had. The example given for Chitra may inspire you. Chitra attended college for two years. She hopes to land a job as a meeting manager, one who arranges conferences and seminars for companies and organizations.

Unpaid-Work Work Sheet

Volunteer job: ____________________

Location: ____________________

____

Supervisor's name, telephone: ____________________

Duties: ____________________

____

Skills learned: ____________________

____

Accomplishments; give concrete examples of each:

____

____

____

Chitra's Unpaid-Work Work Sheet

Volunteer job: Activities coordinator assistant

Location: Peaceful Nursing Home, 18 Grove Lane, Delight, N.M. 35776

Supervisor's name, telephone: Sally Bird, 989/725-5309 or 741/008-3429 (She travels between two facilities.)

Duties: Advance work in planning field trips for nursing home residents; assisted residents on trips

Skills learned: Researching, planning, problem-solving, negotiating, preparing reports, managing groups of people

Accomplishments; give concrete examples of each:
Showed resourcefulness and creative ability by thinking up need for this work, approaching activities coordinator, persuading her to give me a try. She says I am the most helpful volunteer she has ever worked with.

Step 4: Outside Interests Work Sheet

(Use your identity inventory for interests here.)

Make a work sheet—similar to your other summaries—of all extra-curricular activities, hobbies and personal pursuits.

List everything you've done for the past few years. Analyze the information to see which interests helped you develop skills and accomplishments related to the job you want. Put a check mark beside job-related outside interests, and then develop your work sheet like the example.

Outside Interests Work Sheet

A. Interest: ____________________

Skills learned: ____________________

Accomplishment: ____________________

____

B. Interest: ____________________

Skills learned: ____________________

Accomplishment: ____________________

____

C. Interest: ____________________

Skills learned: ____________________

Accomplishment: ____________________

____

D. Interest: ____________________

Skills learned: ____________________

Accomplishment: ____________________

____

E. Interest: ____________________

Skills learned: ____________________

Accomplishment: ____________________

____

Dan's outside interests are wide ranging, as his work sheet illustrates.

Dan's Outside Interests Work Sheet

A. Interest: Writing

Skills learned: Organization of thoughts, self-expression

Accomplishment: Won city-wide essay contest on merchandising with 150 entrants. Block St. Merchant's Assn.

B. Interest: Reading

Skills learned: Awareness of trends

Accomplishment: Read regularly several consumer magazines

C. Interest: Travel

Skills learned: Awareness of various consumer tastes

Accomplishment: Am widely traveled in U.S.

Step 5: Job Target Research

Decide which jobs you want to apply for. Do advance research on each.

For student jobs, find out what the company does—what goods it makes or sells, what services it provides.

If the company has a personnel or human resources department, ask the receptionist if a job description is available for the job you want. You can pick it up in person or telephone and ask that it be mailed to you. Study the job description carefully. List the qualifications (skills, abilities, accomplishments, education) you have that match the job's requirements.

For example, if you know the job requires the ability to read well and to be reliable, identify your reading skills and the times you have shown reliability.

Add this proof to your finished resume. You are giving the employer what the employer wants.

If you can't get a job description, invent one. Ask yourself: If I were hiring a person for this job, what qualifications would I want? Admittedly, this is not an easy task. Family and friends who are in the job market can offer suggestions. You can get more tips by reading related newspaper help-wanted ads, which often go into detail about job requirements.

Whether real or imagined, working from a job description as you write a resume will help you to "get inside the employer's head," and, therefore, present yourself as an applicant well matched to the job in question.

The notes you make on the job—and how you match its requirements—are your *job target sheets.*

Job target sheets can be made in any style you like; an example of a blank job target sheet form, followed by a filled-out job target sheet for Carrie, illustrates the technique.

Job Target Sheet

Company: ______________________

Contact: ______________________

Address: ______________________

Telephone: ______________________

Job Description/Key Elements: ______________________

____

____

____

Carrie's Job Target Sheet

Company: Gary Ford Publishing Co.

Contact: Patricia Ford, Vice President

Address: 2889 Sunburst Blvd., Northbrook, Ill. 76767

Telephone: 499-7777

Job Description/Key Elements: Secretary, Editorial Dept. Strong skills in shorthand, typing, word processing. Knowledge of office procedures and systems. Will provide clerical support for three editors; good interpersonal skills required.

You'll refer to your job target sheets along with your work sheets and identity inventories when you put together your finished resumes.

Resumes? Did we say resumes? That's right. You may write a dozen or more versions after you learn to tailor a resume to a specific job.

Some students do an all-purpose resume and let it go at that. But then, they're not practicing to be expert job seekers.

You can, of course, construct a general resume and use a cover letter to customize your application to each employer. More about cover letters in section 15.

Writing the Winning Resume

You've done most of the work, and now it's time to whip your information together.

Remember: In every statement, your resume will tell employers that you *can* do the job, that you *will* do the job, and that you *will get along* with others while doing it.

Appearance Creates an Instant Image

The appearance of your resume is usually the first impression you make on an employer. How a resume looks says as much about you as its content.

Here are tips on how to look alert:

- *Length.* Hold your resume to one page, two pages at the most.
- *White Space.* Leave lots of space for margins. Leave some space between paragraphs. Use underlining and capital letters to call attention to key points. Short lines are easier to read than long lines.
- *Paper.* Use standard-size (8½" x 11"), quality paper. Stick to white or an eggshell color.
- *Printing.* How should you make copies of your resume?

A copy of your resume that is individually typed is a wonderful way of telling an employer you really care about a job. It shows you went to a lot of trouble because you respect the employer, and you respect the job offer that may be made. It is a subtle compliment.

But typing 50 or more original copies can wear your fingers to the nub. And there's plenty of room to make typing errors.

The answer is to use electronic typewriters or word processors. Often these are available in schools and offices. An electronic typewriter or a word processor automatically types the same resume over and over. Each copy is an original. All the operator does is feed in paper and push several buttons. A resume must be beautifully typed, so if you can't type, find someone who can.

If you don't have access to an electronic typewriter or word processor, should you take your resume to a printer and have it printed professionally?

Some employers do not like printed resumes. They think you must not be a qualified applicant if you need a fancy printed resume to land a job. Other employers think printed resumes are highly professional.

A practical answer is to have first-class photocopies made. The photocopy must be A-1. This means no slick paper, no sloppy inking or washed out spots. This means no extra scratches or dirt flecks on the copy.

The newest wrinkle is the laser resume. Laser printers have set new standards in reproducing written documents. The nearly typeset-quality printing costs far less than traditional typesetting. Most major cities have desktop publishing and laser printing service bureaus where you can rent time on a computer or pay someone to type your resume for you. The laser method can be used with or without a software package that helps you compose the content of your resume.

Laser resumes offer two advantages. First, your resume is word processed, which allows you to change or customize it easily. Second, you can have it printed cheaply and quickly with a clean crisp look that shows you are in tune with the times.

If you can't find a laser printing service, ask at a computer store where you can get your resume printed by laser.

• *Spelling.* Spelling and typing errors ruin the best of resumes. Employers tend to think if you are careless on your resume, you will be careless on the job.

Moreover, do not scribble data in handwriting to correct or update your resume. Start over. Look fresh!

Use Action Words

Use as many action verbs as possible in your resume. Use words like: *managed, coordinated, sold, improved, planned.*

Drop introductory phrases such as "I was in charge of. . ." Just say "Supervised. . ." This way, you save valuable space for additional accomplishments.

The more *I*'s you can make disappear from your resume, the better.

Use Words That Measure

As we said earlier, when describing accomplishments, give concrete examples that can be measured in some way. Use numbers, percentages, amounts, and supreme statements.

Use Job Objectives

Because employers' eyes streak across resumes like comets in the sky, tell them right away what kind of a job or career field you want.

Begin your resume with a job objective—"Wish to work as hotel front-desk clerk" or "Seeking to be assistant at amusement park."

You may hear that stating a job objective limits employment prospects because there may be job openings of which you are unaware. You can minimize the risk by keeping a job objective fairly broad.

Stating your job objective becomes most important later, as you apply for jobs of greater responsibility. Employers are apt to see students as a blank canvas, but after you gain experience, they'll expect to see the color and form that make a recognizable picture of who you are and what you want.

An alternative to using a job-objective statement to begin your resume is to start with a benefits capsule. Here you state what you are offering, such as "Offering typing skills and the willingness to work hard and the ability to learn fast." See resume examples of job-objective statements later in this section.

You are almost ready to begin writing your resume—as soon as you decide which format to use.

Choose Best Format for You

Just as certain colors and clothing styles flatter one person but not another, resume styles can boost or lower your chances for an interview.

Aim for a format—the form used to give information—that is most flattering to you. It will be one that shouts your strengths and keeps quiet about your faults.

Some people say it is dishonest not to mention your faults in a resume. Does this make sense to you? Have you ever read a help-wanted ad like this?

Worker wanted for a company that almost went out of business last year. The boss is a nag. The customers are worse. Co-workers are known for giving beginners a hard time. But the money's good.

Probably not. That's because no one would apply.

During an employment interview, there is ample time to raise any problem you feel you must reveal as an honest person.

Study format choices carefully. Basically, you can choose from one of three types—*chronological, functional* or *hybrid* formats.

Chronological Format

Chronological, of course, means related to the order of time. In this style, you begin with your most recent experiences and work backwards.

The chronological format is best for people who have a steady school and work record showing constant growth.

The chronological format is the easiest to write, but it is not always advantageous. It is a poor choice for those having employment gaps or other problems in their work backgrounds.

Young people rarely have a lot of work experience; listing only one or two jobs is somewhat like putting only one or two pieces of furniture in a big, empty room.

It is possible to highlight your accomplishments—other than work experiences—in a chronological format, but it is hard to do without making your resume look cluttered.

Functional Format

A function is an activity for which one is specially fitted. The functional format groups your qualifications by function—selling, purchasing, organizing, managing, or repairing, for example.

In a functional format, it is not important when or where you gained your qualifications. Dates, employers, and schools are not given.

Perhaps the most valuable advantage for the young applicant is that the functional style makes the most of scant work experience.

A functional format highlights what you can do rather than merely reporting what you have done.

Moreover, it allows you to disregard experiences that do not relate to the kind of work you want. Suppose the job you want requires good spelling skills. You can emphasize the experiences that show your spelling skills and ignore the non-related job where you learned to read sun dials.

Another advantage to the functional format is that it allows you to lead the reader's attention away from a spotty work history or a poor school record.

As useful as it can be, the functional format has two major disadvantages:

1. It can be very confusing.
2. It may make an employer suspicious of your past because it is not straightforward.

Hybrid Format

A hybrid style combines the best features of the chronological and functional formats. For young people, it can be an ideal choice.

You can put together a hybrid resume in one of three ways:

1. A functional summary can be placed on top of a chronological resume (two pages).
2. A functional resume is followed by a short chronological page that gives dates, employers and schools, as well as a summary of each experience (two pages).
3. A page contains functional groupings and is followed by chronological details (one page).

Checklist for Excellence

At this point, stop reading and begin writing your resume. We know it's hard to do, but keep writing.

When you finish, see if you can answer *yes* to all these questions:

1. Overall, does my resume show how an employer would benefit by interviewing me?
2. Does it stress my accomplishments and skills—instead of being a dry list of things I studied and tasks I performed?
3. Is it inviting to read because of good layout, enough white space, good typing, emphasis on key points?

4. Is my writing style action-oriented and clear?

5. Is my resume free of facts unrelated to the job?

6. Does my resume contain only positive information?

7. Are all my claims believable—backed up by concrete, measurable examples?

If you cannot answer *yes* to all these questions, go back to the drawing board and try again.

Keep at it until you succeed. Resume-writing is a skill you will most probably use again and again. And you already know more about it than most people learn in a lifetime.

What About References?

Arrange for personal references by asking people for permission to use their names. Don't list the names and addresses of your references on your resume, but have them ready on a separate sheet of paper.

Use your references only when an employer asks for them. If you overuse your references, they may become weary of saying how outstanding you are and mumble that you're okay.

Examples of Resumes

We know that individuals who write inadequate resumes as students tend to write inadequate resumes as 40-year-olds. They go through life failing to grasp the central idea of resumes.

The central resume idea is to create a document saying you and the job are a good match. A good match means that you know the job's requirements; that you can do the work; that you will do the work; and that you will behave pleasantly while doing it.

The following resumes incorporate this central theme. Each begins with a job objective, telling the reader the type of job being sought. (A cover letter accompanying an all-purpose resume could do the same thing.)

The examples continue with Chitra, Carrie and Dan. Unless otherwise noted, the information about each person has not been previously mentioned.

Notice in Chitra's resume how she gives measurable proof of how she can do the job of coordinating a convention. This job requires handling a zillion details in a hectic environment. Chitra says immediately that she is experienced, competent, and calm. Then she gives examples to back up her claims.

Why did Chitra begin by noting her unpaid work experience rather than her education?

Because Carrie is short on experience, she uses her education as a function. Notice how she takes the positive approach: Carrie's overall class rank was in the bottom one-half. But Carrie stresses her rank in business courses, which is higher and more impressive.

Why does Carrie make a big thing out of being able to work well with others?

Dan's resume is a single page that leads with functional groupings and is followed by chronological details. Notice how he shifts experience in an unrelated field (gas station) to make it seem perfect for retail stores.

Now that you've finished your resume, you've noticed that some of the data you compiled for your work sheets fell on the cutting room floor.

The information isn't wasted. After being dredged up from your memory, it is on standby status in your mind, ready to use during job interviews.

Resume ready, our next concern is how to hunt for a job.

Chronological Resume

CHITRA SAXENA

932 Sandy Lane
Delight, New Mexico 35776

Phone: (989) 234-8021, 6-9 p.m.
Day messages: (989) 234-7878

Seek position as meeting coordinator...to use planning and organizing abilities. Management experience in large and small events. Proven skill in handling many complex details, smoothly and calmly.

EXPERIENCE:

Member, Special Events Committee, University of New Mexico, Albuquerque; 1986-88. As part of the six-person team, was responsible for $100,000 annual budget, and for bringing 27 major performances and 10 speakers to campus. Both years ended with a profit of $25,000 annually.

From Outside Interests Work Sheet.

* Became completely familiar with special event contract negotiations, handling large sums of money, securing facilities, dealing with people.
* Learned to work efficiently under pressure and to handle setbacks in even-tempered, creative manner, according to faculty advisor, Dr. Roger Gomez.

Activities Coordinator Assistant, Peaceful Nursing Home, 18 Grove Lane, Delight, N.M. 34776; 1985-87. Initiated and planned full program of field trips for 25 nursing home residents and accompanied them on trips.

From Unpaid-Work Work Sheet.

* Researched possibilities, negotiated costs, solved transportation problems, managed group of elderly people.
* Showed resourcefulness in seeing need for program. Evaluation study by supervisor Sally Bird showed 100% of participants felt trips were "outstanding."
* My supervisor said I am "The most helpful volunteer she ever worked with."

EDUCATION:

Attended University of New Mexico, 1986-88. Major study: social psychology. Particularly enjoyed research-related courses.

From Educational Work Sheet.

PERSONAL:

Enjoy people, have good social skills...get satisfaction in creating order from chaos.

Functional Resume

CARRIE RICHARDS

27 Girard Ave. 725/870-1245 Caldonia, Utah 98905

Offering excellent skills in shorthand, typing, word processing, knowledge of office machines and systems. Seek to apply these as secretary. Available July 1, 1988.

strong business skills	Accurately take shorthand at 80 and type at 70 words per minute. Can use word processor, dictating equipment, and photocopier. Understand filing and general office systems, as well as correct procedures for telephones	**From Educational Work Sheet.**
typing	Took in part-time typing, arranged by my typing teacher, to earn extra money. Clients were always satisfied with the work and pleased with the speed of its completion.	**From Paid-Work Work Sheet.**
proofreading	Copy editor of high school newspaper, two years; often praised for careful work in spotting errors.	
planning & coordinating	Assisted my father in setting up a new branch office of his company: helped arrange the office, organize the files, negotiate with telephone company for phone system. Worked as a clerk in this office two summers.	**From Outside Interests Work Sheet.**
education: business diploma	High school diploma with four years of English and a concentration in business. Accomplishments: * Take shorthand faster than three-fourths of class. * Received one of only two proficiency certificates awarded among three typing classes. * Selected to aid fellow students on word processor. * Overall rank in business subjects: upper third.	**From Educational Work Sheet.**
work well with others	Directed volunteers to do mailings for a political campaign. We were able to mail 10,000 letters in one week's time, with volunteers enjoying the project and feeling useful.	**From Unpaid-Work Work Sheet.**
	The campaign manager, Will Raindrop, complimented me before the entire staff, saying that I am "an easy person to get along with."	**From Identity Inventory for Personality.**

Hybrid Resume

DAN MAHLUM
1221 Center Street
Pawtucket, R.I. 78888

315/296-0213 (work)
315/296-0069 (home)

Seek manager-trainee position in retail field.

Qualifications include college degree, and ability to handle merchandise and sales transactions responsibly; longtime interest in merchandising.

Education: Bachelor of Arts – English. Emphasis of electives has been on business and marketing.

Sales: At gas service station, handle cash and credit sales for an average of 200 customers daily. Supervisor kept me on when two others were laid off due to shortened business hours, saying I am a "fast learner and hard worker." Missed only one-half day of work, never late.

From Paid-Work Work Sheet.

Merchandising: Won a city-wide essay contest on merchandising with 150 entrants. Sponsored by Block Street Merchants Assn.

From Outside Interests Work Sheets.

Supervising: At variety store, trained 10 new part-time clerks; devised one-week course to orient trainees. Worked in all areas restocking merchandise, making sales, counting receipts.

From Paid-Work Work Sheet.

Awareness: Regularly read several consumer magazines. Have traveled throughout the U.S. with my family and understand differences in consumer taste in various parts of the country.

******

Experience: Service Station Attendant, Exmoor Flagship Service Station, 3881 Market St., New Madrid, R.I. 78888; 314/876-5647; Supervisor, Wes Pumps. Reference checking encouraged as employer knows of my plan to enter merchandising. Sept. '86 to present.

From Paid-Work Work Sheet.

Sales supervisor, Woolwow's, 49 Hand Court, Pawtucket, R.I. 78889; 314/942-5656; Supervisor, Michelle Bryanowski. Sept. '84-Sept. '86 (part-time).

College: Apple University, Carson, P.A.: B.A. 1986. Earned approximately 50% of tuition while student beginning in junior year.

From Identity Inventory for Work Values and Education Work Sheet.

Personal: Often complimented on my appearance and grooming...5′9″...169 lbs....excellent health.

When You Need a Crash Course in Finding Student Jobs

No matter how wonderful your resume, you won't receive a job offer until you've been through a job interview. Resumes help you get interviews, but during the interview you sell yourself as a good match for a job. Sometimes you won't even show a resume until the interview.

The trick is to line up interviews. Here are ways to do it.

Schools

Your campus career planning and placement center is an obvious place to start looking for a part-time or summer job. In some high schools, a counselor or career center specialist maintains a clearinghouse of student jobs. In both colleges and high schools, notices of student opportunities find their way to bulletin boards.

Don't overlook professors in your major field, and teachers who coordinate vocational education work-study programs. Since these educators stay in touch year-round with employers, they may know of opportunities.

Networking

Use contacts to obtain referrals to other people who can direct you to opportunities. Include parents, relatives, neighbors, classmates, past employers, and school and community youth placement agencies, as well as teachers and counselors. Add to your personal contacts log for future reference all new acquaintances.

Direct Application

About one-fourth of all employees find their jobs by going directly to employers and asking to be hired.

Newspaper Want Ads

Check local weekly papers, as well as the metropolitan daily papers for job leads. In addition to help-wanted ads, learn to read business news stories with an eye toward developing job opportunities. Is a new store opening? If so, you could get in on the ground floor.

Employment Services

Community centers, civic organizations, religious groups, city governments, school districts and others often sponsor student job programs.

Y's and similar organizations frequently post help-wanted notices on bulletin boards, as do some shopping centers.

The chamber of commerce may have a list of firms that hire summer workers. A quick reference to these services may be found by checking with campus career planning and placement centers and school counselors.

A call to the mayor's office, or a visit to a large library, may turn up a list of job opportunities.

Some civic-minded private employment agencies post free-of-charge summer student jobs. Don't forget to check with the local public job service office, in many states called the Job Service, which we discuss in detail in section 15.

Timetable for Summer Job Hunting

October to November

1. Identify potential employers: companies, agencies, programs.

2. Research the 20 employers you'd most like to work for; write job target sheets.

3. Write (or redo) your resume to match your qualifications to the requirements of the top 20 job prospects.

November to January

1. Each year a booklet is published that catalogs federal summer jobs. Most jobs are for college students, but some are available to high school students. The booklet, known as Announcement 414, is titled "Summer Jobs in the Federal Government for [year]." Copies are available in Federal Job Information Centers, school career centers and libraries.

Much of the information is constant from year to year. If, by the first of December, you can't locate a current copy, ask for a copy from the previous year. It will tell you to which federal agencies you should apply and help you meet the application deadlines, some of which come as early as January.

In addition to federal jobs, ask your counselor or librarian to steer you to lists of city and state government summer jobs.

2. Over holidays, contact people who can hire or refer you to a job. See as many in person as you can. To others, send letters of application and resumes. Submit applications for special programs.

January to March

1. Meet deadlines for government job applications.

2. Continue to apply for jobs.

March to May

1. Contact all companies and agencies that have not replied. Expand your contacts to as many more prospects as you can identify.

June

1. Push the panic button. Try for any type of summer job. Once again, drop a note to your top 20 prospects saying that you are still available if circumstances should change.

Three Best Ways to Use the Phone to Line up Job Interviews

Using the phone to arrange job interviews is an art. Plunge in now; the practice will do you good and may even eliminate the sensation that your mouth is filled with woodworkers' glue whenever you try to ask someone for a job interview.

There are three top techniques for landing interviews by phone.

1. The number-one method is to arrange to be referred by an official source. This might be a counselor, career center employee or employment service specialist. It could be a teacher or professor. The official source probably has knowledge, or at least an inkling, that the target (person you are calling) is in a hiring mode.

"My name is Roy Pfautch. Charlie Pitman at the Baron University Career Center thought that I might be exactly the person to consider hiring for a summer job. With your agreement, I'd like to stop by next Tuesday at 2 o'clock. Would that be convenient or would after 4 be better?"

Keep it simple. All you want to achieve in this call is to gain an interview appointment. Do not give the target an opening to interview you on the phone. If pressed, say "I really want to talk to you about that face to face. When would be the best time?"

2. The second method is to be referred by an unofficial source—friend, relative, virtually anyone.

"My name is Claire Burns. Dr. Scott, I'm a student at Freemont Community College where I'm studying medical assisting. Our friend Allison Cook asked me to call you. She thinks we ought to meet because one day you may need a reliable part-time assistant and I'd like to be at the top of the list. Knowing how busy you are, I'm asking you to set the time at your convenience. When would be the best day?"

You are saying quickly who you are, who knows you, and what you want. You are implying that someone known to the target asked you to call and that the target will gain a benefit by meeting with you.

Another reason to get to the point quickly is so the target will not begin to worry about important calls being missed because of a busy line.

Marilyn Moats Kennedy, who heads Career Strategies, a counseling firm in Evanston, Ill., points out there are exceptions to the advice of getting on and off the phone in a flash. A lengthier call could pay off if you are a very good talker and can keep the conversation going long enough to entice the target's interest. The target will want to protect the investment of time already spent on the phone with you by following up with a meeting.

3. The third in a trio of effective techniques is the telemarketing call. Never call the personnel department and only say, "Do you have any openings?" It is too easy to say "No, sorry." Instead, try this: (to a personnel department employment interviewer, whose name you got from the telephone receptionist) "Hello, my name is Agatha Wisti. I'd like to stop by your office tomorrow to talk about working part time for your company. Would tomorrow morning around 11 be a good time for your schedule or would after lunch be more convenient?"

Although many of you will take this fairly simple approach, there's still a better way.

Do advance research on the name of the person who has the power to hire you. Usually this is the individual who will supervise you. In a small firm of 25 employees or less, ask for the name of the company manager. In a larger firm, ask for the name of the person to whom you would report.

Practice what you are going to say before you call. If you are given a "no help wanted" answer, don't fizzle out like a punctured balloon—keep talking, keep asking for an interview. If you seem to be talking to a stone wall, ask if you can call back in a few days. Your persistence will make a good impression.

While no one expects you to demonstrate golden tonsils, do get yourself in an upbeat mood before making your calls. Sound as though you are an enthusiastic person who has a high energy level. Your telephone personality is the only basis upon which the employer can judge you at this point.

Here's the kind of technique to use. The example is adapted from the book *Who's Hiring Who* by Richard Lathrop (Ten Speed Press).

"Mrs. Botticelli, I'm sure I can do a great job in your department when a part-time job opens up. May I come in to see you?"

Botticelli resists: "We don't have an opening."

"What I'd like to do is show you that I'm the best applicant to hire the next time you do. May I come to see you?"

If Botticelli asks you about your experience, don't crumple because you don't have any. Instead, turn to related strengths.

"In school I showed that I worked hard, fast and with care. People have always liked the jobs I've done for them."

If Botticelli says that's all very nice but that they need better experience than that, keep your mouth running.

"I learn fast and you can count on the fact that I'll work hard for you. I'd sure appreciate the chance to prove it to you. Can I come in to see you?"

Botticelli may say you've earned an interview and set the date, or she may continue to say no. If so, ask if you can call back in several weeks, and ask if she can suggest someone else who can use your abilities.

After you thank her, immediately call any person to whom she referred you and say, "Mrs. Botticelli suggested I call you. . ."

You have lost nothing. If you did not gain an appointment with Mrs. Botticelli, you may have promoted yourself upstairs to the second best way of using a telephone to arrange a job interview.

Looking Like You Belong

Whether or not you will be offered a job often turns on what happens during the first few minutes of contact in an interview.

The reason may be what psychologists call the *halo effect*—if you excel in one area, it is assumed you excel in others.

Dress and grooming play major roles in creating your halo effect.

Although we'll discuss image in greater detail later, the thing to remember is to look as though you belong in the setting to which you aspire.

As a student, your school clothing may be perfect, but, if there's doubt in your mind, ask a counselor, or reconnoiter the workplace in advance of your interview and see what everybody else is wearing.

How to Make the Interviewer Select You

It's showtime! You have resume in hand and you've arranged a job interview. It's time to show your stuff.

Although it may do nothing to calm your nerves, remember that you will be offered the job or rejected because of the impression you make on the interviewer.

Arrive for interviews about five minutes early—never be late. Nobody cares if you got caught in traffic.

Be friendly and well mannered. Avoid the urge to chew gum or smoke anything. Stand still until you're invited to sit. Project a good handshake and remember that a smile improves your looks.

The biggest favor you can do yourself is to anticipate questions and rehearse good answers.

Some typical questions for student jobs include these brain-breakers:

- Tell me about yourself. (Tip: Keep your answer brief. Cover your education, skills, abilities and work attitudes.)
- What school courses do you like best? least? why?
- In which subjects do you do best? worst? why?
- In what activities have you participated?
- Do you drive? own your car?
- What are your skills?
- What are your career plans?
- What hours could you work?
- Why do you want to do this kind of work?
- Why do you want to work for this company?
- Why should we hire you? (Tip: You learn fast, you work hard and you are reliable.)
- Have you ever failed a course in school? (Tip: If the answer is affirmative, admit it and quickly change the subject to a course in which you did well.)

It would be unusual if you were not nervous during your interview performance. As a student, your nervousness will be overlooked as long as your teeth don't chatter and you don't fidget in your chair. The cure for nervousness is to interview often. Practice makes poised.

Watch for clues that the interview is drawing to a close. The interviewer may stand up, or thank you for coming in.

You, in turn, express your thanks to the interviewer. Ask about the next step:

"This job sounds very challenging and I would be grateful for the chance to show you I can do it. When do you think I might hear from you?"

Another tack you can take at this point eliminates the anxiety of waiting long, fingernail-biting days for the phone to ring with a job offer. Say that you may be hard to reach in the next few days and ask if it would be okay if you check back with the employer on a given date.

Going home and writing a thank-you note to the interviewer for the time and consideration given you is one more way to make a favorable impression. And, in case we forgot to mention it, deduct 15 points from your mythical job interviewing score every time you say, "you know."

For advanced job-interviewing suggestions, turn to section 15.

When You're Not Offered the Job

Suppose you wait a week for an answer. Wait no longer. Pick up the phone and ask the interviewer if a decision has been made, or if there is additional information you can supply. Restate your interest in the job.

When You Are Offered the Job

Lucky you. You're among the top picks. You've got the job. Chances are you'll be asked to fill out an employment application even though you have a resume.

Ask for two copies. Fill them out at home. Use one as a drafting copy. Use the other for the neatly completed application.

Remember, a job application is considered a legal document. It's not advisable to stretch the truth.

When you're filling in the blanks, be smarter than the man who was puzzled by the blank space after "Person to notify in case of accident." He wrote, "Anybody in sight."

Hired! Start Your Job on the Right Foot

Once you land a job, there's a simple way to get off to a good start with your boss. On your first day at work, ask for guidance on what is expected of you and the kinds of achievements most valued.

Say something like this: "I'm going to try hard to be the best person on your team. To be sure I've got my signals straight, will you tell me which duties are most important to you? I want to do things your way but I need to double-check that I know what you prefer."

How to Avoid Flops, Flubs, Failures and Fiascoes

Reasons given by business concerns for not hiring young applicants can double as a guide to success on your student job. On the left are some of the reasons and on the right, the corollaries for good performance.

Negative Factor	Corollary
1. Poor personal appearance.	1. Dress appropriately; be neat and clean. Use deodorant.
2. Overbearing know-it-all.	2. Figuratively speaking, don't rearrange the furniture until you're the boss.
3. Inability to express self clearly, poor diction and grammar.	3. As a Chinese fortune cookie says: "Engage brain, start mouth."
4. Lack of interest, enthusiasm.	4. Focus on the job, get involved, show interest. Being lost in space is better left to starships.
5. Interested only in paycheck.	5. Do a fair day's work, remembering that if you goof off, you'll be fired and someone else will get your job.
6. Unwilling to start at bottom, expects too much too soon.	6. Sweep as fast as you can.
7. Makes excuses, is evasive.	7. When you flub, don't invent excuses that shift the blame. Instead, accept the responsibility by apologizing and if you have an acceptable reason for a mistake, blurt it out.
8. Lack of tact.	8. It's okay to be a bit blunt, but never say that your boss is "actually quite perceptive and not entirely stupid."
9. Lack of courtesy.	9. Show your politeness in every way every day. Never elbow the boss aside when racing for the door.
10. Lack of vitality.	10. When you're a tad tired, pep up by sticking your head under the cold water faucet. Claim it's a new hair style.
11. Little sense of humor.	11. Laugh at everything your boss says, assuming it's supposed to be funny.
12. Lazy.	12. Walk briskly, respond to directions quickly, ask for assignments when you have time on your hands.

∞

More Basics for Beginners

Attitude is the magic word for success in a student job. Employers say it makes all the difference. Attitude covers a lot of ground, including criticism.

When your supervisor criticizes you, accept it gracefully because it's not likely you'll do a near-perfect job in the beginning.

Your work habits will be under scrutiny too. Don't let the company phone grow out of your head by making frequent or lengthy personal calls. Keep personal chats with co-workers to a minimum. A radio is an appliance that belongs in your home. Disappearing acts from your work station may result in your permanent departure.

Most employers go through the roof when you are absent without giving advance notice and getting approval. If you're part of a team, your absence can cause major problems. Whenever you will be late, call as soon as you know you'll be among the missing and explain why.

Be sure to honor the time limits of lunch hours and breaks, and stay until quitting time.

Light-fingeredness is very risky business. Walking out with anything that is not yours is stealing and employers are getting tougher on employee theft.

Refuse no assignment within reason or you'll remind the boss of the message inside a greeting card: "I'd wish you a happy birthday, but it's not in my job description."

What Employers Think About You

A survey of employers reported by VICA (Vocational Industrial Clubs of America) asked three questions. Here are the results.

1. *What do you consider to be the major problem of new employees?*
   - Dependability, responsibility.
   - Lack of motivation, initiative.
   - Attendance, punctuality.
   - Selfish attitudes (wants pay without work).

2. *What is the main reason for terminating an employee?*
   - Poor attendance.
   - Poor job performance.
   - Poor punctuality.
     [Other studies show that interpersonal factors—inability to get along with others and politics—is the number-one reason why people are fired.]

3. *What is important for advancement?*
   - Self-motivation, initiative, extra effort.
   - Willingness to accept responsibility.
   - Dependability, reliability.
   - Interest, enthusiasm.

What to Do When the Boss Verbally Mugs You

It happens to experienced workers, too, but young employees are particularly vulnerable to short-fused or unstable employers.

If you are unfortunate enough to be the victim of unfair, brutal verbal attacks, here's how to flameproof your self-esteem against supervisors who enjoy belching fire.

Initial strategy: Remain calm on the outside. Look directly into your boss's eyes. Smile only slightly. Do not speak unless you are asked a direct question, and then respond with a brief, to-the-point answer. Imagine you are dealing with a child having a temper tantrum, but take care not to come across as insubordinate.

Last resort strategy: No defense works 100 percent of the time. If the outbursts are frequent and you're the special target, you have to defend yourself in a more forceful manner to avoid being psychologically scarred.

"I can no longer tolerate your screaming at me. It gives me an upset stomach. Beating on me with words is unfair and it is unreasonable. I may deserve criticism but I don't deserve being yelled at."

Do not be surprised if you are fired on the spot. If so, go immediately to your boss's supervisor, calmly explain what has happened and ask if you can have a letter of recommendation to take with you before you leave.

Keep a Log of Accomplishments

Buy an inexpensive little notebook and as soon as you've mastered your job, begin writing down any accomplishment or contribution you make to the employer's success.

Every few months, summarize your achievements. Remember the measurement technique.

As you'll recall, there are four basic ways to measure. You can use:

1. *Numbers.* "Saved 200 carry-out food cartons from being dumped by mistake."

2. *Percentages.* "By carefully following maintenance procedures, cut service calls on photocopy machine by 50 percent over previous three-month period."

3. *Amounts.* "In needlepoint store, sold $100 more per week than in previous quarter."

4. *Supreme statements.* "Regional supervisor said this movie theater concession stand is the cleanest of any in his group."

As simple as it sounds, keeping a measurable record of your accomplishments can make a big difference at raise time—and on future resumes. Moreover, it's a valuable habit to develop for later in your career.

Capitalists Prosper (Sometimes) in Own Business

You don't want to work for somebody else? OK. Adventuresome students may decide to get off to a fast start in the business world by starting their own mini-businesses.

Some ideas are simple: furniture refinishing, swimming pool cleaning, lawn mowing. Others involve organization: coordinating local garage sales for a percentage of the profits.

Still others—principally those created by hard-charging college students—are a maxi success. A Stanford University student customized tax and accounting software for companies, grossing $300,000 in sales his senior year.

Business ideas abound in such books as *Money-Grubbing: A Student's Guide to Part-time Jobs & Self-run Businesses* by Patrick and Gregory Crowe (Chicago Review Press) and Brett Kingstone's *Student Entrepreneur's Guide* (Ten Speed Press).

Not all student businesses amount to much. Most don't. In fact, some young business owners have a first-hand opportunity to learn about losing money.

Still, some notable successes remind us of this remark by author John Andrew Holmes:

Never tell a young person that anything cannot be done. God may have been waiting for centuries for somebody ignorant enough of the impossible to do that very thing.

SECTION TWELVE

After High School, What?

W*hat shall you do after high school? That's the question of the year*—preferably of the year in which you are a high school junior. Matters can get hectic if you wait until your senior year to make plans.

Often the question of the year is approached through a series of *should I* questions.

- Should I go right to work immediately?
- Should I wait a year before continuing school?
- Should I attend a vocational school to learn a trade?
- Should I go to a small college or a big university?
- Should I choose a technical or liberal arts major?
- Should I join the Air Force?

This section is the first of three that respond to questions about your direction after high school. It addresses the college-bound student, offering a roadmap of considerations that bear on your future career. Students who are not bound for college can turn to section 14.

Among the topics we discuss are education in a changing world; the case for college in a techno-tomorrow; the dwindling importance of admissions tests in the majority of colleges; coaching and test-taking for competitive colleges; paying for college; rating the colleges; cooperative education programs; college internships; federal service academies; university-affiliated technology parks; and taking the first two years at a community college.

The section concludes with an explanation of what accreditation really means and a checklist for selecting your college.

The Third Year Is for Making Plans

Make your plans during your junior year.

You may want to start even earlier. Many prep school students begin college shopping during the summer preceding their junior year; by the summer before their senior year, they have screened out all but the few institutions of greatest interest.

Wait until seniorhood and you may find yourself dismally facing too many loose ends to tie up before important deadlines.

Coping With Last-Minute Jitters

The senior year seems to bring with it stress, tension and truckloads of assorted doubts.

Are you making the right choice? Can you afford college? Do you have the brainpower? Will you fit into your new setting? Is it the kind of future you really want?

You're not alone in your doubts and confusion. Last-minute jitters are common. They go with the mortarboard and gown.

If you suddenly find yourself up in the air about tomorrow, go back to the beginning.

Reviewing the earlier sections of this book can help you reassess what you want to do and what you can do.

You may decide that you were right the first time, or you may decide that you want to change course.

Education in a Changing World

Hundreds of thousands of jobs in steel mills, textile plants, shoe factories and other traditional smokestack workplaces are slipping into history. Caught in the void of bygone industries are a group of unfortunate people, officially called *displaced workers,* whose jobs are gone forever and who often lack the flexibility and skills to effectively search out employment alternatives.

What does the plight of displaced older citizens have to do with you? You're part of a brave new high-tech world, right? Yes and no.

Your generation will be trained to direct computers, lasers, robots and other wonders, but there's also a strong possibility that you'll come up against increasingly sophisticated, gee-whiz machines that can outperform humans in the operation of lesser machines.

Even now there are computers that program other computers and robots that boss robots.

Super automation may create a new generation of displaced workers. That's a distressing thought, but you can take strong, positive steps to protect yourself against becoming a future casualty of a "brotherhood of machines."

The secret to doing well in a rapidly changing society is to acquire the skill of learning.

Learning is a renewable resource. In the years ahead, you may be required to draw upon that resource again and again. If technology should close one door, it may open another; by consciously developing a flexible attitude and by never hesitating to add to your educational power base, you position yourself among those who can cross over new thresholds.

Whether you join the Army, go to a vo-tech school or obtain an advanced university degree, it is important to master fundamental skills upon which future learning can be built.

What are fundamental skills? There are many definitions, but they certainly include written and oral expression, mathematics, analytical thinking and creative responsiveness to problems.

No matter what basic mix you accept, the point is: From a strong foundation, you can branch out in many directions—as required by changing circumstances.

Learn to think.

Learn to learn.

Why We Favor College for Many Students

You may notice that colleges and universities get the lion's share of attention in this section. There's a good reason for the focus.

A recent U.S. Labor Department study reports that college programs lasting four years or longer provide qualifying training to more workers than all other postsecondary school categories combined.

Even so, remember that not everyone shows championship form in the most traveled waters and you may find your best prospects are not found on college campuses but elsewhere. We'll discuss that later in this section. But for now—college, here we come!

The Case for College in a Techno-Tomorrow

As you envision a lifetime when computers sometimes outthink humans, customers shop by video terminal, and robots do windows, a nagging thought may lurk in the recesses of your mind: Is college as important as it once was?

In the '60s and '70s, mortarboard mania was epidemic; about half of the nation's high school graduates were urged to attend college whether they wanted to or not.

Now, in the closing, highly automated years of the 20th century, you may be pondering the possibility that college is losing its punch as a favorite strategy to reach money, power and status.

If so, you are in the minority. A short decade ago, one-third of the public thought that college was very important. Today? Two-thirds say it's the way to go, according to a recent Gallup survey.

Many college students are choosing job-related curricula. Here is a list of the top 10 majors in the 1980s. Of every 100 undergraduate degrees, this many are for

Business management	23.4
Education	10.1
Social sciences	9.8
Engineering	7.5
Health sciences	6.7
Psychology	4.2
Life sciences	4.1
Visual and performing arts	4.1
Communications	3.8
Letters	3.4

Among the reasons for obtaining a college education, consider the effect on a career.

As a college graduate, you are likely to earn more money than do non-graduates, suffer less unemployment, and hold superior positions. Lifetime earnings of a man with a college degree are nearly 50 percent more than those of a man with only a high school diploma.

The Bureau of Census shows the lifetime earnings picture by educational level. These projections are averages for persons who were 18 years old in 1979 and who will work until age 65.

	High School 4 years	*College 1–3 years*	*College 4 years*
Men	$861,000	$957,000	$1,190,000
Women	$381,000	$460,000	$ 523,000

Even the starting pay for college graduates often outpaces typical earnings for the population as a whole. Median earnings for full-time workers are $20,400 per year. This is the *going* rate of pay for people of all ages, of all educational attainment, whether they have been working for 30 years or just starting out.

Compare that rate to the median *starting* salary offers by major to recent graduates, according to the College Placement Council.

Petroleum engineering	$32,040
Chemical engineering	$30,420
Electrical engineering	$29,400
Mechanical engineering	$28,800
Computer science	$27,000
Mathematics	$26,400
Civil engineering	$24,000
Health professions	$24,000
Biological sciences	$22,596
Accounting	$21,996
Social sciences	$20,448
Marketing, distribution	$20,004
Business	$19,992
Humanities	$19,500
Agricultural sciences	$18,636

College graduates have the edge in job security too. In the late '80s, the unemployment rate for college graduates 25 to 64 years old is less than 3 percent, compared with more than 7 percent for high school graduates.

Various studies report that most college graduates obtain jobs in fields related to their majors; that several years after graduation most male graduates have relatively high status occupations, and that roughly 90 percent of college graduates are satisfied with their occupations.

Other education research calls attention to the benefits of old-school ties. Many employers regard the college you attended as one of the most important considerations in first-job hiring decisions.

Finally, some of the most attractive occupations, such as engineers and teachers, are closed to those who lack a college degree.

Jobs, though, aren't the only reason to study yourself into the ground and perhaps go in debt for an education.

The following comments are by a U.S. Secretary of Education, William J. Bennett. He makes strong points in explaining how you benefit from exposure to all the major disciplines—history, science, literature, mathematics and foreign language. In Dr. Bennett's words:

College should *be a road to your ambitions. But every student should take the time to tread the ground outside his or her major, and to spend some time in the company of the great travelers who have come before.*

Why? Put simply, because they can help you lead a better and perhaps happier life. If we give time to studying how men and women of the past have dealt with life's enduring problems, then we will be better prepared when those same problems come our way. We may be a little less surprised to find treachery at work in the world about us, a little less startled by unselfish devotion, a little readier to believe in the capacity of the human mind.

And what does that do for a future career? As Hamlet said, "readiness is all." In the end, the problems we face during the course of a career are the same kind that we face in the general course of life.

If you want to be a corporate executive, how can you learn about not missing the right opportunities? One way is to read Hamlet. *Do you want to learn about the dangers of overweening ambition? Read* Macbeth. *Want to know the pitfalls of playing around on the job? Read* Antony and Cleopatra. *The importance of fulfilling the responsibilities entrusted to leadership? Read* King Lear.

Even in the modern world, it is still that peculiar mix of literature, science, history, math, philosophy and language that can help mature minds come to grips with the age-old issues, the problems that transverse every plane of life. Students who bring to college the willingness to seek out those issues, to enliven the spirit and broaden the mind, will be more likely to profit in any endeavor.

More Good Reasons for Going to College

As you approach the milestone of high school graduation, you may need help in clarifying your thoughts about college. Here are more reasons to invest in a college education.

Knowledge and Intellectual Development

No overwhelming research *proves* that intellectual development and training to think are nourished by the college experience, but it is logical to assume that few students know less about a subject at the end of a course than they knew at the beginning.

Even so, couldn't you do as well by reading books on your own? Perhaps, but educators say most people will find the college experience far more enriching. Going to class, reciting, asking questions of the professor, being stimulated by other students, reviewing for exams, gathering your thoughts and knowledge to prepare a term paper—all these factors reinforce learning in ways that independent reading can't.

Social Development

College attendance is associated with growing up socially.

Researchers say that college students often become more liberal in their attitudes, more politically and socially sophisticated, and more competent in working with others than do non-students.

Researchers assert that college graduates are more tolerant and exhibit less prejudice toward persons who are different from themselves.

Personal Growth

Individual self-esteem seems to bloom in college students. A theory is that higher education provides a range of resources from which you can build a sound psychological base. You learn, for example, where to find the information you need, which helps you remain open to new ideas.

College—A Good Investment for Many

The case for college attendance to prepare for a techno-tomorrow is a strong one. It is not the only way to prepare—as we discuss later in this section—but it is one of the best.

On the average, college attendance is associated with career enhancement, intellectual attainment, and social and personal growth. Compared with those who have not gone to college, college graduates know more, hold better jobs and earn more money.

College and Students With Disabilities

In 1949 the University of Illinois at Urbana-Champaign was the only institution equipped to accommodate physically disabled veterans returning from World War II. Today, in many ways, the picture is much brighter. Most schools across the country have taken steps to make their campuses accessible not only to physically disabled students but also to sensory- and learning-disabled people.

Moreover, most students with disabilities are admitted to America's colleges on much the same basis as able-bodied applicants with comparable qualifications, according to a College Board study.

Not all disabilities are treated equally in admissions decisions, however. Admissions were lower than expected for learning disabled, visually impaired and physically disabled students, but hearing-impaired applicants were admitted more often than their grades and test scores would suggest.

Read: *How to Choose a College: Guide for the Student with a Disability,* and *Financial Aid and Disabled Students.* Both publications are available free from the HEATH Resource Center, Suite 800, One Dupont Circle, Washington, DC 20036; toll-free telephone: 800-544-3284; District of Columbia residents call 202-939-9320.

Is College for You? Questions and Answers

Q. *My grades in high school were terrible. What college would have me?*

A. No matter how dismal your high school grades, you can find a college that will accept you. Open admissions (the policy of accepting all high school graduates to an institution's limit of capacity) is more prevalent now than it was a decade ago. You will, of course, have to take remedial courses in college to make up for what you didn't learn in high school.

Q. *I hated high school. Isn't college more of the same?*

A. An odd thing happens to many students who thought high school was the pits. Once they get on campus, they find they like it! In high school, teachers and school authorities were breathing down your neck. Even as a senior, you had to follow many of the same rules you faced as a freshman.

In college, the rigid atmosphere is gone. You'll have freedom you've never known before. No one is breathing down your neck or even looking over your shoulder. If you need help, you have to go after it.

Q. *Nobody in my family ever went to college; I am afraid that others will look down on me because I have not had their advantages and we do not have a lot of money. My high school wasn't the best. I sometimes think about going to college, but then I think that I should stick with the kind of life I know.*

A. These fears remind us of fleet-footed huskies pulling sleds in Alaska: The scenery only changes for the lead dog.

Move ahead. In any family, one individual has to pioneer. Can you think of any reason why it shouldn't be you? Sure, there's a possibility that in your first days at college, you'll feel uncomfortable, and even a bit inferior. You're not alone. As you make friends on campus, you will discover that others feel uneasy too. Gaining confidence, you'll begin to think college is a pretty good idea after all.

Here are a couple of common-sense suggestions to help.

If your educational preparation wasn't all it could have been, look into ways to obtain tutorial or special catch-up help. Many colleges offer classes or workshops to strengthen students' academic skills.

As for money, become expert on how the student financial-aid system operates. Do not rely solely on awards from the financial aid officer at your college.

Q. *I just want to have a good time in college. Is it fair to my parents to enroll when I have no intention of exhausting myself studying?*
A. No, it's not fair if your parents are struggling to put you through school.

Q. *I am interested in trying college but to be honest, I never stick with any one hobby or activity very long. What can I do to stay in school once I start?*
A. Campus involvement is the tie that binds. A leading education researcher, Alexander W. Astin, observes that students who rarely make contact with faculty members are good drop-out prospects.

Dr. Astin reports that students maximize their chances of finishing college when they do not commute, but instead go away from home and live in college housing, when they get a part-time job on the campus, when they join social organizations and when they participate in extracurricular activities.

The message is clear: Get involved.

Q. *If I decide late in my senior year that I really do want to go to college, can I still go?*
A. The majority of colleges have openings as late as a *month* before the start of a semester. Once you make up your mind, race to your high school counselor's office.

Many community colleges will accept you as late as the day of registration.

Q. *Will a college degree guarantee me a good job?*
A. No. You cannot be certain you'll get a good job just because you're a college graduate. If you have decided on a major, you can compare the job placement results for similar majors at different schools. Ask career planning and placement offices at various colleges for the figures. If 85 percent of plastics engineers from one college found jobs, but only 45 percent were hired from another school, find out what caused the difference.

The Tests to Take

Test taking for college admission is one of life's necessary evils. Because you usually can't avoid testing if you're campus bound, learn good test-taking practices from a book, a course, or your counselor.

Even when you're well prepared, tension can put knots in your thinking process. Before a test, try to relax. Here's a sure-fire way to take the sting out of stress: breathe slower.

The trick is to slow your breathing to a seven-second inhale and an eight-second exhale. Do four cycles a minute for two minutes and your stress should vanish.

How can you count if you don't have a second hand on your watch? Try a word clock. Put a number in front of a three syllable word to equal one second, like this: *one vic-to-ry, two vic-to-ry,* and so forth.

This stress-releasing technique works for taking tests, and also for other punishing situations, such as making speeches or going on job interviews.

Now, here are the most commonly given tests.

Preliminary Scholastic Aptitude Test/National Merit Scholarship Qualifying Test (PSAT/NMSQT)

This test is administered by the College Board each year, on two days in late October. The test is divided into two segments: verbal and mathematical. Scores on each part range from 20 to 80. This test is designed for juniors, and it is also given to interested sophomores as a practice test.

Scores are reported as a National Merit Selection Index which is derived by doubling the verbal score and adding the math score (2V + M = Selection Index). National Merit Scholarship semifinalists are determined by the Selection Index. Generally, to be ranked as a semifinalist, a student must have an index of 200 or more (this varies from year to year). At a level just below the semifinalists are the commended students who usually have an index of 185 or more.

The test must be taken in the junior year if a student is to qualify for National Merit consideration.

Scholastic Aptitude Test (SAT)

This College Board test includes three sections: verbal, mathematical, and the test of standard written English. Scores on the verbal and math sections range from 200 to 800 per section (a total of 1600 points for both). Applications and test schedules are available at every high school.

Often called the *college boards,* this test is given as many as seven times, depending on geographic location, during the school year. Many students take the test in the spring of their junior year; all college hopefuls should plan to take the SAT before January of their senior year. Students planning to apply for early admissions decision programs should complete all required testing by the end of their junior year. College-bound students usually score at least 800 (out of 1600) total points.

American College Test (ACT)

This test is chiefly used by many midwestern, southern, and western colleges instead of the SAT. It includes scores for English, mathematics, social studies reading, and natural sciences reading. Scores range from 0 to 36. College-bound students usually score between 15 and 21 points.

P-ACT+ (Preliminary American College Test Plus) is a new practice test with added components for career planning. You can take it as a sophomore.

Achievement Tests (ACH)

These College Board tests are administered in 15 subjects: American history and social studies, biology, chemistry, English composition, European history and world cultures, French, German, Hebrew, Latin, literature, mathematics-level I, mathematics-level II, physics, Russian, and Spanish. Scores range from 200 to 800. Not all colleges require achievement tests, and many colleges say they do not use the results for admissions purposes.

Advanced Placement Tests (AP)

These College Board tests are for high school students who are taking college-level course work in certain subjects. The tests are graded 1 through 5. Many colleges award credits, usually three to five, to students who earn high scores. Students decide whether to submit these test results to the colleges.

Test of English as a Foreign Language (TOEFL)

Students—mostly foreign—whose first language is not English take this test. The results will help the college evaluate their verbal ability.

Critics Give Some Tests Failing Grades

Standardized college admissions tests are under fire.

Critics question whether the exams can accurately predict academic performance. They say the tests do not measure aptitude (your potential) but simply achievement (what you already know).

Detractors insist the existing tests measure only minimum levels of skills, factual recall and theoretical knowledge. They say tests ignore such qualities as judgment, ambition, drive and values. Tests do not show how well individuals would apply their knowledge in meeting daily challenges.

Moreover, some critics say the exams are biased against minorities and the poor.

A number of selective colleges, such as Middlebury in Vermont and Union in New York, have made the SAT optional. Some administrators believe students should be spending their time studying Dickens and Shakespeare, not being coached for the SAT.

The National Center for Fair & Open Testing has released a report claiming that women lose out on National Merit Scholarships because the SAT underpredicts their ability to do college work.

In his book, *College: The Undergraduate Experience in America* (Carnegie Foundation for the Advancement of Teaching), former U.S. Secretary of Education Ernest L. Boyer says a majority of deans surveyed do not take SAT results seriously.

The backlash against the aptitude test industry, plus the availability of new technology, is causing testmakers to rush forth a new generation of computerized tests they hope will quiet the critics, although the types of questions most likely will be the same.

One day you may find yourself before a keyboard taking a computer-adaptive test that uses mathematical models to tailor questions to your particular ability.

The computer does not follow the paper-and-pencil style of asking a series of questions based on average capabilities of people taking the test. Instead, the computer adjusts the difficulty of each question to the correctness of the answer you gave on the previous question.

The purported intent of the new computerized custom testing is to more accurately measure your capabilities.

That's not all that's changing in the testing industry. In addition to using computers in an adaptive mode, tomorrow's exams will provide computer-aided graphics, animation and artificial intelligence technology to measure such things as visual, motor, spatial and memory skills.

Doctors, for example, may face computer simulations of lifelike situations before being granted a license. A typical question shows an injured person admitted to an emergency room. The doctor must decide a treatment and deal with the consequences of wrong decisions.

If you're scheduled for a computer adaptive test, ask your counselor for a practice run.

A Contemporary Perspective on Tests and Admissions

The pool of 18-year-olds is shrinking. Except for the top schools—the ones that are harder to get into than Fort Knox—colleges and universities are marketing hard to keep their doors open.

Thus, higher education has moved from a sellers market of a generation ago to a buyer's market today. The change forces colleges to be more flexible about admittance requirements. In news reports, some admissions officials from less competitive colleges straightforwardly admit they are paying less attention to aptitude tests these days in the scramble to fill freshman seats.

What this means is that you can put off having a nervous breakdown because your SAT or ACT scores leave much to be desired. You can get into some college somewhere.

But if you've got your eye on the top of the line, your SAT and ACT scores matter a lot.

When the SAT and ACT Loom Large

Earning very high scores on the SAT or ACT is not of earth-shaking consequence for entrance into most institutions of higher education, except in three instances:

1. When you are trying to get into one of the most selective colleges.
2. When you want to attend a state university (or federal service academy) that limits enrollments by requiring minimum SAT or ACT scores.
3. When you are competing for a merit scholarship.

If you are interested in applying to one of the most highly selective schools, listen to Katie McCabe, a test-prep coach, teacher and writer working in the Washington, D.C. area:

> *The name of the game, at the top level, is a flawless package: an SAT total of 1350 plus [or an ACT total of 31], neatly in line with a 3.8 [out of 4.0] grade-point average (to avoid the fatal "underachiever" label), top-5-percent class rank, stellar essays and recommendations, an impressive leadership record, and a good interview presence.*

While you will want to check college guidebooks for more details on relationships between test scores and specific institutions, McCabe gives a concise overview:

> *Viewed by colleges and applicants alike as an index of raw brainpower, the SAT for 60 years has sifted college-bound students into categories along a 1,600-point yardstick. The national norm is 900. Frequently, the doors to [competitive] state schools open at 1,000 to 1,100, to competitive private colleges at 1,200, to the Ivies at 1,300.*

Comparable figures for the ACT would be: Of a possible composite score of 34.5, the national norm is 18.6. You may get into competitive state schools with a score of 26, into competitive colleges with 29, into the top schools with 30.

McCabe mentioned only the SAT because she was addressing an East Coast audience; the SAT is dominant in the East and in California, Oregon, Hawaii, and Indiana.

In 28 states in the West, South and Midwest, the ACT is the most used admissions test.

The ACT and the SAT are each taken by about one million high school seniors yearly.

A new wrinkle—brought about by institutions trying to enroll the maximum number of students—is the increasing acceptance by colleges of either test. Nearly 1,400 colleges take either SAT or ACT scores, while some 200 accept only SAT and another 300 accept only ACT.

Generally speaking, any college that can afford the luxury of turning away applicants probably will use test scores as a key screening device.

There's one more thing to know about admissions tests. College officials use tests for more than admissions decisions; they use them to help place students once they have been admitted. If, for instance, your math scores are on the low side, you may be required to take certain basic math courses.

Allow plenty of time if you decide you're going to prepare for your admissions tests, remembering the Chinese proverb: Dig a well before you are thirsty.

Can Coaching Boost Your Scores?

Coaching for the SAT and ACT has been available for years, but test preparation courses did not become a growth industry until the early '80s.

A decade ago, several groups, from the federal government to Ralph Nader to Harvard professors, studying the coaching issue affirmed the value of test preparation. In essence, they said "It works."

In Montgomery County, Md., Joseph Monte agrees. In 25 years of counseling students, the former president of the National Association of College Admissions Counselors says he has seen large numbers of students helped by coaching.

Today there's little doubt that coaching does work and that it is possible to turn a student into a "test expert."

In fact, top training groups claim they can boost scores on the SAT by an average of 100 to 150 points out of a maximum of 1,600. We believe improvement of ACT scores is comparable.

Once the word about coaching success spreads, students rush to sign up for courses.

Stanley H. Kaplan, the man who practically invented the coaching business, says, "The more who go for coaching, the more who want it."

At the very least, coaching makes you familiar with the testing process. If you're a person who panics at the mention of the word "test," a dress rehearsal will give you the confidence to score up to your potential.

The cost of test-prep courses—$200 to $600—probably makes you wonder if you can't turn coaching into a do-it-yourself project. Yes, of course you can. The drawback is that while you may learn as much on your own about test *content,* you may overlook important *strategies* known by test-wise instructors.

As one young woman has said, "It would be better to prepare on your own than not at all, but I feel the course gave me a little edge over what I could produce myself. I found questions on my exam that were very similar to what I had been given in the course. You make up so much time when that happens it makes you feel better about the test and you're able to do better overall."

But if you do want to study on your own, here are four of the most popular resources (available in bookstores, libraries or by mail order).

- *Preparation for the ACT* by William Gladstone (Simon & Schuster), a comprehensive study aid with simulated exams.

- *The ACT Assessment Sample Test Booklet and Answer Sheet—Number 2 and Number 3.* Both booklets of actual past tests are available only by mail for a total cost of $4 from ACT Records, Box 451, Iowa City, IA 52243.

- *How to Prepare for the Scholastic Aptitude Test* by Samuel C. Brownstein and Mitchel Weiner (Barron's Educational Series).

- *Ten SATS: Scholastic Aptitude Tests of the College Board* (College Board), a collection of actual past tests.

Although test-prep may be in your future, remember that getting a high test score—after intense preparation—will not necessarily provide the winning ticket in the Great American Selective College Sweepstakes. High test scores alone are unlikely to force admission to a school that wants a total package other than what you offer.

If you want coaching, get it well before the first SAT is taken in the spring of your junior year. Test-prep programs vary in length from five to a dozen weeks.

Because *all* SAT scores are sent to colleges, a single high score is more likely to put a smile on an admissions officer's face than a series of varying scores. The officer has to wonder which score reflects more accurately your academic capacity—"Will the real test score please stand up?"

However, if you have a particular college in mind and you haven't scored in that school's range, it can be worthwhile to retake the tests.

With ACT, the student can specify which score is to be sent to colleges.

How to Choose a Coaching Program

If coaching is going to make a difference for you, it's important to pick the most appropriate program.

Depending on where you live, you may choose from such national test-prep agencies as the Stanley H. Kaplan Educational Centers or the Princeton Review, or from regional or local educational services. Some high schools offer coaching courses. In a number of communities you'll find special programs for learning-disabled students, as well as computer-based SAT courses.

Begin shopping test-prep courses with a visit to your school counselor, who will probably refer you to a number of services.

We suggest you make a chart to compare features of each service. Here are things you want to know:

Comments

Guarantee. Some coaching agencies offer a guarantee to raise your test score by a specified amount. If it doesn't happen, the guarantee may include a promise to let you retake the course without charge, or to give you a refund. Other agencies don't offer a guarantee in the same sense, but do allow you to take the course as many times as you wish without additional cost for as long as one year. Still other agencies offer no guarantee, retakes or refund.

It's a mistake to choose a course on the basis of score guarantees alone. If you think about it, nobody can guarantee that you will achieve a score gain—it's up to you. Guarantees are merely a marketing approach. Be sure you read the terms of the guarantee and fully understand what rights you have to a refund or to take the course over. Remember, too, schools prefer a single strong score rather than several varying scores.

Tuition Cost. Here are some typical costs: $400 for 11 classes/44 hours, plus unlimited use of a test and tape learning lab for up to one year; $550 for 10 classes plus extra-help sessions; $250 for eight classes plus access to tapes; $175 for eight classes plus a computer software package.

The most expensive course may not be the best for you. The cost usually is based on the number of students in the class, the number of sessions and the package of learning materials. There is no easy guide to value. Your best gauge is to decide how hard you want to work and for how long.

Ask, too, whether you must pay the full amount in advance or if installment payments are acceptable.

Scholarship Availability. If you can't pay for coaching, don't hesitate to ask for scholarship assistance. A good coaching program will evaluate your situation and give you a helping hand if you really need it.

Duration of Course. How long can you keep your nose to the test-prep grindstone? Courses last from 5 to 11 weeks. Most provide supplemental learning materials—audio- or video-tapes, computer software and other self-drill exercises. Homework assignments may be scant or take eight hours a week. If you have a short attention span, you need a condensed course, but—and this is important—don't confuse condensed courses with cram courses that are of little value with their formula-memorizing routines. When you have severe knowledge-flow problems, stretch out the course as long as possible.

Class Size. Stanley Kaplan feels strongly that the class should not exceed 20 students, with 15 being ideal. In his observation, too-small classes of six or seven students can lose the stimulation of interaction among classmates. One-on-one tutoring may be what you need, but expect it to be more costly than group study.

School Address. A permanent address suggests stability. Be cautious of a test-prep agency that operates out of a post office box or telephone answering service.

Test-Prep Comparison Chart

Guarantee ______________________________
(retake, refund, no)

Tuition Cost ______________________________
(amount; payable in advance or installments)

____

Scholarship Availability ______________________________
(yes, no)

Duration of Course ______________________________
(number of weeks)

____

Class Size ______________________________
(under 25, over 25, private tutoring)

School Address ______________________________
(street address or box number)

____

Content, Strategy Mix ______________________________
(emphasis on one or the other, or blend)

____

Learning Materials ______________________________
(cost, availability, type)

____

Course Currency ______________________________
(when course last updated)

____

Instructor's Background ______________________________
(college degree; experience in coaching SAT, ACT)

____

Class Frequency, Homework Assignments ______________________________
(how often is class and how many hours of homework)

____

Accessibility ______________________________
(near, far)

____

Computer Instruction ______________________________
(software only provided, or combined with instructor's tutoring)

Content, Strategy Mix. While it's important to understand when and how to use guessing strategies, having a genuine knowledge of test content will serve you better in the long run.

Content is the subject matter you are trying to learn.

One test-prep agency, operating on the theory that the tests are beatable, focuses on strategies. This approach can be of some benefit for top students but does a disservice to average or below-average students whose lack of fundamental knowledge may cause them to go blank when confronted with unfamiliar material.

The best courses blend test-taking strategy with test content preparation.

Learning Materials. Is the cost of materials included in the tuition fee? If not, how much more must you spend? If you have access to a learning center, is it conveniently located?

Course Currency. Be sure your course is using current test programs. Ask when the course was last updated.

Instructor's Background. Ask the test-prep agency who will teach the course and whether the instructor is a college graduate. Find out how much experience the instructor has had with SAT or ACT; a rookie may know the technical side of the course but contribute little advice about test-taking skills.

Class Frequency, Homework Assignments. Expect to attend weekly classes and receive homework assignments. The instructor should monitor your progress each week.

Accessibility. Is the test-prep program 50 miles or a bike ride away? A lengthy commute is inconvenient and may invite absenteeism.

Computer Instruction. A criticism of SAT or ACT computer workshops is that the software packages are lax on strategy, do not reflect actual test questions and fail to include paper-pencil practice. Some courses get around that by combining software packages with tutoring and throwing in paper-pencil exercises.

WHAT COLLEGES LOOK FOR

Selective institutions—also called competitive institutions—can afford to be choosy. They enjoy swarms of applicants, many more than they can absorb.

The number of selective colleges in the United States is disputed. We agree with most education authorities who use the figure of 50 to 60 institutions. Others maintain that 117 institutions are in the most selective category—those that accept less than half of their applicants.

Studies show that while two college admissions committees rarely paint on the same canvas, most picture the following criteria as the major factors influencing their decisions.

The two big numbers are *grade point average* (GPA) and *class rank.* Next comes *admissions test scores.* If you've got lousy grades, you usually can save the day with great test scores; if your test scores are weak but your GPA is impressive, you still can look like a desirable student. In a selective college, academic factors range from between 50 percent and 75 percent of the overall evaluation.

Your school's *academic challenge* receives consideration. Top grades from a secondary school known for the rigor of its studies command more respect than top grades from a school thought to be mediocre. This is why prep school students often have an advantage over public school students in seeking entry to competitive colleges.

Course selection counts too. Students who have labored through tough courses are more impressive to admissions people than students who have taken soft loads. Admissions appraisers also frown on those who loaf through their senior year because slacking off does not keep you in training for the college work load.

Advanced placement and *honors courses* add a few gold stars to your application.

After GPA, class rank and admissions test scores, admissions evaluators are interested in your *extra-curricular activities*—and in this case, less may be more.

Rather than hopping all over the activities map, concentrate on doing a few things extremely well. The qualities you want to show are persistence, that you can follow through on a project with significant results, and that your activities have focus. Leadership positions in school organizations are ideal for this.

Next on the college entry scale comes *recommendations* from teachers, counselors and alumni. While glowing references do make a favorable impression, run-of-the-mill references may not count for much because recommendations no longer are confidential. Fearing a lawsuit, reference givers are reluctant to say anything bad about you and admissions people know this.

What about personal interviews? Don't they count in the admissions process? Surveys say not. In a recent study by the Educational Testing Service, colleges reported they place little credence on personal interviews in admissions decisions. Use your meetings with admissions officers to gather information about institutions.

If you are asked to write an essay, choose a personal topic, perhaps an event that affected your life, rather than an abstract subject such as world peace.

Beyond basic criteria, some students enjoy what can be called an "ace in the hole." When all else is equal, they may have an edge. Who fits in this elite group? Sons and daughters of alumni, minority students, athletes, musicians and others with notable talents.

When the time comes to set facts to paper, keep a couple of common-sense points in mind.

Fill out your applications neatly. Hard-to-read forms are annoying. Set aside enough time to write or type a legible, clean, grammatical, properly spelled and altogether well-done application.

The same rule applies to essays, if you are asked to write one. When college representatives ask you to submit an essay, count on its being read.

Sometimes it will pay to include documentation along with your application. If you are a musician, it may be wise to send a tape of your music. If you are an artist, enclose a couple of slides of your best work. Be very selective in sending supplemental materials.

Suppose you are not setting your sights on a highly competitive college and you know that most colleges will welcome your application. Does this mean you can offer less than your best presentation?

No way. It may be just your luck to set your heart on Podunk U. on the outskirts of the end of the world, only to find that overnight Podunk U. has blossomed into a hot school and suddenly is turning away applicants, including you.

Do more than your best. Read up on admissions dynamics in such books as *Peterson's Guide to College Admissions* by R. Fred Zuker and Karen C. Hegener (Peterson's Guides).

Paying for College

The cost of a four-year degree at a private, upscale college runs $60,000 or $70,000, sometimes more. At state schools, the total tab adds up to $20,000 or $30,000.

Paying college bills is far too broad a subject to discuss here in detail, but we offer several basic start-up tips.

- Learn the student financial aid system. Although most aid is directed toward those with the greatest financial need, millions of dollars are awarded in merit scholarships.

Education dollars do not always go to the student most entitled to receive them. They go to the student most expert at finding and applying for them.

Among the many student financial aid guides on the market, an inexpensive primer that provides an overview of the aid system is *The College Financial Aid Emergency Kit* by Dr. Herm Davis and Joyce Lain Kennedy. It's available only by mail for $4.50 from Sun Features Inc., Box 368M, Cardiff, CA 92007.

Another inexpensive guide is *Need a Lift? To Educational Opportunities, Career Loans, Scholarships, Employment.* Published annually, it's available for $1 from the American Legion Education Program, Box 1050, Indianapolis, IN 46206. (The price is subject to increase for the 1988-89 edition.)

For a full listing, see a library copy of a major reference like *Scholarships, Fellowships and Loans* by Dr. S. Norman Feingold and Marie Feingold (Bellman Publishing Co.).

- Become an educated borrower. Most American families today must borrow to finance college. They obtain loans from the federal government, state agencies, colleges themselves and commercial institutions.

- The first place to begin prospecting for funds is at a college's financial aid office. The aid officer controls a wellspring of benefits.

- Timing is of utmost importance. Not only do students lose out because they miss application deadlines but also because much aid is awarded on a first-come, first-served basis. Apply for aid early in January of the year you enter college and don't wait until you have all your tax forms—estimate your parents' income from the previous year.

The freshman year of high school is not too soon to discover how the student financial aid system works.

- Apply to a favorite college even if it looks like it's too rich for your pocket. When there's a chance you'll stand in the upper 25 percent of the freshman class, you'll be seen as a valuable recruit and it is reasonable to assume you'll be offered generous aid. If it doesn't work out, at least you'll have the satisfaction of knowing you gave it your best shot.

- Be realistic but not intimidated in your expectations. Student aid comes in packages—a mix of loan money which you pay back, scholarship and grant money which you do not pay back, and student job opportunities.

If two schools of otherwise equal appeal offer differing financial aid packages, obviously you'll choose the most beneficial to you. If you really prefer the school with the lesser financial aid package, you might negotiate an improved offer—no school likes to lose a new recruit to a direct competitor.

If you feel the aid offer is drastically under market and you want to attend the college, never hesitate to appeal the award to the school's director of financial aid. Many students think an award offer is set in concrete. It's not. It may be negotiable. Remember, higher education is a buyer's market.

AMERICA'S COLLEGES

From sea to shining sea there are more than 3,200 higher-education institutions.

How many are two-year colleges? At last count, 1,270.

How many are four-year colleges? Approximately 1,850.

How many are universities? Only 156.

Now that you know the numerical shape of higher education, according to the Center for Educational Statistics, what direction will you pursue—liberal arts or vocationally oriented studies? Which environment will be most compatible—urban, suburban or rural? Traditional, contemporary or avant-garde? Coed or single-sex? Large or small? Public or private? Selective admissions requirements or less-selective? How far away from home are you willing to travel—20 miles or 2,000? North, east, south or west?

It's a tough choice, all right. Later, we offer a step-by-step guide to help you make the right one. First, a few considerations as you explore options in a land rich with higher education opportunities.

Classifying the Colleges and Universities

Traditionally, the difference between colleges and universities has been that the latter provide graduate education. It's no longer easy to tell what's what. Bryn Mawr College in Pennsylvania offers doctorates; the two-year Bassist College in Oregon offers master's degrees; Miami University (Middletown Campus), a two-year college in Ohio, offers associate degrees.

Nevertheless, understanding that different categories of institutions of higher education exist can be useful in determining which type best meets your needs.

Here is a representative cluster developed by the Carnegie Foundation for the Advancement of Teaching.

Four-year Institutions

(Graduate programs require one or more additional years of study.)

- *Research Universities*—oriented to research, receiving many government and private research grants; focus on graduate education; national in scope.
- *Doctoral-Granting Institutions*—focus also on graduate education, but less oriented to research; national or regional.
- *Comprehensive*—in addition to liberal arts, these institutions offer one or more occupational or professional programs; national or regional.
- *Liberal Arts*—colleges offering the classic broad education favored for fundamental knowledge; national or regional.

Two-year Institutions

- *Community Colleges, Junior Colleges, Technical Institutes*—although termed two-year colleges for convenience, occupational programs may last from one year to three years; transfer programs are two years; regional or local.

Rating the Colleges

Which are the nation's best campuses for undergraduate study? Stock answers and certain school names leap to mind, but why not develop a deeper understanding of the issue?

The real answer to the best-colleges question depends on who is doing the rating. Is it academicians—faculty, deans, college presidents? Or is it students, alumni, employers?

Sometimes academicians recognize that a college has shot up in quality, passing longtime favorites; employers, however, may not get the word for years.

Most authorities agree that the number of the best undergraduate colleges ranges between 300 and 350; and at the very top, there probably are no more than 50 to 60 institutions.

As you gather data on various colleges, jot down each institution's degree of difficulty for entrance. Here's a simple scale:

1. Highly selective (most difficult to enter).
2. Selective (choosy).
3. Traditional (most people can qualify).
4. Liberal (a minimal academic orientation is okay).
5. Open (anyone can enroll).

If you want to know the best schools, here are several places to look.

Peterson's Competitive Colleges (Peterson's Guides) contains comparative data on more than 300 colleges that consistently attract a surplus of undergraduate applicants. Profiles of freshman classes indicate each school's degree of entrance difficulty. Published annually, the introductory text offers valuable advice:

Far too many students choose colleges for the wrong reasons. For example, many go to a local university, not because they know it will contribute to their intellectual and professional development, but because of convenience or territorial chauvinism.

Thousands of high school juniors receive the guide free, but if you miss out, you can buy it in bookstores or directly from the publisher.

In odd-numbered years, the editors of *U.S. News & World Report* magazine ask college presidents to choose the nation's best campuses. Survey results appear in the magazine in late November, and in a book, *America's Best Colleges and Professional Schools* (U.S. News & World Report, Inc.).

Two well-known books are by *New York Times* education editor Edward B. Fiske: *Selective Guide to Colleges;* and *The Best Buys in College Education.* Both books are published by Times Books/Random House.

Another useful book is *A Student's Guide to College Admissions: Everything Your Guidance Counselor Has No Time to Tell You,* by Harold G. Unger (Facts on File).

Recently, a number of lively books about the academic and social life on many campuses have appeared. Several in particular are zippy reading, but as you read, ask: Does the author have a background in education and did the author survey academicians, students, alumni or employers?

Small or Large?

Some institutions are small—more than 700 colleges have fewer than 500 students. Others are huge—more than 100 institutions enroll 20,000 students or more.

The attraction of a large institution is fairly obvious: It's a shopping center of educational programs and offers name recognition, superior resources and, often, famous faculty members.

A huge college can be a fast, somewhat impersonal track and best suits students who feel comfortable in a crowd.

By contrast, a small college can be bountiful to people who like to know their neighbors. The residential nature of a small campus, plus the intense focus on students, can nurture emotional as well as academic growth.

Attending an institution that boasts a Nobel Prize winner is exciting, but does the winner teach or are instructional chores assigned to a teaching assistant? At small colleges, professors are often more accessible, perhaps even inviting students majoring in their subjects home for tea and enlightenment.

Can you climb high and fast if you attend a small school that's not exactly a household word? A graduate of Eureka College in Illinois has done well. His name is Ronald Reagan.

Schools That Are Different

In Olympia, Wash., unorthodox courses are common at Evergreen State College. A program on technology focuses on whether it helps or hinders society. The school gives students narrative evaluations of their work rather than grades.

Berea College in Berea, Ky., charges no tuition. Each student must perform some of the labor required to maintain the institution, "thus gaining an appreciation of the worth and dignity of all the labor needed in a common enterprise."

St. Andrews Presbyterian College in Laurinburg, N.C., a private college of 800 students, offers an innovative curriculum and has such a commitment to people that its new campus was specifically built to attract and serve students with disabilities.

Armed with a $175 million endowment, Trinity College in San Antonio aggressively goes after top students with offers of generous scholarships and recruits renowned faculty with offers of superior pay. Quality is the name of the game at Trinity, which aims to become one of the strongest liberal arts schools in the Southwest.

Smith College in Northampton, Mass., offers dual degree programs in liberal arts and engineering. The purpose is to allow the strong math/science student the opportunity to obtain a Smith College liberal arts education, while pursuing an engineering discipline at the University of Massachusetts.

If you like marching to a different drummer, you can find compatible bandmates on a campus somewhere.

Cooperative Education: College Programs That Can Boost Your Career

Have you seen this bumper sticker on cars?

I owe, I owe, so off to work I go.

How true, how true. As a college student, would you like to have a job that kicks in $6,500 to $7,000 of your yearly budget? Would you like to have a job that has an excellent chance of leading to a permanent position after graduation?

About 200,000 students in 900 college co-op programs are saying "yes" to these questions.

Although there's money to be made, the economic benefits of co-op study are secondary to the educational aspect. In cooperative education, the objective is to *learn*—and earn while you're at it.

It is this objective that sets co-op education apart from campus work-study jobs, which emphasize earning over learning.

Co-op jobs can be highly responsible assignments. Students supervise production lines, manage customer accounts, write software instruction manuals, represent federal departments at meetings or supervise architectural job sites, to give you an idea of the career-experience league you can expect.

In a four-year program, usually you spend the first year in school, after which you follow some pattern of study-work rotation based on the school's academic calendar. If attending a two-year college, you might work mornings or afternoons, or you might alternate semesters of study and work until you accumulate a year or more of work experience. Details vary among co-op programs.

On the downside, you may find you have limited time for studies outside your discipline, and, in several schools, it can take as long as five years to get a bachelor's degree. (If you want more of the academic spectrum, you can always take night classes after you're settled in a good job.)

All things considered, cooperative study is a superb approach to education; you bridge the gap from school to work more easily, and you may be more motivated to do your best in school because you better understand how what you learn can be applied to your entire life.

Studies show that 40 percent of co-op graduates turn their last student job into a permanent position; 40 percent enter the career field in which they prepared and most of the remaining number enter graduate school.

If you decide you want to try out a career field in advance, look for a cooperative education program that is well organized, well financed, well promoted, well filled and well regarded. You may be disappointed if you are one of only a few co-op students on campus and the college administration treats the program with indifference.

Check, too, the job descriptions for students in your intended major. Do they sound educationally meaty or more like a very casual learning opportunity? Liberal arts co-op assignments may be difficult to assess, requiring the help of a seasoned co-op education professional to determine whether any real career exploration and development can take place.

Need more information? Two publications, *Co-op Education,* which describes the learning experience and how it works, and the *Co-Op Education Undergraduate Program Directory* are free from the National Commission for Cooperative Education, Box 999, Boston, MA 02115. The directory of programs in colleges and universities shows where the programs are located and the disciplines involved.

College Internships: Another Way to Test Career Goals

An internship is a short-term job that allows you to explore a career interest. You can try out work that interests you, make contacts and acquire experience.

You may work for a famous journalist, a state governor's office or a major corporation; internships are everywhere—private companies, public agencies and non-profit organizations.

You may be asked to stay on the job when your internship ends. You may accept or, after the experience, decide your interests are elsewhere.

Find out whether schools you're interested in have a strong track record in arranging student internships. While you can uncover or create them yourself, it is a time-consuming task.

Two guides of interest are:

1. *The National Directory of Internships,* published annually by the National Society for Internships and Experiential Education, Suite 207, 3509 Haworth Dr., Raleigh, NC 27609. Check the publisher for current cost.
2. *Internships,* an annual directory of thousands of job training opportunities for many types of careers, published by Writer's Digest Books, 9933 Alliance Road, Cincinnati, Ohio 45242. Check the publisher for current cost.

College Abroad

If you fancy crossing an ocean to study for a year or more, you can do it in one of two ways. You can enroll directly in a foreign university, or, as most Americans do, go under the sponsorship of an American college.

Before becoming an American at Munich or elsewhere, be certain to compile all the pertinent facts. Will lectures be exclusively in the host country's language? If the university doesn't award credits or transcripts, how can your educational progress be documented for American credentials? Do you have to pay in American dollars or can you save by paying expenses in local currency?

American college-sponsored programs are abundant, and many are delighted to accept students from other schools. More than 1,100 are listed in *Academic Year Abroad,* the annual catalog of the Institute of International Education, 809 United Nations Plaza, New York, NY 10017. Check the publisher for cost.

For anyone interested in overseas study, this publication is essential reading. It includes a great deal of wide-ranging information on how to plan for foreign study.

Military Academies Are Tuition-Free

If you're willing to serve your country for several years, you might attend college free and be paid while doing it.

Four U.S. military academies offer the option to complete college with an officer's commission.

U.S. Naval Academy
Annapolis, MD 21402

U.S. Military Academy
606 Thayer Road
West Point, NY 10996

U.S. Air Force Academy
Colorado Springs, CO 80840

U.S. Coast Guard Academy
New London, CT 06320

Each of the federal service academies—the U.S. Air Force, U.S. Military (Army), U.S. Naval and U.S. Coast Guard—offer four years of college leading to a bachelor of science degree. Cadets and midshipmen receive tuition, medical care, room and board, plus a monthly stipend to help pay for uniforms, books, and incidental expenses.

Upon graduation, commissions are conferred for an active-duty period of no less than five years. Of course, the Pentagon brass hopes that after receiving a first-rate education on your fellow citizens, you'll choose the military for a lifetime career. If you decide that military life is not in your long-term game plan, however, you need not stay beyond your required duty period.

The academies look for evidence of character, scholarship, leadership, physical aptitude, medical fitness, goals and motivation. In evaluating scholarship, they look closely at SAT and ACT scores, as well as school records.

Admission to the U.S. Air Force, U.S. Military and U.S. Naval academies is by nomination. Most who win appointments do so through nominations from members of the U.S. Congress, although other sources of nomination are available through affiliations with the armed forces. In the fall of your junior year, contact the office of your U.S. representative or senators to obtain details about how you can be nominated. It is not necessary to know the congressional member personally to receive a nomination.

Appointments to the U.S. Coast Guard Academy are handled differently. Students who wish to attend the Coast Guard Academy must enter the nationwide competition held each year for the spaces in the freshman class. Write to the Coast Guard Academy for information.

There's another way to receive personalized, current information about service academies. Ask your counselor or a military recruiter if there's an academy liaison officer in your area. In Palos Verdes, Calif., Leon R. Busby, a Delta airline pilot, also is an Air Force reserve officer who spends many hours identifying and encouraging outstanding students to consider the Air Force Academy. Because there are many more applications than openings, Lt. Col. Busby's role is more like that of a college admissions counselor than a military recruiter.

If you feel you have the "right stuff," a service academy could serve both you and your country.

University-Affiliated Technology Parks

New business relationships are springing up between academia and industry—it's a trend that could ease your entry to a fast-track technology career.

Forty universities are operating or developing technology parks and 10 more schools are said to be planning them, according to *High Technology* magazine.

If you're interested in science or engineering, these institutions should be high on your list of preferred colleges. Not only is the academic environment likely to be crisp with innovation, but the companies in residence are built-in employers.

Physically speaking, the technology parks are real estate developments usually adjacent to a campus. Corporations—most of which are research oriented—build facilities, hire staff that includes faculty and students, and sometimes fund research programs at the affiliated university.

The companies participate to obtain a steady labor pool of bright minds. The universities' motive for tying the knot with industry is to stop what they call "brain drains." University administrators have learned they must enhance income opportunities for faculty and students or risk losing their best people to the corporate world.

Here is a roster of university-affiliated technology parks. Note that in a few instances several universities relate to the same park.

Before you enroll in one of these universities, ask the dean of the school of engineering or an appropriate science for an up-to-date list of the companies in residence, including the size of each company's workforce (does the company offer 20 jobs or 2,000 jobs?) and its product lines (you may be interested in computers when the company specializes in biogenetics).

Technology Research Parks

Arizona State University Research Park
2105 Elliot Rd.
Tempe, AZ 85284

Engineering Research Center
(University of Arkansas)
College of Engineering
University of Arkansas
Fayetteville, AR 72701

Stanford Industrial Park
Lands Management, Stanford University
209 Hamilton Ave.
Palo Alto, CA 94301

University of Connecticut—Storrs
University of Connecticut
Administration Services, Gulley Hall
352 Mansfield
Storrs, CT 06268

New Haven Science Park
(Yale University)
Science Park Development Corporation
5 Science Park
New Haven, CT 06511

University Research Park at Lewes
(University of Delaware)
University of Delaware
Newark, DE 19716

Innovation Park
(Florida State University & Florida A&M)
1673 W. Paul Birac Dr.
Tallahassee, FL 32304

Northern Kentucky University Foundation Research/ Technology Park
Northern Kentucky University Foundation
Highland Heights, KY 41076

Maryland Science Technology Center
(University of Maryland)
University of Maryland Foundation
University of Maryland
Adelphi, MD 20783

University Park
(Massachusetts Institute of Technology)
Rm. 12-192
Cambridge, MA 02139

Geddes Center
(Eastern Michigan University & University of Michigan
3040 N. Prospect
Ypsilanti, MI 48197

Ann Arbor Technology Park
(University of Michigan)
Wood & Company
21C Ft. Evans Rd.
Leesburg, VA 22075

Dandini Research Park
(University of Nevada)
Desert Research Institute
Box 60220
Reno, NV 89506

Miami Valley Research Park
(Wright State University, University of Dayton, Sinclair Community College, Central State University)
Mead Corporation
Courthouse Plaza
Dayton, OH 45401

Swearingen Research Park
(University of Oklahoma)
Real Estate Development Office
University of Oklahoma
1000 Asp Ave., Rm. 210
Norman, OK 73019

University City Science Center
3624 Market St.
Philadelphia, PA 19104

Carolina Research Park
(University of South Carolina—Columbia)
South Carolina Research Authority
Box 12025
Columbia, SC 29211

Tennessee Technology Corridor
(University of Tennessee)
Tennessee Technology Foundation
Box 23184
Knoxville, TN 37933

Texas A&M University Research Park
Research Park, Texas A&M University
College Station, TX 77843

Central Florida Research Park
(University of Central Florida)
11800 Research Pkwy.
Orlando, FL 32826

University of Florida Research & Technology Park
University of Florida
Progress Center, Grinter Hall
Gainesville, FL 32611

Advanced Technology Development Center
(Georgia Tech)
Research & Communications
430 Tenth St., NW
Atlanta, GA 30318

Evanston/University Research Park
(Northwestern University)
1710 Orrington Ave.
Evanston Inventure
Evanston, IL 60201

Purdue Industrial Research Park
Purdue Research Foundation
Hovde Hall
W. Lafayette, IN 47907

Princeton Forrestal Center
Princeton University
Princeton Forrestal Center Administration
105 College Rd. East
Princeton, NJ 08540

University of New Mexico Research Park
Scholes Hall
Albuquerque, NM 87131

Rensselaer Technology Park
(Rensselaer Polytechnic Institute)
100 Jordan Rd.
Troy, NY 12180

Research Triangle Park
(University of North Carolina, Duke University, North Carolina State)
Research Triangle Foundation
Box 12255
Research Triangle Park, NC 27709

University Research Park
(University of North Carolina—Charlotte)
University of North Carolina—Charlotte
Charlotte, NC 28282

University Research Complex
(Ohio State University)
University Research Complex
1314 Kinnear Rd.
Columbus, OH 43212

University of Utah Research Park
Research Park
505 Water Way
Salt Lake City, UT 84108

Virginia Technical Corporate Research Center
220 Burruss Hall
Virginia Technical
Blacksburg, VA 24061

Washington State University Research & Technology Park
Research Park
432 French Administration Building
Pullman, WA 99164

Morgantown Industrial & Research Park
(West Virginia University)
1000 Dupont Rd., Bldg. 510
Morgantown, WV 26505

University Research Park
(University of Wisconsin—Madison)
946 WARF Building
620 Walnut St.
Madison, WI 53705

Source: Urban Land Institute, Washington, D.C.

The research parks listed here are either operating or under development. Other parks are in early planning stages.

Study the First Two Years at a Two-Year College and Save Money

Jennifer Turner says a funny thing happened on the way to a four-year degree. She became a community college student.

Jennifer opted to live at home and do her first two years of college at a nearby public community college. She saved a bundle, and she had the fun of a couple of extra years with her close-knit family.

Soon she'll receive her bachelor's degree from a four-year college. All her community college credits transferred; Jennifer was alert—she had confirmed with the four-year institution in advance the transferability of her credits before she enrolled in the two-year college.

At a time when tuition costs at baccalaureate institutions have zoomed, it makes sense to consider the cost advantage of the community college. The average annual tuition of less than $700 is about half of the price charged by a full-fledged university.

Living at home helps keep the costs down even more, and most community college students do live at home.

The academic programs at community colleges are much like freshman and sophomore programs at four-year institutions and are designed to let you earn transferable credits.

To avoid annoying surprises—like repeating a year of study—you'll make certain that courses will transfer to a senior institution, won't you?

There is a negative to attending a community college. With a little effort, you can overcome it. Students often build relationships with each other starting in the freshman year. You will miss establishing friendships from day one of your college career—friendships that can be of value later in life when you find the need to use contacts. The remedy: Make extra friends and contacts during your last two years.

One more consideration: employers. Do they care where you spend your first two years of college? Not many give it a thought. What they want to know is from which college you were graduated.

Besides public community colleges, there are public and private junior colleges. Public junior colleges are similar to community colleges. Private junior colleges are usually residential schools and sometimes are church-related. Their traditional purpose has been to prepare students for transfer to a senior institution, although many have switched their focus to career preparation. The cost of attending a private junior college is considerably higher than that of a public community or junior college.

Learn more about two-year colleges in section 14.

Getting a Line on Four-Year Colleges

There are six basic ways to find out about particular colleges.

Reading. Standard annual guides include those published or written by Barron's, Cass & Birnbaum, the College Board, Lovejoy and Peterson's. These references include statistical profiles of colleges, providing such data as the size of the student body, major fields of study and average test scores.

Another type of guide is *Peterson's National College Databank* (Peterson's Guides); it lists colleges that meet specific criteria. You can, for instance, identify colleges that offer ROTC programs, non-need scholarships, open admissions, evening and weekend degree programs and study abroad.

Study the college bulletins and catalogs. These may be available in your school media or career center, or you can write for those of particular interest. Don't expect an objective presentation—often you'll see a glamorized picture of smiling students standing in front of impressive buildings under a blue sky. Read the text with a critical eye.

Computer Search. Your high school may have the equipment to do a computerized search of colleges. Ask your counselor. Among the best known software programs are Discover, Explore, Guidance Information System, and Peterson's.

The programs offer a similar choice of criteria. You can search by major, location, type of institution, degree requirements, costs, student body type, enrollment size, campus setting, entrance difficulty, sports, student ethnic-geographic mix and other factors. You establish the criteria you want and, in essence, direct the computer to print a list of colleges that meet your requirements.

Video Laser Disc. This new technology is beginning to appear at high school media and career centers—if the school has a sufficient supply of prospective college students to make it cost-effective.

By watching television screens, students see filmed presentations of various colleges. It is not necessary to sit through an entire disc—you use a remote control to call up any of the colleges recorded on a disc.

After spotting a school you like, you can obtain more information by mailing the response card provided with the discs.

The technology was pioneered by College U.S.A., a firm headquartered in Gaithersburg, Md. Other companies reportedly plan to provide similar services.

The institutions are selling a lifestyle as well as an education. New England colleges are resplendently portrayed with autumn leaves while the Sun Belt colleges are shown aglow with surfers and hang-gliders.

A video tour can help narrow your field of choice but should not be the basis of a final decision.

Asking Others. Alumni may remember—from the distance of time—their college days with overly fond memories, whereas present-day students, dealing with the here and now, give a more reflective picture of the campus. Business friends can give you an idea of a college's reputation.

College Fairs and Representatives. Most high schools are visited by a number of college representatives on recruiting tours. They may give solo presentations to an audience, or a dozen or more reps may gather in a gym, set up tables, unfurl banners and hold a college fair.

You'll want to attend as many as possible of the presentations and fairs, bearing in mind that asking a college rep if he or she thinks the institution is for you is like asking a barber if you need a haircut.

Campus Visits. Americans traditionally think of college as a promise of ivy-colored halls, rah-rah spirit, all-night fraternity parties, wisdom-infused profs and winning football teams.

Many students, assuming this is how things will be, sign up and never lay eyes on the college of their choice until they report for freshman orientation week, a few short days before classes begin.

This is an error. Your choice may work out, but then again, it may not. Would you buy a car sight unseen, or pick a mate by computer?

Even if the college is a good fit on paper, each institution is unique and has its own personality and environment. Only by being on the campus can you find out if a college is up your alley and down your street. Go there!

Perhaps you can combine a family vacation with visits to colleges, or join a tour of colleges conducted by a parent or paid guide.

Make an advance appointment with admissions offices so there will be time for an adequate discussion. You may have to visit during the summer, but it is infinitely more rewarding to tour the school when classes are in session so that you can talk with students and get a feel for the "real thing."

If you need low-cost accommodations, ask about the possibility of booking rooms in the residence hall. Take along information about yourself—your high school record and test scores. Don't hesitate to discuss finances, including scholarship, loan and work opportunities.

If you're applying to a selective school, feel free to ask for an estimate of your chances for admission, but don't expect a firm commitment at this point.

After your visit, if you like the college and have not yet applied, do so immediately.

A Word About Accreditation

Accreditation is a concept of potential significance to your career and you should know about it.

Accreditation is a form of consumer protection. Experts who know how a school should be run, or what a program should be teaching, make judgments about the competence of an institution or curriculum.

The fact that a school or program is accredited does not mean it is top-notch. Accreditation means that evaluation experts believe it is providing the services it says it is providing.

Graduation from an accredited school or program is generally required for advanced study, or to qualify for professional practice.

How would you like to tunnel through four years of college work only to be refused admission to law school because your undergraduate degree is not from an accredited college?

Accredited institutions usually will not accept credits from non-accredited schools.

How would you like to transfer after one year from a non-accredited college to an accredited institution only to be told that none of your credits are acceptable and that you can look forward to spending an extra year in school?

Some employers, particularly those who employ technical personnel, will not hire new graduates of a non-accredited institution.

Still another benefit of attending accredited institutions is that you can be pretty sure the school is concerned about its reputation and product.

Broadly speaking, there are two basic types of accreditation.

1. Institutional, or regional accreditation, which applies to the entire institution. It is awarded by one of nine regional accrediting commissions. They are:

- Middle States Association of Colleges and Schools
- New England Association of Schools and Colleges (Commission on Institutions of Higher Education)
- New England Association of Schools and Colleges (Commission on Vocational, Technical, and Career Institutions)
- North Central Association of Colleges and Schools
- Northwest Association of Schools and Colleges
- Southern Association of Colleges and Schools
- Western Association of Schools and Colleges (Accrediting Commission for Community and Junior Colleges)
- Western Association of Schools and Colleges (Accrediting Commission for Senior Colleges and Universities)

In addition, national associations accredit institutions that are single purpose in nature. These include:

- American Association of Bible Colleges
- Association of Theological Schools
- Association of Independent Colleges and Schools
- National Association of Trade and Technical Schools
- National Home Study Council

2. Specialized or program accreditation is given by national organizations that represent a specific career area. The organization usually accredits a particular program within an institution and not the entire institution. Examples are:

- American Dietetic Association
- Liaison Committee on Medical Education
- Society of American Foresters

When in Doubt, Check It Out

Two resources can aid in determining whether the school or program you are considering meets the standards of a recognized accrediting body.

1. COPA (Council on Postsecondary Accreditation) identifies and monitors accrediting bodies. A free list of its members can be obtained from COPA,

Suite 305, One Dupont Circle NW, Washington, DC 20036.

2. The U.S. Department of Education also keeps a list of accrediting organizations. If you hope to receive educational grants or loans from the federal government, the institution or program you choose must be accredited by an organization recognized by the Department of Education. A free list of recognized accrediting bodies can be obtained by writing to the Division of Eligibility and Certification, U.S. Department of Education, Room 3030, ROB 3, 400 Maryland Ave. SW, Washington, DC 20202.

If an accrediting body is listed on either the COPA or the USOE list, you can write to the body asking for the roster of schools or programs that it has accredited.

Although the two resources overlap somewhat, COPA is chiefly concerned with the maintenance of educational quality, while the federal government's target is to make sure public funds are not squandered on substandard education.

What about the term *VA-approved* attached to the advertising of certain study courses? All the term means is that eligible veterans can use their military educational benefits to pay for these courses. *VA approved* certainly does not mean the course offers quality training.

In many states, a school or program must be state-approved to operate. To find out exactly what this means in your state, contact your state department of education.

If you don't want to waste time and money on questionable education, do your homework to determine what a school or program really means when it claims accreditation.

College Prospecting Checklist

General Perspective

- Are you comfortable with the college's culture (emphasis on scholarly or social pursuits, religious affiliation, competitive or laid-back atmosphere, single-sex or coed student body)?
- What is the school's reputation?
- By which associations is it accredited?
- What do you think of students you meet on campus (are they on your wave length)?
- Is public transportation available, or is a car needed?
- Do you prefer a specialized (such as engineering), liberal arts or comprehensive (liberal arts and vocational studies) institution?
- If you plan to enter graduate or professional school, what percent of the college's graduates enter advanced study (for instance, what percent are accepted at a top-rated school of law)?
- Is there a counseling center with qualified personnel to help with school or personal problems?

Career Perspective

- Does the college operate an aggressive career development and placement service?
- Does the community offer adequate job opportunities for students?
- Does the school philosophy favor internships?

- Are co-op education programs available?

- Have recent graduates in your future major found related jobs?

Academic Perspective

- Is the college a leader in the career fields that interest you? How many courses are regularly offered in areas in which you may wish to major—do they thin out after survey courses, or are in-depth study opportunities such as senior seminars available?

- What courses are required? Is there a requirement you are unable or unwilling to meet?

- What's the typical student-teacher ratio? If some courses are given in auditoriums, what provision is made for giving special help if needed?

- How many faculty members actually teach? Is much of the teaching done by graduate students?

- How accessible are faculty members?

Location

- Do you want to stay close to home or handle the expense of travel several times a year?

- Is the slower pace of a college town or the hustle-bustle of a big city best for you?

- Is the locale saturated with people who majored in your field of interest (in case you want to stay in the area after graduation)?

- Does the locale offer the resources you prefer for leisure time activities (mountains, oceans, desert)?

- Is climate important to you? What kind?

Size

- Would you rather know everybody or be a face in the crowd?

- If you come from a large urban high school, would a small college bore you?

- If you come from a small high school, would a large, impersonal university intimidate you?

Expenses

- Can you, with student aid and working, afford a private college, or does a public college seem more practical?

- Have you counted in all of your expenses—books, social life, laundry, trips home?

Campus Concerns

- Do you want to live in a dorm or in a private apartment? (You may not have the choice as a freshman.)

- Does it matter socially if most of the students live on campus and you live at home?

- Are there fraternities and sororities? Are they big deals? Do you have to be a "Greek" to be included in most social events?

- Do you want an athletic program in a particular sport?

Academic Requirements

- Do you have the academic track record to be accepted at competitive colleges?

- Would you prefer an easier school?

- Have you double-checked the application procedure, including deadlines, entrance exams and fees?

College Comparison Form

Name of College (address, phone, contact)	High School Grades Preferred	Class Rank Preferred	Freshman Average ACT or SAT	Majors of Interest	Cost/Tuition Fees, Room

Special Data (Note here all criteria of interest to you; see previous checklist.)

College Reminder Calendar

9TH GRADE:

Fall

Date ____________ Discuss your academics/career plans with your counselor.

Date ____________ Become familiar with the resources available in your library and/or career center.

Spring

Date ____________ Discuss your academic progress and plan your program for next year with your counselor. Remember your GPA begins in 9th grade for some colleges; others compute your GPA for 10th and 11th grades only, sometimes requesting the first semester of the 12th grade.

10TH GRADE:

September

Date ____________ Sign up for the P-ACT+

November/December

Date ____________ Take interest survey if offered.

Spring

Date ____________ Work out schedule of next two years with counselor. Consider taking practice PSAT/NMSQT if offered.

Summer

Date ____________ Visit colleges with parents. Preliminary screening.

11TH GRADE:

September

Date ____________ Sign up for the PSAT.

October through May

Meet with college admissions representatives who visit your school.

March/April

Date ____________ Plan next year's program.

Early Spring

Date ____________ Register for college admission tests.

Spring

Date ____________ Attend college fair and school-sponsored programs. Confer with your counselor about college.

Date ______ Explore college materials in the career center.

Date ______ Narrow final list of colleges to five or six schools.

Summer

Date ______ Visit colleges with parents. Make selective list of colleges you are definitely interested in.

Late Summer

Write for college applications.

12TH GRADE:

Late September

Date ______ Register for college admission tests.

Date ______ Familiarize yourself with your school's transcript procedure.

October through December

Date ______ Talk to admissions representatives who visit your school.

Date ______ Seek letters of recommendation if needed.

Date ______ Take achievement tests if required by target colleges.

January

Date ______ File financial aid forms.

NARROWING THE FIELD

Each application to a college costs a non-refundable fee of $10 to $30, and sometimes even more. A practical approach is to narrow your choices to six institutions.

Your first and second choices can be long shots—colleges you prefer but aren't sure of your chances.

Your third and fourth choices can be probables—colleges that offer a solid chance of acceptance.

Your fifth and sixth choices can be sure things—colleges that offer excellent chances of acceptance.

Six isn't a magic number and, in many cases, you need not apply to that many.

Be sure you and your family agree about the amount they are willing to finance and how much you are expected to come up with. The College Talk is a ritual you can't ignore.

Want to apply as soon as possible? Early-decision admissions are becoming regular admissions in some competitive colleges. In these schools, the majority of freshmen are admitted on an early-decision basis.

A book to help families cover the college ground is *The College Guide for Parents* by Charles J. Shields (Surrey Books).

* * *

Your college choice is made and you're all set to enter school the next semester. This is a good time to glance over the glossary of educational terms in the Appendix. The next section looks at ways to make the most of your campus life.

SECTION THIRTEEN

MAKING THE MOST OF COLLEGE

T*his section is devoted to the college experience: It begins with advice* on acclimating yourself to college culture—getting along with the faculty and students, and learning to function within the institution's rules and regulations.

The topics include freshman orientation, roommates and food, choosing advisers and professors, study tips, high-performance reading, writing research papers and passing exams.

Next come career-related curricula considerations: the value of the liberal arts major in the job market, self-designed education programs, and double majors.

We look at the importance of practicing power skills, making career contacts and gaining work experience as an undergraduate.

The section concludes with a look ahead to graduate and professional education, concentrating on business administration, law and medicine.

College: How to Make Sure Your Mind Never Returns to Its Original Size

Oliver Wendell Holmes said: "The mind, once expanded to the dimensions of larger ideas, never returns to its original size."

That's what will happen as a result of your college experience, assuming you don't fritter away these invaluable years.

Pay close attention to the personal achievement tips and the career-related advice that follows.

So Your First Choice Turns You Down

Contrary to popular thought, students who attend highly selective colleges do not learn more than students who attend less selective institutions. Nor, according to research, do students appear to develop fewer competencies because they do not attend a top-tier college.

Certainly you will be unhappy if your number-one college choice rejects you, but it is largely up to you whether you receive an excellent education wherever you enroll. Enthusiasm lights its own fire.

Second-choice doesn't mean second-class. It only means that's how the marbles rolled.

The Roommate and Food Concerns

Let's be honest: Students tell us their two biggest pre-college worries are not academics and personal growth, but roommates and food. The questions we hear sound like this:

"Can I go back for second helpings of food in the cafeteria?" "Where can I get food late at night?" "How will the school choose a roommate that I will like?" "Suppose my roomie doesn't like the same kind of music that I do?" "What do I do if I get stuck with a real nerd?"

For openers, you have a head start on building a good relationship with a roommate if you make up your mind to work at it. Learn some communication skills and anticipate areas that may cause problems.

As for the food, well, chow hounds, we don't know how to solve that problem except to say that we know of no student who left college just because of food. Also, we hear having a hot-air popcorn popper in your room is worth its weight in kernels during all-night study sessions when no pizza stand is open anywhere.

If you need more help in managing interpersonal relationships and other college concerns, read *How to Succeed in College* by Marcia Johnson, Sally Springer and Sarah Sternglanz (Wm. Kaufmann Inc.).

Go to Orientation

Should you go to freshman orientation? (Do bees buzz flowers?) Of course. It may be tempting to skip orientation for another week at the lake, but the no-show would be a ghastly mistake. You meet most of your new friends at orientation. Dyan Colvin, a college senior at the University of California, San Diego, describes it as "the two most worthwhile days of my early college career."

Find an Adviser You Admire

You are not stuck with the adviser assigned to you by the college (usually a faculty member in your declared major), if you find another professor with whom you feel more compatible. Ask the professor of your choice to be your adviser and for guidance on how to take care of any paperwork the change may require.

Be thoughtful: Read the college catalogue and plan your program before asking for your adviser's time.

If you're having trouble with coursework or study habits, your adviser can help.

For personal problems, go to the college's counseling center.

Pick Your Professors

In some ways, professors are like bosses—they are the gatekeepers of your future.

It makes sense to pick those who will best facilitate your education. You can't always choose which courses you take, but you can always try to register for the classes of well-regarded teachers. How will you know who's the best? Keep your ears open; word gets around.

When you have a choice between a convenient time period with a so-so professor and an inconvenient time period with a superior professor, go for quality.

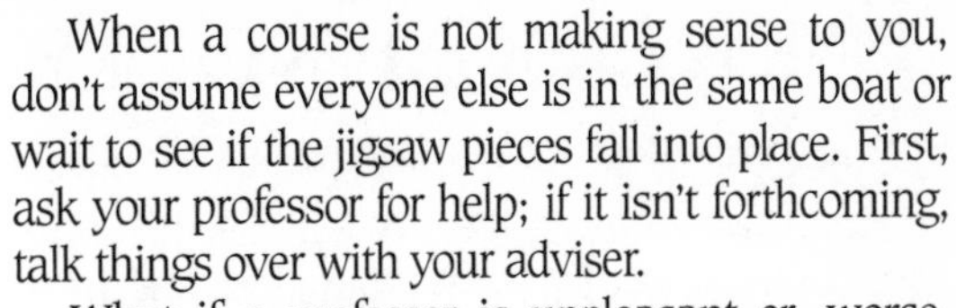

When a course is not making sense to you, don't assume everyone else is in the same boat or wait to see if the jigsaw pieces fall into place. First, ask your professor for help; if it isn't forthcoming, talk things over with your adviser.

What if a professor is unpleasant or, worse, insulting (such as a sexist)? Generally, it's a mistake to drop a course merely because you dislike a professor's personality. Sometimes the difficult professor will be the one whose class is most helpful.

When in doubt, ask yourself, "Am I mastering this subject?" If so, put up with the professor's irritating idiosyncracies. If not, take your troubles to your adviser, and, if necessary, to the dean.

Some students, particularly in engineering schools where there is a shortage of engineering professors, have encountered foreign-born faculty members whose English language skills leave much to the imagination. If you cannot understand the language spoken by a professor, you've got a legitimate beef.

This education is costing your family and you a lot of money and you have the right to get what you pay for.

Classes: Show up for Them

Some professors use lectures to cover material not found in reading on which they will base an exam. Others use lectures to stress key points. You never know when a professor will use either tactic. Skip at your own risk.

When you must miss, get notes on the lecture promptly.

Take Good Notes

- Use a loose-leaf notebook and date your notes.
- Condense what you hear or read. Do not write down every word. Jot down main ideas and flesh them out later.
- Review and revise your notes as soon as possible. Time is your enemy. Highlight key ideas. All this writing burns the data in your brain.
- Study your notes before the next assignment and class.

Read Effectively

- Read the summary first—even if it's last in a chapter. This tells you what the chapter is about.
- Read headings.
- Read the entire text until the headings make sense. Write the major points of each heading in your notes.

When the Grade on a Research Paper Disappoints

Why eat worms when you receive a poor grade on a research paper? Instead, analyze what went wrong.

Here are a few reasons why your grade sinks your spirits.

- You waited too long to start the paper and your research is so skimpy it's a laugh.
- Your organization of material is illogical. Again, time is the villain; three hours is the minimum period you need to organize materials.
- Your writing style suffered from poor planning and use of your time. You should spend at least 10 hours rendering your paper readable.
- Necessary corrections were not made because they were too much trouble. Arizona State University professor Claude Olney, creator of a seminar on smart study methods, says students who use word processors for research papers score as much as a full point higher than do students who use typewriters. There's no mystery—it's easy to make corrections on a word processor and the finished paper looks neater.

When you honestly don't know why your grade was so disappointingly low, politely ask the professor to enlighten you, explaining that you are not challenging the grade, but trying to understand how you can do better in the future.

Tips for Exams

- Go all the way through an exam, doing the easiest questions first; then return to the more difficult ones.
- If the test is in essay format, read the question carefully, make a quick outline of major points, then write on each one of the points in your outline.
- If the exam is oral, ask a friend to rehearse you with anticipated questions.

Time Management

Is this your problem?

Although your semester grade is hanging by the thin thread on tomorrow morning's exam for which you feel ill-prepared, you don't know how to say "no" to friends who ask you to join them for the movies tonight.

Chris Laramore faced the situation as a college student. He says:

In the beginning I squandered time as though

I had an unlimited supply. I had poor study habits, daydreamed a great deal and got mixed up in unrewarding personal relationships. Then everything hit me at once. If I hadn't changed my way of living I would have flunked. A GPA is much harder to bring up than it is to lower. You need to sit down and organize. Find a time for study and stick to that time.

What Chris is recommending is the practice of time management.

In a simple form of time management, you first establish a semester calendar (months and weeks) and write in long-term assignments and final exams.

In addition, you prepare a weekly calendar for regular study and short-term assignments. Allot time for classes, relaxation and chores as well as study. A sample of a weekly calendar follows.

Sample Time Management Weekly Calendar

	Monday	Tuesday	Wednesday	Thursday	Friday	Saturday	Sunday
8:00	Math	Economics	Math	Economics	Math	Clean Room	Sleep
9:00	Free	Economics	Free	Economics	Free	Clean Room	Sleep
10:00	Chemistry	Chemistry	Chemistry	Chemistry	Chemistry	Laundry	Church
11:00	Chem. Lab	Chem. Lab	Chem. Lab	Chem. Lab	Chem. Lab	Laundry	Church
Noon	Lunch	Lunch	Lunch	Lunch	Lunch	Lunch	Lunch
1:00	Study English	Study Math	Study English	Study Chemistry	Library	Free	Free
2:00	English	Study Math	English	Study Chemistry	English	Free	Free
3:00	Library	P.E.	Library	P.E.	Library	Free	Free
4:00	Free	Free	Free	Free	Free	Free	Free
5:00	Dinner	Dinner	Dinner	Dinner	Dinner	Dinner	Dinner
6:00	Study	Study	Library	Study	Free	Free	Study
7:00	Study	Study	Library	Study	Free	Free	Study
8:00	Study	Study	Library	Study	Free	Free	Study
9:00	Free	Study	Study	TV	Free	Free	Free
10:00	Free	Free	Study	Free	Free	Free	Free
11:00	Free	Free	Free	Free	Free	Free	Free
Midnight	Free	Free	Free	Free	Free	Free	Free

∞

THE FRESHMAN BLUES

What's the remedy if, after several months on campus, you feel you've made a bad choice and want to transfer to another college?

In most cases, your best bet is to hang in and wait for your change-of-heart to change back again. The disenchantment is probably an adjustment problem that will pass. Alumni who did not throw in the towel during a siege of freshman blues tend to confirm they made the right decision in staying.

It's a different story for students whose expectations are at wide variance with the realities of the campus. They are misplaced students.

Misplacement usually comes about as a result of the student's inadequate research and preparation—both are key activities you need to master to be a successful college student. The selection of a college is a good place to begin developing investigative and planning skills.

If you believe you really are misplaced—rather than suffering the freshman blues—a long talk with your adviser and parents is in order. The best action may be to cut your losses and transfer elsewhere.

"I'LL BE OKAY" MAYBE YES, MAYBE NO

The aunt asked her college-bound niece: "Do you have a focus yet?"

The niece replied that she plans to enter law school after achieving her undergraduate degree. The aunt asked the young woman if she were aware there is a surplus of lawyers, many of whom are having a hard time establishing a practice or getting on someone's payroll.

"Oh, well, yeah, sure...I've heard about the lawyer glut, but I'm sure I'll be okay."

Some people would call the niece's attitude one of confidence, others would call it naive.

REFLECTIONS ON A LIBERAL ARTS MAJOR

Year after year, new graduates with technical majors dramatically outperform liberal arts majors in the job market, both in numbers of job offers and salaries.

Obviously, there are shades and nuances. Most technical programs, for example, are enriched by substantial doses of arts and humanities, social and behavioral sciences and natural and mathematical sciences, collectively known as the liberal arts. Many liberal arts programs, on the other hand, boast strong vocationally relevant options.

Basically, a liberal education is preparation for the non-vocational aspects of life, including intellectual endeavor, aesthetic enjoyment, personal adjustment, and responsible citizenship.

You can make your liberal arts degree pay off *if you are willing to become a job-hunting expert,* and if you enter a field for which there are no rigid entry requirements, such as banking, sales, insurance, human resources, fund-raising, and lobbying. Entrepreneurship is another possibility.

We recommend liberal arts graduates follow these steps to ease into the job market.

- Be sure you have at least one internship experience in the field you want to enter.
- Take a double major.
- Add specialized or technical courses—accounting, computer science or statistics, for instance—to your liberal arts stew.

In the long-term, in some work settings, liberal arts majors, especially those who have acquired further education, may be able to bypass vocationally oriented majors. In meritocracies, such as

American Telephone and Telegraph, studies show that humanities and social science majors were promoted more rapidly than technical graduates.

There is no easy answer to the liberal-arts-major question. After reading an article in a business magazine extolling liberal arts education in the workplace, a New Jersey father responded to the publication's editor with this opinion:

CEO Roger Smith of General Motors, taking a view from the top, sees the great value of a liberal arts education in business. Yet when his directive arrives at the hiring gate, the message is clear—where are the accounting or comp-sci (computer science) majors? As a French major in the business world, I advise my children to pursue business degrees and hope they'll develop a taste for literature and the arts along the way.

If you decide to pursue a liberal arts major, consider vocationally oriented education at the graduate level. Some bachelor's degree graduates enroll in community colleges to acquire job-related skills.

For a glimpse of how you can apply your liberal arts education in the job market, turn to section 15.

What You Can Do With a Major in...

The following list shows how some graduates have applied their education to work. Observe that a number of jobs bear little relationship to the major, such as the biology major who became a computer programmer. Take into account, too, that some of the jobs listed require advanced education or additional training.

Accountancy
actuary
credit analyst
economist
insurance claims examiner
market research analyst
real estate agent/broker
securities trader
trust officer, bank

Art History
archaeological assistant
archivist
artist
art therapist
cartographer
critic (art, drama, film)
curator
graphic designer
private business owner

Biology
chiropractor
computer programmer
dentist
hospital administrator
insurance claims examiner
laboratory technician
medical doctor
microbiologist

Chemistry
chemical engineer
chemist
laboratory supervisor
marketing manager
medical technologist
production manager
systems analyst
toxicologist

Economics
administrative officer
auditor
bank officer
buyer, retailing
corporate lawyer
cost accountant
Internal Revenue Service agent
investment analyst
statistician

Education
audiovisual specialist
librarian
principal or superintendent
recreation director
rehabilitation counselor
speech pathologist
teacher
tutor

History
customs officer
foreign service officer
intelligence specialist
lawyer
public relations worker
research assistant
training specialist
writer

(continued)

Management and Marketing
brokerage house partner
cost accountant
credit and collection manager
financial planner
insurance underwriter
product distribution manager
public relations
purchasing agent

Mathematics
auditor
bank officer
industrial engineer
mission controller
real estate agent
special agent, FBI
tax administrator
writer, technical

Modern Language
advertising manager
immigration inspector
musician
saleperson, wholesale
scientific linguist
stockbroker
systems analyst
teacher

Philosophy
anthropologist
editor/journalist
foreign correspondent
hotel/restaurant manager
museum guide
psychologist
research assistant
sales manager

Physics
aerospace engineer
astronomer
business executive
oceanographer
patent attorney
physicist
private business
seismologist

Political Science
financial analyst
guidance counselor
investigator, criminal
lawyer
police officer
publisher
securities trader
writer

Psychology
job analyst
occupational therapist
physician
probation officer
public survey worker
speech pathologist
statistician
travel agent

Sociology
anthropologist
criminologist
management trainee
personnel manager
public health educator
recreation director
statistician
urban planner

Is the Self-Designed Major of Minor Benefit?

During the '70s, the self-designed major was a popular innovation. Tailoring a curriculum to meet your declared goal is a good idea on paper and may even be a superior educational idea.

The problem is that the self-designed major can be hard to sell in the job market. Employers don't like guessing games. They are more comfortable with familiar degrees because they know what you had to learn to obtain them.

Unless you have a commanding reason to design your own program, pass up the opportunity.

Doubling Your Chances With a Double Major

The chief reason to take a double major is marketability after you graduate.

In mathematics, for instance, a pure math major leads to teaching jobs, limiting your options. That's why it computes to do a double major (or a strong minor) in such fields as statistics, actuarial work, data processing, systems analysis, economics or finance.

Other common combinations: history and economics, English and accounting, foreign language and education.

If you have a hunch you'll have trouble hitting employment targets with your present major (such as English literature or anthropology), consider adding another arrow to your quiver. Visit a counselor at your campus career planning and placement center. Ask for an opinion as to whether you should retool with a double major.

The Rewards of Student Jobs

We discussed at length the benefits of part-time student work in section 11.

You have much to gain by working 10 to 20 hours a week as a college student. Whether it's an internship, co-op education stint, work-study employment, or something you lined up on your own, a job gives you money and experience, career try-outs and contacts.

Jobs on Campus

Your campus may be a wellspring of jobs. Students at Duke University who participate in a program called Student Labor Services make the point vividly.

SLS's 500 students are temporary office workers, banquet waiters and bartenders, concert set-up crew members, football game marshals and more. They are paid $4.00 to $5.25 per hour.

The program began in the early '70s when a group of enterprising students proposed the service to the college's administration.

SLS aids departments where work varies on a seasonal basis. Students are hired during short periods of intense activity to supplement the permanent staff.

Contacts: Your Partners in Success

Stretch out your hand often during the campus years. The people you get to know through classes and extracurricular activities can be human bridges to the job market. You never know who will open a door for you one day.

Many professional organizations have student divisions; join those in your interest area and attend meetings. Volunteer for projects. You'll be noticed. Your investment in contacts now will pay dividends after graduation.

Get a Headstart on Power Skills

You hear a lot about team spirit making you a valued employee. You hear less about power skills that make you an influential leader. Maybe you won't use power skills your first day on the job, but you'll be in a better position to make the transition from team player to leader if you begin to raise your power consciousness now.

Real power is not ordering everybody out of the pool, or doing sneaky, manipulative things.

Real power is the clout to get things done. Power comes in different packages. *Derivative power* comes from your connection with an office or institution, or from association with a powerful person. Without the student governing office, the student council president is just another person on campus. You will not develop your own power skills if you rely too much on powerful campus friends for stature and acceptance.

Gaining expertise in an area is a better basis for power. Becoming an expert frames you as influential in your own right.

Other avenues to power include making yourself stand out from the crowd. Offer to write your campus club's minutes, handle the public relations for a club event, or prepare the fraternity newsletter—all practical ways to be useful and, not coincidentally, gain power.

Some people do marvelous things with *perceived power.* Others think you have it, whether you do or not. If you take on a job, do it well and appear collected and competent, you will give off an aura of being an expert in your endeavor.

Being powerful does not always equate with being popular. When you are in charge and have to reject another person's pet idea, expect friction.

Once you accept the fact that you can't please everyone all the time, you're on your way to learning how to understand power and how to use it when the time is appropriate.

Stop! Think About Graduate or Professional Study

The term *advanced study* describes both graduate and professional study.

Graduate study means post-baccalaureate education in a given academic field—such as history, chemistry, literature or a foreign language. It is a time for in-depth education and for learning the style and method peculiar to a given discipline. The doctor of philosophy (PhD) is tops in the line of graduate academic degrees.

Professional study stresses the practical application of knowledge and skills—in business, law, architecture and medicine, for instance. Examples of doctoral degrees in these fields are the doctor of business administration (DBA), doctor of jurisprudence (JD), doctor of architecture (D Arch) and doctor of medicine (MD).

A doctorate usually is sought to teach at the college level or to do research.

Between the baccalaureate and the doctorate stands the master's degree. Generally, a master's requires two years of post-baccalaureate study, although some programs can be finished in one year and others take three years to complete.

Many students obtain a master's degree and go on to earn a doctorate. Others skip the master's degree and head straight for the doctorate. Still others stop with a master's degree, either because they can't or don't want to continue on toward a doctorate, or because their chosen fields don't require it for employment. Examples of fields in which a master's is normally the highest degree of choice include the master's degree in business administration (MBA), master's degree in fine arts (MFA), master's degree in library science (MLS) and master's degree in social work (MSW).

The distinctions between traditional graduate academic programs and professional programs are not clear cut. To get up to steam on the topic, thumb through a reference work like *Peterson's Graduate & Professional Programs* (Peterson's Guides, published annually).

Review Your Reasons for Advanced Study

When you're scouting a career field requiring advanced academic or professional study, start exploring your options well before the time you hope to enter the hallowed halls of advanced learning.

Usually, an 18-month lead time is sufficient. But if you are applying for national scholarships—or your undergraduate school has an evaluation committee through which you are applying to the same institution's business administration program or law school—you'll need two years to prepare.

An advantage to planning for advanced study while you're a college sophomore or junior is that you'll have time for a course correction if your undergraduate education is not on the right track for the graduate/professional school of your choice. Determine requirements of the programs you may want to enter, then double check that your undergraduate studies meet them. What a revolting development it would be, at the last minute, to discover you are shy three hours of organic chemistry or six hours of statistics.

Not all paths leading to graduate/professional study are non-stop. Many students work for several years before picking up the books again. In some cases, this is a prudent idea. Educators say having a few years of work under the belt boosts motivation, commitment and diligent pursuit of knowledge.

On the other hand, stepping out of school may make it very tough to pick up the study reins again, especially if you're trying to shuffle job, school and, possibly, family obligations.

Whether you enter advanced study as a 21-year-old or later in life, be sure you're going onward and upward in academe for one of two reasons:

1. The career field you choose, such as medicine, librarianship, law or college teaching, requires advanced education.
2. You plan to become an expert in a given field and you need more education in it either for career goals or personal rewards.

Do not—repeat, do not—pursue advanced study to please someone else; because you assume spiffy jobs with status and money will be your automatic rewards; because friends are headed for graduate school; or because you want another three-year ride on your parents' tab.

Remember, your values, goals and decisions are what count.

Oh, Those Tests!

Colleges and universities usually require a specific graduate or professional admission test, and departments may have additional test requirements. The most frequently used tests for graduate school are the Graduate Record Examinations (GRE) and the Miller Analogies Test (MAT).

Professional schools may want you to take a specific discipline-related admission test, such as the Dental Admission Test (DAT).

Nearly all graduate and professional schools ask students whose first language is not English to take the Test of English as a Foreign Language (TOEFL).

Graduate Schools With National Reputations

Is graduate study on your agenda? If so, what should you look for in choosing a program? Here are three criteria suggested by Dr. Kenneth B. Hoyt, distinguished university professor at Kansas State University.

1. Where will you get the best assistantship package?
2. Will you receive individual help from at least one professor with academic interests and a national reputation in the area of your specialization?
3. What happened to previous graduates of the

program? Have they been successful in finding employment in career fields for which they prepared?

What about the relative prestige of the nation's research universities? Here are some of the major-league institutions grouped by discipline. The list is not complete, but it will give you a starting point in finding a national quality graduate program.

Biological Sciences

Biochemistry
Massachusetts Institute of Technology
Stanford University
Harvard University
University of California, Berkeley
University of Wisconsin, Madison
Yale University
Rockefeller University
Brandeis University
University of California, San Francisco
Cornell University
University of California, San Diego
University of California, Los Angeles
Duke University

Botany
University of California, Davis
University of Texas, Austin
University of Wisconsin, Madison
University of California, Berkeley
Cornell University
University of Michigan, Ann Arbor

Cellular/Molecular Biology
Massachusetts Institute of Technology
California Institute of Technology
Yale University
Rockefeller University
University of Wisconsin, Madison
Harvard University
University of California, San Diego
University of California, Berkeley
University of Colorado
Columbia University
University of Washington, Seattle

Microbiology
Massachusetts Institute of Technology
Rockefeller University
University of California, San Diego
Johns Hopkins University
University of Washington, Seattle
Duke University
University of California, Los Angeles
University of Chicago
University of Illinois, Urbana-Champaign
University of Pennsylvania
University of California, Davis
University of Wisconsin, Madison
Columbia University
University of Michigan, Ann Arbor

Physiology
Rockefeller University
University of California, San Francisco
University of Washington, Seattle
Yale University
University of Pennsylvania
Harvard University
University of California, Los Angeles
Duke University
University of Michigan, Ann Arbor
Washington University, St. Louis

Zoology
Harvard University
University of California, Berkeley
University of Washington, Seattle
Yale University
Duke University
University of California, Los Angeles
University of Wisconsin, Madison

Engineering

Chemical Engineering
University of Minnesota
University of Wisconsin, Madison
University of California, Berkeley
California Institute of Technology
Stanford University
University of Delaware, Newark
Massachusetts Institute of Technology
University of Illinois, Urbana-Champaign

Civil Engineering
University of California, Berkeley
Massachusets Institute of Technology
University of Illinois, Urbana-Champaign
California Institute of Technology
Stanford University
Cornell University
University of Texas, Austin

Electrical Engineering
Massachusetts Institute of Technology
University of California, Berkeley
Stanford University
University of Illinois, Urbana-Champaign
University of California, Los Angeles
Cornell University
University of Southern California
Purdue University
California Institute of Technology
Princeton University

Mechanical Engineering
Massachusetts Institute of Technology
Stanford University
University of California, Berkeley
California Institute of Technology
University of Minnesota
Princeton University
Purdue University
Brown University

Humanities

Art History
New York University
Harvard University
Yale University
Columbia University

Classics
Harvard University
University of California, Berkeley
Yale University
Princeton University

English Language and Literature
Yale University
University of California, Berkeley
Harvard University
University of Virginia
Cornell University
University of Chicago
Johns Hopkins University
Princeton University
Stanford University
Columbia University

French Language and Literature
Yale University
Princeton University
Columbia University
New York University
Cornell University
Indiana University, Bloomington

German Language and Literature
Yale University
University of Wisconsin, Madison
Princeton University
Indiana University, Bloomington
University of California, Berkeley

Linguistics
Massachusetts Institute of Technology
University of California, Los Angeles
University of Massachusetts
University of Texas, Austin

Music
University of California, Berkeley
University of Chicago
Princeton University
Yale University
Cornell University

Philosophy
Princeton University
University of Pittsburgh
Harvard University
University of California, Berkeley
University of California, Los Angeles
Stanford University
University of Chicago

Spanish Language and Literature
University of Pennsylvania
Harvard University
University of Texas, Austin
University of California, Berkeley

Yale University
University of Michigan, Ann Arbor
University of Wisconsin, Madison

Math and Physical Sciences

Chemistry

California Institute of Technology
University of California, Berkeley
Harvard University
Massachusetts Institute of Technology
Columbia University
University of Illinois, Urbana-Champaign
Stanford University
University of Chicago
University of California, Los Angeles
University of Wisconsin, Madison
Cornell University
Northwestern University
Princeton University
Yale University
Purdue University

Computer Science

Stanford University
Massachusetts Institute of Technology
Carnegie-Mellon University
University of California, Berkeley
Cornell University
University of Illinois, Urbana-Champaign

Geosciences

California Institute of Technology
Massachusetts Institute of Technology
University of California, Los Angeles
Columbia University
Stanford University
Harvard University
University of Chicago
Princeton University
Yale University

Mathematics

Princeton University
University of California, Berkeley
Harvard University
Massachusetts Institute of Technology
University of Chicago
Stanford University
New York University
Yale University
University of Wisconsin, Madison
Columbia University
University of Michigan, Ann Arbor
Brown University
Cornell University

Physics

Harvard University
California Institute of Technology
Cornell University
Princeton University
Massachusetts Institute of Technology
University of California, Berkeley
Stanford University
University of Chicago
University of Illinois, Urbana-Champaign
Columbia University
State University of New York, Stony Brook

Statistics/Biostatistics

Stanford University
University of California, Berkeley
University of Chicago
University of Wisconsin, Madison
Iowa State University, Ames
University of North Carolina, Chapel Hill

Social and Behavioral Sciences

Anthropology

University of Michigan, Ann Arbor
University of California, Berkeley
University of Chicago
University of Pennsylvania
University of Arizona, Tucson
Stanford University
Yale University

Economics

Massachusetts Institute of Technology
University of Chicago
Stanford University
Princeton University
Harvard University
Yale University
University of Minnesota

University of Pennsylvania
University of Wisconsin, Madison

Geography
University of Minnesota
Pennsylvania State University
University of Wisconsin, Madison
University of California, Berkeley
University of Chicago

History
Yale University
University of California, Berkeley
Princeton University
Harvard University
University of Michigan, Ann Arbor
Stanford University
Columbia University
University of Chicago
Johns Hopkins University
University of Wisconsin, Madison

Political Science
Yale University
University of Michigan, Ann Arbor
University of California, Berkeley
University of Chicago
Harvard University
Massachusetts Institute of Technology
Stanford University
University of Wisconsin, Madison

Psychology
Stanford University
Yale University
University of Pennsylvania
University of Michigan, Ann Arbor
University of Minnesota
University of California, Berkeley
Harvard University
University of Illinois, Urbana-Champaign
University of California, Los Angeles
Carnegie-Mellon University
University of California, San Diego
University of Chicago
University of Colorado
Indiana University, Bloomington
University of Oregon, Eugene
University of Wisconsin, Madison

Sociology
University of Wisconsin, Madison
University of Michigan, Ann Arbor
University of Chicago
University of North Carolina, Chapel Hill
University of California, Berkeley
Harvard University
Stanford University
University of Washington, Seattle
Columbia University
Indiana University, Bloomington
University of California, Los Angeles

International Education

Are foreign lands calling your name? The U.S. Department of Education administers about 700 fellowships related to foreign languages and international relations—the Foreign Language and Area Studies Fellowships and the Fullbright-Hays Doctoral Dissertation Awards.

Check out these and other funding possibilities with your institution's financial aid office.

Should you pack your bags for an overseas study tour?

Upside answer: Living in a foreign culture stimulates the senses, producing a heightened awareness of the world in which you live. It is a sophisticating experience and one which may be a high point in your life.

Downside answer: Living in less developed nations can be a culture shock that prevents you from maximizing your educational experience. If you make an unwise selection, the educational credential, such as degrees granted by certain foreign medical schools, may be of little value in the United States.

If you decide to study abroad, try to learn the language before you go. That way you can avoid repeating the experience of a student in a lavish

Parisian restaurant who, pointing to an item on the menu, said, "Waiter, bring some of this." The waiter replied, "Monsieur, the orchestra is now playing it."

* * *

To B-School or not to B-School? That's the next question.

Business School: Is It Music to Your Ears?

Sing hey, hey, the MBAs,
Can't you see we're the latest craze?
Hey, hey, the MBAs
Having fun earning twice our age.

These lyrics from the song "Born to Run Things" hint at the spectacular rise of the MBA (master's in business administration degree) and the explosion of B-schools (schools of business administration) over the last two decades.

Each year, a record-breaking 69,000 newly minted MBAs burst forth from campuses across the land. The number is nearly a fifteenfold increase from 1960 when only 4,800 received the degree. And more are on the way: 200,000 students now are studying for MBAs.

Women have caught on to the trend for business study, too. In 1962, fewer than 300 of new MBAs were female. Today, women are taking nearly one-third of the new MBA degrees.

To meet the demand of young movers and shakers, B-schools arose seemingly overnight. Twenty years ago, fewer than 200 schools received standardized test scores for admission to graduate programs of business administration. Today, 650 do. But of this number, only one-third are accredited by the American Assembly of Collegiate Schools of Business.

Why the craze for the MBA? In the '70s, the MBA degree became, in essence, a prerequisite for many corporate positions. The degree was widely thought to be embossed with magic—a reliable ticket to the executive suite and the riches and power that go with it. Other than medical school, it seemed the quickest route to a six-figure income.

When anything becomes as popular as the MBA, it acquires fad status and, as you know, most fads eventually fade away. Executives started disparaging MBAs, saying the young marvels may know a lot of management theory, but not much about the realities of running a company. Critics said students were narrowly educated, arrogant, and prone to job hopping, and that they expected to get ahead too fast.

One critic doesn't mince words. In describing recent Harvard MBAs, he says: "These kids are smart. But I'd as soon take a python to bed as hire one. He'd suck my brains, memorize my Rolodex [file of contacts], and use my telephone to find some other guy who'd pay him twice the money."

The combination of a tidal wave of graduates and increasing disenchantment with MBAs' performance has made competition for good jobs keen. Some experts believe the phenomenal production of MBAs during the past 20 years may have created a glut in the market for both MBA schools and graduates. Many major corporations already have become far more selective about the schools at which they recruit, and the caliber and kinds of MBAs they hire.

Although the MBA no longer carries the cachet it once had, guess what executives recommend to their own children?

In a recent survey, 600 senior business leaders were asked: "If your son or daughter were planning a career in business, would you advise him or her to get an MBA, or not?" A whopping 78 percent said "yes."

MBAs: Dollars, Sense and Sectors

Obviously not all employers rate the MBA as pampered and overpriced. Most new graduates are offered annual starting salaries in the high $20s and some do even better. Among top business schools, $30,000 to $45,000 is the range of the average offer to new MBAs. The highest offers range from $49,000 to an incredible high of $85,000.

The knock-your-socks-off salaries generally go to MBAs who amassed working experience between their undergraduate and professional studies, have sought-after technical backgrounds, or were successful in courting the glitter and gold of investment banking or consulting. The big Wall Street firms and national management consulting companies have a reputation for outbidding other types of employers for the best and the brightest of new MBAs.

Apart from money, some people zero in on the degree for defensive reasons. They believe—with good reason—that when merit and abilities are equal, people with MBAs often get promoted faster than people without the degree. That's why someone with a master's degree in economics or banking may go back and finish an MBA program.

For women in particular, the degree may be seen as proof of sincerity, commitment to career and probably the single best tool for getting ahead. Experts do not agree about the specific value of the MBA for women, but the weight of opinion seems to be that it's important for a woman to enter corporate employment with all the credentials she can get.

Although no one—man or woman—*has* to have an MBA to become a fast-lane speed demon in business, most observers agree that MBAs from well-regarded schools do have an edge in the beginning. Once in a position, advancement depends on how valuable you are to the company. Performance preempts education as the measure of promotability. When you change jobs, however, education often comes up in the hiring decision. "He's a Stanford MBA" or "She's a Harvard MBA" may be part of the behind-the-scenes hiring discussion.

What jobs do MBAs take? Half or more of all new MBAs work in finance and accounting or marketing. Others toil in general management and administration, information management, operations and production.

They perform these functions in many industries—banking, data processing, accounting, consulting, insurance, food and beverage, automotive, financial services and consumer products.

A Report Card on Business Schools

Harvard Business School is the second-oldest B-school in America—but it is the largest, the richest, the most prestigious and the most imitated. The school's $200 million endowment is said to be larger than that of all other graduate B-schools combined. It has the nation's largest alumni base—nearly 31,000—and boasts more top chief executive officers than any other school.

As the pun goes, "There's no B.S. like H.B.S."

Despite Harvard's preeminence, many observers say that Stanford University's graduate management school is becoming—or already is—number one.

Arguments about who's tops fly back and forth but mercifully, there's far greater agreement on the general ranking of B-schools. Think of a pyramid. Approximately 20 institutions are at the apex. Another 30 or so rank on the second tier. Perhaps another 50 schools are on a third tier, and, at the base of the pyramid, are hundreds more schools flying the MBA banner.

Which graduate schools of business have blue-chip reputations? The following universities often head up various surveys of top programs:

University of California at Berkeley, University of California at Los Angeles, Carnegie-Mellon University, University of Chicago, Columbia University, Cornell University (Johnson), Dartmouth College (Amos Tuck), Duke University (Fuqua), Harvard University, University of Illinois, Indiana University, Massachusetts Institute of Technology (Sloan), University of Michigan, University of Minnesota, New York University, University of North Carolina, Northwestern University (Kellogg), University of Pennsylvania (Wharton), Rochester Institute of Technology, Stanford University, University of

Texas at Austin, University of Virginia (Darden) and Yale University.

Tip: There are probably good quality schools not presently accredited by the American Assembly of Collegiate Schools of Business, the official accrediting body, but we advise you to select an AACSB-accredited graduate school of business. To obtain a list of more than 230 accredited graduate programs, write to AACSB, Suite 220, 605 Old Ballas Road, St. Louis, MO 63111.

As you have deduced, not all MBAs are created equal. An MBA graduate with mediocre grades from a mediocre school will not be touched with the sword of corporate acceptance and raised to a comfortable knighthood. More likely, the lackluster graduate will have to pound the pavements, jostling mightily in job market tournaments.

The B-school you attend not only affects how many job offers you get and how much you initially earn, but how you will go about running things down the road. Many of the leading schools teach the making of business decisions by quantitative (quantity, numbers) analysis and computer (mathematical) modeling. Others stress leadership skills and communications, or blend both approaches.

Beyond the differences in status and philosophy, there are other factors to consider when choosing a B-school. Let's say you do not enroll in a nationally known institution. Consider a highly regarded regional MBA program; its graduates often are first picks of neighboring businesses.

If your focus is fixed, you may wish to attend a specialty program, such as the graduate business program at Northeastern University in Boston, which is designed to ready managers to run high-tech companies (business management, not technical project management). The University of South Carolina is applauded for its international business program. The University of Illinois at Urbana-Champaign profits from its reputation for accounting courses.

As a rule, MBA programs are spread out over two full-time academic years, or the equivalent.

A large number of institutions offer external degree (off campus) programs. Most offer night sessions. Some train MBAs in weekend programs. And a growing number of companies tell B-schools what to teach in programs tailored to meet individual corporate needs; not all are MBA-qualifying but some, such as the one produced by General Electric with Purdue University's Krannert Graduate School of Management, are accelerated programs leading to an MBA.

The rich diversity of ways to gain the degree has grown from pressures on B-schools to remain competitive. Some business educators fear the MBA market may be approaching saturation and speculate that a shakeout is ahead in which weak, unaccredited B-schools will close, perhaps hundreds of them. One observer remarked, "It may be a situation in which the stronger schools get fatter, and the marginal ones fail."

Competition for students among B-schools is so intense that some of the savviest make it easy for students to connect by installing toll-free telephone numbers for admissions offices, such as the one at the University of Virginia: 1-800-UVA-MBA-1. To determine whether an institution has a toll-free number, dial the information directory: 1-800-555-1212.

Wherever you attend, you can expect to have a "30-pound paperweight" on your desk—that's student slang for the personal computer you include with your gear, or one supplied by the university.

What else? Bring money. Tuition ranges from about $6,000 a year at state universities to about $12,000 a year at private uppercrust institutions. This doesn't include living expenses—count on at least $20,000 per year for everything.

What Top Business Schools Look For

The vast majority of B-schools need your business, so getting in is no big deal. The best schools, however, are selective—Stanford accepts only 9 percent of its applicants, Indiana, 34 percent. Duke University, by contrast, accepts 67 percent of those who apply—but that's a reflection of its recent intent to enlarge its MBA program.

How do selective schools decide who will pass through their portals and perhaps gain fame and fortune on the stage of business?

Informal surveys of admissions directors reveal that vital signs of future B-school success include leadership in undergraduate extracurricular activities, work experience, grades, test scores, essays and recommendations.

Even so, not all admissions directors kick in the same chorus line. Some institutions place enormous emphasis on work experience, particularly several years at a large corporation. Some, including Harvard, no longer use the standardized admission test. Some are not wowed by grades, preferring to back writers of well-written essays.

If your sights are set on a particular school, contact the institution's admissions office and ask for a statement of how each selection factor is weighed in the decision-making process. As best you can, structure your application to fit the stated preferences.

If you learn that working experience is prized, get some. Ask whether the school will grant you a deferred guaranteed-admit option, or even help you find a job with a friendly corporation for a couple of years. If you discover that essays are unusually important, give the task four times your normal effort.

Find out how your favorite school tries to determine academic competence, management potential and personal characteristics. You can do this by asking the dean's office for a statement of selection criteria. Try to package yourself to fit the requirements of the casting call.

Don't worry about characteristics you can't change, like your undergraduate major. Although graduate schools of business discourage business undergraduates, the undergraduate major seems to have minimal effect on who passes through the top B-school portals.

The GMAT and Other Management Tools

The Graduate Management Admission Test (GMAT) is required by most schools of business. It's an exam with the same format as the SAT, but with harder questions. Practice tests are included in the *Official Guide to GMAT.*

The *Official Guide to MBA Programs,* edited by Charlotte Kurst, describes the particulars of programs offering a graduate degree in business.

Both publications are published by the Graduate Management Admission Council and distributed by the Educational Testing Service. The publications are available in bookstores and libraries, or order directly from ETS, Princeton, NJ 08541.

Should You Get an MBA?, by Albert Hegyi (Prentice Hall), answers many of the questions you may have about management, which is really the art of getting other people to do all the work.

How To Turn Your MBA Into a CEO, by Robert Lear (Macmillan), suggests how to choose the right courses and land the all-important first job. CEO means chief executive officer.

Is Graduate Business Study For You?

Before exchanging two years of life for an MBA, reflect on your ultimate career goals.

If you want to be a corporate alpinist scaling the sheer cliffs of top management, an MBA is a must. If you want to rate as a management consultant or investment banker, get an MBA. If you seek powerful contacts, you can begin developing them in an MBA program. If you have a liberal arts degree and need marketability, an MBA will help. If you've got a technical undergraduate degree and you seek broadening managerial horizons, go MBA.

The ideal approach is to work hard to get into the best school you can and graduate near the top of the class. Warming up with a couple of years of working experience will help you understand the practical problems of applying what's taught in the classroom.

If you can't justify day school, you can get an MBA at night or on weekends. Try to find employment with a company that will pay for your studies.

A graduate school of business can help you acquire not only technical business skills, but communicate the lifestyle and values needed to move up in organizations that hire MBAs who would be kings—or queens.

A LAW DEGREE CAN LEAD ALMOST ANYWHERE

Lawyer bashing is nothing new.

"The first thing we do, let's kill all the lawyers," said Shakespeare's Henry VI.

"Can we bar lawyers from coming to the New World?" asked explorer Balboa of King Ferdinand in 1523.

"I would be loath to speak ill of any man, but I'm afraid this man is an attorney," said English author Dr. Samuel Johnson.

Attorneys have been under indictment from the public throughout history but charges seem to be flying faster than before. In the past decade, an uncomfortable number of lawyers—a very small minority, true, but enough to blister regard for lawyers as a group—have been accused of everything from courtroom blunders and fee gouging to outright crookedness.

As a result, only 12 percent of people in a recent Louis Harris survey expressed "a great deal of confidence" in law firms, down from 24 percent a decade earlier.

Against this backdrop of modest public esteem for lawyers, it could be assumed that the profession has lost appeal for bright young minds.

A reasonable assumption, but a wrong one.

America is teeming with lawyers. Some people say there's a glut of them. Across the land, licensed lawyers total 650,000, double the number only 15 years ago.

The boom is off the rolls of new law students by about 10 percent, yet a sizable army of young persons continues to march into the nation's 174 accredited law schools, which contain 124,000 students, compared with 63,000 in the late '60s. Each year more than 35,000 new lawyers graduate and begin seeking domain in the professional marketplace.

Researchers speculate that by the mid '90s, there will be one million practicing lawyers, one for every 300 Americans.

Women have taken to law like judges to gavels; about 40 percent of today's law students are female. Moreover, the U.S. Supreme Court has ruled that law firms must comply with federal employment discrimination laws when deciding who moves up from employee to partner, which is good news for women.

A small number of lawyers clerk for judges, but this is usually a short-term stop on career paths into other areas of the profession. The trend is away from one-lawyer firms, although 47 percent of lawyers in private practice work alone. About 70 percent of all lawyers are in private practice, some as employees or partners in law firms. Other lawyers work for corporations or government agencies.

As we mentioned in section 1 the legal profession does not guarantee affluence to its members. Legal aid lawyers often earn less than $15,000 yearly. Law clerks, solo practitioners and young law firm associates may have to make do on less than $25,000 a year.

Most government lawyers are paid according to civil service scales, rarely earning more than $65,000 a year, even after decades of service. Corporate lawyers have earnings comparable to other company executives, which can top $100,000, or dip under $30,000.

The real money machines are found in prestige law firms, particularly in New York City, Washington, D.C., and other major cities. Partners in top firms can command a quarter-of-a-million dollars annually, or much, much more—better than a million dollars in a good year.

What about starting out? If you do very well at a leading law school and go to work for a prestigious New York law firm, you will be paid about $80,000 a year to start. This happens to only a few lucky graduates. If you don't do so well at an obscure law school, you probably will have trouble finding your first job in law.

Where you go to school is more important in law than it is in many other professions. Years after graduation, a lawyer looking for a job will be asked about his or her law school and rank in class.

Other than the hope of high earnings, what attracts hordes of people to the law? Sometimes it's idealism. Sometimes students decide that lawyers have special handles on the nation's power levers and they want to pull them. Sometimes they can't think of any other profession to enter. Sometimes training in the law seems useful whether it is to be practiced or not.

A law degree can lead to almost anything—the law, politics, business.

Howard Cosell, who was trained as an attorney, laid down the law to become a well-known figure in the sports world. Former International Ladies Garment Workers President Sol Chaikin used his law degree to look for and find the union label. CIA chief (and former FBI head) William Webster began his illustrious career as a lawyer.

From the corridors of government power and the sky-hugging office buildings of New York, Houston and cities everywhere, to the suburban shopping malls and the commercial districts of small towns, lawyers are everywhere, into everything.

What Lawyers Do

Litigating, negotiating, securing and *counseling* are the four broad activities that lawyers can pursue.

The litigators are the courtroom warriors who parachute into the fray and blast away until a particular point of view has been pressed as vigorously as possible. The negotiators settle conflicts short of courtroom battle, reconciling divergent interests and opinions. Securers use communication skills to nail down contracts and other agreements that keep society running by a set of rules. The counselors advise clients on a broad spectrum of personal and business problems—they're in the "preventive litigation" business.

Not all lawyers do all of these things. Although most states prohibit lawyers from claiming a specialty, lawyers do say things like "focus on—" or "limit my practice to—." You can build a practice emphasizing any number of concerns such as tax, criminal, antitrust, immigration, high-tech, patent, personal-injury, divorce, employment, communications and real estate law. You may spot dozens of other law specialties by reading the telephone yellow page directories under "Attorneys Listed by Fields of Law."

Schools Where You Learn to Think Like a Lawyer

With lawyerly class, the degree you get after three years of law school—or four years in a part-time evening program—has been changed from the traditional LLB (bachelor of law) to JD for *juris doctor.*

Choosing a law school requires the same thought and research skills as choosing an undergraduate institution. You need to cross-examine the question with care because where you go to law school has much to do with where you will practice the profession and how successful you'll be in your legal career.

Some well-established firms recruit new lawyers only from law schools attended by the firms' present members or from law schools they consider their state's best. The toniest big-city firms often recruit new associates only from graduates of the nation's top law schools.

Schools often mentioned as being on the first tier are Harvard University, Yale University, University of Chicago, Columbia University, Stanford University, University of Michigan, Northwestern University, University of California at Berkeley, University of Pennsylvania, New York University, University of Virginia, University of Texas, Duke University, Georgetown University, University of Southern California, University of Minnesota, University of California at Los Angeles, University of Illinois and University of Wisconsin.

It's worth noting that many law schools offer joint-degree programs in which you obtain a second degree from an affiliated institution in less time than it would take to complete both degrees separately. The most common programs combine law and business administration, or law and public administration, but you can also team law with economics, history, urban planning, medicine, social work, international relations, journalism, public health and more. You should be certain that such specialized programs will be useful to your career; if in doubt, *don't* get a two-fer. A solid law degree can be widely applied.

Students have always been encouraged to attend law school in the region where they wish to practice because it is easier to find a job when you're home-trained talent. This is still a good idea, but in today's mobile society, fewer and fewer students know with certainty where they want to hang a shingle after graduation.

If that's your dilemma, simply aim for the most highly regarded school you can get in and don't lose sleep over geography.

If you are accepted by more than one school, consider carefully before making your decision. It is an uphill battle to transfer from one law school to another.

Since the choice of a law school can have significant consequences, ask experienced lawyers and your college's prelaw adviser for guidance on which schools match your aspirations.

The only law schools you should consider attending are those approved by the American Bar Association. In nearly every state, graduation from an ABA-approved law school is required for admission to the bar. For all practical purposes, you can't become a lawyer in the United States without earning a degree from an approved law school.

Once you're in school, work hard. Employers put a lot of emphasis on a candidate's grades; being near the top of the class is more important than it is for graduates in many other fields. Everybody wants a "smart" lawyer.

How To Look Good to Your Favorite Law School

Some law schools now have to campaign hard to fill all their seats, which means that if you can handle the academics, you probably can get into a law school somewhere.

If you want to wear the school tie of a very selective institution, you must unveil the mysteries of its admissions process. The big-time law schools, still under siege from would-be students, can afford to be picky about whom they accept.

In general, the selection criteria are the same as those used by admissions committees at professional schools of all types, with one notable difference: The standardized admission test may be taken more seriously by law schools than are standardized tests in other career fields, with the possible exception of medicine.

The importance of each selection factor depends on the law school's admissions policy, but it is commonly believed that the Law School Admission Test (LSAT) is the single most significant element. The scoring scale is 10 to 48; you need a score of 45 to be considered a front-running candidate for the top law schools.

Grades are a close second on the academic measuring stick. Easy, pushover courses don't count as much as respectably difficult studies.

References and recommendations may be influential. A recommendation from one of the school's alumni benefactors could tip the scales in your favor if your qualifications are first-rate. Strong academic references from approving professors can help a lot, too. But if you've got a 1.5 grade point and a 28 LSAT score, you may be turned down even if you have a father who can contribute the west wing of a new library, as well as endorsements from three former U.S. presidents.

Extracurricular activities are frosting on the cake. The activities that reflect most favorably are those requiring communication skills, like public speaking, debating and writing.

If you're a member of a minority group, be sure to mention the fact: There may be special programs available that work to your advantage.

To bask in the light of acceptance from your favorite law school(s), the appropriate strategy is obvious: Keep your grades up, and study for the LSAT. Yes, you can prepare for it.

Here's a Starter Law Library

The Law School Admission Council (Box 2000, Newtown, PA 18940) is a kind of one-stop shopping center specializing in materials that collectively tell you everything you ever wanted to know about law school. Two key publications are *The Official Guide to U.S. Law Schools* and *The Official LSAT Sample Test Book.* The Council also publishes smaller works on choosing the right law school and financing a law school education. Write for a catalog.

Inside the Law Schools: A Guide By Students For Students, by Sally Goldfarb (Dutton), offers an unofficial look at the nation's legal education system.

Is a Law Career Really You?

To be an effective practicing lawyer, you know you need strong communication abilities, but did you know you need a high tolerance for ambiguity?

Some students enter school thinking the law is filled with order. They are surprised to learn that law does not contain that kind of certainty. Lawyers must always take a judicial look at all sides of an issue. An individual with a rigid mind-set will be uneasy in an atmosphere of multisided disclosure.

How do you rank on patience? In law, you have to dig in and spend long hours chasing a single legal point, then shape the facts into a persuasive argument.

Then there are real-life games of scruples. When you have tough calls to make—defending a confessed criminal, writing lopsided contracts for clients—you may be creating inner turmoil you can't handle.

How do you feel about generous participation in charitable, educational and community activities as a way of attracting clients? In some communities, new lawyers regularly run for political office, not to win but to advertise their services.

Ambiguity, patience, scruples and public visibility are only a few of the factors you should consider before making a decision in favor of the law.

Medical School: Fewer Knocks on the Door

Today your chances of getting into medical school are 50 percent better than they were only a few years ago.

Until recently med schools enrolled one out of three applicants; now it's one out of two. The institutions wonder why fewer would-be physicians are standing on their doorsteps. The two most obvious reasons: the chilling cost of becoming a physician, and the general realization that medicine is an overbooked profession.

The nation has more than 550,000 licensed physicians, a third more than a decade ago. If trends hold, there will be 26 doctors per 10,000 people by the end of the century, compared with 17 in 1976. Most of the surplus is concentrated in urban areas and in certain medical specialties.

Today a third of the students entering medical schools are women, up from fewer than 10 percent 20 years ago. Except for surgery, every specialty field has a large number of women residents. Presumably, women aren't wild about cutting, preferring such non-invasive specialties as primary care.

Minorities? Other than an increase in the number of Asian-American medical students, there's been little enrollment movement up or down by minorities in the past few years. The total minority enrollment in medical schools in the late '80s runs about 17 percent.

Virtually everything is changing in American medicine. A must-read look at the medical revolution is found in *Newsweek*'s cover story, January 26, 1987:

> *Consider the shifts of the last five years alone. Hospitals have changed from overcrowded to underused; hospital financing has shifted from cost-plus to fiercely competitive; delivery of services has been effectively deregulated, leading to ambulatory surgical clinics, physician advertising...and the return of the house call.*

The oversupply of hospital beds and doctors and the government lid on Medicare/Medicaid expenses haven't yet financially weakened physicians as a group, unless you think average net earnings of $118,000 are anemic. Even so, the days when doctors "wore the golden ring"—some earning half-million-dollar yearly incomes—may be history.

What must you invest in a medical career? You may pay up to $20,000 annually if you enroll at a private medical school. After four stressful, hardball years there, you're ready to move on to three or more grueling years of residency, where you are a doctor in training. The average debt of a medical school graduate entering residency is $33,000—and debt loads more than twice that amount are not uncommon.

Now that you finally are earning money, how much will you get? The average resident earns $22,000 yearly. Not all are that lucky. A recent study shows that 200 medical residents—often graduates of foreign medical schools—have agreed to work for free because they are desperate to gain a foothold in a crowded profession.

If you still have med school in mind, the most important thing you can do right now is contact the premedical adviser in your college. Most colleges and universities have designated a faculty member—usually in health sciences, chemistry or biology—as the adviser for premedical students. The office of the dean of liberal arts and/or sciences usually can refer you to the premedical adviser. If your institution does not have such an adviser, contact the registrar or admissions officer at a nearby medical school.

Examining the Medical Schools

Two types of physicians are trained in the United States. One has an MD (doctor of medicine) degree and the other has a DO (doctor of osteopathic medicine) degree. MDs outnumber DOs about 20 to 1.

The difference between the two is in their approach to medicine, but training for both MDs and DOs is similar in timing and professional requirements. MDs study in allopathic medical schools, DOs in osteopathic medical schools.

Of the nation's 128 allopathic medical schools, 127 are accredited by the Liaison Committee on Medical Education, the official accreditation group for MD programs. In addition, 16 Canadian programs are accredited.

All 15 osteopathic medical schools in the U.S. are accredited by the American Osteopathic Association, the official accrediting group for DO programs.

Accreditation, important to future licensure, is virtually universal among North American medical schools, which means you ought to obtain quality training in any one of them—after all, American physicians are the best in the world. Even so, certain institutions are more notable than others.

We asked numerous medical authorities which institutions they think rank in the highest tier of medical schools. Certain names came up consistently.

Among allopathic medical schools, the institutions most often mentioned include Johns Hopkins University, Duke University, Harvard University, Stanford University, Washington University, University of Chicago, Columbia University, University of California at San Diego, University of California at Los Angeles, University of California at San Francisco, University of Texas at Dallas, Yale University, University of Pennsylvania, Cornell University, University of Chicago, University of Iowa, University of Michigan and Vanderbilt University.

Among osteopathic medical schools, the Kirksville (Mo.) College of Osteopathic Medicine is the pioneer institution, frequently and favorably mentioned. Others are the Philadelphia College of Osteopathic Medicine, Chicago College of Osteopathic Medicine, Michigan State University, New Jersey School of Osteopathic Medicine and Texas College of Osteopathic Medicine.

The big-name allopathic medical schools have far more clinical facilities and research capacity than do the best known osteopathic medical schools.

The book to read about allopathic medical schools is the *Medical School Admissions Requirements,* published annually by the Association of American Medical Colleges, Suite 200, One Dupont Circle NW, Washington, DC 20036.

Information about osteopathic schools is available from the American Association of Colleges of Osteopathic Medicine, Suite 405, 6110 Executive Blvd., Rockville, MD 20852.

Because the majority of medical schools are state related, restrictions will be placed on the number of out-of-state applicants who can be accepted. The University of Kansas School of Medicine, for example, will give preference to applicants who are graduates of undergraduate colleges in Kansas before considering applicants from other states.

In brief, you should apply to medical schools within your state, and to a reasonable number of private medical schools and a small number of state medical schools outside your state.

Getting Into Medical School

If you knew before you entered college that you wanted to attend medical school, you probably chose your undergraduate institution with that goal in mind.

That's smart planning. Graduating from a college affiliated with a medical school can be advantageous. Medical schools tend to select graduates of particular colleges when they've been happy with past choices from those colleges. Attending a nationally known college maximizes the probabilities of your acceptance to a nationally known medical school.

But if you're already in college when the thought of becoming a physician enters your mind, make sure your curriculum meets all academic requirements for the premed track.

Rush to read an excellent resource for premed students: *Preparing For Medical School: A Guide to Requirements, Admission, Financial Aid, and More,* by Brice W. Corder. The book was published in 1983 and some figures may be dated, but as a counseling guide, it's the best we've seen. If you can't find the book locally, order in paperback from the publisher, Ambleside Publishers, 2122 E. Concorda Drive, Tempe, AZ 85282. The cost, including postage, is $8.95 prepaid.

After you're into the routine of making good grades in the courses required for admission, you'll probably be debating with yourself whether you should apply to medical school as a three- or four-year applicant. If you try to speed up your education by entering medical school after three years of study, you will be the one out of ten who does so. More than 90 percent of students entering American medical schools have completed at least four years of college.

Preparing for the Medical College Admission Test (MCAT) makes good use of your spare time. With notable exceptions—Johns Hopkins no longer requires the MCAT—the standardized admission test is one of the two big numbers medical schools' admissions committees use for preliminary screening. Take the MCAT during the preceding spring, not the fall, of the year in which you plan to apply to medical schools. If you delay until the fall, you could be at a disadvantage at a school that uses a rolling admissions process, because the longer you wait, the more individuals you must compete with for a place in the freshman class.

An essential book to read on the topic of the admission test is *The New MCAT Student Manual,* published by the Association of American Medical Colleges. You can buy it in most college bookstores or order it through your premedical adviser's office. The book contains helpful hints and practice tests.

Many premed students enroll in review courses such as those offered by the Stanley H. Kaplan Educational Centers.

The other big number used by school admissions committees for screening is the grade point average.

To have a reasonably good chance to get into a medical school that receives more applications than it can handle, you must have a good GPA and impressive scores on the MCAT. What's "good"? What's "impressive"? You want at least a 3.6 GPA in both science and non-science courses, and high MCAT scores. Some schools, particularly state institutions, will take into account an upward trend in the GPA; you may receive a nod of approval even if your GPA was sluggish for the first two years of college if it shoots up once a decision is made to pursue medicine.

Generally speaking, you will need better numbers at private and out-of-state schools than you will for medical schools in your state. A student with a GPA of around 3.0 and MCAT scores in the 60 percentile who is accepted into an out-of-state school is a lucky person—it doesn't happen often. It can happen at in-state schools.

Osteopathic medical schools aren't interested unless you have a minimum 3.0 GPA and 50 percentile MCAT scores.

Once medical school committees move from screening to selection, a number of factors are considered, which is why you should read detailed admissions guidance such as that given in Dr. Brice Corder's book. Selection criteria vary somewhat from school to school, but usually the factors include interviews, references, faculty letters, minority goals, and political pressure from alumni.

Not Getting In

It's a black day when your last thin letter says, "Sorry, you didn't make it into our medical school." You feel rage, shame, not good enough. How you handle these reactions is critical to your entire future.

Wrestle with the demon of lowered self-esteem. Realize that the rejection is only career related, not self-worth related. It's pointless to paralyze yourself by making rejection a creed.

End of pep talk. Now decide what you're going to do: reapply next year or make an alternative career choice. Foreign medical schools are no longer a good alternative, according to Dr. James G. Price, chairman of family medicine, University of Kansas School of Medicine. Their graduates are likely to have trouble getting licenses and residency appointments.

Act on your decision!

Operating in the Profession: Choices

You may start out in medical school with a definite idea of the specialty area you want to pursue. The odds are strongly against your sticking with your original choice when the time comes—during your fourth year of medical school—to declare your residency field. Premedical advisers say that as many as 90 percent of students have second thoughts about their original choices.

Here are the medical specialties recognized by both the allopathic and osteopathic sectors of the profession. Each September, the *Journal of the American Medical Association* publishes a medical education issue that includes this information and much more.

Allergy and immunology
Anesthesiology
Colon and rectal surgery
Dermatology
Dermatopathology
Emergency medicine
Family practice
Internal medicine
Neurological surgery
Neurology
Nuclear medicine
Obstetrics-gynecology
Ophthalmology
Orthopedic surgery
Otolaryngology
Pathology
  Blood banking
  Forensic pathology
  Hematology
  Neuropathology
Pediatrics
  Pediatric cardiology
  Neonatal-perinatal medicine
Physical medicine and rehabilitation
Plastic surgery
Preventive medicine, general
  Aerospace medicine
  Occupational medicine
  Public health
  Combined general preventive medicine/public health
Psychiatry
  Child psychiatry
Radiology, diagnostic
Radiology, diagnostic (nuclear)
Radiology, therapeutic
Surgery
  Pediatric surgery
  Vascular surgery
  Thoracic surgery
Urology

Should There Be a Doctor in Your House?

In addition to wanting to help others, people are attracted to medicine for many reasons. Financial security and success are two of them. Add to the list of motivations intellectual challenge, the ability to exercise authority, independence, and social status.

At the bottom line, we hope you'll be candid. Are you going into medicine for reasons that are right for you?

As Dr. Stuart Scott, a highly successful internist in Gaithersburg, Md., says:

Some people feel that doctors will always do well, that the money will take care of itself. That used to be true, and, to a degree, still is, but recent financial dislocations are causing controversy within the profession.

Government and private insurance plans are turning compensation schedules inside out, favoring high payments for physicians who do invasive procedures [surgery and other work inside the body], and penalizing physicians who perform intellectual, diagnostic services.

The inequity is being addressed forcefully by several medical specialty associations. Regardless of the outcome, there is one constant: The real rewards, the daily uplifting satisfactions go to the sincere and diligent practitioner. Anyone who is focused on the bank statement should not be in the profession.

SECTION FOURTEEN

An Educational Catalog: Pathways to Success

J*ust as there's more than one way to dance, and more than one kind of* music to dance to, there's more than one way to attain a satisfying career.

You don't have to pursue a traditional four-year college education to position yourself for the good things in life. You do have to develop job skills that are in demand and, with rare exceptions, the only way to get those skills is through comprehensive training.

This section describes the spectacular array of specialty training and skill-learning options you can choose from—both now and later as you update your competencies to remain competitive throughout your career years. Included are vocational-technical schools and community colleges, as well as opportunities in home study, external degree, continuing education, employee training and military training programs.

You will find information on programs offered by professional societies, trade organizations, community organizations, churches and synagogues, libraries, museums, seminar sponsors and summer institutes.

Apprenticeships, formal and informal, are described. The section concludes with suggestions on how to choose a skill-learning option.

Feast on a Banquet of Job-Training Programs

A young friend says she chose between two vocational programs—cosmetology and medical assisting—by tossing a coin. Before we could close our astonished mouths, she explained:

"When you flip a coin in the air, that's when the truth hits you of how you hope it will come out."

Fortunately, from our friend's point of view, the coin landed right side up. She likes her work. But there's a better way. Do the necessary homework on yourself and on the job market before signing up to learn specific job skills.

Ask yourself: Am I really interested in this work? Will there be demand for the kind of work I want? Are there more people training for my kind of work than there are jobs? Do potential employers say there is a local need for workers in the career field I'm considering? If prospects are poor for working locally but are better elsewhere, am I willing to move to where the jobs are?

Think about these kinds of things as you choose from an appetizing feast of skill-learning options.

Heads or tails—can you believe that!

Schools Where Students Pay to Learn Paying Jobs

If you're the sort of person who likes to get straight to the point, you may be a candidate for vocational-technical (vo-tech) education. One option: the nation's network of 6,000 private profit-making vo-tech schools that send graduates into the world with a marketable set of work skills.

Another 1,300 vo-tech schools in the private sector are set up as non-profit institutions that have the same mission and operate in ways similar to the profit makers.

Together, they comprise about 80 percent of the nation's 9,200 or so postsecondary vo-tech schools.

The private schools offer pure and lean training programs that usually can get you into a paying job within a year, although some programs last two years. Private courses skip over academic subjects, unless they are necessary to do the work. They emphasize solving everyday work problems similar to those found on the job.

Most private vo-tech institutions aren't cheap. Costs run from about $800 for nine-week programs, such as manicuring, to more than $6,000 a year for longer programs—computer sciences, for example. If the school is accredited by an agency recognized by the U.S. Department of Education, you can apply for federal and state student aid—loans, grants and work-study programs—just as college students do.

Who attends private vo-tech schools? The typical enrollment mix might include these fictional but representive people: Kevin, a high school graduate who is fed up with conventional education; Marsha, a college graduate who finds her academic credentials aren't helping her obtain a well-paying job; Jonathan, a midcareer switcher who wants to change his line of work; Tiffany, a homemaker who wishes to return to the job market but needs skills quickly; Rob, who lost his job in an auto plant and is forced to find a new way of earning a living.

Logically you may ask why spend the money for a private school when you can learn the same job skills in a less expensive public vo-tech school or a community college? Good question. Here are the pluses of private vo-tech training.

Advantages of Private Vo-Tech Schools

• Some students choose the private route for a basic reason: job first, culture later. They just want job training, not academic enlightenment. They don't see themselves as college oriented, but feel they need additional training to land jobs.

• Students can usually enroll any time in a private vo-tech school; they need not wait until the semester or quarter break. Because these schools offer short-course units—with nearly instant intervals of completion and success—students who did not do too well in high school often get their first sweet taste of accomplishment in a private vo-tech school classroom. This feeling of success may help them as much as the content of the course in preparing to work in skilled jobs.

• An attractive feature at some private vocational schools is a performance evaluation policy that permits you to leave when you know the material. Such a school is said to have an open exit philosphy. If you can pass the test—for instance, tune an engine—you can leave immediately as a graduate, rather than wait out the full term.

• Classes are usually small. The teachers may give extra attention, doing their best to see that a student doesn't drop out, because for them a dropout is a lost sale.

• Private vo-tech schools usually are very concerned about their placement records and business reputations. They must satisfy their customers, or eventually they will go out of business. Staffs tend to work hard to place graduates and to cultivate the esteem of local employers.

Disadvantages of Private Vo-Tech Schools

• A drawback to private vo-tech study is that the school may not have the extensive classroom, laboratory and recreational facilities that a government-supported school does. If you are considering a private vo-tech course requiring hands-on experience with various tools, such as auto mechanics, be sure you are learning on up-to-date equipment.

• Beware of the "dream schools," institutions that feed on individuals chasing unlikely dreams in glamour careers.

The never-ending stream of would-be stars has spawned an industry of dream merchants who operate schools for actors, artists, authors, baseball and basketball players, comedians, disc jockeys, models, musicians, race car drivers and songwriters.

No matter how well-intentioned the dream merchants, the fact is that very, very few of their students reach the crests they seek. As one psychiatrist says, "Many people set themselves up for failure by training all year for the next football camp or the next movie tryout and avoid getting on with their lives."

• Very, very few courses at a private vo-tech school will transfer for academic college credit. You may eventually want a college degree; don't be surprised when you can't apply vocational studies to an academic degree program and have to start at the beginning.

• The best private vo-tech schools can provide skills necessary to get good jobs and to advance more quickly. Unfortunately, some schools are operated by "Fast Eddies" who promise high-paying jobs and rosy futures they cannot deliver. If you don't want to be fleeced by a gyp operator, do your homework in checking out the school. How do you find a good school? Follow this guide.

Choosing a Private Vo-Tech School

• Check the advertising. A school's advertising should communicate that *students* are sought, not employees. Ads recruiting "trainees for immediate openings" are not straightforward.

What You Can Learn in Vocational-Technical Schools

Look over this abbreviated list of programs offered by both private and public vocational schools to get an idea of career fields you can learn.

- accounting
- administrative assistant training, health
- advertising art/design
- agricultural management
- air conditioning, heating, refrigeration service
- aircraft maintenance technology
- airline and travel career training
- audio and recording technology
- automated office administration
- automated system service technology
- automotive body repair
- automotive mechanics

- baking
- barbering
- bartending
- biomedical equipment technology
- blood bank technology
- blueprint reading
- bricklaying
- broadcast technician training
- building maintenance
- burglar and fire alarm technology
- business administration
- business communications
- business computer systems
- business machines maintenance

- cardiovascular perfusionist training
- carpentry
- cartooning/animation
- cat grooming
- charm training
- chemical technology
- child care
- coin-operated machine repair
- communications electronics
- computer graphics
- computer information systems
- culinary arts

- data processing
- dental assisting
- dental laboratory technology
- diagnostic medical sonography
- diamond and gem cutting
- diesel technology
- digital electronics
- distributive education
- dog grooming
- drafting, computer-aided design
- dressmaking and design
- driver education

- electricity, construction
- EKG technology
- electrolysis
- electromechanical technology
- electronic technician training
- electronics technology
- engineering technology
- equestrian studies
- esthetics (cosmetics and skin care)

- farrier training (horseshoeing)
- fashion design
- fashion illustration
- fashion merchandising
- fiber-optic technology

- finance
- fine arts
- floristry
- fluid power technology
- food service technology (includes catering)
- forestry technology

- gemology
- geriatric assisting
- golf instruction
- graphic arts
- greenhouse management
- gunsmithing

- heavy equipment operation
- hematology
- histological technology
- home furnishings sales
- home health aide training
- horticulture
- hotel and motel management

- illustration
- income tax
- industrial electronics
- information processing
- institutional management
- instrument repair
- interior decoration
- international trade

- jewelry design
- jewelry repair
- kennel management
- landscaping/gardening
- laser technology
- legal assisting
- locksmithing

- machine tool operations
- manicuring
- manufacturing technology
- marine mechanics
- marketing
- massage therapy
- medical assistant training
- medical records technology
- microcomputer repair
- mobile communications
- modeling
- multi-image production

- nuclear medicine technology
- nurse aid training
- nursing, registered
- office assistant training
- office machines operations
- optical technology
- orthotics
- paperhanging
- paralegal assisting
- patternmaking
- photography, commercial
- plastics technology
- plumbing, construction
- private investigation

- radiation therapy technology
- radio and TV broadcasting
- radio and TV repair
- radiologic (x-ray) technology
- real estate sales and management
- receptionist training
- record engineer training
- records management
- recreation and tourism
- respiratory care
- robotics
- roofing, construction

- sales management
- secretarial studies
- security management
- sheet-metal trades
- shipbuilding
- sign painting

(continued)

- small business management
- small engine repair
- solar energy technology
- stenography
- supermarket management
- surveying and mapping

- tailoring
- telecommunications electronics
- textile design
- tool and die design
- toxicology
- travel personnel training

- truck driving
- turf management
- typing

- upholstering
- veterinarian assisting
- VCR repair
- violin making
- water technologies
- welding
- woodworking/cabinetmaking
- word processing
- yacht design

• Watch out for guarantees. Steer clear of a school that guarantees you a job, or insists that there's "a place for you in____field." Avoid schools that suggest you'll be anything other than a trainee after graduation.

• Don't fall for hype. Resist pressure to sign an enrollment agreement quickly in return for a discount. You're looking for quality training, not a bargain. In many instances, the so-called discount is a myth. Most states have a cooling-off period of several days that allows you to cancel a contract without financial penalty.

• Be very clear about the fine print in the enrollment agreement regarding payments and tuition refunds if you drop out. For instance, if the agreement says you'll get a refund if you withdraw because of an emergency, will you get it if a parent becomes ill and you must quit to work full time, or is an emergency refund given only if you become ill? Ignore verbal assurances from a school's representative. Get clarifications or modifications to the agreement in writing.

• Request placement figures. What percentage of graduates find jobs related to their studies? The average is said to be about 80 percent.

As a practical matter, you have no way to verify the school's placement rate. That's why contacting recent graduates is important. Ask for the names of a dozen and get in touch with four or five. Try to reach graduates who live in your geographic area so you can talk face to face.

• Determine employer views. Ask employers such key questions as: Would you hire this school's graduates? Have you hired any during the past year? Were they hired because of school training? Did that training make any difference in starting salary?

• Talk to students privately. Ask if there's a time when you can visit the school and speak to them on a random basis. See how they evaluate the training they're receiving.

• Verify licensing. Most states require licensing by the state's postsecondary school licensing body. Your state's department of education can confirm whether a particular school is licensed.

• Verify graduation credentials. Because they specialize in specific job fields, vo-tech schools usually do not give academic degrees. When you complete the program the school will give you a certificate or diploma attesting to your newly learned skills. Find out if completion of the program qualifies you to take the state certification examination, if there is one for your field, such as cosmetology, real estate or certain medical technologies.

- Ask whether the school is accredited and, if so, by what group? Accreditation should be given by an agency recognized by the U.S. Office of Education. A school can be a fine institution without being accredited, but if you're considering attending an unaccredited school, you should do extensive research on it before signing up. For a quick check on accreditation, obtain free guidebooks from these two groups: *National Association of Trade and Technical Schools,* Box 10429, Rockville, MD 20850; *Association of Independent Colleges and Schools,* Suite 350, One Dupont Circle NW, Washington, DC 20036.
- Get catalogs from at least three institutions and compare them. You can look up names and addresses of vo-tech schools in a library copy of *Vocational School Manual,* issued annually by Chronicle Guidance Publications, or the *Directory of Postsecondary Institutions, Part 2 (Occupational Programs),* published every two years by the Center for Educational Statistics, U.S. Office of Education.

Public Schools Where Students Train for Jobs

"Dear Mom and Dad," the letter from the college student began. "It's been a whole month since I've heard from you. Why not drop me a check so I'll know you're okay?"

Does this sound like something you might come up with? We heard it from a college student's parents, but the student is at a special kind of college—a *job college.*

Just as some students go away to academic colleges, others go away to state-supported residential vocational-technical schools, also called residential technical colleges or residential technical institutes.

In the following pages we tell you more about live-in job schools, as well as other types of public vo-tech schools.

"Stop right here!" you say? You're all set to be a philosophy major at Old Ivy U. and you may as well skip this portion because it doesn't apply to your immediate plans. Please keep reading. You won't be wasting your time learning something about public vo-tech education.

Point 1: Higher education costs today run somewhere between extraordinary and impossible. You may face a choice between a skyscraper of debt and working your way through college. Without work skills, you likely qualify only for minimum-wage jobs. With skills, such as hairdressing or automotive technology, you can earn far more.

Point 2: A changing world is sending more and more adults into vo-tech classrooms for retraining. You may not be interested in vo-tech education now, but you could be very interested later.

Point 3: Your plans may change. Roughly half the students who enter college don't cross the finish line four years later. Moreover, college grads sometimes decide they'd rather chuck office jobs to do such things as cabinetmaking or running swimming pool services.

From any angle, you're ahead of the game when you know where to find inexpensive schools that teach marketable job skills.

Secondary Public Vo-Tech Schools

Most high school districts operate job training programs that are open to adults. These vo-tech programs and courses are designed to provide skills, knowledge and techniques that prepare you for employment immediately upon leaving school.

A large number of programs operate elaborate skill centers that boast the latest equipment and industrial techniques.

AVTSs are area vocational-technical schools that teach technical skills ranging from "soft" specialties such as floristry, to "hard" technology like electronics. The schools' prime purpose is to deliver vo-tech education in a wide range of occupations to students in the area's high schools, but most offer adult education programs at night. Study requirements for these programs range from several weeks to two years.

Comprehensive high schools offer vocational-technical programs in several or all of these areas: agricultural, business, distributive and industrial education, as well as home economics. Programs vary widely in length, but two years is common.

Technical high schools are found most often in large cities. Their programs, usually lasting three or four years for high school students, may be condensed to a year or two for adults. Studies tend to be on the technological side, such as computer science and plastics molding, but programs are offered in such traditional trades as upholstery.

You may have noticed there's an overlapping of skill-learning options among secondary institutions. Don't worry about whether the school is called an AVTS, a comprehensive high school or a technical high school. If you want vo-tech education at the secondary level, just call the board of education in your community and ask about available opportunities wherever they may be.

Postsecondary Public Vo-Tech Schools

Actor Jack Lemmon says the best advice he ever received was from his father, an executive of a company that manufactures bakery goods. In encouraging Lemmon to follow his heart, his father said: "The day I don't find romance in a loaf of bread, I'm going to quit."

What the father meant was that what you are doing is not as important as loving it.

Loving the idea of practical, rather than theoretical, work is one of the reasons—probably the best reason—that students enroll in the 2,000 postsecondary public job training institutions across the nation.

The institutions offer programs ranging in length from one to four years, most often two years. Typically, they have institutional titles like *technical institutes, vocational-technical institutes, area vocational-technical institutes* and *technical colleges.*

To add a note of confusion, a number of postsecondary public vocational-technical education institutions are known as—are you ready for this?—*community colleges* or *state colleges.*

Some are regionally based, like the Lake Washington Vocational Technical Institute in Kirkland, Wash., serving the northwestern portion of the state, while others are state oriented, such as the North Dakota State School of Science at Wahpeton.

By any name or area, public postsecondary vocational-technical schools are designed to provide relevant, effective and efficient job training at nominal cost to students; a $2,000 course at a private vocational school might cost $200 at a public vocational school.

Collectively, public institutions offer the full range of occupational programs listed earlier in this section. No school offers all fields any more than all colleges offer all majors. Whether you're interested in business machines or photography,culinary arts or truck driving, you'll have to look around for schools offering appropriate training programs.

You can ask a school counselor, career center specialist or reference librarian for the names of vo-tech schools appropriate to your needs. You also can write to the postsecondary education specialist in your state's education department to request a list of vo-tech programs within your state.

Do students ever make education and career selections the other way around—hearing about an excellent vo-tech school and then selecting one of the career fields the school offers? Yes. Sometimes the reverse method of decision making works out, sometimes it doesn't.

Earlier we mentioned that the vast majority of

vo-tech programs offer certificates and diplomas, not academic degrees. There are exceptions. Institutions that include a general education component in a program lasting two years or more may award associate degrees similar to those offered by community colleges.

If you are going for training, rather than for retraining, it's wise to consider a program that contains some general education. Technologies die; knowledge remains.

In describing the need for students to be flexible throughout their careers, Larry W. Johnson, chief executive officer of the Vocational Industrial Club of America, argues against education that is sliced too thin.

We need to educate our young people broadly enough that they have the ability to cope with changing requirements in the workplace. This means we need to be teaching them not only job skills they can use immediately; we also need to be teaching them to learn—they will need to continue learning all their lives to live in our new world.

Let's look now at a special group of exciting postsecondary public vocational schools—the job colleges we mentioned earlier.

Live-In Job Colleges

A parent writes:

Dear Registrar: Our son, Rob, is the kind who can find 50 uses for a paper clip, has helped his dad build and wire three houses, works on his sports car constantly, and will be captain of the football team his senior year. But he has no interest in four long years in a college. Please rush a brochure on your school to Rob.

The letter is typical of the thousands received each year by the registrar of Oklahoma State University, Technical Branch in Okmulgee, Okla., the nation's largest residential technical college campus. Housed in an impressive spread of modern buildings, the institution provides a learning experience that places equal importance on educating hand and mind.

OSU Tech looks and operates much like most state colleges, except that its graduates emerge with immediately marketable skills and are inundated with job offers in such fields as computer-integrated systems service, automotive technology, electronics, air conditioning and other technologies.

The live-in job college, as represented by OSU Tech, is not a second-best choice for second-best students. On the contrary, it is the very best choice for thousands of very fine students.

OSU Tech, for example, has a 160-acre, multimillion-dollar campus, more than 4,000 full-time students each year who come not only from Oklahoma, but every other state and several foreign countries, nearly 200 full-time, industry-experienced instructors, many millions of dollars in instructional equipment for student use and a national reputation for excellence.

Like academic colleges, the school has campus dorms, clubs, intramural sports, a student center, medical facilities and other familiar college attractions.

Programs are divided into trimesters and range in length from four months to two years. Students can enter in early January, mid-April or late August. Programs are open to male and female high school graduates; non-graduates who are at least 17.5 years old are admitted as special students.

All coursework is offered for college credit, and all five- and six-trimester programs lead to the associate in applied science degree.

Costs are equivalent to many state-supported schools; in-state students pay less than $400 tuition a trimester, out-of-state students pay more, but less than $1,500.

At OSU Tech, students can choose from more than 40 career programs. A catalog is available from Oklahoma State University, Technical Branch, Okmulgee, OK 74447.

Our research turned up a mere handful of residential vo-tech institutions that, like OSU Tech, are considered on a par with state colleges where you live on campus and receive comprehensive training in job skills. Here is the list we developed:

North Georgia Vocational-Technical School
Clarkesville, GA 30523

South Georgia Vocational-Technical School
Americus, GA 31709

Ferris State College
Big Rapids, MI 49307

Southeast Community College
Milford, NB 68405

North Dakota State School of Science
Wahpeton, ND 58075

Texas State Technical Institute
Waco, TX 76705

In choosing a public postsecondary vo-tech school, use some of the same guidelines recommended for selecting a proprietary institution. You want to know if the instruction and equipment are up to date, whether the faculty is first-rate and if there's a demand for the occupational skills you will learn. To find out, query employers, students, graduates and counselors.

We've never heard anyone speak of vo-tech education in terms of skylarking poetry, presumably because it is, after all, a practical pursuit leading to practical career skills. Remember, though, that in choosing this option, you make a real contribution to others as well as to your own career prospects.

A vision without skills is a dream;
Skills without vision is a grind;
A vision and skills is achievement.

The Two-Year College: Opportunity With Excellence

Community, technical and junior colleges are a vast and growing force in America. They enroll a stunning 55 percent of all first-time freshmen in institutions of higher learning across the country today. Approximately 8 percent of all adult Americans will take one or more classes in an American community, technical or junior college this year. These institutions are acting out and modeling our national commitments.

—Dale Parnell in
The Neglected Majority

In the last 30 years, community colleges have sprung up throughout the United States, putting one within commuting distance of almost every citizen. Now numbering about 1,200, there aren't many more locations to put a two-year educational institution that prides itself on being available to large numbers of students at low cost.

Each year about five million students, part-time and full-time, teenagers to octogenarians, attend community colleges. They pay an average annual tuition of less than $700, about half the tuition at a public four-year college and one-tenth the tuition at a private university. Living at home helps keep the costs down, too, and most community college students do commute to classes.

More than half the students who attend community colleges have a specific purpose: they want to learn job skills that lead to employment in a specific career field. Are you interested in acquiring specific job skills? Depending on the course, you can graduate with a two-year associate degree, or a certificate in a specialty area, which usually is awarded for a program lasting one year or less. In either case, you will be prepared to start working at the technician or paraprofessional level, assisting or reporting to a professional-level worker.

Terms, Those Pesky Terms

For convenience, we use the term *community college* to mean all associate-degree-awarding institutions offering programs lasting two years or more, but less than four years, regardless of whether the institution's name includes the title *technical institute, technical college* or *junior college.*

Technical institutes, you'll remember, are included in the previous pages on vocational education because most originated as vo-tech schools. As increasing numbers of technical institutes award associate degrees, rather than diplomas and certificates, they may be classified under the community college banner.

Technical institutes teach many of the same subjects as other vo-tech schools, but the training tends to be more intense, and to require advanced math and scientific theory courses. Graduates are considered technicians and usually have a potentially higher level of responsibility on the job than do graduates of some vo-tech schools. Technical institute programs typically run from one to three years, most often two years.

According to the American Association of Community and Junior Colleges, the term *technical college* refers to an institution that primarily offers associate in science or associate in applied science degrees aimed at employment after graduation. A *junior college* primarily offers associate in arts or associate in science degrees aimed at transfer to a baccalaureate-degree-granting institution after graduation. The term *community college,* in AACJC usage, denotes a comprehensive institution that primarily grants associate degrees in technical (work related) or academic (transfer oriented) areas.

You've figured it out—there are no absolutes in educational terminology.

In many states, associate degrees reflecting technical training come in two forms. They are: the associate in applied science (AAS) and the associate in occupational studies (AOS). The AOS generally requires fewer liberal arts courses.

Either the AOS or the AAS may stand alone or may reflect specific studies in the title, such as AAS in computer technology, or AOS in scientific data processing. Other titles used in technically focused programs include associate in business, associate in a specific occupation, and associate in applied arts and sciences.

The choice of skills you can learn is vast, from automotive technology to word processing. Among popular programs are business and management, health occupations, electronics and police work.

A community college can also teach you advertising, agricultural technologies, art education, drafting and design, recreation and leisure services, wildlife management and more.

Another large group of students attend community colleges with the plan to switch later to a four-year college. The core programs at community colleges are much like freshman and sophomore programs at four-year institutions and are designed to let you earn transferable credits.

The appropriate degrees for transfer students often are the associate in arts (AA) and associate in science (AS). The AA degree is appropriate to those majoring in the social sciences, humanities, arts and like subjects. The AS is for students who want to major in engineering, agriculture, or the sciences with heavy undergraduate requirements in math and science.

Whether you have an associate in arts or an associate in science degree, you should be accepted as a junior-level transfer student in baccalaureate-degree-granting institutions. Associate in applied science and associate in occupational studies programs are another matter; because the programs are planned as complete units of study, many of the credits you earn in them will not transfer to a four-year college.

If you think you can stand one more perplexing point, hundreds of four-year colleges offer associate degrees. Credits from your associate degree years theoretically should be valid for a bachelor's degree at the same college, but don't take chances—ask about baccalaureate degree requirements in advance of your first day as a freshman.

The community college, being a uniquely American creation, has felt free to invent itself. Instead of fielding a rigid curriculum during working hours on weekdays on a quadrangled campus, the community colleges operate at all hours in all kinds of places, from store fronts and movie theaters to office buildings and modern classrooms. As writer Jeremy Main has said, "Students in search of ivied halls or a boozy fraternity social life won't find them at community college."

What they will find is opportunity with excellent teaching in many colleges. In study after study, students report they experienced the best teaching of their college careers in a community college. If strong teaching matters to you, include community colleges on your list of best bets for education.

To recap, you have many choices in a community college. You can take a couple of courses for personal satisfaction in subjects like scuba diving or gourmet cooking. You can take a two-year academic program that ends with an associate degree or credits that can be transferred to a four-year school. You can enroll in a technical program leading to a certificate or associate degree.

When you've got a caviar taste for knowledge and are on a casserole budget, check out your community college.

What You Can Learn in Community Colleges

Here is a sampling of the programs available in community colleges throughout the nation. Not all schools offer all programs.

- accounting
- advertising
- aerospace sciences
- African studies
- agricultural business
- agronomy
- aircraft maintenance
- American studies
- animal hospital technology
- animal sciences
- anthropology
- archaeology
- architectural technologies
- art/fine arts
- astronomy
- automotive technologies
- aviation administration

- behavioral sciences
- biological sciences
- biomedical technologies
- black studies
- botany
- broadcasting
- business administration
- business education
- business machine technologies

- carpentry
- cartography
- ceramic art
- chemical engineering technology
- chemistry
- child care studies
- child psychology

- city planning
- civil engineering technology
- communication equipment technology
- community services
- computer information systems
- computer programming
- computer science
- computer technologies
- conservation
- construction management
- consumer services
- corrections/prison management
- cosmetology
- court reporting
- creative writing
- criminal justice
- culinary arts
- cytotechnology

- dance
- data processing
- deaf interpreter training
- dental services
- dietetics
- drafting/design
- drama therapy

- early childhood education
- ecology/environmental studies
- economics
- educational media
- electrical/electronics technologies
- electrical engineering technology
- emergency medical technology
- energy management technologies
- English
- environmental health sciences
- ethnic studies
- equestrian studies

- family services
- farm/ranch management
- fashion design
- fashion merchandising
- film studies
- finance/banking
- fire science
- fish/game management
- flight training
- food marketing
- food sciences
- food services management
- forensic sciences
- forestry
- French
- funeral services

- geography
- geology
- German
- gerontology
- graphic arts
- Greek
- health education
- heating, refrigeration/air conditioning
- Hebrew
- Hispanic studies
- history
- home economics
- horticulture
- hospitality service
- human services
- humanities

- illustration
- industrial administration
- industrial arts
- industrial design
- industrial engineering technology
- industrial equipment maintenance
- instrumentation technology
- insurance
- interior design
- Italian
- Japanese
- jewelry/metalsmithing
- journalism
- labor relations
- laboratory technologies
- landscape architecture

(continued)

- law enforcement
- library science
- marriage counseling
- materials sciences
- mathematics
- mechanical engineering technology
- medical assistant technologies
- medical illustration
- medical laboratory technology
- medical records services
- medical secretarial studies
- metallurgical technology
- meteorology
- Mexican-American studies
- military science
- mining technology
- museum studies
- music
- Native American studies
- natural resource management
- natural sciences
- nuclear medical technology
- nursing
- nutrition
- occupational safety/health
- occupational therapy
- oceanography
- operating room technology
- optometric technologies
- ornamental horticulture
- painting/drawing
- paper/pulp sciences
- paralegal studies
- parks management
- photography
- physical education
- physical therapy
- plumbing
- practical nursing
- printing technologies
- public administration
- public relations
- publishing
- quality control technology
- radio/TV studies
- radiological technology
- real estate
- recreation/leisure services
- rehabilitation therapy
- religious studies
- respiratory therapy
- retail management
- robotics
- Russian
- safety/security technologies
- sanitation technologies
- science education
- sculpture
- secretarial studies
- social work
- soil conservation
- solar technologies
- Spanish
- speech/public address
- sports administration
- sports medicine
- statistics
- surveying technology
- taxation
- technical writing
- telecommunications
- textile arts
- theater arts
- tourism and travel
- transportation technologies
- urban studies
- veterinary sciences
- vocational education
- water resources
- welding
- wildlife management
- women's studies
- wood sciences
- zoology

Home Study Schools: You Ring the Classroom Bell

Captain Patricia A. Brown is a Florida Army National Guard helicopter pilot who successfully navigated through required communications electronics courses, thanks to correspondence study programs. Louisiana insurance executive James Moye III earned his professional credential, the prestigious Chartered Life Underwriter, with knowledge acquired in a home study program.

Why does home study appeal to Brown and Moye? Why might it appeal to you? Control and convenience are two cardinal reasons.

When you learn at a distance from the campus, you learn at your own pace in your own home. You determine the time when you will use textbooks, workbooks, audiotapes, videotapes, exercises, projects and other materials the institution supplies. You determine when you will complete and return lesson assignments for grading and credit by the institution's faculty. Within reasonable limits, you control the clock and you control the calendar of when and how fast you learn.

As Pat Brown says, "I feel that correspondence courses have greatly helped my educational efforts. I always keep a course segment in my car, one in my briefcase and one in my flight bag. You never know when the opportunity will present itself to enrich your education."

Home study is different from self-study in that you receive responses from a faculty member who provides information, advice and explanations of points that aren't immediately clear to you. You can write or telephone your instructor to receive answers to your questions.

The range of courses available is similar to an exotic bazaar teeming with colorful items, heady fragrances and interesting activities. In the more than 2,000 courses offered through correspondence schools, some are not available at most conventional institutions—diamond grading, doll repair, yacht design, color analysis, exercise studio management and outdoor sporting goods repair.

Are home study courses really helpful in starting a career such as income tax counseling or business management? While we don't advocate learning brain surgery by mail, home study can be a highly desirable way to acquire skills for many kinds of business, trade and industry occupations. In a study of 1,800 correspondence school graduates, 54 percent said they won jobs related to their courses, and when asked if they would take a correspondence school course again, 85 percent said "yes."

Every major research study on correspondence education in the past half century has shown that home study students achieve and perform as well as, if not better than, resident-trained students who studied the same subject. How can this be? Various reasons are suggested, ranging from greater personal discipline to selection of courses by home study students in which they have a special interest and aptitude.

Despite the fact that home study does work, how do employers feel about skills you acquire in this manner? No definitive studies probe employer attitudes, but the proliferation of correspondence courses by colleges and universities, corporations, labor unions, professional groups and government agencies suggests a wider acceptance that the point is what one knows—not where or how one learned it.

A U.S. Navy study says the cost of home study is 10 percent to 25 percent of the cost of resident systems. Home study courses, running from four weeks to four years, range in price from about $100 for a basic electronics course to $4,000 for a sophisticated robotics course complete with hardware.

Can you get college credit, or even degrees by mail? Yes, although most degrees available exclusively through home study are associate degrees; baccalaureate degrees more often are awarded through the broader concept of external degrees, discussed later in this section.

Two guides will help you locate home study courses.

- *The Directory of Accredited Home Study Schools* is available free from the National Home Study Council, 1601 18th St. NW, Washington, DC 20009.

- More than 70 colleges and universities that are members of the National University Continuing Education Association offer correspondence instruction. You can find them in *The Independent Study Catalog: The NUCEA Guide to Independent Study Through Correspondence Instruction.* The book is available by mail for $10.70, postage and handling included, from Peterson's Guides, Dept. 6217, Box 2123, Princeton, NJ 08543.

More than three million people enroll in correspondence courses each year. Since 1900, approximately 75 million Americans have taken courses by mail, including U.S. President Franklin D. Roosevelt, "Peanuts" cartoonist Charles Schulz and newscaster Walter Cronkite.

Home study can be a fine way to learn, but this method isn't for everyone. Ask yourself these questions:

- Do I have strong motivation in whatever I do?
- Do I learn most easily by reading and trying to understand by myself?
- Do I have an excellent ability to concentrate?
- When working by myself, can I set up and follow my own schedule?
- Do I have a quiet place at home where I can read?
- Am I able to understand most subjects that interest me?
- Do I prefer to learn things on my own?

If your answers are "yes," you probably would be a successful home study student. If you decide there's a school in your mailbox, match your needs with the right institution.

How to Select a Home Study School

1. Write to many schools that teach the subject you want to study and ask for catalogs and brochures. Examine them with saucer eyes. Be certain you understand exactly what you are buying. Compare learning objectives, subjects taught, length of the course, materials provided, tuition and various services.

2. Many excellent schools are not accredited, but the single best assurance of product reliability is accreditation. The Accrediting Commission of the National Home Study Council, recognized by the U.S. Department of Education, accredits home study schools. This organization checks to see if a school advertises truthfully, has a quality staff, a sound curriculum, and shows evidence of student success.

   All of the colleges and universities offering correspondence study that are members of the National University Continuing Education Association are accredited by appropriate organizations.

3. Evaluate the institution's refund policy. Accredited institutions offering correspondence courses have a liberal refund policy. Understand your obligations when you sign the enrollment contract.

4. Get an estimate of how long it takes for the course to be completed by a typical student. Before you enroll, decide how much time you're willing to devote.

5. For vocational courses, find out if the training really qualifies you for the job you want. Contact employers who hire in the industry for which you are preparing. Would they recognize training from specific home study schools? Ask if they would hire someone who acquired their skills in a correspondence school.

6. Be sure the school is properly licensed. Your state department of education will know whether the school complies with appropriate laws and regulations. Check the school's reputation through your area's better business bureau.

7. If you're taking the course to transfer credits to a local college or to an external degree program, check with the registrar at the degree-granting institution to be sure it will accept the credits and that the credits will apply toward the specific degree you seek. College policies on acceptance of credits differ.

Apprenticeship programs allow you to earn while you learn. You usually start a job at about 50 percent or more of journeyworkers' pay and move progressively up the wage scale to as much as 95 percent of journeyworkers' pay during your last six months of training. Time frames and percentages differ by occupation and program, but here is a sample wage schedule.

Three-year Apprenticeship Program

1st six months—50% of journeyworkers' wages
2nd six months—60% of journeyworkers' wages
3rd six months—70% of journeyworkers' wages
4th six months—80% of journeyworkers' wages
5th six months—90% of journeyworkers' wages
6th six months—95% of journeyworkers' wages

How to Learn and Earn Through Apprenticeship

As the carpenter said to the yardstick, let's get a couple of things straight up front.

1. In everyday conversation, you may hear someone say he or she is an *apprentice,* when, in fact, the correct term is *trainee.* Being an apprentice means you are enrolled in a formally structured program designed to give you A-to-Z knowledge of a particular occupation.

2. Apprentices are hired by employers, not by labor unions. Some apprenticeship programs are operated by employers and labor unions in partnership, but it's the employer partner who signs the paychecks. Employers run some apprentice programs without the participation of labor unions.

Now that we have these two points squared away, visualize yourself moving in on an apprenticeship opportunity.

An apprenticeship combines on-job training under the supervision of certified journeyworkers, plus 144 hours of related technical instruction per year, usually in a classroom setting. The training can be as short as one year or as long as six years, with most trades requiring four to six years.

Apprenticeship programs may be registered with the U.S. Department of Labor's Bureau of Apprenticeship and Training (BAT) or with a federally approved state apprenticeship agency.

Registration is like accreditation for schools in that it indicates the program meets minimum standards of quality and fair admission practices.

Conditions are spelled out in writing in the apprenticeship agreement. Pay, training and supervision are all clearly described, along with other particulars of employment. The apprentice and the employer sign the agreement. The employer promises to make every effort to keep the apprentice employed and to comply with standards established for the program; the apprentice promises to work faithfully and to complete the required study. Laws to protect the rights of minority groups are part of the apprenticeship agreement.

Apprentices who successfully complete registered programs receive certificates of completion from the U.S. Department of Labor or a federally approved state apprenticeship agency.

Registered programs offer apprenticeships in more than 770 occupations, 40 of which have been added in recent years. New programs include such occupations as firefighter, radiation monitor, tumor registrar, truckdriver, paralegal assistant and emergency medical technician.

When an employer and a union work together to operate a training program, a joint apprenticeship committee is formed to oversee the program's progress. An apprentice who participates in a joint apprenticeship program is accepted for membership in the co-sponsoring union. The vast majority of programs registered with BAT are operated by employers without the participation of a trade union.

What's best—getting into a union apprenticeship or a non-union apprenticeship? It depends on where you live and how heavily the state is unionized. The money, benefits and retirement security are likely to be superior for journeyworkers who are members of trade unions. The opposite side of the coin reflects the preference of many employers to hire less costly non-union journeyworkers whenever they can. If you live in a state without a strong union presence, you'll find more openings without a union card, but the opposite is true in states where organized labor is strong. The question becomes moot where there are few apprenticeship opportunities open—you may want to grab whatever you can get.

Sometimes special opportunities arise to enter apprenticeship, or to get credit for what you know because of linkages with other institutions. You may receive apprenticeship credit for the skills you learn in the military. Some community colleges sponsor programs that award academic credits as well as apprenticeship credits to apprentices. Skills acquired in a vo-tech school can count for apprenticeship credit. High school seniors in many of the states can apply to participate in school-apprenticeship linkage programs as part-time apprentices, assuming full-time apprentice status after graduation.

Women face unique obstacles to apprenticeship, a traditionally male preserve. Not infrequently they are hassled and harassed. Why are women willing to suffer hostility from earlier settlers in the world of journeyworkers? For the money, of course. As a journeyworker, a woman can earn triple what she gets as an unskilled worker.

Even if you decide apprenticeship is an ideal learning option, all may not be smooth sailing. The competition for an apprentice opening can be intense. After you take an aptitude test, produce a high school diploma or equivalent, meet an age requirement, pass occupationally essential physical requirements, show acceptable school grades and come through an interview with flying colors, you may still have to go on a register, or waiting list. The wait on the register can last months or even years.

The flood of qualified applicants for some trades has reached discouraging numbers on many registers of local apprentice programs. Although about 60,000 openings occur across the nation each year, hundreds of thousands of people want them.

Once you're in, you could face unemployment if the sponsoring employer runs out of work temporarily. Beginning apprentices may feel their work is menial or boring, and advanced apprentices may feel their pay is less than what they could earn elsewhere with their skills.

Other than above-average earnings, what's the incentive for the crowds of people who clamor to climb aboard the apprenticeship system? Mastery of a skilled trade sets you apart from other workers, is often satisfying and rewarding, and is a marketable asset.

Apprenticeship bestows versatility by giving you exposure to all aspects of a trade, and transforms you from inexperienced outsider to experienced insider.

A study of construction apprenticeship graduates and other construction workers in six cities concludes that apprenticeship training provides construction workers considerable advantage over those trained by informal means. Apprenticeship grads in the study were more educated, worked more

Jobs You Can Learn Through Apprenticeship

Registered programs offer apprenticeship in more than 770 occupations. The following list—by no means all-inclusive—indicates the range of jobs. Over half of all apprentices are in construction trades.

aircraft mechanic
airframe mechanic
automobile body repairer
automobile mechanic
baker
biomedical equipment technician
blacksmith
bookbinder
bricklayer
cabinetmaker
carpenter
cement mason
chemical laboratory technician
coin machine service repairer
cook
cosmetologist
custom tailor
dairy equipment repairer
dental laboratory technician
drafter, mechanical
dry cleaner
electrical repairer
embalmer
engraver
farm equipment mechanic
firefighter
floor layer
glazier
instrumentation technician
jeweler
laboratory technician
landscape gardener
leather stamper
locksmith
machinist
millwright
model maker
operating engineer
optician
orthotist
painter
patternmaker
photoengraver
plasterer
plumber
prosthetics technician
roofer
sheet-metal worker
shipwright
sign writer
silversmith
stationary engineer
stonemason
TV and radio repairer
tile setter
tool-and-die maker
transmission mechanic
upholsterer
welding technician
X-ray equipment tester

steadily, learned their trades faster, and were more likely to be supervisors than were those who picked up their know how here and there.

It is said that "learning is better worth than house or land." If so, apprenticeship is especially valuable because you get paid while you're learning.

Formal apprenticeship gets an A in our grading system.

Where To Go For Help

1. *Your School.* Look for information about apprenticeship programs in your school library, guidance office, career center or vo-tech department.

2. *Public Employment Service or Job Service.* Ask about local apprenticeship programs and available literature.

3. *Bureau of Apprenticeship and Training.* There are BAT offices in every state. If you can't find one in your city (look in the telephone book under U.S. Government, Department of Labor), ask at a library or public employment service office. If you're still stuck for information, contact the headquarters office: Bureau of Apprenticeship and Training, U.S. Department of Labor, 200 Constitution Ave. NW, Washington, DC 20210.

4. *State Apprenticeship Agencies.* Offices are located in 27 states, the District of Columbia and Puerto Rico. A BAT office can tell you if there is one for your state.

5. *Labor Unions.* If you are interested in a particular trade, contact the union to see if there is a joint apprenticeship committee in the trade that reviews applications for apprenticeships and interviews applicants.

CAREER TRAINING IN THE ARMED FORCES

If your values do not conflict with military service, the excellent and free career training you get in the Armed Forces might be the way to go. Make no mistake, when you join Uncle Sam's Armed Forces, you are first a defender of your country, and secondarily a government employee perfecting career skills.

You face long periods of time away from your family and friends. You follow orders with no lippy backtalk. You go to boot camp, where you run miles with a full backpack, crawl through slimy mud, wade through icy streams and, in general, show that you can take the physical stress of battle training.

Other than that, military life provides you with room, board, paycheck and training that can be superb, simply superb.

It begins with basic fitness and the military regime. After that, you begin learning the skills and acquiring the knowledge you need to do your assigned job. You study in classrooms and on the job in programs that last from a few weeks to more than a year, depending on the skills needed for the occupation.

You'll probably receive additional training as you move on to new responsibilities. Whatever you study, you can be assured you are the beneficiary of state-of-the-art training. Each military service spends hundreds of millions of dollars making sure personnel get the best possible instruction.

You'll be given a duty assignment—a job—when you finish your training. All services make an effort to fulfill the enlistment contract, but understand clearly that you may not get the job or the place you want. As in the civilian world, you may or may not get the job, even when there is an opening, if someone else has better qualifications. Further, your test scores and educational history will be used in determining whether you are suited for a particular opening.

Armed Forces ABCs

The Army, Navy, Air Force, and Marines are part of the U.S. Department of Defense.

The Coast Guard is part of the Department of Transportation.

During time of war, the Coast Guard may be placed under command of the Navy—within the Department of Defense.

All five services offer employment and training opportunities. But not all services offer every kind of occupational training. Determine if the service you prefer offers the job training of your choice.

About three military jobs in four relate to a similar job in civilian life. The fourth job is specifically combat-related.

Test scores? You'll have to take an aptitude test—the Armed Services Vocational Aptitude Battery, or ASVAB for short—that classifies you according to the career areas for which you qualify.

Here's a key point: *You don't have to enlist until you find out to which occupational training programs you may be assigned.* If you're not happy with the fields that are available to you by virtue of your ASVAB scores, don't join the service.

Remember, though, there are *no guarantees.* Even if your ASVAB scores qualify you for the training program of your choice, there are no assurances that an opening will occur at the time you need it.

Our advocacy is for career training. That's why we recommend you try for a job that has a civilian counterpart. The only transferable skill you acquire as a tank driver is the ability to steer a float in the Rose Bowl Parade. By contrast, the experience you acquire as a military air traffic controller rolls over into a civilian air traffic controller's position.

Beyond getting you ready to do the job, the training you receive in the military may count toward academic credit at a civilian college. Each college makes its own decision, but the American Council on Education has recommended that about 10,000 military courses be considered for conversion to academic credit.

Some training in the Army, Navy and Marine Corps—machinist, hydraulic equipment mechanic and heavy equipment operator, for example—can be credited toward a registered apprenticeship. If you leave the service, this type of training gives you a head start in the civilian world. You have to sign up for the apprenticeship credit option when you begin training, and it is available in a limited number of fields. Be sure to ask about it if you consider military enlistment.

A Sampling of Enlisted Military Jobs

Each year the five Armed Forces hire nearly half a million young men and women. High school graduates are preferred. Collectively the services offer training and jobs in 134 military occupations. We clustered the occupations into the 12 groups listed below with samples of the civilian-related jobs found in each.

Administrative
court reporter
computer operator

Construction
building electrician
plumber and pipefitter

Electronic and Electrical
aircraft electrician
data processing equipment repairer

Engineering, Science, Technical
air traffic controller
computer systems analyst

Health Care
operating room technician
physical therapy specialist

Human Services
caseworker and counselor
recreation specialist

Machine Operation and Precision Work
printing specialist
water and sewage treatment plant operator

Media and Public Affairs
graphic designer and illustrator
TV camera operator

Personal/Public Service
firefighter
detective

Transportation and Material Handling
flight engineer
truck driver

Vehicle and Machinery Mechanics
automotive body repairer
office machine repairer

*Combat Specialty**
artillery crew member
tank crew member

*For jobs in this category, there are no matching jobs in civilian work life.

Off-Duty Study Bonanza

Education is the "golden handcuffs" of the military services. No other employer can match the educational fringe benefits they offer.

Here's an example of how you could cut college costs by enlisting to serve on active duty for three or four years: Take college courses during off-duty hours. The military will pay 75 percent of tuition costs. Make sure all the courses will transfer to a four-year college degree program. Accumulate college funds through the G.I. Bill. At discharge you may have credit for two years of college and a tuition fund of about $9,000 to help pay for the last two years of college. Get a job during your last two years and you'll graduate debt free. Yes, you'll be two years or so older than the traditional college student, but you'll have greater maturity and work experience—two attributes employers prize.

The variations of military educational benefits are beyond the scope of this book, but recruiting officers will be tickled red, white and blue to tell you all you want to know. Start with the Army—it has the most generous education benefits.

The Officer Route

You can become a military officer in a number of ways. One is by graduation from one of the four service academies described in section 12.

You can also prepare through an ROTC program.

If you are a senior in high school—or are already in college—and know you want to enter the military as an officer, you may be eligible to receive financial assistance while still in school. Scholarships are offered through Reserve Officers Training Corps programs to cover tuition, fees and books. Campus ROTC officers can give you the particulars.

Once commissioned as an officer, the outstanding training will continue. The courses you attend are determined by your assignment.

Exploring Careers in the Military Services by Robert W. Macdonald (The Rosen Publishing Group) will throw more light on life in uniform.

Education and Training, Employer Style

OJT is the number-one source of training for obtaining jobs and improving skills.

OJT... What's OJT?

OJT is the *on-job training* you obtain by working. It's like the young bank officer who rushed into his supervisor's office, gasping in desperation:

"I have lent a foxy businessman $100,000 and he has not given me a receipt. What can I do?"

"Something like that happened to me once," his boss nodded in sympathy. "Here's what to do. Write and firmly demand a receipt for $200,000."

"I guess you didn't hear me," objected the troubled bank officer. "I told you it was only $100,000."

"I know," agreed the boss, "and your borrower will indignantly write and tell you so. Then you will have your receipt."

When experienced supervisors and co-workers share know-how with newcomers, that's OJT! They teach individuals with lesser experience how to do things. They explain the tricks of the trade and the best way to handle the job. Many people are surprised to find that OJT is the most common source of training for qualifying skills to get a job, and for improving skills to move up in the ranks.

Jobs You Can Learn on the Job

Here are some of the most popular occupations you can enter without prior training.

auto mechanic
bookkeeper
bus driver
carpenter
cashier
computer operator
cook
electrician
insurance sales worker
machine operator
machinist
nursing aide and orderly
plumber
police officer
production supervisor
secretary
telephone installer
truck driver
typist
waiter and waitress
welder

The U.S. Department of Labor says OJT dominance is a fact.

Not wanting to be a passenger in an airliner where the pilot is learning to fly, you understand that some jobs lend themselves more readily than others to OJT; see the accompanying list of occupations commonly learned on the job.

Employer training programs come in many stripes.

- The job training may be informal, where you pick up knowledge as best you can. It may come in a formal package, inside the workplace or at a school.
- The training may be *qualifying*—the type you need to do the job. It may be *skills improvement*—what you need to move up in the ranks.
- Courses may carry no academic credit, or may carry academic credit for a bachelor's, master's or doctoral degree. Some employer-sponsored training earns continuing education units, or CEUs. Basically, one CEU is awarded for every 10 classroom hours of participation in systematic, supervised learning. In the job market, it's helpful to have your course work summed up in CEU terms.

Business Educates Workers

Estimates of the amount business spends each year to train workers range from $30 billion upward, about half the amount spent by all colleges and universities. Although some of the corporate money goes to colleges, most of it is spent inside the companies themselves on courses tailored to build specific skills companies need.

High school equivalent courses for employees include such basics as arithmetic, effective listening, grammar-spelling-punctuation, statistical typing, letter- and report-writing skills for technical staff, algebra, effective reading and English for the foreign educated.

Management and executive courses usually fit into four categories: managing people, time, money or production and operations. Student workers learn how to motivate employees who don't want to be motivated, how to manage time and get the important tasks done, how to handle the old bugaboo, budgeting, and how to keep the executive's operation profitable. Courses may be taught in-house, or executives may travel to executive seminars, sometimes located in beautiful conference centers in scenic places like Aspen, Colorado, and Harper's Ferry, West Virginia. Some companies work directly with universities to custom design courses for their employees.

Some companies buy prepackaged programs. Others create their own, teaching them live or through such technologies as laser videodiscs that can be made interactive with a worker/student. Interactive video systems combine still-frame and moving video images, sound and computer-generated overlays of text and graphics. When you use an input device, such as a touch screen, the videodisc systems become personal teachers.

Postsecondary formal corporate education has become so sophisticated that some businesses and professional associations have set up institutions accredited to award the bachelor's, master's and doctoral degrees once viewed as the sole prerogative of traditional universities.

An example is the National Technological University, a Colorado school created by a group of universities with corporate support. The school has no campus or faculty. Instead, the more than 125 participating corporations pay up to a quarter-of-a-million dollars each in basic fees plus additional tuition per student to offer their employees courses live, by satellite or on videotape by professors from 24 major universities. One to three years are needed to complete a master's degree program.

The degree-granting institutions spawned as an effort to train employees or upgrade their skills commonly are called *corporate colleges.* In *Corporate Classrooms* (The Carnegie Foundation for the Advancement of Teaching), author Dr. Nell P. Eurich says the corporate colleges have three general types of sponsors.

1. Institutions established by individual business corporations are illustrated by McDonald's Hamburger University.
2. Industrywide interest and concern is reflected in the textile mills' creation of the Institute of Textile Technology.
3. Professional, research and consulting organizations have launched such degree-granting institutes and programs as think tank RAND Corporation's Graduate School.

Many of these companies are not aiming to replace traditional institutions of learning, but to continue education where the schools leave off.

Corporate Colleges

Institution	Degrees Awarded	Sponsor/Status
American College 270 Bryn Mawr Bryn Mawr, PA 19010	MS in: • Financial Services • Management	Financial services industry and individuals. Independent, non-profit.
American Graduate School of International Management 15249 N. 59th Glendale, AZ 85306	Master of International Management	Banks, individuals and U.S. government. Independent, non-profit
American Institute of Banking at Boston 50 Charles River Plaza Boston, MA 02114	Associate of Business Administration in Banking Studies	American Institute of Banking at Boston. Independent, non-profit.

Institution	Degrees Awarded	Sponsor/Status
Arthur D. Little Management Education Institute Acorn Park Cambridge, MA 02140	MS in: • Administration • Management	Arthur D. Little, Inc. Subsidized by corporation.
GMI Engineering & Management Institute 1700 W. 3rd Ave. Flint, MI 48502	Bachelor of: • Mechanical, Industrial, or Electrical Engineering • Management Systems Master of Manufacturing Management	Established by General Motors; in 1982 became independent, non-profit. Some 300 corporations sponsor undergraduate cooperative education students at the college.
Institute of Textile Technology Box 391 Charlottesville, VA 22902	MS and PhD in Textile Technology	Cooperative program of textile industry in U.S. and Canada. Independent, non-profit.
MGH Institute of Health Professions 15 River St. Boston, MA 02108	MS in: • Dietetics • Nursing • Physical Therapy • Speech, Language Pathology	Massachusetts General Hospital Corporation. Integral to corporation, non-profit.
McDonald's Hamburger University Ronald Lane Oak Brook, IL 60521	AAS in Business Management	McDonald's Corporation. Integral to corporation, non-profit.
National Technological University Box 700 Fort Collins, CO 80522	MS in: • Computer, Electrical, Industrial, or Mechanical Engineering • Engineering Mgt.	Major business corporations, U.S. government and Association for Media-Based Continuing Education for Engineers. Independent, non-profit.
RAND Graduate School 1700 Main St. Santa Monica, CA 90406	PhD in Policy Analysis	RAND Corporation. Integral to corporation, non-profit.
The College of Insurance 101 Murray St. New York, NY 10007	MBA and BBA with major in insurance; BS in Actuarial Science, as well as certificate and diploma programs	Insurance Society of New York. Independent, non-profit.

Reference: Based on a list in *Corporate Classrooms* by Dr. Nell Eurich.

More Avenues of Education

Educana strikes us as a word the language needs. Were there such a word, it would mean the seemingly endless variations of learning opportunities inherent in education. The ones we've mentioned thus far, from colleges to employee training programs, are the options most likely to be chosen by large numbers of young adults.

Countless other learning options exist in educana, many of which are used more often by adults in the workforce than by young people starting out. Here are some of them.

External and Non-Traditional Degrees

Higher education used to be *four-square and five-five.* Society chiefly recognized the kind that takes place in colleges with four walls and two five-month semesters.

All that changed in the early 70s when college lecture halls began spinning off brightly colored pinwheels of fresh ideas. The innovations whirl from conducting college classes on commuter trains to academic credit for life experience learning. For simplicity, the new ideas can be described as *external degree programs* or *non-traditional degree programs,* and their similarities stand out more than do their differences.

Both types of programs require little, or even none, of your three-dimensional presence on campus to obtain credits toward a degree. In fact, there may not be a campus, only an administrative office. One difference: Institutions that offer external degrees usually provide instruction for off-campus learning, while institutions that offer non-traditional degrees may accept credits from a variety of unrelated sources.

Degree requirements can be met through a combination of proficiency exams, college course work, military service schools, courses sponsored by professional societies and home study, to mention only a few of the vibrant vanes in the pinwheel of innovative ideas. Be certain to select an accredited institution if you pursue an external or non-traditional degree program.

One of the nation's top authorities on this type of study is Dr. John Bear who tells all in the 10th edition of his reference book, *Bear's Guide to Non-Traditional College Degrees* (Ten Speed Press).

Continuing Education

In the careers context, continuing education is learning that prepares you for entry into new fields or for advancement in present fields. Continuing education takes place in many of the settings noted in this section and it covers the gamut of career interests.

Two types of credit are available in continuing education. *Certificate/degree credit* is used as a measure of terminal programs for which formal credit may be awarded. If you complete the program, you receive either a certificate or an academic degree in the discipline you studied.

CEU (continuing education unit) credit is, as mentioned earlier, a nationally recognized, standard unit of measurement awarded by colleges and other institutions for participation in qualified continuing education programs. It also is a means by which professional organizations measure and keep track of required continuing education of their members. Upon completion of a program, you might receive two CEUs, for example. CEUs do not lead to a certificate or academic degree, but you might obtain a transcript of your CEU credits. Some professional associations record members' CEU credits in the ACT National Registry Service, a continuing education record-keeping service operated by the American College Testing Program. A number of colleges and other accredited institutions also use the ACT National Registry Service.

Tip: Programs that award neither certificate/degree nor CEU credit will do little to romance your resume in the job market. That's because employers want to know—in measurable terms—your educational qualifications. Take a non-credit course for pleasure or professional improvement, if you wish, but don't expect it to enhance your marketability.

Adult Education Programs

Teaching of adults didn't begin yesterday. Aristotle, Plato, Socrates and the other great historical teachers taught adults, not children. The lessons of the ancient teachers swept around ideas and values. Now, in industrialized nations, a renaissance of lifelong learning has sent adults scurrying for training. Many people choose the learning options offered through evening programs at high schools, vo-tech institutions or community colleges. Libraries often compile listings of local educational offerings.

P.S. The term *adult education* usually refers to basic and secondary education, whereas *continuing education* usually refers to postsecondary education.

College/University Extension Centers

Most colleges and universities have both day and evening classes or divisions. College/university extension centers may provide courses outside the main campus.

A laudable example is Purdue University's statewide technology program given in a number of Indiana communities apart from the main and regional campuses. It is designed to aid adults who see their jobs becoming obsolete, or who want to upgrade skills, or who want to assume a leadership role without giving up their jobs to move to a college town. The program offers an associate or bachelor's degree in specific technologies such as electrical, computer-integrated manufacturing, industrial and mechanical. This ultra extension-center approach provides valuable and tangible help to workers whose jobs are sliding into history.

Extension centers often reach out to the adult market, establishing programs in community centers, store fronts, libraries and school buildings that have been closed.

In considering flexplace education, be alert to a number of factors. Will up-to-date instructional aids and equipment be on hand? Is parking adequate and safe? Can the required books be purchased at the extension center? Do library facilities exist?

When centers are operated by a high-quality institution like Purdue, they can be passports to better jobs. But be certain you get all the facts. Some students are disappointed to find that their extension center gives them inferior instruction for only part of a curriculum, the rest of which must be taken on the main campus several states away.

Professional Societies

Membership organizations are an important sector of educana. The Air Pollution Control Association offers correspondence instruction for professionals in the field. The American Institute of Chemists sponsors lectures and symposia for members. The American Law Enforcement Officers Association offers conferences, courses and seminars to police officers. The American Society of Pension Actuaries holds workshops for members at various locations. The Society of Real Estate Appraisers fields a full schedule of conferences, courses, seminars and workshops for those who assess land and building values. These examples illustrate the incredible variety of training available from peers once you've entered a career field.

College by Electronics

Computer services now bring college education to the comfort of your own home or workplace. Instead of hauling yourself to class every morning or evening, you need traipse only as far as your computer.

Here are sterling examples of electronic colleges.

- The American Open University of the New York Institute of Technology (Central Islip Campus, Central Islip, NY 11722) offers complete four-year programs leading to a bachelor's degree in behavioral sciences, general studies or business administration. The national toll-free number is 1-800-222-6948. New York state residents call 1-516-348-3300.

- Connect Education Inc. is the on-line university sponsored by the New School for Social Research in New York City. Through Connect Ed, you can earn a master of arts degree completely by computer. Undergraduate courses can be taken and may be accepted by other colleges and universities. Specially designed computer software links students to professors and each other. Using a microcomputer, a telephone and a device called a modem, the student attends lectures, takes tests, receives feedback from professors, attends conferences with fellow students and accepts assignments.

The assignments are blipped through the telephone wire, traveling up to a satellite and down to Connect Ed's computers. For information, write to Connect Education Inc., Suite 6F, 92 Van Cortlandt Park So., Bronx, NY 10463. Telephone: 1-212-548-0435.

- The electronic blackboard program offered by the University of Illinois at Urbana-Champaign is sci-fi sophisticated but simple to use. Specially designed surface-sensitive boards, regular telephone lines and standard TV monitors are used by workers at company worksites. The instruction leads to a master's degree in mechanical engineering, general engineering, or theoretical and applied mechanics. For details contact the University of Illinois at Urbana-Champaign, Office of Continuing Engineering Education, 422 Engineering Hall, MC-268, 1308 West Green Street, Urbana, IL 61801. Telephone: 1-217-333-6634.

Telecourses and Points Beyond

Educational Telecommunications—ET—creates glorious learning opportunities not bound by time and space. A leading ET player, the Public Broadcasting Service's Adult Learning Service, built on the efforts of pioneer educational television broadcasters and began demonstrating ET's technological potential in 1981. ALS distributes more than 30 different telecourses, produced by academic experts, colleges and universities, instructional designers and experienced producers. Already ALS productions are a smash hit for the more than 180,000 tuition-paying students who watch each year.

ALS telecourses—often as visually lush as major motion pictures—instruct students in topics of wide appeal: *The American Adventure, ComputerWorks, Economics U$A, The Story of English,* and many more. Each course includes integrated video and print materials (texts and study guides), and sometimes audio and computer components.

Colleges and universities work with their public television stations to broadcast courses in many fields of learning. If you want college credit through television viewing, enroll in a local college, pay tuition, study under the guidance of an instructor, probably attend several class meetings, communicate more frequently with the instructor by phone, watch the programs at home or at work, read the print material, complete assignments and exams, and receive grades.

The easiest way to find out what's available locally is to call the education/adult learning department of the public television station and ask which telecourses will be offered for the coming semester and which colleges/universities are participating.

If the idea of becoming a "multimedia megalearner" is appealing, give a wave to The Annenberg/CPB Project. It was created in 1981 by a gift of $150 million from The Annenberg School of Communications to the Corporation for Public Broadcasting to develop college-level instructional materials and to demonstrate the power of technologies in higher education.

Going beyond quality-rich telecourses, The Annenberg/CPB Project funds educational innovations that can make it easier for students learning via television to communicate with professors and even with other students.

Among the innovations are an awesome array of electronic aids that can be fused with various telecourses. You might say it's a case of "electro-learning meets teleteaching." The goal is to make learning interactive—a two-way street—as it is in the best classrooms. Examples of electrolearning aids are videodiscs and electronic mail, as well as computer simulations, networking and conferencing.

Non-traditional students—over 25 and often employed—now make up 40 percent of all college enrollments. Their need for flexible educational scheduling to accommodate busy lives suggests a growing reliance on educational telecommunications.

Other Places to Learn

The treasures of educana go on and on:

• *Seminars.* Short programs are offered in every community to help adults enhance their job knowledge or skills. They may be sponsored by trade associations, professional societies, universities, profit-making companies or other entities. At least two companies help seminar users locate, compare and select appropriate offerings of professional education opportunities across the country: Seminar Clearinghouse International (630 Bremer Tower, St. Paul, MN 55101), and The 1st Seminar Service (88 Middle St., Lowell, MA 01852).

• *Summer Institutes.* Many colleges and universities offer special short-term summer institutes that focus on topics ranging from the University of Denver's renowned Publishing Institute to the University of Chicago's wide variety of summer workshops for professionals in social work and other helping fields. Locate them through professional or trade associations.

• *Public Libraries, City Recreation Departments, Churches, Synagogues, Community Centers, Y's, Museums.* With a telephone call, you can find out about the special classes or courses these institutions offer. Newspapers and radio and television stations report educational offerings.

After seeing much of what's available in educana, you'll have to agree: If you want to learn, there's no shortage of opportunities.

Ways to Make Good Decisions

Having a clear purpose in mind makes it easier to select the right training. If you're muddled, try writing down your reasons for seeking studies and course work.

Choose a program that meets your needs. Maybe you need college. Maybe you need a vocational-technical program. Maybe the training you need is available through employer-sponsored schooling. If the occupation you're considering requires licensure, such as nursing or architecture, find out from its professional organization what kind of program would be best.

Compare job market outcomes for those who approach an occupation in different ways. For instance, you may find that a private vocational school is so superior that it's worth every dime, or you may find it makes little difference which program—private or public—you attend as far as employability is concerned.

Most important, don't make the poor decision of thinking you can bumble your way through high school and catch up later in advanced technology such as robotics. If you can't read and you can't do math, you can't make it in the emerging workplace.

One final thought: Never give up trying to learn in some way. Unlike stupidity, ignorance is curable.

SECTION FIFTEEN

Looking for Your First Full-Time Job

L*ike learning to dance or to drive or to cook, learning to find a good* full-time job is a specific area of knowledge you must master.

This know-how is especially important for new graduates including any

- college graduate
- vocational graduate
- high school graduate
- military service graduate.

The following section discusses the basics of what you must know to become an expert job seeker. It examines the job search skills you need, building on insights you acquired about student jobs in section 11. As a student, you did not need to learn the complex or subtle concepts of a successful job search; now you do.

Your First Full-Time Job: The Art of Getting Hired

Let's get down to business. After blissful years on campus perfecting the role of student, your approaching or recent graduation means that this is the time to begin getting into your new role of moneymaker.

It's an enticing prospect: No more hitting up Mom for a fast $20; no more wondering if you ought to sell your blood to get through the semester.

Just as you learned the complexities of freshman English composition, you can learn the nuances of job search skills. A sterling performance in school is rewarded with grades; in the job hunt market, it's rewarded with dollars.

On your way to the bank, however, you must master the role of expert job seeker. Learning to market yourself now will pay off handsomely throughout your career. Here are several reasons why:

1. Expert job seekers often snare the best jobs, beating out competitors who actually have superior technical skills. This is because expert job seekers know the mechanics of making good contacts, and they know how to present themselves in the best possible light. Individuals who have only technical skills and little job search savvy may not be in the right place at the right time, or if they are, may not know the right things to say.

2. Expert job seekers are confident of their ability to reach out for a more important position. They are not glued to a job merely because they do not know how to find another. On the contrary, they have mobility. Possessing job search skills is like owning a car: you can travel further when you have wheels.

3. Expert job seekers are their own best unemployment insurance policies. Should sudden joblessness strike, they don't go to pieces—they go out and find another position as good as or better than the one that folded.

By choosing to become an expert job seeker, you gain a clear understanding of job search skills.

Three Broad Categories of Job Search Skills

While there are many ways to view these skills, they can be grouped into three broad categories:

1. Knowing *what you have to sell,* which means self-assessment reflected in resumes.

2. Knowing *where to make the sale,* which means job market strategies and sources.

3. Knowing *how to make the sale,* which means job interviewing and follow-up.

What follows is a streamlined course on getting hired. The information is organized into the three broad categories we just described.

A close reading of this section can pay huge dividends. You may have heard that the job market is about to turn around, that employers are going to be banging on campus doors, begging and wooing graduates to join them. Maybe so. Maybe not.

Predictions like these are based on the fact that your generation is smaller than the swollen babyboom generation before you. Fewer job seekers do mean less competition for available openings.

All this is true, but there are wild cards in this guessing game: How many older workers will decide to stay on the job? How many homemakers will decide to go back into the market? How many jobs will be lost to automating effects of high technology?

We think it's unwise to count on being begged and wooed to join anybody's team. And, if you don't shop the market, how will you recognize the best opportunity when you see it?

Take control of your career by becoming an expert job seeker. Here's how.

Knowing What You Have to Sell

Are You Who Your Resume Says You Are?

Now it can be told. When we discussed the techniques of composing a resume for student jobs in section 11, we went into more detail than you needed.

We confess we had ulterior motives. For the same reasons champion athletes begin their training young, we wanted you to get a head start in thinking about your strengths and how to verbalize them.

We wanted you to form the habit of thinking about your accomplishments in the measurable terms that impress employers.

We wanted you to become comfortable thinking about how to create a paper document that reflects the very best you.

Look again at the principles explained in section 11. Building on that foundation, you can create new resumes reflecting your growth and maturity.

Examples can be instructive. Two follow. The first is incredibly weak, the second is powerful.

A Losing Resume

The resume on the next page was sent to one of the authors. The writer's name and certain facts have been changed to protect the job hunter's identity. The young man who wrote this resume said he had "not had very good luck finding a job using my education." Why do you think he's having problems? Would you invite him for an interview?

A Powerful Resume

By contrast, the hypothetical resume on page 339 is a powerful advertisement of a young man's qualifications. In fact, the resume's creator, Richard Lathrop, prefers to call it a *qualifications brief* to focus attention on the need to stress your qualifications for the job. It is adapted from Lathrop's outstanding book, *Who's Hiring Who* (Ten Speed Press).

Special Tips for New Graduates

- Don't date your resume; when you don't find a job quickly, a dated resume makes you look as though nobody wants to hire you—as though you are a leftover.

- You'll use your resume to line up job interviews. Target it to the person who has the power to hire you. Usually that's the head of the department where you want to work. But new graduates often enter through the doors of the director of college relations or another manager in the company's human resources (personnel) department. Research!

- As a new graduate, your education counts more than your work experience. List it first, after your objective.

Write the name of your educational institution; the type of degree, diploma or certificate you received; the date of your graduation; and courses relevant to the type of work you want.

Mention—as primary education—only the most advanced institution from which you graduated.

An exception to the rule is when you have an advanced (master's or doctoral) degree, or a professional (such as medical or law) degree. In this

ROBERT J. GLUM

Education:	Bachelor of Science in Mathematics (with a minor in Economics), from South State College, South Fork, Florida, in December 1982.
Career Objectives:	To find a challenging position in which I can use my education and work experience.
Work Experience:	February 1983 to August 1984 – Computer Operator at Haig Foodservice in South Attleboro, Mass. February 1985 to August 1985 – Computer Operator at Happy Farmer Corporation in Bedford, Mass. December 1985 to Present – Assistant Manager for Tastee Fried Chicken Corporation, Framingham, Mass.
Work Skills:	Extensive knowledge of the Hewlett-Packard 3000 Series III Computer System
Programming Courses Taken:	Basic I, II Fortran I, II Cobol I, II Statistical Packages – SPSS, BMPD
Hobbies:	Participate in most sports, especially basketball and golf.

References/Placement Papers will be furnished upon request from South State College Placement Office in South Fork, FL.

JOHN BROWN
2923 Clink Street, Ajax, Washington 92361
206/257-5777

Objective	Editorial, management or research assistant in an organization concerned with public affairs – especially where an analytical approach, broad writing ability and a major in human factors are needed to assure strong development of articles, studies or programs.
Education	Bachelor of Arts, University of Washington, 1987. Major: history and government. English minor. Edited campus newspaper. Swim team captain. Graduated in top 10 percent. Earned all expenses.
Analysis of office operations and experience	Served as clerk with the Gulf, Colorado & Santa Fe Railroad. Handled all routine functions of a RR disbursing office – office machine operation, voucher recording, routing, etc. (Summer, 1986) Primary gain: Obtained practical experience in handling large volumes of routine office work. Observed factors that contribute to high operating costs and resistance to improved methods. Chief clerk's comment on our parting handshake: "Best yet."
Successful work-crew supervision and public relations	During previous summer vacations, served as a counselor in a seashore camp for 100 teenagers. After the first year served as a senior counselor. Directed the staff (most of whom were senior in age) in all recreational activities. Supervised 10-member crews in construction, maintenance and deactivation of all camp and waterfront facilities. One result: Returning campers increased 45 percent from season to season. (Summer, 1982 – 1985) Primary gain: Learned how to elicit strong cooperation from others (including an occasional irate parent) and how to schedule work crews for best results. According to the director, the strong reputation of the camp during these years was largely based on my performance.
Personal data	Born 1966...single...presentable...health excellent...Enjoy good music, all aquatic sports.
Other facts	Aiming for employment that will enable me to create my own opportunities and accept responsibility for results...energy and drive...successful in relationships with others...heavy interest in national and international affairs.

case, record all your degrees—professional, graduate and undergraduate.

All pertinent special courses, seminars, workshops, and vocational-technical training can be listed under "Other Education."

- Emphasize a strong overall grade point average. If your overall GPA isn't anything to brag about, highlight the grade point average in your major.

Studies show that grades aren't reliable predictors of success on the job, but many employers feel an impressive academic record indicates ability and drive. If you barely squeaked by, omit on your resume any mention of grades.

In fact, a negative factor of any sort has no place on your resume. When you must admit to anything that weakens your chances of being hired, save it for the job interview where you can interpret the sticky wicket in the least damaging way.

Remember, on your resume you are advertising yourself, not letting it all hang out.

- Mention any scholarships you received and briefly state the criteria on which they were awarded.

- Because you have little experience, you should compress your resume onto a single page, but two pages are acceptable. Personnel executives tend to pronounce one-page resumes as obligatory because they can be scanned in a wink. While you should try to be accommodating, remember this important point:

You and company recruiters do not share the same goal. Their goal is to effectively screen applicants as quickly as possible. Your goal is to make the strongest sales presentation of yourself.

If it takes two pages to get the job done, so be it.

How To Write an Electronic Resume

A technological breakthrough makes it possible to apply for a job unshaven and uncombed, wearing shorts or jeans, and still receive serious attention in personnel offices. This is because a few employers, such as the MITRE Corp. in Bedford, Mass., and Fairchild Industries in Germantown, Md., accept applications and resumes transmitted by personal computer.

In addition to on-line transmission, electronic resumes are stored in databases operated by electronic registry services, such as Career Placement Registry Inc., in Alexandria, Va., and the CSI Career Network in Baltimore, Md. Employers and recruiters pay the registries to review the resumes in their databases. In the early '80s, electronic registry services were heralded as new-age marvels in connecting jobs and job hunters. But the innovation proved unprofitable as various registry service firms lost millions of dollars. After the shakeout, only a few electronic registry services remain.

No one knows if the electronic job market will revive in the near future. But if you have sought-after engineering or other technical skills, you may find it an advantage to use electronic resumes as an additional tool for marketing your self.

Whether you plan to store your electronic resume in a home computer and send it yourself—or release it through the computers of professional electronic registry services—be certain to focus on accomplishments, abilities, skills and other qualifications.

The error many make is to assume automation overcomes the need for effective self-selling. The tools—not the rules—are changing. A weakly worded, computer-sent resume will land in electronic limbo as quickly as a poorly prepared paper resume will end up in the employer's wastebasket.

Focus only on specific experiences sought by the employer to whom you are responding, or on achievements you want to call attention to. Think in terms of *key descriptors,* such as college, major, grade point, engineering specialty, specific experience, language fluency, and salary range. Stress accomplishment; don't waste time with a laundry list of duties and responsibilities.

The format of the electronic resume is trending toward a modified functional style rather than the traditional chronological. This allows you to skip irrelevant data and, without hiding anything, to emphasize only the facts of your background that really count.

Learn to describe in as few words as possible the thrust of your key experiences and abilities. Shakespeare said that "Brevity is the soul of wit." It also is the body of electronic resumes.

In summary, remember that electronic resume registry systems are designed to make it easier for employers to pick out the most qualified candidates. They find people for jobs, not jobs for people. If your credentials—education, experience—do not fit the desired mold, your resume will languish in some impersonal electronic warehouse and you will not have a fighting chance to exhibit social skills, intellectual characteristics, enthusiasm, motivation, easy cheer and all the other human qualities that do not come across in a computer match.

Want an Interview? Write a Cover Letter With Snap

Along with your resume, send a cover letter that calls attention to specific reasons why you should be interviewed.

Include four sections in your cover letter: why you are writing, what you want, why your qualifications might interest the employer and how you plan to follow up.

Responding to Help-Wanted Ads

Hundreds of hopefuls send resumes for an advertised position, but only a handful receive an interview.

Why? And what can you do to assure a place among the chosen?

A major reason why many who answer ads do not receive invitations for interviews is that they fail to include an appropriate cover letter with their resumes. When cover letters are included, many are overblown or, conversely, reminiscent of the adolescent thank-you notes you wrote to Aunt Margaret for birthday gifts.

Take as much care with a cover letter as you do with your resume, advises Jack Erdlen, president of Management Dimensions Inc., a human resources consulting firm in Wellesley, Mass.

Cover letters that boil down to "I saw your ad and I'm looking for a job and here's my resume," are duds.

The objective of a cover letter is to highlight your credentials. The cover letter should always supplement and support your resume. Because a resume is seldom aimed specifically at any ad, the cover letter must be individualized and tailored to the job advertised.

Here are tips from Erdlen on writing cover letters:

1. Type on white bond business-letter size paper. Use correct grammar and spelling. Be brief and succinct.
2. Save the best information for the interview. Write just enough to entice the person designated in the ad.
3. You may gain more attention by not being in the first wave of responses; don't feel compelled to mail your package the day the ad appears.

In general, open enthusiastically, mentioning the advertiser's need and how you meet it. Use industry jargon when possible. Close with the action step—a suggestion of an interview. The sample cover letter on page 342 serves as an example.

An Unsolicited Cover Letter

You follow the same principles, but phrase your letter differently when you are writing to an employer who has not advertised a job opening.

The key is to attract the reader's attention immediately by a personal tie-in. Perhaps you read a professional article the employer wrote, or met the employer through a campus activity or—best of all—have a mutual friend. An example of an unsolicited cover letter appears on page 343.

Sample Cover Letter Responding To An Ad

Ms. Vi Bradley Felton
Manager
Revenue & Treasury Systems
NDJ Telephone Company
3000 Goodview Blvd.
Rockville, MD 20857

Dear Ms. Felton:

Your ad asking for a production analyst trainee with a background in marketing and finance made my day. It seems to be exactly what I am looking for in the telecommunications industry.

In several weeks I'll have my MBA from George Washington University; my concentration is in marketing and finance. I may be exactly what you are looking for and I'd like to meet with you to talk about my qualifications.

I've had mainframe and microcomputer experience, both in my classwork and as a graduate research assistant to a senior professor of marketing. My resume more fully describes how I might fit into your department.

I will call you next week to see when we can meet.

Sincerely,

Ryan R. Bodman

Ryan R. Bodman

Sample Unsolicited Cover Letter

Mr. Clayton Byers
Manager
La Ritzy Country Club
4321 Pacific Palisades Road
Bel Air, California 90088

Dear Mr. Byers:

You may remember my mother, Irene Lark, who worked as your secretary 20 years ago. You were her all-time favorite employer, a fact which encourages me to contact you now.

As a new graduate of the Dana Point, Calif. Community College hotel and restaurant management program, I am very much interested in working in the club management industry, perhaps starting as an assistant club manager. Would it be possible to arrange an interview with you to discuss this? Obviously, I would be delighted to have the opportunity of working at a prestigious club like yours, but if there isn't a job opening at the present time, perhaps you could refer me to a colleague.

I am not a beginner. Prior to my graduation at Dana Point, I worked for three years in food-and-beverage management in the Army, serving the non-com clubs. I am energetic and do not have family duties so my hours can fit the needs of a club. People say I inherited my mother's cheerful disposition. I have enclosed my resume, which provides specifics.

I will call you later this week to see if an interview can be arranged.

Sincerely,

Georgina Lark

Georgina Lark

As you portray the most favorable version of yourself on paper or electronic screen, never lose sight of the central resume idea mentioned in the student jobs section. It bears repeating:

The central resume idea is to create a document saying you and the job are a good match. A good match means that you know the job's requirements, and that you can do the work, that you will do the work, and that you will behave pleasantly while doing it.

Knowing Where to Make the Sale

The job market is where the money is, but the terrain can prove tricky to maneuver.

Its potholes and pitfalls help explain why, in the abstract, the job market often is portrayed as a swamp of infinite options, confusion and danger.

How often have you seen the job market illustrated as a maze with frustrating twists and turns, or as a roadway with crazy signs pointing in all directions, or as a jungle with scary animals lurking in the bushes waiting to pounce on the unsuspecting traveller?

There's a certain truth behind these visualizations, but as an expert job seeker, you will not attempt a job hunt without drawing up a plan of attack. Let's talk strategy.

Choose a Strategy

Three strategies cover the bases of looking for a job.

1. The target approach is by far the best strategy. You go after selected jobs that fit into your overall career plan. You learn the jobs' requirements and set a course destined to prove to specific employers that you and the jobs are a good match.

The pure target approach works most easily for job seekers who are graduates of vocationally focused education, or who have a pretty good idea of what they want to do.

The target strategy is superior because you take greater control of your future. As outplacement counselor Roderick Deighen observes, "Why let your career drift down the river like a log? Put a motor on it. Steer it. Be in charge of it."

2. The second strategy can be called the oyster approach, as in "the world is my oyster." The premise is that the job seeker can do anything. An underlying belief is, "I can think and so I can learn to do any job."

To operate by this strategy, you locate and apply for all job openings that are vaguely in your ball park. Who knows what lucrative hidden job might turn up?

Many liberal arts graduates pursue this strategy.

The advantage to oyster advocates: This strategy maximizes your opportunities. You cast a wide net. The disadvantage: Not all oysters contain pearls.

3. The third strategy is the combination approach. In it, you join the best elements of both the target and oyster approaches.

Our advice is to place primary emphasis on the target approach, spending maybe 80 percent to 90 percent of your time tracking jobs that fit into your career plan. Use the remainder of your time to look at anything and everything that comes your way.

Hire Yourself to Look for a Job

Some unfortunate people start off in the wrong job and, after establishing a pattern, keep repeating the same unhappy choice job after job.

Make an effort to avoid a false start. Do this by spending an absolute minimum of 35 hours a week on your search (assuming you're out of school and unemployed). Anything less and your efforts are recreational.

The chief mistake most people make is to throw out a few hooks, read a few ads, sign up with an employment agency or two and then go home and wait. Unfortunately, the wait can be a long one. The better plan is to take the offensive in the job market.

Plan to see at least five employers a week. Be prepared to interview time and time again. If you have 50 interviews, certainly you have a much better chance than if you have only a few. It's a matter of numbers. Like the ads for the lotteries say, "You gotta play to win."

Commit enough of your personal resources to do the job of getting the job you want. If time drags by and nothing much seems to be happening, don't throw in the towel. Remember the words of Winston Churchill: "There are two kinds of success: immediate and ultimate."

Keep Track of the Jobs You Apply For

Even when jobs are not hard to get, the better the job, the stiffer the competition. Don't allow opportunities to slip from your memory.

Keep detailed records of all your job search moves. Write down the name of the person or organization you apply to; who interviews you; the name of the interviewer's secretary; who referred you; what was discussed; what follow-up action you took, and to whom the interviewer referred you. Include phone numbers, addresses, job titles and comments. Immediately after an interview, jot down pertinent details before you forget.

Make a List of Employers

Who is going to be the lucky recipient of your talents? Make a list of employers worthy of that honor.

Your list of prospects can be as elaborate as you like, but at minimum, it must contain the name, address and telephone number of the prospective employer, and the name of the person who can hire you, or at least get you through the door.

Where will you get good leads for your prospects list? From looking at all available sources, of course.

The Bushes to Beat for Jobs

Here are the sources (and resources) to turn to when you look for job openings.

School Sources

High school graduates should check in the work experience or career center office for possible job openings.

Vocational-technical schools usually help place graduates in their first jobs.

Colleges and Universities

If you're a graduate of a two- or four-year college or university, your school's career planning and placement center can offer specific knowledge of job openings. Typical job openings include those for engineers, accountants, and management trainees in insurance and retailing.

Even if you find nothing to your taste in the current openings file, you could still benefit from it. Call the contacts listed for jobs you don't want; say you are interested in another type of position, and ask if you could drop by for a talk.

Your alumni office is another job-hunting ally. Its directory of past graduates can be an excellent source of contacts. You need not overdo the school spirit routine; just call to say you are about to graduate from the alum's school, need help breaking into the job market and would appreciate a chance to talk. Leave several copies of your resume with alumni.

The placement office and the alumni office may work together for your benefit; find out what services they offer jointly, as well as individually.

Campus organizations and senior classes may sponsor lectures and workshops with business people; this is a fine chance to meet individuals who can brighten your future. Some campus groups produce books containing resumes of prospective graduates that are distributed to employers.

Professors often work as consultants to business organizations; frequently they are asked to recommend appropriate students, or you can take the initiative by asking them for suggestions of whom you might contact.

Campus recruiters are looking for graduates who are the cream of the crop. Because it's costly to send professionals to college campuses around the country, the recruiters usually represent major corporations and local employers.

Recruiters are selective. They are interested only in graduates of high-demand fields: engineering, computer science, math, accounting and other technical majors. Liberal arts students get the nod from banks, insurance companies, retailers, fast-food chains and utilities.

Do not put all your chips on the campus recruiting crew because you may miss a whiz of a job in a medium-size company in another city.

You may be interested in a glamour or competitive field that virtually never recruits (media, films, travel, and fashion design, for example).

You may be left on the shelf until the unemployment plague is upon you. Of college graduates, about half leave school without a full-time job, according to a study by the Chicago-based outplacement firm Challenger, Gray & Christmas, Inc.

Go forth and seek on your own initiative after you and the recruiters have talked things over.

Networking

Networking is meeting people, asking around for information you need, and being referred to others. It's making and using contacts. It's developing to a fine art whom you know, even if it's knowing someone who knows someone who has an uncle.

Perhaps you're having lunch with that friend who happens to mention that his uncle is looking for someone to be his construction assistant for a new luxury apartment complex. This someone has to be willing to live for a year in Paris.

Or perhaps you're having lunch with that friend who happens to mention that her aunt, a software genius, will soon have openings for entry-level employees at her submicron integrated circuit firm.

Maybe we got carried away with the examples, but our point should not be missed: Networking brings you insider's news to act on.

You have a head start. Do you remember back in section 5 when we asked you to begin keeping a personal contacts log? We hope you followed our advice because this is payday. Dig out your log and list the people who you already know can play a role in your job search. Consider them your varsity team for networking.

Build on that base by adding others to your networking team. Make systematic contacts with people who can give you a break.

Even when an interview fails, ask to be referred from one manager to another, always with a recommendation, until you and your job meet.

There's no doubt about it: The coattails of contacts are a powerful way to travel in the job market.

Direct Application

When your strategy is the target or combination approach, you'll spend a lot of time making unsolicited approaches to employers.

Many jobs are won by just asking. Sometimes a job has not been advertised or sent to the personnel department because it is still on management's drawing boards—this is what is meant by the term *hidden job market*.

You learn about the hidden job market either by networking or by direct application.

What's the best way to make a cold call on an employer—make an appointment by letter or telephone, or just pop by and hope you can get in to see the boss?

We suggest you write or call for an appointment; whether you use the mails or telephone depends on which one best fits your style.

If you can't seem to wrangle an appointment, and you really want to see someone, you might try getting past the receptionist. Here's how to handle it:

You are making a cold call on a company. By research, you've learned that Julian H. Miller is hiring applicants with your kinds of skills. You ask the receptionist to see Mr. Miller.

The receptionist asks if he is expecting you. When you admit that he is not, the receptionist says that Mr. Miller never sees anyone without an appointment and that he's busy all week. The receptionist asks that you leave your resume.

Don't do it. The resume could make a round trip to China before you'll receive a response.

Instead, reply pleasantly that you'd rather give it to Mr. Miller yourself because there are items you need to explain. Moreover, you have some questions of your own. Say you need only a few minutes of his time.

At this point in the conversation, use your carrot. Say that you will come back tomorrow to find out when Mr. Miller could see you. Add that you appreciate the receptionist's help in arranging the appointment.

This tactic shows you value the receptionist as an important person and a potential fellow employee. You are trying to create an ally and an advocate.

A further point: We mentioned that the misuse of informational interviewing by people who saw it as a gimmick to get a job ruined the technique with many employers. Here are excerpts from a letter to one of the authors from a young man seeking a job in microbiology. For confidentiality, several names are changed:

I have read and done most of the exercises in several contemporary career guides. While they were thoughtful, interesting and fun to read, I do not think they helped me very much in finding a job. Perhaps it is just the highly competitive nature of the scientific-technical job market, but when I have approached a potential employer with an unsolicited inquiry or attempted "interviewing for information only," I get nowhere.

If you are lucky enough to talk with the person with the power to hire, he or she is extremely rushed, will not want to talk to a stranger for more than five minutes or in any detail about what they are doing, and will not hire anyone until an opening occurs.

Several years ago I spent my one-week vacation in the Philadelphia area doing informational interviewing. Company X's secretaries would not let me speak to anyone, Company Y's secretaries would let me speak only to the personnel staff, and so on.

After these experiences, I decided to sneak into the back door of a pharmaceutical company and act like I worked there. Unfortunately, I did not know whom to speak to and had to approach a secretary for information. She asked who I was, how I got in and there was a big uproar, with a guard eventually seeing me out.

Another example of impractical advice is that one should thoroughly research a company, uncover their problems and show how you might solve them. Most high-tech or scientific companies are as secret as the CIA and as accessible as Ft. Knox. Except for the financial statements and stockholder information that exists for larger companies, virtually no printed information exists on these companies' research activities or problems.

Advice on this order really is not that practical, at least for science majors.

We agree that no one approach works for everyone and that's why we're giving you the whole spectrum of job search.

Direct Mail

In days of old, circa 1960, job market experts commonly advised sending out *broadcast letters.* The idea was to compile huge lists of prospective employers—as many as 1,000—and write to them outlining your qualifications and asking for an interview.

The letters were expensive and usually didn't work, critics say.

Today most job market experts view direct mail buckshots as being wasteful of time and money.

We think direct mail is worth considering under certain conditions:

1. Your strategy is the target or combination approach and you are highly selective about whom you write. You obtain the name and title of the decision-maker.

2. You write a persuasive cover letter for your resume; or, you write a broadcast letter, which combines the highlights of your cover letter and resume.

Still, chances are slim. One man told us that he sent out more than 2,000 broadcast letters, received 13 replies, four job-interviews and no offers.

Newspapers

In addition to leads picked up by reading the news sections of daily papers, follow the help-wanted ads. Many appear in the classified sections, others are found on sports or business pages and still others are collected in special career groupings. Read the ads daily, not just on Sundays, because many ads first appear during the week.

Ads are useful because they tell you about jobs that somebody wants to fill immediately. Are they effective for professional jobs? You bet.

Most professionals are hired through recruitment advertisements, according to a survey conducted by the Employment Management Association (EMA), a professional organization for personnel executives. The response indicated that an average of 30 percent of their total of new, experienced hires were recruited through advertising in newspapers, trade journals and other media.

The other major sources of recruitment were employee referrals, 27 percent; employment agencies, 24 percent; and direct contact, 8 percent.

Although you aren't in the experienced category of potential new hires, you see why ads are near the front of the job market parade.

Here are tips on answering help-wanted ads, as suggested by EMA officials.

1. Put yourself in the position of the person who receives your letter and resume. Ask yourself: What information about someone's background would induce me to invite that person for an interview? Be sure that your reply sparks the reader's interest.

2. Tailor your response to fit the ad. Highlight experiences and accomplishments that directly relate to the specific opening.

3. Limit yourself to a single page. Keep your correspondence brief and use the resume to spell out your qualifications. The reviewer cannot be expected to examine your credentials in depth.

4. Should you answer the ad immediately or wait a few days before responding? Employment experts have trouble agreeing which timing has the best chance of receiving interest—the early response or the resume arriving after the deluge of replies has diminished. [The authors favor waiting two or three days before replying to a help-wanted ad.]

5. Avoid references to salary requirements. This point is controversial, but at this stage it is advisable to indicate that your requirements are open. A compensation figure that is either too high or too low can eliminate you from consideration despite your experience or attractive credentials.

6. Address the reply exactly as it appears in the advertisement. These ads are usually coded, so they can be handled promptly.

7. Indicate why you have an interest in the company whenever the employer is identified in the ad. Including this information will require that you do some homework to learn about the organization, its products and services.

8. Send in a second reply if you have not heard from the company after two weeks. Resumes are often lost, misplaced, or misread. A follow-up telephone call is recommended.

Although EMA reports that eight out of 10 employers use ads, the large response they attract can drown the individual in a sea of applicants. This means your replies to ads should be the strongest you can produce.

Associations and Trade Journals

Most job fields are covered by at least one trade journal. Some are published by private firms, while others are products of trade associations and professional societies.

Trade journals may include ads for jobs. Some trade associations and societies operate a job clearinghouse, in addition to staging meetings where you can find jobs through formal employment booths, or through chance meetings. Ask whether a trade organization offers a directory or list of its members who are working in the job field that interests you.

Employment Services

You have several different types of employment services to consider.

Private employment agencies. Placement firms—commonly known as employment agencies—are matchmakers. Their purpose is to put people seeking jobs with job openings that employers have listed with them to fill.

When a firm makes a match it is entitled to a fee. Usually the employer pays; occasionally, the newly hired employee pays.

The choice is yours. You can tell the firm that you will consider (a) only fee-paid jobs; (b) that you are willing to pay the total fee for the right job; (c) that you will split the fee with the employer; or (d) that you will pay the fee, or a portion of it, provided the employer agrees to reimburse you after you've been on the job a year or so.

Even if you sign a contract agreeing to pay for a job, unless you accept one the firm finds for you, you owe nothing. And if you do pay a fee, find out what the placement firm's policy is on refunds if you should be laid off before a year has passed.

The fact that it is the employer who most often pays the fee is at the root of many misunderstandings.

What job seekers don't focus on is that the placement firm is primarily responsive to the bill payer and provider of repeat business—the employer. The firm is usually recruiting good people for listed job openings, not scouting openings for job seekers.

The slant changes somewhat if you agree to pay a fee. It then is reasonable to expect the firm to develop leads to jobs for you. But whether a firm's consultant actively markets you by canvassing employers depends largely on how busy the consultant is and how motivated.

Once you realize that you have no grounds to insist that a firm act as your personal representative, your expectations will be more realistic.

When choosing employment agencies, these suggestions can prove useful.

- Determine whether the firm is a member of a state employment agency association (names vary from state to state) or of the National Association of Personnel Consultants (1432 Duke St., Alexandria, VA 22314). Members agree to abide by specific business ethics.

  It's a bonus if your consultant has passed rigid exams and met experience requirements to become certified by a state or national association. The national credential is *Certified Personnel Consultant.*

- Call placement firms to ask which specialize in your field. Unless there's only one in your community that handles the kinds of jobs you want, sign up with several firms. No one employment agency is in touch with all possible employers.

If you're highly marketable, let each firm know it has competition for your placement; each consultant will want to be the first to put you before employers.

If you're not so marketable, you need all the help you can get, but, unless you are asked outright, keep it to yourself that you are registered with a dozen placement firms.

Your strategy is to make each consultant feel prime responsibility for your employment status.

It is the employment agency's consultant working directly with you who counts most. Good employment consultants draw out your background, work record and career goals before rushing you to specific jobs.

Private contingency firms. A close relative of the private employment agency is the contingency firm. Sometimes called *technical recruiters* and sometimes *headhunters,* these recruiters tend to specialize in engineers and other technical personnel. Their fee is always paid by the employer. Although you may put your resume on file with a number of technical recruiters, their operating motto is "Don't call us, we'll call you."

Executive recruiters. A recruiter or executive-search firm does not work on a contingency basis. Executive recruiters are paid in advance to search for middle and senior managers with specific credentials and experience. They also are known as headhunters. Don't bother contacting executive recruiters until you've got a track record.

Public employment service. Tax dollars support the public employment service, also called the Job Service. Run by the state employment security agencies under the direction of the Labor Department's U.S. Employment Service, the 1,700 local Job Service offices offer a range of services without charge.

Job matching and referral services are of the greatest interest to most people. Interviews pinpoint the type of work for which you show interest and aptitude. If you know the kind of work you are qualified for, you can look over a computerized listing of job openings called the *Job Bank* that is updated daily. Job Bank listings include positions in private industry as well as in government agencies. If you spot something you like, ask a Job Service staff member for details on the job and arrange for an interview.

Counseling and testing services are available if you need help deciding what kind of work you want to do.

Veterans, by law, get priority in interviewing, counseling, testing and job placement. If you're a vet, ask to see the veterans' employment representative.

If you decide to try the Job Service, here are three suggestions.

1. While many of the jobs in the files of the Job Service offices are positioned on the low end of the career scale, only you can decide whether this source is worth your time. A couple of visits to look over Job Bank listings will give you an idea of whether your kind of work is included.

2. Critics charge Job Service personnel with being bureaucratic and inept. We don't agree. Like private employment services, the quality of help you receive depends on with whom you deal. Many Job Service counselors are talented and dedicated. Go with an open mind.

3. Be assertive. If you do not feel you are receiving good service, don't hesitate to ask the Job Service manager to reassign your search to another staffer.

To find the public employment office nearest you, look in the state government telephone listings under "Job Service" or "Employment."

Teleconferencing

Another new-wave recruiting development is teleconferencing.

Here's how it works. A teleconference is held between high-demand seniors at colleges and universities, and companies that want to hire them. After the companies make a recruiting presentation via satellite, the students ask questions. This creates a two-way dialogue.

Liberal arts graduates can forget this one. What teleconferencing employers are looking for are engineers and computer science graduates.

Your college placement office will know if teleconferencing is available in your area.

Books

Bookstores and libraries are stacked high with job search guides; for more suggestions, turn back to section 8.

Summing Up on Sources

We've reviewed the most used sources for finding beginning employment. Which should you pursue first?

We recommend:

1. School and college placement offices; employers list immediately available openings with them.
2. Help-wanted ads in newspapers and trade journals; they contain news of immediate openings.
3. Employment services; they offer immediate openings.
4. Networking; contacts, while extremely effective, may take longer than you can wait to find a job.
5. Direct application; you may have to market yourself longer than you can wait to obtain employment.

How much emphasis you should place on each of these five channels depends on your strategy and goals.

If you want to work in films, don't waste your time on help-wanted ads or employment services. Filmmakers don't have to recruit.

If you're in one of the business fields, help-wanted ads and employment services are key sources. Think about it.

Let's look now at several special concerns and what to do about them.

How To Break Into Competitive Industries

Some job fields seem to be surrounded by insurmountably high fences.

These are the fields that drip with glamor, pay big money, or both. You probably have thought about one or two of them yourself.

How do you become a television talk show host? A film producer? A recording engineer? A sports team publicist? A literary agent? An auto designer? A travel tour packager? A fashion photographer? A rock star?

While particulars change from field to field, all share certain characteristics. Here are tips for climbing over the fences that shut you out of competitive industries.

1. When you can't lasso your immediate job target, try to snare the most closely related job you can while continuing to move toward your goal. Even film producers need people to act as housekeepers, baby sitters and gofers.
2. While you are gaining related experience, change your status from outsider to insider. You do this by becoming a regular in the circles in which you'd like to work. Make friends with people who can give you advance word of job openings. Read the field's trade press regularly. Join pertinent associations and attend their meetings and annual conventions. Volunteer for committee

work to gain exposure and contacts. Go wherever the people you want to join gather. Every contact, every piece of related information helps you move from outsider to insider.

"Persistence pays" is a cliche, but cliches usually have a basis in truth. Keep calling on employers even when they say there won't be an opening for the next five years. Employers have no idea who might walk out tomorrow—and there you are, waiting in the wings, ready to step on stage.

LIBERAL ARTS MAJORS: WHAT CAN YOU DO?

Year after year, technical majors dramatically outperform liberal arts majors in the job market, both in offers and salary.

This is why it is essential for liberal arts graduates to become expert job seekers and to concentrate on fields in which there are many jobs that do not have precise entry requirements. Such fields include banking, telecommunications, sales, insurance, human resources, fund raising and entrepreneurship.

A study by the Association of American Colleges offers examples of positions a liberal arts graduate, after gaining work experience, can aspire to. They include credit analyst, merchandiser, underwriter, marketing representative, purchasing manager and public relations specialist.

The same study reports that a history major became a molasses trader. A student who combined a Russian studies major and a dance minor found work as an assistant trust officer in a bank. An American studies major became an administrator at a real estate company specializing in condominium development and sales. An English major found employment as a renewal and collections supervisor for a national news magazine. A psychology major blossomed into a personnel recruiter for a department store. A Spanish major uses only English in his pharmaceutical sales job servicing small groceries and drug stores.

Mount Holyoke College, a liberal arts institution, tracks its graduates from time to time. Here's a sampling of jobs obtained by some liberal arts graduates. They show how a four-year investment in a liberal arts education can pay off. Remember that not all of the people in these examples went to work directly after obtaining their bachelor's degrees. Some pursued advanced degrees in the field of their undergraduate majors. Others chose professional work in an entirely different field, such as law or library science.

Art/Dance/Music/Theater

Art editor, book publishing company
Curatorial assistant, White House
Page and guide, television network
Dance teacher, community center
Computer programmer
Junior high art teacher
Teacher of music, public schools
Assistant traffic manager, television station
Editorial assistant, medical journal
Missionary in Hong Kong
Social caseworker
Buyer trainee, retailing
Prop maker, opera company
Securities analyst, bank
Tourist department assistant, Colonial Williamsburg

Anthropology/Psychology/Sociology

Foreign service officer
Social worker
Probation officer
Public relations assistant, hospital

Rehabilitation counselor
Research correspondent, bank
Research analyst, television network
Financial management trainee, major corporation
Trainee in market research, advertising firm
Regional sales manager, motion picture company
Field director, Girl Scouts

Biological Sciences/Physical Sciences/ Mathematics

Research technician, medical school
Researcher, publishing company
Buyer trainee, large retail chain
Editorial assistant, book publisher
Copy editor, newspaper
Engineering analyst
Lecturer, science museum
Management trainee, insurance company
Systems engineer, computer company
Patent researcher
Management trainee, bank

Classical and Foreign Languages

Assistant to managing editor, book publishing
Bilingual secretary, U.N.
Director of independent school program for study abroad
Management trainee, life insurance company
Correspondent, foreign department of bank
Underwriter, insurance
Marketing trainee, major corporation
Management trainee, retailing
Editorial copywriter, magazine
Research assistant, investment firm
Communications coordinator, industrial firm
Sales, telephone company

Economics/Geography/Political Science

Investment administrator, bank
Legislative aide, U.S. Representative
Management trainee, Federal Reserve Bank
Portfolio analyst, brokerage firm
Cartographer, CIA
Writer, political journal
Reporter, suburban newspaper
Operations research, consulting firm
Claims adjuster, insurance
Assistant editor, foreign agricultural magazine
Research assistant, Foreign Policy Association

English/History/Philosophy/Religion

Researcher, international division of news magazine
Assistant fund raiser, Sierra Club
Computer programmer trainee, insurance company
Editorial assistant, children's division, book publisher
Youth worker, YWCA
Map editor, publishing house
Guitar instructor, public schools
Paralegal assistant
Field representative, college admissions office
Sales, paper company
Editor, insurance company public relations
Reporter, daily newspaper
Tax auditor, IRS

Looking for a Job Far Away

Whether you intend to return to your home base or relocate to a completely new locale, a little planning can ease your long-distance search.

Before you are hired, you'll have to be present for interviews. Set a time at least two months away when you will be in the distant city.

Network to find the names of decision-makers or influential people who can refer you to decision-makers. Among those this group might include are business executives, civic leaders, religious leaders, bankers and stockbrokers.

If you don't know a soul in your target city, you may have to develop contacts in two phases:

1. Obtain the names of reputable residents of the city and ask for a referral to decision-makers.

2. Write to the decision-makers or influential people and ask for an appointment.

Your request letters should not put pressure on recipients. Communicate that you are a new graduate, that you want to take the business pulse of the city, and that you would appreciate a 10-minute meeting. During interviews ask about the business climate, job market, and the community as a place for young adults. Mention your chief skills and abilities, too. Ask, "Can you recommend where I might find (a job, a place to live, who's hiring in my field, and so forth)?" People like to recommend.

Personal referrals can make all the difference in whether your search gets off to a brisk start or limps along.

Some experts think all this will be academic in the not-too-distant future. They believe we'll soon be doing two-way video interviews routinely, and that employer and employee will not meet each other until the first day of work.

We're not so sure. We think employers and job seekers will always want to be in the same room, shaking hands, "feeling the flesh," as a way of sizing up the professional relationship that each might be embarking upon.

Disorganized? Discouraged? Try the Buddy System

Sometimes you just can't seem to pull your job hunting head together. You mean to get organized, but before you know it the clock is striking four and another day is shot.

When you can't be your own best career friend, find a buddy. Use the mutual support system.

In tandem with another new graduate, share leads, review each other's resumes, do practice interviews, boost each other's morale and—most important—keep each other on your collective 20 toes.

Want to give it a try? There are only two rules: Communicate daily, and agree that the buddyship doesn't break up until both partners have a job.

During the times when nothing seems to be clicking and nobody seems to want to hire you, remember that rejection doesn't mean failure; it means try harder.

Knowing How to Make the Sale

Selling is persuading people to act—convincing the customer to buy.

Selling yourself is convincing employers to buy your skills.

Happily, you've got a running start on your sales effort. Now that you've finished your resume and mapped out your search, there's only one more function to master before you can call yourself an expert job seeker: interviewing.

Okay? Now we'll show you how to bypass the big red lights and the roar of boos on your way to making interviewers choose you.

Facing the Interview

No matter how superb your resume and how organized your campaign, the interview is the magic moment when you sink or swim.

Actually, the magic moment is more like 30 minutes, although some interviews may stretch out to more than an hour. Knowing that your future's on the line during these crucial periods is likely to produce anxiety and a few psychological blips. That's the downside.

Here's the upside: The interviewing experience need not give you a rash if you take the time to learn the ropes. Once you understand interviewing and its methods and madnesses, you'll know that you're not dealing with normal, everyday behavior.

All the face-to-face chats you must survive to get a job are about 10 percent reality and 90 percent theater.

Interviewing is drama, so shape your performance to fit the role. Knowing what's expected and what you should say will make everything much, much easier.

Despite your best efforts, suppose the worst happens and you blow an interview for a job you really want? Unless you are touched by angels, interviewing disasters will happen in your life. To keep the right perspective, call a failed interview a learning experience, and vow to do better the next time.

Remember that while flubbing interviews can make you want to pound sand, events far more upsetting can happen in your career. As former Montreal Canadian hockey goaltender Jacques Plante once said: "How would you like a job, where if you make a mistake, a big red light comes on and 18,000 people boo?"

Preparation is the Great Relaxer

Is it important to research a company before the interview?

Is it important to turn the tables and pose questions to the interviewer?

The answer to both questions is "yes." Based on a survey of personnel directors of 100 large companies, 84 percent feel it is important for applicants to demonstrate that they have made an effort to learn something about the company prior to the interview.

The study, by Accountemps, a temporary help firm, also found that a whopping 98 percent of the personnel managers believe applicants should ask specific questions about both the company and the position for which they are applying.

When you bone up on a company in advance, you meet both criteria. Additionally, the research gives you something in common with the interviewer. Don't you like best those friends with whom you have the most in common? Interviewers react in the same manner.

The key reason, however, for finding out what's happening at a potential employer's organization is that it gives you the basis of information to suggest how you might fit into the organization.

When you are unprepared, you tend to talk about you and what you want. When you are prepared, the talk can focus on the employer's needs and how your skills match them.

No one expects a new graduate to be a walking encyclopedia, but your school's placement office will usually have literature available about companies that are recruiting on campus.

You may also obtain a copy of the company's annual report at the placement office or a business library. Read the president's message and the financial figures. You'll get an indication of the company's priorities.

Whenever you want to be a cut above the crowd, research your target to the hilt. Try to chat with the company's employees, read the industry's trade press and check for clippings at a large library.

After you gather the information, use it judiciously. Don't walk in and discuss reorganizing the company. Coming across as a know-it-all and attempting to tell the employer how to run the business are deadly sins.

A Sneaky Tip

Books written for the job hunter are helpful but books written for the *interviewer* are eye-opening. These manuals tell the interviewer what questions to ask and what responses to watch for.

One such book is *The Evaluation Interview* by Richard A. Fear (McGraw-Hill). Another is *The Interviewer's Manual* by Henry H. Morgan and John W. Cogger (available only by mail from the publisher: Drake Beam Morin Inc., 100 Park Ave., New York, NY 10017; query publisher for current price).

The interviewer is taught to word questions so that you may self-destruct without knowing it. For instance, it's unwise to volunteer weaknesses to an interviewer, but the interviewer may try to finesse you by asking innocently, "What did you do less well?" instead of the more direct question for which you prepared, "What were your weak subjects in school?"

Save the Best for Last

A common mistake is to arrange interviews with your best prospects before you have had enough practice at interviewing to do well. You can't control campus recruiting schedules, but you can work out some of the bugs by mock interviewing with friends.

Use the Truth-In-Telling Rule

Bogus information is everywhere.

A woman's magazine advised its job hunting readers to "fudge facts" when necessary.

A men's magazine said that job hunters "sometimes should lie," and implied that advice to the contrary is hopelessly naive.

A professional resume writer suggested in a newsletter to fellow professionals that they should change a client's job titles to "more accurately reflect what the client did for an organization."

One headhunter in the Seattle area says he can't recall a single recruiting search in the last five years where he didn't uncover at least one education falsification.

What about it? Has the code of ethics in the American job market changed *that* much? Are you likely to be caught and punished by the deceived employer if you take liberties with the truth?

The answer to the first question is "no." Mainstream ethics have not changed; it's still wrong to obtain employment under false colors.

The answer to the second question is "maybe." You may get away with lies, or you may be discovered in a fabrication that could seriously damage your career.

If your lie is revealed during a reference check before an offer is made, you can forget that job.

Suppose your breach of integrity isn't discovered and you are hired. In that case, you live with a time bomb that could go off at a bad time in your career. If it does, what then?

Many companies will let you keep your job if you are doing it well. Here are typical comments from employers reflecting this philosophy:

"When we find falsification, we confront, not dismiss."

"Dismissal would result only if it were a serious lie."

The problem is you can never be sure what will happen. In opposition to the "fess-up-and-forgive" view is the personnel chief of another company who says:

"When we want to terminate a problem employee, we go through the legal application form looking for lies."

An executive for another large company sees matters in a similar vein:

"We were about to transfer the guy when we found out he claimed two phony doctorates and we dismissed him."

If you lie, you take your chances. In our opinion, lying siphons your concentration by making you nervous trying to remember exactly which lie you told.

As we see it, claiming fake job titles or unearned educational degrees is dumb. Be wise enough to tell the intelligent truth. Here is the truth-in-telling rule for interviews that we recommend.

When it helps your cause to reveal a fact, do so in glowing detail.

Keep negative information in your pocket unless you are concealing an impediment that would prevent you from doing a fine job.

What Employers Look For

Which factors turn an employer's head? Here are several that employers say are high on their lists of hiring criteria.

Enthusiasm. An Administrative Management Society survey says that the trait employers like best is enthusiasm. You don't show enthusiasm by responding with a steady stream of "oh, wows" in the interview, but by paying close attention, smiling, maintaining eye contact, asking appropriate questions and stating your interest in the job.

Grades. If grades were everything, you could mail them in and recruiters wouldn't have to spend vast amounts of time and money traveling from campus to campus. People who hire want to see the three-dimensional you in the flesh.

Having said that, you know that grade point averages will open or close certain doors. Standout grades indicate to many employers that you are motivated and swift of mind. If you attend an obscure educational institution, it is particularly important that you obtain high grades to be considered for the best jobs.

Communications Skills. Information has to pass with clarity between you and others or the job will suffer.

Interpersonal Skills. Employers want to be sure you will fit into their organizations so they watch for clues that you get along well with others.

High Energy Level. Your physical behavior during an interview—a spring in your step, sitting up straight—leads employers to speculate whether you have the physical stamina to work quickly and hard.

Judgment. Unless you're a child actor, kid behavior and business don't mix. Employers want employees who behave in an adult manner. They want people whose suggestions reflect judgment, not just mere opinion.

Which Self Should You Be?

Many job hunt experts tell you the way to behave in an interview is to "be yourself" and "act naturally."

Which self? What's natural?

Don't you behave differently in differing circumstances? Are your shiny shoes natural? Combed hair? Clean fingernails?

Earlier we stressed that an interview is mostly theater. There's nothing real about compressing a lifetime in a 30-minute conversation. The best role to play is the one that most closely matches what you understand the requirements of the job to be. Your behavior would be different when applying for a job as a bank loan officer than when auditioning for a job as a television quiz show host.

The best self at any interview exudes self-confidence, even if you don't feel it. When you have no confidence in yourself, others won't either.

Echo Your Interviewer

Earlier we discussed the question of "which self" to be when you are "being yourself." Here's more on the topic.

Try to get a handle on the interviewer's style. If the interviewer is one who speaks in short clips, don't rattle on and on. If the interviewer seems laid back, don't come on like gangbusters. If the interviewer is formal, don't be casual. Once more, the point is: It's human nature to like people who are like ourselves.

Within the framework of your true personality, hum the interviewer's tune.

Drake Beam Morin, a major consulting firm specializing in human resources, says there are four basic types of interviewers. A quick but careful glance at what the interviewer is wearing and how the office is arranged will give you clues about how to present your answers.

Reinvent Yourself: The Miracle of Videotape

Before you set off on interviews, study your image in living color and if you don't like the picture, improve it.

Videotaping makes it easy to evaluate and upgrade your performance in a job interview. Camcorders are dropping in price, but you don't need to own the equipment—many school media centers maintain videotaping equipment students can use.

When you see yourself on tape, you may be surprised at how often you scratch your head, pop chewing gum, crack all 10 knuckles, swing your eyeglasses like a New Year's Eve noisemaker or commit other interviewing errors. By seeing and eliminating such irritating mannerisms, you dramatically boost your chances of being hired.

Four Styles of Interviewers

Interviewer	Personality Profile	Identifying Tips	Interview Focus
Senser	Present-oriented, responds to things that can be touched or felt.	Cluttered desk, disorganized office; casual dress.	Your ability as a problem-solver.
Feeler	Relies on emotions and gut reactions. Thrives on human contact, enjoys people.	Family photos, souvenirs, awards; fashion-conscious.	Your relationships with others, how you will enjoy the job.
Thinker	Logical, systematic, orderly, data-oriented.	Neat desk, sterile office; presence of charts or computer detail is possible; conservative dress.	Facts and figures (i.e., grade point average). Respond to the thinker with as much detail as possible.
Intuitor	Future-oriented, goalsetter.	Books and reports stacked on the desk, projection charts on the wall; far-out dressers, apt to look like absent-minded professors.	Your long-term objectives and goals; try to relate your past to the future demands of the position and the movement of the company.

Ask a friend to play the role of the interviewer, feeding you questions until you respond comfortably with good, solid answers.

In hands-on and service industries, such as construction or health work, the dress of the day appropriately could be clean jeans, sweat shirt or uniform.

Shaping your image can be one of the major rewards—and investments—of your career.

How You Look

Image is a business tool. Image is how you walk, talk, present yourself and behave. Definitely, it's what you wear and how you look.

When your appearance is contemporary and attractive, the interviewer is likely to credit you with better-than-average awareness of the world at work.

The opposite is true, too. If you appear as though you never notice what others are wearing, the interviewer may question your awareness.

You do not have to project the image of a fashion plate if you are not in a fashion industry, but it is important to be perceived as one who is tuned into today's tempo. Aware people are smart enough to know what's happening and care enough to be a part of it.

Magazines regularly include articles on the latest ways to dress for business. Read them. In brief, there are only two basic principles to bear in mind.

1. *Dress appropriately for the job you seek.*
2. *For most jobs, project a conservative, businesslike image.*

In non-conservative companies, business clothing means costuming, according to image consultant Jane Segerstrom.

If you are an artist, writer, photographer, musician or other creative type, or one who sells to the youth market, your office wear could be quite different from the three-piece suit.

- Men may opt for pirate, polo, Western, ivy league, sport or turtleneck shirts. Vests or jackets may top jeans, cords, slacks or drawstring pants.
- Women may choose overblouses, shawls, sweaters, wide and wild belts, scarves, vests, pants or skirts of all descriptions. Jewelry can be bold. Extreme hairstyles complete costuming at its height.

Body Language Can't Keep a Secret

Body language sometimes reveals true feelings that may be contrary to what a person says.

Gain a secret weapon. Learn the basics of non-verbal signals and use them to your advantage.

A number of books on non-verbal communication are available. From them you can learn such things as how to know when an interviewer is bored and that it's time to change the subject of your conversation.

How can you tell when an interviewer is bored? Among the clues: playing with an object on the desk or tapping fingers. If this happens, stop and simply ask for direction. Say something like this: "Would you like to hear more about about my minerals economics studies or about my computer lab work?"

Another sign that an interview may not be going well is when the interviewer crosses arms in front of the body and leans away from you.

A positive sign that you're coming across well is when an interviewer leans forward in the chair.

Once you learn to read body language, you'll be more aware that non-verbal movements, mannerisms and gestures reveal what's on your mind, too.

Tugging at your skirt or jiggling your keys makes you look nervous and short on self-confidence.

Reaching up and touching the back of your head when an interviewer asks if you have a given skill may suggest you really don't—that you are disturbed or startled by the idea.

Looking at the ceiling as you collect your thoughts may cause an interviewer to view you as vague or even insincere. If you have trouble keeping eye contact, look at the bridge of an interviewer's nose. It will appear that you are looking the interviewer straight in the eyes.

As a child, somebody probably told you never to point at anyone. Even kidding around, never point at an interviewer—it's rude.

The combination of attentive listening, thoughtful speaking and the ability to interpret non-verbal signals is a step toward power.

In every interview, try to show a pleasing temperament and a high energy level. Lethargy is the quicksand of job hunting.

Job Bias: What to Do if It Happens to You

It's the law: When you apply for employment, you can't be discriminated against because of your race, color, national origin, religion, sex, age or, in some cases, physical or mental disabilities. The point is to give everyone an equal chance at jobs.

On paper, the issues are straightforward. In practice, they become fuzzy. Discrimination law is ever changing and complex.

In addition to federal discrimination laws, many states and some cities or counties have fair employment practices laws. They vary widely. Some of them flatly prohibit employers from asking certain questions. You can get a list of suspect questions from state or local labor and human rights agencies that administer anti-discrimination laws in your area.

Contrary to popular belief, there is no such thing as a list of illegal questions forbidden by federal law. Other than questions about arrests, employers can ask anything they wish to know. *The key is what use the employer makes of the information. If it is used to discriminate against you, the question becomes illegal.*

Which set of laws takes precedence in employment rights cases? When the federal law is stronger, it prevails; state and local statutes prevail when they are stronger than the federal versions.

One thing you should know: Questions that might be judged discriminatory in pre-hire situations may be valid once you're employed. Employers often are required to collect personal information for affirmative action programs and insurance plans.

Thin-Ice Questions

Interviewers usually stay up to date on employment laws and away from sensitive topics, but some may be so busy juggling a variety of duties that they ask risky questions out of ignorance. Here are examples of questions to look out for.

Race or color. Neither should be commented on in any way during an interview, nor should you be asked for a picture when you apply for a job.

National origin. If fluency in another language is relevant to the job, the interviewer shouldn't ask whether the language is your native tongue or even how you acquired your fluency if that might reveal information about your national origin.

It is okay to ask if you are a U.S. citizen; if you are not, it is acceptable to ask if you have the legal right to remain and work in the U.S.

Sex and marital status. You should not be asked about your marital status, whether or where your spouse works, or even whom you'd like an employer to notify in case of an emergency. Other risky questions are those about children, child care arrangements, the probability of pregnancy and your views about birth control.

A rule of thumb. What basic compass can you use to assess whether employers are getting too nosey? Just ask yourself:

Is this information relevant to my doing the job?

All pre-hire questions should be relevant to a given job. And the questions—the same questions—must be asked of all applicants, regardless of sex, age, race, religion or national origin.

Good Answers to Poor Questions

Pretend you are in the interviewer's office, ready to begin the interview and prove you're the best qualified for the job.

The interview starts and suddenly the interviewer shoots you a question that seems irrelevant. Your indignation is soaring. How will you handle the situation?

You have three basic choices.

1. Answer the question and don't make waves.
2. Finesse the issue or politely explain that the question doesn't seem related to your ability to do the job.
3. Tell the interviewer you understand laws prohibit employers from considering potentially illegal information in evaluating job applicants.

The last option is not advisable if you want the job. The first option may be acceptable to you if the interviewer's questions seem to come from ignorance rather than bias.

The second option is our preference. The moderate response shows that you are accommodating, but that you also are an aware, thinking person.

Here are a few sample answers using the second option.

Q. *Do you plan to be married?*

A. That decision is still in my future. I haven't made it yet.

Q. *I see that you speak Spanish. Where did you learn it?*

A. I studied Spanish in school. What opportunity would I have to use it in this position?

Q. *What does your father do?*

A. I would appreciate it if you would clarify for me how this question relates to my ability to do the job. Then I would have a better idea of the type of information you're looking for.

Q. *What's your credit rating?*

A. I haven't been out of school long enough to establish one. But. . .I didn't know I'd be handling money.

Q. *Do you want to be addressed as Ms., Miss or Mrs. Smith?*

A. Joan Smith is fine, thanks.

If Discrimination Threatens You

Should you find yourself involved in a blatant case of discrimination, you may want to get advice from your state or local labor or human rights agencies, or from an office of the Equal Employment Opportunity Commission.

What About Employment Tests?

Many people think equal opportunity and affirmative action laws made employment tests illegal. Not so. These tests become illegal only when they are used to discriminate on the basis of race, color, national origin, religion, sex, age or disabilities.

The upshot is that when you're asked to take an employment test, agree to do so if you want the job. Make the best of the situation and greet the test-giver, often a psychologist, as an alert, well-adjusted, happy person.

Here are several tips on selling yourself in employment tests.

- Avoid absolutes, such as "always" or "never." These are red flags to psychologists who then try to determine if you are straying from the truth. The reasoning is that anyone who "never stole anything" probably pinched cookies as a kid.
- On timed tests, attempt to answer all questions. On some tests, you may be limited to several choices and find that none describe the action you would take in a hypothetical situation. Choose the option closest to your way of thinking. Try to be consistent in your approach.
- Should you guess? Guess answers to anything you don't know when there is no penalty for wrong answers. Guessing may pay off even if there is a penalty. Typically, you will receive a full credit for every right answer and be docked only a fraction of a credit for every wrong answer. Figure your odds.
- Sentence completion should be upbeat. You know better than to end the sentence, "Work is..." with "the pits." Another illustration revolves around the notion of mice playing when the cat's away. The right ending to "When the boss came in..." is not "everyone worked harder." A better answer is "everyone smiled."

If you're worried about taking psychological tests, your library may have sample tests for practice.

Screening and Selection Interviews

In organizations large enough to operate a personnel department, interviewing usually is a two-stage process.

A representative of the personnel department conducts screening interviews designed to weed out all but the best-qualified candidates. Survivors are passed to the person who has the hiring authority, often a department head. The recommended behavior at a screening interview is simple: Be pleasant, be bland.

You have nothing to gain by risking strong opinions that may conflict with those of the screener.

It is the screener's job to check that your credentials are satisfactory—that you can do the job and that you will do the job.

The screener does not make the decision on how you'll fit in with the rest of the team. If your credentials are acceptable and you don't make waves, you probably will be passed on to the hiring authority.

At the selection interview, you'll be dealing with the decision-maker, and, perhaps, one or more colleagues. The decision-maker probably is the person you will be working for, so now is the time to express your best personality.

You've got to hit it off with the decision-maker, but if you rub each other the wrong way, it's better to discover the fact up front and continue your search. (A point of interest: Campus recruiters usually are conducting screening interviews.)

If you want a sophisticated understanding of the differences between the two types of interviews, read H. Anthony Medley's *Sweaty Palms: The Neglected Art of Being Interviewed* (Ten Speed Press).

Please Come In...

The moment has arrived. Your interview is about to begin. You smile, make eye contact, shake hands and introduce yourself, "Hello, I'm ________."

Be ready with initial pleasantries and safe small talk—"What an interesting painting on your wall," or "What a handsome view from this office." Avoid all personal references, such as comments about the interviewer's appearance or family photographs.

Try to project businesslike warmth and friendliness. Your aim is to make the interviewer like you. Many recruiters say far more people are turned away for personality factors than for lack of capability.

By personality factors, we mean "vibes"—the non-verbal communication and other under-the-surface factors that make people like you or dislike you.

In the final analysis—assuming your qualifications are adequate for the position—what convinces an employer to hire you over someone else can be boiled down to two words: liking you.

If things go well in the first few minutes, you'll create the halo effect, which, as we explained, means if you shine in one area, it is assumed you shine in others. Interviewers are cautioned not to let the halo effect cloud their judgment. But you know how it is—if you like a person, you tend to see everything the person does in a favorable light.

The Most Important Question in the Interview

As early as possible, ask the interviewer to describe the scope of the job and the qualifications of the ideal person for it. Keep your antennae up and your headlights on. The information you receive is the key to the entire interview.

Listen carefully. Take notes if you wish. If an ideal qualification is careful attention to detail, give the interviewer examples of how carefully you pay attention to detail. If an ideal qualification is to organize massive projects, give the interviewer examples of what a great organizer you are. If an ideal qualification is the ability to solve problems, give the interviewer examples of your problem-solving skills.

Throughout the meeting take every opportunity to remind the interviewer of the link-up between your qualifications and the ideal person the interviewer described.

To be blunt, you will feed back what you have been fed. You will show how your qualifications match what the interviewer wants.

Do not interpret this basic strategy to mean that it's okay to fabricate information. Cynical parroting might work—but not for long.

A Special Tip to Minority Applicants

Minority students often wonder how much should be said about minority-oriented extracurricular activities.

As an example, a young black woman asked whether she could mention her participation in black organizations when she graduated and applied for accounting jobs.

Our answer: If the activities support your objective of being hired, mention them.

If they do not add anything to making you look good for the job, why clutter your image?

In seeking an accounting job, there's not much value in pushing the point that you played on an all-black basketball team, or on any basketball team, for that matter, because basketball is unrelated to accounting. The exception would be if it is the only activity that shows teamwork experience and the ability to get along with others.

But suppose you were president of the state black studies club. Play up the experience. It suggests you possess leadership potential and are academically minded.

Bring up any topic that strengthens the relationship between your background and the job's requirements.

Basic Reminders

Try to use the interviewer's name several times during the meeting. Don't smoke even if the interviewer lights up; if you're a non-smoker, don't imply criticism of the habit. Gum-chewing is out of place. Stand until you're invited to sit.

You may run into an oldtimer who uses what is called the *stress interviewing* method. You're asked to sit in a chair with uneven legs, or placed so that you face the sun or are subjected to similar childish gambits to see "how well you stand up to stressful situations." Leave these people to their own amusement and look for work elsewhere.

Questions You May Hear

Most questions can be slotted into one of three categories. They are:

A. Questions that show you can do the job; these relate to skills, education and experience. Examples:

Why should I hire you?

Why do you want to work here?

Which subject in school did you like best and why?

B. Questions that show you will do the job; these relate to positive work attitudes, ability to cope and motivation for success. Examples:

What would you like to accomplish in the next 10 years?

What is it that you want to do?

Why did you major in ______?

C. Questions that show you can get along with others; these relate to interpersonal relationships, focus, flexibility and personality. Examples:

Can you describe an ideal working place in terms of your co-workers?

If I called your former adviser, how do you think you would be described?

What three people in public life do you admire most?

50 Questions Recruiters Ask College Seniors

Here are 50 questions asked by employers during interviews with college seniors. The list was compiled by Northwestern University's Placement Office.

A job interview is not the best place for surprises. That's why it would be time well spent to go over these questions, placing them in one of the three above categories. *Some questions you may want to place in two—or even all three categories.* It's a matter of individual interpretation. This is not a right-or-wrong quiz, but merely a device to help you consider each question in turn.

Category (A,B or C)	Questions
______	1. What are your long-range and short-range goals and objectives; when and why did you establish these goals and how are you preparing yourself to achieve them?
______	2. What specific goals, other than those related to your occupation, have you established for yourself for the next 10 years?
______	3. What do you see yourself doing five years from now?
______	4. What do you really want to do in life?
______	5. What are your long-range career objectives?
______	6. How do you plan to achieve your career goals?
______	7. What are the most important rewards you expect in your business career?
______	8. What do you expect to be earning in five years?
______	9. Why did you choose the career for which you are preparing?
______	10. Which is more important to you, the money or the type of job?

_______ 11. What do you consider to be your greatest strengths and weaknesses?

_______ 12. How would you describe yourself?

_______ 13. How do you think a friend or professor who knows you well would describe you?

_______ 14. What motivates you to put forth your greatest effort?

_______ 15. How has your college experience prepared you for a business career?

_______ 16. Why should I hire you?

_______ 17. What qualifications do you have that make you think that you will be successful in business?

_______ 18. How do you determine or evaluate success?

_______ 19. What do you think it takes to be successful in a company like ours?

_______ 20. In what ways do you think you can make a contribution to our company?

_______ 21. What qualities should a successful manager possess?

_______ 22. Describe the relationship that should exist between a supervisor and subordinates.

_______ 23. What two or three accomplishments have given you the most satisfaction? Why?

_______ 24. Describe your most rewarding college experience.

_______ 25. If you were hiring a graduate for this position, what qualities would you look for?

_______ 26. Why did you select your college or university?

_______ 27. What led you to choose your field of major study?

_______ 28. What college subjects did you like best? Why?

_______ 29. What college subjects did you like least? Why?

_______ 30. If you could do so, how would you plan your academic study differently? Why?

_______ 31. What changes would you make in your college or university?

_______ 32. Do you have plans for continued study? An advanced degree?

_______ 33. Do you think your grades are a good indication of your academic achievement?

_______ 34. What have you learned from participation in extracurricular activities?

_______ 35. In what kind of work environment are you most comfortable?

_______ 36. How do you work under pressure?

_______ 37. In what part-time work are you interested? Why?

_______ 38. How would you describe the ideal job for you following graduation?

_______ 39. Why did you decide to seek a position with this company?

_______ 40. What do you know about our company?

_______ 41. What two or three things are most important to you in your job?

_______ 42. Are you seeking employment in a company of a certain size? Why?

_______ 43. What criteria are you using to evaluate our company?

_______ 44. Do you have a geographical preference? Why?

_______ 45. Will you relocate? Does relocation bother you?

_______ 46. Are you willing to travel?

_______ 47. Are you willing to spend at least six months as a trainee?

_______ 48. Why do you think you might like to live in the community in which our company is located?

_______ 49. What major problem have you encountered and how did you deal with it?

_______ 50. What have you learned from your mistakes?

How to Answer Major Questions

You can bet that several of these questions are going to be asked at most interviews. Here are illustrations of good responses.

"What Can You Tell Me About Yourself?"

This is the bone crusher of all interview questions. Memorize a short answer. Summarize your background quickly and then narrow the focus to discuss your qualifications for the job at hand. Here's an answer for a marketing trainee position:

I graduated from the University of Southern California last June with a major in marketing. I was in the top 10 percent of my class. I was on the tennis team. I was elected treasurer of the marketing club. Through student jobs, I earned 60 percent of my school expenses. I'm a self-motivater and generally a pretty happy person. I like people.

"How Much Money Do You Want?"

As a beginner, you'll have little control over the salary you command, but you have a shot at negotiating if you don't name a figure. Respond to the question with a question of your own. That is: "What do you think would be fair pay for this job at the starting level, and what do you see as the long-term compensation potential?" Ask for a hair more than the offered figure to show you're an above-average candidate.

"What Are Some of Your Strengths and Weaknesses?"

Try to present strengths without seeming to brag:

Other people tell me I am effective at getting the job done.

I pride myself on meeting deadlines. I work well under pressure.

I enjoy working with others and have good relationships.

I am told I am a person who can come up with creative solutions to hard problems.

I am a team worker.

Present a weakness as a strength:

Although I try to do everything assigned to me in a professional manner, I would get bored if I did nothing but routine work everyday.

Some people say I should allot more time to social activities.

People tell me I'm too thorough.

I become impatient in non-productive meetings.

(Never say anything like, "I'm not too well organized.")

"Why Should We Hire You?"

If you haven't researched the company, you're going to have a hard time with this one. After research, you can say this:

I've checked out your company and it appears to be a good match with my qualifications and would probably result in a long-term relationship.

* * *

Could you use more help answering questions? Read Jeffrey G. Allen's *How to Turn an Interview Into a Job* (Simon & Schuster).

Questions You Should Ask

At various times during the interview, it will be your turn to play quizmaster. Your questions also can be grouped in three categories. They are:

1. Questions that demonstrate knowledge of the field.

Will company expansion occur more rapidly in the Ohio or Texas divisions?

In the researcher-writer position, would I have the opportunity to use my history knowledge by working on the forthcoming Civil War series?

2. Questions that show you are paying close attention.

Could you explain a bit more about the new department you mentioned?

In connection with the sealing process, what is the time allotted between design and manufacture?

3. Questions that help you decide whether the job is for you.

As I understand the position, the title is _______, the duties are _______, and the department is called _______. I would report directly to _______. Is that right? (You are making sure your facts are straight.)

What became of the last person who held this job? (You are trying to find out if it's a stepping stone to bigger things or a road to nowhere.)

You mentioned company training. Would that be formal or informal and how long does it last? What skills would I learn?

Is travel involved? If so, approximately what percent of my time would be spent traveling?

What do you see as opportunities for advancement in this job? (You are double-checking advancement potential.)

How is job performance evaluated? (You are trying to find out if performance evaluations and hence raises and promotions, are based on objective criteria that employees know and understand.)

What is the compensation level for this job? Does that figure include employee benefits? (If you are offered the job and nothing is said about salary.)

Ask for the Job—Or at Least Leave the Door Open

When it's time to go, the interviewer may stand up or inquire whether you have any further questions about the job. This is your cue to close with an approach that encourages an offer, or at least leaves the door open. In marketing circles, this is called *asking for the order* or *closing the sale.*

Use the following script as a guide in choosing your own words.

I'm very excited about this job. My qualifications seem to fit it very well.

Follow this assertion with a summary of your qualifications. Although you've mentioned them throughout the interview, people forget what they hear. Next, attempt to draw objections out in the open.

Do you see any gaps between my qualifications and the requirements for the job?

If any shortcomings are mentioned, try to overcome them. If the objection is that you have no experience, say you learn fast and will work as hard as it takes to get the job done. Continue to show interest by asking if you've missed any points.

Do you have any further questions or concerns about my background, qualifications or anything else? I'm very interested in this job and I'd like to be sure you have all the information you need to assess how I might fit in here.

You may even have the opportunity to ask the brass-ring question: "Do I get the job?" Opinion is divided on whether experienced people should ask to be hired. After you've held a couple of full-time jobs and established a track record, you may not find it advantageous to look too available. Enthusiasm is irresistible in beginners, however, and you may as well make it work for you by being straightforward if you want the job.

In any event, don't leave without asking when a hiring decision will be made. Remember, if the answer is fuzzy, ask if you may call back to check on the status of the job.

In the final moments, remember the halo effect looks as good going away as it does coming. Be certain to express your appreciation for the time the interviewer spent with you.

Interview Thanks: Is It an Outdated Idea?

Some people say thank-you notes to employers for interviews are relics of earlier times. Are they right?

In a competitive situation, anything you use as a tactic to call attention to why you should be hired is never out of date. Here are the viewpoints of two executives who evaluate many applicants:

From a supervisor of professional employment for a manufacturer in Cleveland, Ohio:

Having recruited for positions at the entry- as well as upper-level, I favor notes of appreciation from individuals interviewing for lower-level jobs. Competition for these jobs can be fierce and a thank-you letter will often help me remember a person.

For higher-level positions, a thank-you note might be viewed as unprofessional or unnecessary.

Thank-you letters should be sent promptly, within 24 hours of the interview, and should be brief, concise and sincere. Flowery or verbose letters tend to signal oversell.

From a manager of human resources for a defense contractor in Carlsbad, Calif.:

Thank-you notes are an excellent means for reminding the interviewer of the person applying. A grateful, warm, personal note is a plus in the process. In addition, a reminder of skills and qualities and a suggestion as to where the person could fit in is helpful.

Both personnel executives are suggesting that at the professional level, you should use a follow-up letter for more than a thank you.

You can (1) impart a sense of urgency, (2) offer new information, or (3) restate your benefits.

Examples:

Urgency

I've had other interesting discussions, but your organization is tops on my list. I've got to make a decision within two weeks. May I have the opportunity of seeing you again next week to provide any additional information you may find useful in making your final decision?

New Information

After reflecting on our meeting, I realize there is a strong linkage between the areas of specialized knowledge you need and the technology I have studied. You mentioned that the company intends to enter the fiber optics market. Although I mentioned that I have completed six courses specific to fiber optics, it occurs to me that I did not elaborate on their content as it relates to your needs. I'm enclosing a brief statement of my fiber optics education and would be glad to meet with you again this week to amplify my qualifications.

Restate Benefits

The description of the work your organization is doing was helpful in reviewing my qualifications in light of your requirement... (restate your benefits)... *I'm sure we could work together profitably and productively. Can we meet this week and finalize matters?*

If you miss out on a job, you can still bank on the future when you write.

I was disappointed that I did not get the job but I appreciate your time and consideration. If you again find a similar position open, I would be grateful for a chance to compete for it.

View thank-you letters not as an exercise in good manners, but as an effective follow-up tactic; the higher the job level, the more sophisticated your communication should be.

Interviewing is a Numbers Game

Graduates in high-demand fields may connect with a job from among a half-dozen interviews. Liberal arts graduates should not be discouraged if they go through dozens of interviews without an offer.

The main thing is not to lose heart. The more interviews you experience, the better you'll become at talking about who you are and what benefits you can bring to an employer. You might have to suffer through 100 "no's" before getting one good "yes."

SECTION SIXTEEN

CHOOSING AND SUCCEEDING ON YOUR FIRST FULL-TIME JOB

After putting forth a herculean effort in your job search campaign, let's assume you made all the right moves and earned your reward—one or more job offers. Now that employers have said they want you, it's your turn to be selective.

This section tells you how to recognize the offers you should refuse and the one you should grab. It discusses what employers expect of you, the importance of hitting it off with your boss, and techniques you can use to win recognition, promotion and raises. We offer information for dealing with sexual harassment.

The discussion concludes with a consideration of knowing when it's time to find greener pastures, and how to look good to the boss you leave behind.

Stick to Your Career Plan

If a job doesn't boost your career aims, let someone else have it.

There are major exceptions: Some job is better than no job when you need rent money, your car requires an engine overhaul, your education loans are coming due, your roommate is threatening to stop paying the food bill, or your parents are about to throw you out of the house.

As a guideline, don't take a job in supermarket operations when you really want to be a leader in travel and tourism. Stay close to your field and watch where you step.

Ask yourself: "Will this job *position me* for future advancement in my field?"

Position you? What's that? Positioning is an important ingredient in career success, and it means putting yourself into a situation where opportunity may salute you. It means gaining exposure to various types of work that exist in your field. It means being visible to higher-ups who have the power to single you out for advancement.

Here is a brief example of career positioning.

Imagine you have a degree in business, emphasizing marketing and finance. You have two job offers. One is with the accounting department of a solar energy equipment manufacturer where you would be assigned to a regional office. In the other job, you would be a traveling consultant working for an association of mortgage bankers.

The solar job would qualify you to do other financial work in the solar industry, and probably qualify you for financial work in other industries. Not being at the headquarters office, you would be away from top management and have less chance of being noticed by higher-ups. Unless you make a concerted effort to read industry news and attend industry meetings, you'll not be exposed to other areas of work in the solar field. It's possible you eventually could be the vice president of finance for the solar maker, it's also possible you could be locked into a career closet.

The traveling consultant job would position you to learn about many opportunities in financial marketing. You would see and be seen by influential bankers who could offer you a good job. Two years on the road could provide your lucky break.

A less obvious situation in positioning analysis is the offer that on the surface seems distant from your goals but in reality can set you up for better things. An example is: "I-don't-wanna-sell insurance." Maybe not. But maybe you do want to be in the public relations field. Insurance companies have sizable public relations staffs. Positioning could help your goals see daylight.

Be sure the job you accept is in the right ball park even if you have to push back the fences a bit, and be sure the position you play offers benefits.

Big Company, Small Company: Which Is Best for Your First Job?

True, you gain professional breadth more quickly by wearing several hats at a small firm than by specializing at a large company, but we suggest that you *think big.*

Large corporations usually offer excellent training programs for career development. Small firms can't afford them.

Large corporations may be willing to move you around, giving you a chance to try out work or at least observe various tasks at close range. Rotating assignments can give you access to a wide range of ideas and people outside the company.

Moreover, it's easy to move from prestige large to obscure small, but not as easily done the other way.

Generally speaking, the larger the company, the larger your training opportunity; the greater the company's reputation, the greater your career clout.

What often happens is that new graduates take the expensive training offered by a giant and run, frequently to a more responsible job at higher pay in a smaller company.

If a large company doesn't book your maiden career voyage, look on the bright side of working for an organization of lesser size. Small businesses employ about half the non-government workers in the country and small firms have provided virtually all new jobs in the U.S. for the past several years.

By working for a small company, you get greater exposure to senior management, faster advancement and more opportunities to become involved in corporate goals and directions.

Job Offer Evaluation Checklist

Miracles never cease. You have a job offer. What a relief. You were beginning to wonder if anyone would ever invite you aboard. You may be tempted to snatch the first job offered, but slow down. As with anything else done in haste, the results can be disappointing.

Instead of saying "yes" or "no" on the spot to a job offer, express your gratitude in a warm and friendly manner and then ask for a day or two to consider the opportunity.

You will make your own decisions, but we think the most important criteria in evaluating a job offer are, in this order: your new boss, the work content of your job, the positioning opportunities, the company, and, lastly, the salary.

Use the following checklist to explore what you think about a job offer. Remember to focus on the items most important to you.

The Job

_______ In my best guess, will I get along well with my boss?

_______ How will I be managed? Will I have more than one boss?

_______ Do I clearly understand the nature of the work?

_______ Do I know specifically what I will be doing? Are my responsibilities reflected in my job title?

_______ Is the position itself interesting and challenging?

_______ Can I make final decisions affecting my work?

_______ In my best guess, will I get along well with co-workers?

_______ Will I need more training? Will the company pay for it?

_______ Will overtime be necessary or available? Night work? Weekends?

_______ Will I travel? How much? Where?

_______ Will I relocate? Where? Will the company pay moving expenses?

(continued)

_______ Is there reasonable job security?

_______ Will I be proud to tell my friends what I do?

Positioning

_______ Could this job result in a significant promotion?

_______ Is the background I'm building too narrow to be of interest to most other employers?

_______ In contrast, will this job help broaden my experience and build a saleable background?

_______ If this isn't my dream job, can it be a springboard to something better as I acquire experience and skills for advancement?

_______ Does this job give me exposure to other opportunities in my field?

_______ Will I be visible to decision-makers?

_______ How frequent are my performance reviews? (Important for improving your performance and being rewarded for a good one.)

The Company

_______ Is the organization too large and rigidly structured for my personality?

_______ Is the organization too small to offer room for advancement or impressive credentials for a future resume?

_______ Is a written personnel statement available that describes vacations, sick leave, cause for dismissal, etc.?

_______ Is the company growing faster than its competitors? Is its financial position healthy?

_______ Is there a high turnover of personnel? If so, why?

_______ Is the company's location convenient?

_______ Is the commuting time acceptable?

_______ Is the physical setting acceptable? (Enough light, ventilation, cleanliness.)

_______ If I relocate, do I like the lifestyle the company's location offers? Are desirable community, cultural, religious, shopping, and recreational facilities available?

_______ What is the firm's reputation for fair treatment of employees?

_______ Is the organization in a growth industry? If it's in a shrinking industry, do I have reason to believe the industry can still offer good opportunities over my working lifetime?

Financial Rewards

_______ Is the salary competitive? (Does it pay the market rate or more?)

_______ If it is not competitive, is it possible to get an early review and an increase before one year?

_______ Do I clearly understand the method of payment—salary, hourly wage, commission, wage and tips, by the piece, fee?

_______ Are raises based on merit, length of service, formal exams?

_______ Are employee benefits competitive? Do I receive any of these common benefits?

- Insurance: health, dental, life.
- Memberships: professional societies, trade associations, health clubs.
- Free parking.
- Time off: vacation days, holidays, sick days, maternity leave.
- Retirement plan. How much does the company pay and how much do I pay?

_______ Do I receive any of these less common employee benefits?

- Company car.
- Clothing allowance for special uniforms required but not provided by employer.

- Expense account.
- Employer-paid tuition for college.
- Travel to conferences, conventions.
- Subscriptions to professional and trade journals.
- Profit sharing or stock purchase program.

much leverage as a beginner, you might negotiate minor concessions.

In our observation, there is no such thing as a perfect 10 job. If you find one, tell the employer you'd be as happy as a clam at a shellfish singing contest to come aboard. Is yesterday too soon?

Rate the Offer

You may find you lack enough information to even guess at some of these questions.

In that case, telephone the person who made the hiring offer, saying you have several questions and would appreciate a chance to clear them up. Ask when you can drop by for a brief meeting.

Once in the employer's office, take the curse off your hesitancy by saying that while you're 99 percent sure the job is perfect for you, as a conscientious person, you intend to make a serious career commitment to the position. For that reason, you have to be sure there are no loose ends.

Not having adequate facts on which to weigh a job offer the moment you receive it is another reason to ask for time to reflect. Once you accept an offer, renegotiating is difficult, often impossible.

But some gains may be possible before you accept a job. Once all the data are in, compare the offer with your job objective.

Unless you enjoy complex computations, keep it simple. A scale of 1 to 10 works well for many people.

If the offer rates less than 6 on your scale, the job probably isn't for you. You want to do better than break even, don't you?

If the offer scores above 6 points, a majority of its factors appear to meet your requirements. What's missing in the offer? What would bring it closer to the top of your scale—a little more money, a bit more visibility? Although you won't have

Discover the Best Companies to Work For

What makes a company good to work for? Surveys of executive recruiters and studies by business writers show several common characteristics.

Excellence. A study by *Money* magazine says the quality of excellence seems to be what sets the best companies above others. The term refers to all-around excellence in products, research, marketing, management and people. A company that operates on sound values and gives good value seems to spur the enthusiasm of its employees to conquer the marketplace.

Somewhat Higher Pay and Employee Benefits. Compensation is often a bit higher at the best companies. They appreciate good employees and want to keep them.

Sensitivity to Human Problems. The top companies pay more than lip service to the fact that human resources are as important as capital and products. Doors are open, promotions are made from within. Management builds team loyalty by being fair and competent.

Among the leaders, the Xerox Corporation is a vivid example of caring about people. In 1971, Xerox announced that each year it would let about 20 employees have up to one year off with full pay and benefits to pursue social projects in their communities. Employees work in concerns of their own choosing, such as drug addiction, civil rights, literacy and penal reform. Hundreds of people have had leaves since 1972 at an average annual cost of up to $500,000 in replacement salaries.

Want to know about other corporate standard bearers? A ready reference is *The 100 Best Companies to Work For in America* by Robert Levering, Milton Moskowitz and Michael Katz (New American Library).

Steelcase Inc. is one of the companies highlighted in the book. The office furniture manufacturer's benefits are extensive: from an innovative child-care referral program, to an eight-week program for spouses and employees soon to retire; from a 1,100-acre employee campground, to company sponsored recreation programs in sports, hobbies and wellness.

Not only do husbands and wives often work at Steelcase, but the company offers employees' children student loans, summer jobs, and priority status on full-time work.

That's not all: Steelcase offers high quality dining-room food at cost, superior pay, and profit sharing. A flextime policy allows employees to structure their own working hours. If you like a family atmosphere, you can't beat Steelcase, Inc. in Grand Rapids, Mich.

Other companies frequently named in the top group are such well-known giants as IBM, Procter & Gamble, Eastman Kodak, 3M, General Electric, Weyerhauser, Cummins Engine, DuPont, Hallmark Cards, Hewlett-Packard, Northwestern Mutual Life and Citicorp. This listing is by no means complete but it does give you some idea of enlightened corporations and how they operate.

By contrast, what makes a company not so good to work for? Always make your own judgments based on individual assessments, but, as a general rule, executive recruiters warn against companies with a high turnover, a rigid management unsure of itself, or a management with many layers. Recruiters also advise you to carefully check companies that are family-owned, and companies that are run by an autocrat. While such companies often pay better than average, they may offer little satisfaction or security.

Right about now you may be thinking, "Oh, yeah, sure... it would be great to go with the pennant winners but there isn't room for everyone in the best companies. I might not get in the door."

That's true. Neither is there room for everyone in the worst companies.

It's good to know the difference.

Government Jobs: A Spectrum of Career Opportunities

Government jobs are found at the federal, state and local levels. Each level has its own hiring process.

The most visible government workers are elected officials and appointed high-level advisers—the people you see on news programs.

Although they're in the spotlight, such people are a small portion of the 17 million employees throughout all levels of government.

About one worker in seven has a government job. There are hordes of engineers, secretaries, health specialists, journalists, law enforcement officers, firefighters, teachers, historians, biologists, labor economists, hydrologists, foresters, social insurance representatives, artists, lawyers, food service workers, intelligence agents, diplomats, accountants, laborers, bankers and more.

Virtually all occupations that flourish in private enterprise exist in the government sphere.

The money is adequate and the benefits are excellent, but don't count on buying a yacht if you opt for the public sector.

Our general advice is to choose the business world for your first job, unless you intend to spend your entire career in government service. If you begin in government, you may find it difficult to switch later to a corporate position. The reason is that many business executives are reluctant to hire former government workers, feeling that they care too little about making money for commercial establishments.

The viewpoint is reflected in the comment of former Secretary of the Treasury W. Michael Blumenthal: "The difference between business and government is that the government has no bottom line."

Another reason you may not want to consider government employment for your first job is that a federal job hunt typically takes a year or more between start and hiring. The time frames for state and local job hunts vary.

P.S. If you ever want to work for the federal government, Neale Baxter's *Opportunities in Federal Government Careers* (VGM Career Horizons) gives you a quick fill-in. You are introduced to the kinds of jobs available and offered excellent suggestions on how to obtain them.

It's Attitude Adjustment Time

As a school senior, you were at the top of your profession (of student). Now you're starting over. It's back to square one—you're a freshman, a beginner, a rookie. Entering the working world is almost like being a newcomer in a foreign land: You'll have to adjust to a new culture, different behavior, unfamiliar customs, and, if technical jargon is spoken where you work, a new language.

Be aware of the need to change your perspective. While your intellectual floor may be the average person's ceiling, don't give in to the temptation to behave in ways that cause co-workers to see you as elitist, superior or overbearing. Adopt the attitude that you are bright enough to know you have much to learn, but you can do it with time and effort.

Reliability is another area that may require an adjustment in your attitude. In school, when you didn't feel like going to class, you may have stayed at home. It's different at work because others depend on you. The consequences can be severe if you continue to exercise the independence that was yours as a student.

Another difference between school and work is the weight of your responsibilities. In class, a partially right answer may have brought you partial credit; if you flubbed an exam, usually you could make it up by scoring a higher grade next time.

An employee doesn't have a similar latitude. Being half-right or flubbing a question can result in horrendous costs, or downright disaster. Suppose, for example, you take a job as an engineer who makes recommendations for evaluating the catalyst in a nuclear reactor, or a quality assurance technician who checks pacemakers for human hearts, or a mutual fund analyst who researches million-dollar transactions in the stock market. The outcome of "oops" could be overwhelming.

The attitude adjustments you'll have to make are many, but simply recognizing this fact can smooth the transition.

A misstep at school usually was repairable and forgivable. At work, the end result could be much different, depending on the severity of the goof. The following warning, posted in offices across the nation, is exaggerated, but it gives you the general idea:

To err is human, to forgive is not company policy.

The Boss: Gatekeeper to Your Future

Many people don't fully comprehend that the person they call "boss" has make-it-or-break-it power over their work life.

Your boss can be a friend or enemy, mentor or tormentor. Your boss evaluates your performance and recommends you for promotion or good riddance. You won't get a raise unless your boss agrees.

Even after you leave the organization, your boss's power reaches out from the past in the form of references.

We know it is impossible to maintain a good relationship with some supervisors, but if ever you see a rift developing, act quickly and try your best to mend it.

Here's a good idea on how to do this. We learned the technique from Mary Ann and Eric Allison, who wrote *Managing Up, Managing Down* (Simon & Schuster/Cornerstone Library).

"The Boss and You" Analysis Chart

Analyze the personal factors between you and the boss. Draw a chart listing these items down the left side of the paper: *Age, Race, Sex, Background, Preferred method of communication* (in person, memo...), *Frequency of communication, Style of dress, Prejudices, Sense of humor, Willingness to take risks, Acceptance of change, Preferred personal presentation style* and *Time of day when at one's best.*

Now make four columns to the right of the traits listed. The headings are: *You, Your manager, Match?* and *Action needed?*

Using any detail you wish, write the important things about yourself in each trait category, then contrast them with the characteristics you see in your boss. The areas of conflict will stand out.

Under *Time of day,* for instance, if you're a lark who is wide awake in the morning, and your boss is a nightingale who functions best after noon, it won't do to rouse your manager with questions and reports while the boss is still trying to wake up.

Age is another minefield. If you're 23 and your manager is 59, you note there is no match. The action needed may require that you understand the boss feels you're too young for the responsibility you have and that maybe you should keep mum about winning at racketball.

Suppose under *Sense of humor* your Irish boss tells Italian jokes and you're Italian and you don't like it. There is no tactful way to tell the person who signs your merit review that his or her taste in jokes is lousy or prejudiced, but taking the problem into consideration in your planning can help prevent a blow-up.

After completing your analysis, let a few days pass before you begin to plan formal actions. Do well on this exercise and you've taken strong positive steps toward a bright beginning.

First Days on a New Job

Yes, every newcomer is just as nervous as you are at starting a job. Here are tips to help relieve the tension and create a good beginning impression.

• Personality is a powerful influencer of career success. No longer is it safe to wallow in grouchy days as you may have at school, to exhibit coolness, abrasiveness or insensitivity to others. Positive traits, such as enthusiasm, cooperativeness and self-confidence will ease your way.

• Give top performance on the job. One of the shortest routes to success is to show your boss you can get things done and that you place company concerns before personal pleasures.

• Ask questions until you know what you're doing. For small, routine questions, ask the boss to name a "shepherd," or "buddy," for you. When you want to know how to order supplies or where the files are, you can say to your shepherd, "The boss said to ask you my newcomer's questions." The shepherd is doubly flattered at being asked by the boss and you.

• Watch the use of first names. Simply ask your boss, "Shall I call you Mr./Ms.______?" If the boss wants you to use first names, you'll be told.

• Ask your boss how an assignment is to be handled—with regular progress reports or contact only when you're stumped. You need to know how much responsibility and authority the boss is willing to delegate to you.

• Remember that people like other people who are like them. If your boss's office looks like a garbage can, yours can be neater but not pin-perfect. If your boss shows up a half hour early each morning, you make the great sacrifice and do so too.

• Follow office etiquette. A sharp listener will soon pick up on the special office language that's used to answer telephones, in office memos, and to address co-workers personally.

• In dress, take an employer's lead. When you're in doubt, dress conservatively until you know what's accepted.

• Learn new ways. Be receptive to co-workers who offer advice on work techniques although this may mean changing old habits. Accept criticism gracefully.

When you are criticized, avoid being defensive. Simply ask your critic to be specific—"Can you tell me where my work falls short?" If the criticism is fair, own up to it—"You're right. . .I'll pay more attention to this point from now on."

As long as you are not defensive it's okay to explain why a criticism is off the mark when you feel it is unfair.

• Arrive at work on time. Staying late does not make up for a tardy arrival. Your morning absence may play havoc with the work schedule of others.

It's just as important to arrive at work ready to work. Be sure grooming and eating are finished before you cross the office threshold. Eating lunch at your desk can create an image of dedication while eating breakfast at your desk makes you look disorganized and uncommitted.

• Go slow in changing your work area. Watch how others organize their workspace and follow their example.

• Lunch with different groups. You want to avoid being linked with an inappropriate group and need time to figure out who's who.

• Chances are you'll be introduced around. But if not, take advantage of naturally occurring meeting opportunities—in the elevator or at the water fountain, for instance—to introduce yourself.

• Learn the artful use of the memo. You may have to write a memo as a proposal to persuade someone to take an action, to report on an assigned project, or simply to protect yourself by getting an incident on paper and in the files. Remember to ask yourself, "Why am I writing? What is the problem? Why is it important? What do I want done about it? Who will make the decision?"

Your memo must answer those questions, and the fewer words it takes, the more likely it will be read and acted upon.

If your memo is not addressed to your boss, be certain he or she knows what you are doing and approves it. Don't ever appear to be sidestepping your boss's authority.

- Be cautious about socializing after hours. As journalist Wes Smith has observed, "Going out for a drink with the boys after work every night is a bad idea. Notice that the boss doesn't go. That's why he's the boss and they're still the boys."

Dealing With Sexual Harassment

Sexual harassment is a problem working women faced for decades, but only in the early '70s did women managers and employees begin to discuss harassment openly.

What is sexual harassment? Here is what the National Organization for Women and the Working Women's Institute say:

Sexual harassment is any repeated or unwarranted verbal or physical sexual advances, sexually explicit derogatory statements, or sexually discriminatory remarks made by someone in the workplace which are offensive or objectionable to the recipient or which cause the recipient discomfort or humiliation or which interfere with the recipient's job performance.

In the worst instances, a sexually harassed victim complies with a supervisor's demands or is not hired, is not given a raise, is not promoted, is given unattractive duties or is fired.

The victim is in a no-win situation.

Studies show that nearly half of all working women have been harassed or know someone who has. Yet, not all victims are women. According to a two-year study of federal employees by the U.S. Merit Systems Protection Board, 42 percent of the 694,000 women questioned and 15 percent of the 1,168,000 men said they had been sexually harassed.

What can you do if it happens to you? Here are two important points:

1. *Seek advice and counsel from friends and co-workers. Don't ignore the harassment.*

2. *Keep a log or diary in a safe place, not your desk. You will need the data if you file a formal complaint with a government agency.*

Another option is to write a letter to the harasser, keeping a copy for your files. State every instance of harassment, and conclude by saying that you want the relationship to be totally professional from that point on. The tone of the letter should be rational, not angry.

Dr. Mary Rowe, a labor economist, advises that this is a very effective way to stop harassment. She says: "The typical reaction [to a letter of this type] from the harasser was no reaction. The harassment just stopped."

For more information, ask at a library for such books as *Sexual Harassment on the Job* by Constance Backhouse and Leah Cohen (Prentice-Hall).

To contact the appropriate government agencies for information or to file a complaint, look in your telephone directory under "U.S. Government

Offices" for a local office of the Equal Employment Opportunity Commission. Look under state and city government listings for state and local human rights agencies.

How to Get a Raise

You may receive a raise without asking for one after you've been on the job for a year. Then again, you may not.

If this is confusing, a little background will help you better understand pay trends today.

For the past several decades, the typical compensation policy of American corporations has been for managers to conduct annual performance reviews of each staff member and, as night follows day, conclude the reviews by awarding salary increases.

The review-raise process has been such an established routine that unless you had bombed the CEO with water balloons at the company picnic, you were sure to be rewarded for time served and loyalty rendered.

Automatic raises that are tied to performance evaluations continue to be the norm in many corporations, but growing numbers of large employers are becoming cost-conscious, especially in service industries where payroll expense is the biggest financial drain.

The cost-containers are looking at the relationship between productivity and pay. Their recommendations can boil down to giving no automatic raises, or more frequently, to stretching them out to 18 or 24 months, rather than the former 12-month review.

More large employers are relying on merit raises—increases given only to the most productive employees.

Find out what the compensation policy is at your company. If it has dropped automatic increases in favor of merit rewards, prepare to actively campaign for regular and generous raises.

How much should you expect? Compensation specialists say typical increases range between 5 percent and 7 percent when inflation is below 5 percent. If you change jobs, expect a boost in pay between 15 percent and 20 percent.

How can you prepare? As we said before: Maintain records. From the first month on the job, keep a journal of your achievements. Write down any contribution to the employer's success that can be used to win a raise. Spend 5 or 10 minutes of your own time every Friday jotting down your ammunition; summarize it every six months.

Rehearse your negotiations with a friend. Tape record the practice sessions. If your arguments seem weak, devise more persuasive points.

What if you are turned down on the basis of performance? Ask what you need to do to be rated as outstanding and make sure your manager sees you writing down the advice. Request another review in three months. Improve your performance and at the second review, refer to your notes to explain how you have met the standards set by your manager. Ask if you now can be rated as an outstanding worker (and, not incidentally, qualify for a merit increase).

Large corporations aren't the only places where automatic increases are under attack. A change is in the wind for small companies, too, according to Peat, Marwick, Mitchell & Co., an accounting firm that studied the issue along with *INC.* magazine.

The study concludes that growing numbers of salary increases in smaller companies are based on achievement of goals. As an official of the accounting firm explains, "Just coming to work and continuing to draw breath doesn't warrant a 12 percent annual increase anymore."

If you'd like additional strategies to increase your compensation, read a booklet by one of the authors. *Higher Salaries: How to Get Them* by Joyce Lain Kennedy is available for $3.50 only from the publisher: Sun Features Inc., Box 368-D, Cardiff, Calif. 92007.

When You've Chosen the Wrong Job, Quit

Sometimes a job goes sour and you wonder what happened. Where did you go wrong? You thought you did everything you were supposed to do. You researched the company. You filled out the job-offer evaluation checklist. You felt you were on the same wavelength as your boss.

Despite everything, the job turned out to be a huge disappointment. After only three months, you are certain you have made a monumental false start.

How long do you have to stick with such a job? Stay only as long as it takes you to find a better job.

Cut your losses and try again. One or two years of your life is too stiff a price to pay for a miscalculation.

Analyze what went wrong. Somewhere there's a gap in your prior plannning. Be more careful about which job offer you accept next time. You don't want to build a reputation as a quick-change artist.

If You Bow Out, Do It Gracefully

All things eventually end, even satisfying first jobs. Either you'll be selected for promotion in your company, or you'll move on. If your career is in a holding pattern, about two years is a benchmark for knowing when it's time to pack up and get out.

When you go, depart in style, leaving behind an image of you as a classy person.

Tell your immediate supervisor first; follow up with a letter of resignation. Then tell subordinates because they will be affected by your leaving. Next, notify higher-ups in writing. Last, share the news with your associates and clients.

How much notice should you give? Two weeks to one month is appropriate.

About your leaving, explain that you have mixed feelings. You're pleased to be tackling a new challenge, but you'll miss the people with whom you currently work.

The exit-interview can be a booby trap. A manager asks you to be frank and let your hair down about your views toward the company and why you're leaving. It's a mistake to assume you're finished with this company and attempt to clear the air with your gripes. Limit your remarks to positive reasons—you liked your job and the company, but you received an offer you couldn't pass up. You can never tell when negative words will haunt you. People talk—sometimes to other people with whom you will be dealing. In addition, you might be invited down the road to rejoin the company at a higher level if your file is filled with kind words.

Try to finish projects and establish a line of transition with co-workers for tasks you can't conclude. Offer to serve as a resource for your successor and to do everything possible to make the changeover go smoothly.

On departure day, thank everyone for opportunities, loyalty, support, courtesies and favors. Put your appreciation in writing to your boss and top management.

It is not unheard of for employers who can't

handle rejection to fire you once you resign. The day you give notice becomes your last day.

Reputable companies don't behave in such a second-rate manner, but if you have any hint that it could happen, here's a tip to protect yourself.

When accepting a new job, prepare the way with your future employer. Say, "I will, of course, offer two weeks' notice, but it's possible that my boss will be willing to release me sooner than that. Would it be okay if I let you know in a few days the exact date I can start with you?"

Should it turn out that your boss demands you leave the moment you resign, you're covered. With dignity, call your new employer to say you were able to work it out so that you can start work immediately. Offer no explanations, and never refer to the jerk who didn't play by the rules. Doing so would reflect unfavorably on you.

SECTION SEVENTEEN

YOU CAN OWN THE 21ST CENTURY

I*n tomorrow's 21st century, career paths will not be as well marked as* they were for previous generations.

Expect twists and turns along the way, some pleasant, some unpleasant. Once you get a toehold in the success market, there's still a great deal you'll need to know about getting ahead and staying out in front of the crowd.

Of course, we can't lead you through all the minefields in your first job, but we can point out some important basics of career success.

One way to achieve that success is to give your career regular checkups. This section tells how to do this and continues with a treasury of success pointers gathered from respected sources.

A Regular Career Checkup Keeps You on Course

A lot of toil went into finding your first job. It wouldn't be surprising if after getting it under control, you feel that it's time to relax, to lighten up. After all, it will be several years before anyone trusts you with managerial responsibility. Right?

Wrong. This kind of thinking will keep you from wanting to show up at your class reunion a decade from now.

Never is there time in your career to coast. This is true on your first job, your second job, and every job thereafter.

While there is a legal age for certain things—voting and registering for the draft, for instance—there is no legal age for seizing opportunities. Good career chances could come your way at any time of your life, starting now. If you're busy taking it easy, you may miss some humdingers.

Beginning with your first full-time job and continuing throughout the course of your working years, devote a corner of your life to the management of your career.

Set aside a regular time—say, a half-dozen times a year—for the purpose. Use the time to review where you've been, how you're doing and where you're headed. It's useful to map out a plan, one that includes

- goals
- objectives
- obstacles to be overcome
- activities to achieve objectives
- a timetable

(To refresh your memory about goal-setting, turn back to section 9.)

Because career and life planning is not a one-time proposition, view your plan as flexible. Be ready to amend it if you get wind of changing situations, developing disasters or unexpected opportunities.

You may ask, "Why write a plan that isn't set in stone?" The mere act of planning puts structure and substance into your career management. Planning makes you think.

During your career checkup, assess your progress and make revisions to your plan, when needed. Here's a list of questions to ask yourself:

Career Checkup Questions

1. Am I meeting my objectives on the timetable I set for myself? If not, why not? What am I going to do about it?

____

____

____

2. Do I have enough experience to advance in my field? If not, what can I do to get more? Would I gain by asking for a transfer to another department within the company? Would it be possible to work on an interdepartmental task force?

____

____

____

3. Do I have enough education to continue to advance in my field? If not, what specific additional education do I need? Can I get it without quitting my job? Will my company pay for it? If not, can I afford to pay for it?

____

____

____

4. Am I satisfied with this job? Do I enjoy the daily functions and responsibilities? Does this job meet my personal values requirements? If not, is it time to start looking for another job?

____

____

____

5. Does this job have a future? Can I expand my responsibilities (with a promotion in mind)? Is the company growing and is it financially stable? Is the industry stable or expanding? If negatives exist, can I reasonably expect the situation to improve within the next year, or should I look for other opportunities?

____

____

____

6. Is my career on the right course? Are my earnings what they should be compared to others at my level in the field? Are my benefits up to par? Do I enjoy good interpersonal relationships with my boss and co-workers? If there are problems, what can I do to resolve them?

____

____

____

Points to Check

1. If your career is not moving along at the right pace, reconsider whether your goals and objectives are realistic. Perhaps your timetable is too ambitious. Maybe you need to take a hard, objective look at your qualifications for the job.

2. Suppose you are in financial marketing and find that you are blocked from moving up because you lack experience in mainframe computers. A candid discussion with your supervisor, asking for advice, is a good place to start overcoming your experience deficiency.

3. Assume you are employed as a case worker for a public social agency. You have a bachelor's degree. You want to be the agency director one day. You will need at least a master's degree and perhaps a doctorate. Ask about the agency's policy for employer-paid tuition programs, and about available educational grants from outside groups.

4. If a job is personally unfulfilling, be sure the trouble isn't really within yourself. Many people who believe the clouds will float away and the sun will shine again once they have a new job need to take a closer look at the sources of their unhappiness.

5. Anticipate which way the highway you are following will branch and branch again in the distance. Some jobs provide 10 years of experience. Other jobs provide one year of experience 10 times. Read business publications and trade journals for your industry to help you look around corners.

6. When you don't know what you should be earning (your market value), do research. Depending on the type of job you have, you can contact executive recruiters, private employment agencies, college career offices and the public Job Service.

Study help-wanted ads in newspapers and trade journals. Professional societies and trade associations often have local salary figures or know where to get them.

The reference librarian at a major library can direct you to private salary studies such as those conducted by the Administrative Management Society, the American Management Association, or books about what people earn, such as *Paychecks* by David Harrop (Harper & Row).

As for employee benefits, compare your employer's package with that offered by most other companies, as given in the table on the next page.

Keeping track of how you're doing places you on a career trampoline to spring higher and higher.

How Do Your Fringes Compare?

These figures are from a survey conducted by the Chamber of Commerce of the United States, to which 1,507 firms responded.

Fringe Benefits	% of Companies that Provide It	Average Annual Amount Paid by Employer	What Your Employer Pays for You
Life, hospital, surgical, medical, major-medical insurance	99%	$1,274	$________
Social security and unemployment compensation	98	1,543	________
Paid vacation time	86	902	________
Pension plan	83	1,040	________
Paid holidays	81	533	________
Paid sick leave	75	244	________
Paid periods for lunch, travel, rest and so forth	67	523	________
Education (tuition refunds and so forth)	63	46	________
Dental insurance	53	83	________
Long-term disability insurance	50	58	________
Christmas or other bonuses, service awards	49	62	________
Employer's contribution to thrift plans	26	80	________
Profit-sharing payments	23	218	________
Meals furnished by employer	21	24	________
Discounts on goods and services bought from the company	15	17	________

Source: *Employee Benefits*

The Success Market

We hope that by now you've developed a fascination for career ambition.

Be as ambitious as you like. As Mark Twain once said: "I'm against millionaires but it would be dangerous to offer me the position."

We can't be sure what lies beyond the calendar horizon of January 1, 2000, but it is customary for authors and commencement speakers to solemnly inform each new crop of graduates that the challenges they face are greater than any since the Ice Age. In your case, it's true. That's because of the technological speedup that is occurring as you read this page.

You are going where no generation has gone before. But isn't that the same for everyone? Yes, but what's different for you, and why your challenge is greater than that of, say, your parents, is that your crystal ball is almost fogged over as a result of the *rate* of change: It's happening in fast-forward motion.

When you consider that about 90 percent of all scientists and engineers ever born are alive today, and that you'll be working in an era of space travel between planets, living in a time when machines think like humans, and experiencing years in which the science of biotechnology changes life itself, you can see that your future is not going to be business as usual.

Even so, there are enduring and anchoring wisdoms that can light your way today, next year and through a million galaxies tomorrow. Here are some of them.

Time and You

Besides the noble art of getting things done, there is the noble art of leaving things undone. The wisdom of life consists in the elimination of non-essentials.

—Lin Yutang

Time is a non-renewable resource. We cannot stockpile it; the best we can do is manage it well.

Start each day with a list of things you want to do. Separate the list into "must do today" and "can wait." Chances are you will have "can waits" left over each day. If a "can wait" gets pushed to the next day five times, consider whether you need to do it at all.

A good expenditure of your time is to spend several hours pursuing a time management course or a book on the subject. You'll learn about such things as the "80/20 trap," which holds that the majority of people spend 80 percent of their time on activities that produce only 20 percent of their results.

For one week, keep a log of how you spend your time. You will be amazed at how many precious moments you can save.

Build Power Alliances

In virtually every organization, there are two kinds of power systems—formal, which appears on the organization chart, and informal, which is a system of alliances.

Even as a new employee, begin to build power by participating in alliances. If there's a problem or opportunity in the wind, you'll probably hear about it through your alliances. If the change could affect you, the advance notice buys time to plan a strategy in response.

FIRED!

One day you may be fired from a job. Before going to pieces, remember that you lost only a job. You didn't lose your intrinisic worth. The sun will rise tomorrow.

Many people are fired at least once during the course of their careers. They just don't tell you about it. You are young. You are resilient. You will find a better job.

LINE VS. STAFF JOBS

Line jobs are those that earn income for an organization. Often they involve the making or selling of a product or service. In banks, loan officers hold line jobs; in manufacturing, plant managers are line personnel; in newspapers, reporters are in line slots. In one way or another, they fatten company coffers. Line jobs generally are viewed as being on the fast track.

Staff jobs are support positions that spend money rather than earn it. Staff expenses are necessary to keep the business afloat or to promote the general profitability of the enterprise. You'll find staff people in human resources departments, recruiting and devising benefits; in communications, writing and lobbying; in management information systems, analyzing data and preparing reports.

Support staff provides an organization's accounting and legal services, advertising and administration. Many people view staff jobs as being on the slow track.

Historically, the top executive suite jobs have gone to line people who "knew the business." In recent years, several studies have come along to claim aides-de-camp can become heirs to their bosses' jobs. Moreover, lawyers and financial specialists not infrequently rise to the number-one job in their companies. Still, the weight of opinion appears not to have changed dramatically. Business school wisdom still says that if you want to fly an airplane, get a job in the cockpit, not in the maintenance hangar.

The type of company also affects how far you can go. In an accounting firm, accountancy is line work; in a corporate internal communications department, a reporter holds a staff job.

Being a staff worker is not without luster. In a large corporation, the top of the staff ladder is a department or division head, and, upon occasion, an executive in the upper echelon of management. The vice-presidential level of staff jobs can be impressive in money (six figures), power, status and recognition. A human resources or communications VP might, for instance, direct the activities of hundreds of people. The scope can be wide enough to prevent a hint of boredom; an administrative vice president might oversee food services, security, facilities, purchasing and information management. The limit to advancement in some staff jobs is at a lofty level.

In small firms, a staff worker can rise to owner, partner or head.

One problem about staff jobs is that when times turn lean-and-mean, they are more likely to be cut back than are line jobs.

Staff skies can be friendly, but if you are determined to become a high-flying captain, line jobs are the safest choice.

GETTING NOTICED

Many young people assume that if they work hard and are loyal, they'll be rewarded. That's not necessarily true. Your management may be so involved with its own concerns that you remain a face in the crowd.

Don't make the mistake of keeping your professional qualifications a secret. If you are ambitious, execute a personal image-building campaign.

Here are tips on acceptable horn-tooting from public relations expert David Drobis:

1. Get your name in the newspaper, perhaps as a consultant to an editor on topics involving your specialty.
2. Speak on radio and television talk shows as an expert on some topic.
3. Garner magazine publicity with by-lined articles. (Write a piece for your company publication.)
4. Join a club and contribute visibly.
5. Give a speech and arrange for your organization's public relations department to publicize it.
6. Give a presentation to management showing your department's problem-solving capabilities.
7. Use written internal communications to publicize your accomplishments. (But be careful not to sound like a braggart.)
8. At work, plug into the interpersonal communications grapevine, join committees and speak at luncheons.
9. Win an award and see that it is publicized.

How To Be Lucky

Keep your personal contacts log, discussed in section 5, up to date. Contacts are not a substitute for competence, but the fact remains that the more well-placed people you know, the greater the number of opportunities that will come your way.

In *The Luck Factor* (Macmillan), journalist Max Gunther, who has interviewed more than 1,000 people about what made them lucky or unlucky, says you can exercise a degree of control.

The basic difference between lucky and unlucky people, he says, is that "lucky people have a spider web network of friends and contacts, and unlucky people tend to be loners. Most of the big lucky breaks in life come through knowing people. The more people you know, the more chances you have to get lucky."

Professional societies and trade associations are excellent places to begin. Find out what groups operate in your field and join today.

Learn the Art of Compensatory Responding

Answer questions and requests from strength. Never answer an employer's query with a naked "no" and let it end at that. Build your answer on a "yes."

For example, if an interviewer should ask whether you ever worked in the hotel field and you reply, "No, I haven't," add something like this: "but I've worked in the restaurant field and I know a good deal that is common to both of these related industries."

If your boss should inquire if you are willing to take a stab at preparing next year's budget and the thought petrifies you, never say so. Instead tell the boss that while the budget drafting is new to you, you're willing to give it your best shot and would appreciate guidelines.

For a young person, the art of compensatory responding means finding ways to overcome a lack of experience. Compensate by focusing on your high energy, your fine education, your flexibility, your willingness to work hard and your ability to learn fast.

When you apply the art of compensatory responding to your answers, you let others know you are a "can-do" person.

Handle Money, Manage Technology

If you're a private who wants to be a field marshall in the 21st century, learn to handle money and to manage technology. This is a high-performance team of talents.

This is the MBA who is comfortable with computers. This is the electrical engineer who understands high finance. This is the accountant who is clear on the mechanics of water resource management.

Perhaps you learned about money or technology your first time through school. Why not pick up the other half during evening or weekend studies?

Money and technology are an unbeatable combination.

Getting More Money

What is the single most important thing you can do to receive a higher salary when you start a new job as an experienced worker?

Delay talking about money until you've been offered a specific position. Before that time, you are the seller and the employer is the buyer. After the offer, you negotiate as equals settling the price of a commodity. You are discussing value for value.

If you're asked too soon in a job interview how much money you want, say you're sure salary will not be a problem once you both understand the dimensions of the position and the quality of the contributions you'll be expected to make.

Can you imagine an interviewer saying the job is trivial? That an idiot could do it? No, you're likely to hear it is an important assignment and that a superior performer is required.

Once you show you are a superior performer for an important job, your value is up. And your price is up.

Support Your Local Boss

Being at war with your immediate boss is like turning cartwheels on an ice floe: Dangerous with a capital D.

If you and your boss don't see eye to eye, maybe you can escape to a new job. Otherwise, act unilaterally to solve the problem.

Why? Because the boss holds the power. The boss controls the quality of your daily life. The boss can keep you from passing through the gate to praise, a raise, promotion or glowing reference. Unfair, perhaps, but true.

One reason people flub boss relationships is a fear of authority carried over from childhood. This tends to make us treat the boss as a kind of god rather than as another adult who has needs and problems, fears and values.

If there's tension on the job, make a research project out of the boss and analyze the conflict with as little emotion as you can manage.

Note body language. Listen for hidden meanings. Read between the lines. Once you get a glimmer of why the boss acts in a particular manner, you gain a measure of control over the situation.

Look for a Job When You Have a Job

One of the big "never's" in the success market is "never quit a job until you have another job." Or, looking at it another way: The best time to look for a good job is when you have a good job.

With the exception of new graduates, employers like to hire people who already are on somebody else's payroll. This is assurance that somebody wants you. It is much harder to find employment when you're jobless.

This means you often have to keep your job hunt a secret.

When you need to make a quiet search, bear in mind these tips from Robert Half, the author of *Robert Half on Hiring* (Crown Publishers):

- Don't take longer lunch hours than usual.
- Keep personal phone calls to a minimum.
- Maintain your normal level of communication with management—staying out of sight is a clue that you're ready to move.
- Don't start coming to work dressed noticeably better than usual.
- Don't begin clearing your desk of personal effects.
- Don't make a sudden change in your vacation pattern.
- Don't be less aggressive in the office than normal.

Robert Half says that usually as soon as your company suspects that you're getting ready to leave, you can consider yourself as good as fired.

But in some cases, employers will make you a buy-back offer—that is, make you an offer that will induce you to stay. The career management skills come in knowing whether it is to your advantage to keep your search quiet or to let it be known.

Coping With Crisis

One of the best rules I know is, when a crisis occurs or is in the process of occurring, don't react. Just say you'd like to think about it.

Once you have analyzed the crisis in terms of its potential for disaster, then you can respond. This at least allows for clearheadedness in dealing with the problem, and if you're savvy about what's going on and haven't become caught up in crisis yourself, it may present a very interesting edge.

This advice comes from Mark H. McCormack in his book *What They Don't Teach You at Harvard Business School* (Bantam Books).

When McCormack says "don't react," he does not mean you should stand still and let the office burn down.

He does mean keeping your cool in an emergency. Have you noticed that movie heroes never seem to be out of control even in a disaster film? In reality, you may be panic-stricken when a crisis occurs, but do your best to maintain a calm facade. The more unflappable you appear, the more people will follow you.

Learn to Follow Money

To find jobs, find industries, businesses, private institutions, and government agencies that are expanding. To find these organizations, follow money.

Bankers and investment counselors know about money. Ask one of them who is spending it. Or ask two.

John L. Munschauer, who wrote those words, in *Jobs for English Majors and Other Smart People* (Peterson's Guides) is right. Even in recessions, the turnover rate for American corporations is around 15 percent.

As Munschauer says:

Prospering and growing organizations need money to finance growth. Bankers, who make money by lending it, make it a point to find organizations that are growing and need to borrow. Organizations that are growing need talent... You can't ask bankers to discuss their business, but you can ask them to nominate employers that are generally regarded... as progressive and growing.

Make Decisions as if You Owned the Company

Robert Townsend, who turned Avis Rent-A-Car corporation into the nation's best-known No. 2 rental company, wrote a best-selling book, revised as *Further Up the Organization* (Alfred A. Knopf).

His many wisdoms include this sage advice:

Make every decision as if you owned the whole company. All your colleagues will be making their decisions in ways designed to make them look good or to give the boss what they think he wants to hear. In your case you'll be giving the boss what's in the interest of the whole company for him to hear even if he won't like hearing it. This approach will give you backbone when it's needed—and you'll begin to stand out among your peers. Don't overdo it... Be pleasant. The worse the news you bring your boss, the bigger your smile should be.

Make Yourself Obsolescence Proof

The pupfish is a sort of quick-change artist that makes evolutionary modifications in response to environmental changes.

For 40,000 years, the pupfish has lived in the Death Valley area, where—although it is only an inch long—the piscatorial creature has amazed scientists with its ability to adapt and survive in desert waterholes.

The pupfish reconciles itself to rigorous conditions of wide extremes, and you can learn from its example: Expect inevitable change and minimize the risk of your own job-market obsolescence.

Accept the idea of continuing education as a way of life for all your life.

You need not take formal coursework each year, but make it your style to read, watch educational programs on the tube, and attend industry meetings where new trends surface.

Just as you work out to keep fit, get into the habit of doing an information workout on a regular basis.

The dogged pupfish survived by moving with the times; you can too.

In the Race to the Top, Who Wins— Scramblers or Stabilizers?

Getting to the top used to be a straight path. You worked for 30 years with the same company, showed unswerving loyalty and were promoted. You stabilized.

"No more. Today large numbers of men and women at the top have gotten there by working for five businesses in 10 years, dedicating themselves totally to their own advancement and to getting a better and better job. These corporate zigzaggers are scramblers," says career consultant and educator Dr. Elwood N. Chapman. In his book, *Scrambling—Zigzagging Your Way to the Top* (J.P. Tarcher/Houghton Mifflin Co.), Chapman concludes that scrambling is the wave of the future for career advancement.

Not everyone agrees. Some advisers say that today's chief executive officers (CEOs) are the type of people who have long-term time horizons.

In a study of people holding the top jobs for the nation's 800 largest companies, Arthur Young Executive Resource Consultants found that CEOs average 24 years' employment with their companies. About one-third of the people studied had only one employer, and just 10 percent of the people had more than four.

Both viewpoints have merit. You'll have to choose the path that best fits your personal temperament—scrambling or stabilizing.

The scrambler places self above organizational interest. The stabilizer is devoted to the organization for which he or she is working.

In the past, traits exhibited by scramblers caused critics to label them as opportunists, job hoppers and hustlers, but it is a mistake to assume that scrambling techniques are something nice people don't do.

Suppose you decide on the scrambling route. If you are challenged by an interviewer who suggests you've been job hopping, turn a negative to a positive and speak enthusiastically of the advantages of your *diversified* experience.

Become an Expert

How can you become a person who makes things happen?

A key suggestion offered by management consultant Dennis J. Kravetz is to become an expert. In his book, *Getting Noticed—A Manager's Success Kit* (Wiley Press), he advises:

Become highly knowledgeable in your specialty. Be the most expert accountant, programmer, mechanical engineer, or middle manager. Others will seek your advice when they want to do things correctly, because they know you are the best source of information they have.

When you've mastered your own specialty area, keep going. Master another area, then a third and a fourth, until you know all the ins and outs of the company, including areas you're not responsible for. Get to know the people in other departments, divisions, and even regions. Learn how their operations run. More and more people will seek your counsel, and the reputation you build will increase your control over your future.

No Job Gives You Everything

While you're not expecting too much to want a great career, you are going to be disappointed if you expect any occupation to fill all your needs.

There's always a glitch, always something you wish were not a part of the job. A letter from a 40-year-old electrical engineer working in the aerospace industry illustrates:

I have always found engineering to be personally satisfying and stimulating, but the only defense against career frustration seems to be well-nourished cynicism and a bit of plain resignation.

This apparently negative attitude isn't unusual, but rather more the norm. Believe me. I've been in the trenches a long time, and I've met a lot of other guys shoveling alongside me that feel the same way.

There really isn't any such thing as the "corporate advancement ladder" for engineers. As you get older and smarter, you get more responsible job assignments, your title changes occasionally, but one is still an engineer. Okay, fine. That's what I wanted. The rewards, to get to the bottom line, are ultimately financial—the paycheck.

Which way is up? Supervision? No thanks. I've worked for a lot of people, and I wouldn't trade jobs with any of them. Private consulting? Ask the Small Business Administration what the failure rate is. Besides, I'm no businessman. I'm an engineer. Transfer within the company? Different frying pan, same fire. Quit, and work for another large company? Same pattern after the initial hire-in inducements. Small company? I've tried it. Aside from having to be a jack-of-all-trades, work man-killing hours, and hope the outfit doesn't fold up, it's all right. There is the one advantage of being close to where money decisions are made.

Get out of engineering? Many have. My choice? Stick it out. I like engineering and besides, I'm probably too stubborn for my own good.

Thanks for letting me sound off.

Don't anticipate getting everything you want from work. Total satisfaction is no more assured in your career than in any other area of life. There are days, weeks, even months when things go well—or badly.

Many jobs have great moments, but they are not eternal. Most jobs have bad times, but they pass.

Try to appreciate the personal rewards in your work, because deep satisfaction in your career is more likely to come from the journey than the destination.

Position Yourself for Promotion

Are you too smart to be ensnarled by the "task-busy trap"? That's when you indiscriminately try to do each task 100 percent perfectly—and lose sight of the larger question.

The larger question is, "Are you positioning your performance in a way that will advance your career, as well as boost the company's fortunes?"

Why gilt-edge an assignment that doesn't rate a footnote in management circles? Save your heavy firepower for jobs that significantly benefit the company, and which, not so incidentally, focus higher-ups' attention on your exceptional capabilities. Get-ahead executives actively seek crucial projects big-wigs will notice. Call it positioning, political awareness, or enlightened self-promotion, but call it to mind as a strategy for moving up.

Keep Your Ears Up

Employment experts John D. Erdlen and Donald H. Sweet say you are not expected to know everything, and that you cannot learn without asking. That's one of the reasons you have supervisors. It's always better to ask questions than to risk making a costly mistake.

And you'd better learn to listen carefully. In their book *Job Hunting for the College Graduate* (D.C. Heath and Co.), the authors report:

The biggest problem most people have in whatever they do is the failure to listen. This is compounded when, in an effort to demonstrate ability and effectiveness, the new employee rushes to get a job done without knowing fully what has to be done or how it is to be accomplished.

The Success Image

It's the status-behavior perception area where you may need coaching.

In *Market Yourself for Success* (Prentice-Hall/A Spectrum Book), career counselor Richard A. Payne says many people get ahead in large measure because they give the appearance of being successful.

These people may not [be] the quickest, the brightest, or more importantly, the greatest contributors in their jobs. But they sure knew how to play the role inherent in their job title. And whammo, they were promoted ahead of others who offered more long-term benefits.

As for behavior, never let others think you are loafing. If you have a job you could finish daily by 10 A.M., be resourceful about looking busy. Write letters, create projects, attend meetings. Don't be seen as one who reads personal magazines on company time, takes long coffee breaks, lingers in the hallways or makes lengthy personal phone calls. Act as though somebody were videotaping your day to play it back before your company's board of directors.

By the way, if you should find yourself with a job that has few real duties, first try volunteering for extra assignments; if that fails, get out of there before you yawn yourself to death.

Some observers argue that image (how you appear to do the job) is more important than your technical skills (how you actually do the job). We're not willing to go that far (witness the brilliant professor who walks around wearing socks of two different colors), but there is no question that a high-performance image is jet fuel for moving up.

Extend Your Range

When you can't find a job you want in your home town, consider relocating.

When your company offers a promotion but it's in a faraway community where you don't know a soul, consider relocating.

When you have close personal ties to your college town and you'd like to stay on after graduation, consider relocating.

Sometimes you've got to be courageous and push yourself out into the world. To use an aeronautical metaphor, if you want to build airplanes, you have to go where they build airplanes.

There is no getting around the fact that if you stubbornly refuse to consider relocating to greener pastures, you drastically cut back the number of jobs you could get—perhaps by as many as 90 percent of job openings.

How can you evaluate whether it's worthwhile to change scenery? You weigh advantages against disadvantages, including income against expenses. You review your priorities and values, as well.

If, after reading this advice, you still intend to spend eternity right where you are, reflect on the admirable little coyote, a strong example of the benefits of following the winds of opportunity.

In this country some years ago, the coyote was found only in the western states. When humankind began building houses and shopping centers on enormous sections of rural land the small wolf called home, the long-time canine resident was squeezed out. It had to make a move or perish. The coyote solved the immediate problem by extending its range and fanning out to all of the 48 contiguous states.

Although a spouse's job or other family considerations will eliminate some relocation options, your basic stance should be a willingness to consider a change of geography when the change is a stepping-stone to your goals.

Think about it: How wide-ranging is *your* habitat?

Make 'Em Laugh

(To customer who drove 40 miles out of the city to inspect your plant):

I guess this place is pretty far off the beaten track. It's not the end of the world, I always say, but you can see it from here.

Anytime you can ease awkward moments with an amusing line, you're ahead of the game. While you need not be the office clown to use humor as an advancement tool, a tasteful joke helps you admit your own mistakes and papers over minor problems. Just be sure the butt of the gag is yourself, not others.

The More Mentors the Merrier

A mentor is someone who teaches you, advises you or promotes your career.

The mentor who teaches you is likely to be your immediate boss. The mentor who advises you may be your boss or a co-worker—or even someone outside your company. Some people develop relationships only with those who can enhance their careers.

The mentor who promotes your career is in the sponsor or "godfather" category and is likely to be a higher-up in your company, or someone connected with your company or industry who is powerful and influential.

Although you need at least one mentor, gratefully take as many as you can get. The more people you have pulling for you, the better.

Timing Is Everything

Time itself is the essence of this pointer from James A. Newman and Roy Alexander. They wrote *Climbing the Corporate Matterhorn* (John Wiley & Sons). Alexander relates an incident:

A colleague said to me recently: "Jim, you're a great believer in punctuality. When you have a meeting at 8 A.M., you bisect the dot. You don't get there early, you don't get there late."

It's true. I believe in punctuality. You'd better, too. Nothing will give you poorer marks quicker than tardiness... Being late makes you flustered and full of apologies—not a good way to start—rather than calm and confident.

I know what you're thinking: "On the face of it, five minutes is a fairly minor sin." Yet it indicates something bigger.

The rising executive is expected to be punctual...

Oh, there are *reasons for being late. But they'd better be damned good ones. Not the heavy traffic on the way over. Not the shortage of cabs or a place to park. Those are things you plan for. Or at least the real upward mover does.*

Getting the Golden Worm

Perhaps the most important tip is the one at the focus of this book: *Think early about your career goals.*

As 35-year-old multimillionaire entrepreneur and co-founder of Apple Computer, Steve Wozniak, tells job market beginners in *Graduating Engineer:*

Realize that you have more energy now than you will later, and that you'll lose that after a while. If you want to really move up, this is the time to put in a few more hours. Make your job Number One, and work it like a pyramid, building on a strong base.

This Is Goodbye

After reading this book, you are better equipped than most of your friends to plan how your dreams and serious ambitions will fit into the maze of life's choices.

While you may not have a completely clear idea of everything your dreams encompass, chances are they involve love, respect, happy days, enough money to live the kind of life you want, and good health.

As you prepare to make your dreams real, we ask you once again to remember that whatever your choice, it's not always the salary or stature or security that counts most *for you.*

A healthy regard for the future and a rainy day is basic. Beyond that, your work must give you personal rewards—excitement and involvement and purpose. In other words—*Do something you'd do for nothing.*

APPENDIX A

Study Terms Beyond the High School Level

As you move higher in your education, you'll hear terms with which you may be vaguely familiar, but are not positive about their meaning. Here's a glossary so you'll be sure.

Acceptance Candidate is admitted. Colleges notify students in early April. Students should reply as soon as possible whether they will or will not attend the college. (For details see "admissions programs.")

Accreditation The process by which a non-governmental accrediting association or professional organization grants public recognition to an institution or particular course of study. Generally, accreditation guarantees that certain minimal educational standards are met. Periodic evaluations are carried out to ensure the standards are maintained.

Admissions Programs

Early Action A plan allowing students to know the decision on their admission application before the standard April notification date. It differs from "early decision" in that students are not required to accept admission immediately.

Early Admission A program in which a college accepts enrollments of high school students before they graduate from high school. Admissions standards are more stringent for early admissions.

Early Decision A plan in which students apply in November or December and learn of the decision on their application during December or January. This plan is suggested only for students who are academically strong and know where they want to attend college. If accepted, early-decision students are often required to withdraw their applications to other colleges and must agree to matriculate at the college accepting them.

Early Notification A program in which applicants must file their papers by December 1 in order to receive an admission decision by February 1.

Midyear Admission An option allowing applicants who were placed on the waiting list for fall admission and not admitted to allow them to start classes in the second semester.

Rolling Admissions A program in which admissions applications are evaluated upon receipt and applicants are immediately notified of the decision.

Many colleges employ more than one of the admissions programs described above.

Admissions Testing Program (ATP) A program of College Board entrance tests that includes the Scholastic Aptitude Test, Test of Standard Written English, Achievement Tests, and the Student Descriptive Questionnaire.

Admit-Deny Candidate is accepted but denied financial aid.

Advanced Degree A degree beyond the associate or bachelor's degree. First professional, master's, and doctor's degrees are usually considered advanced degrees.

Advanced Placement Admission or assignment of a freshman to an advanced course in a certain subject based on evidence that the student has completed the equivalent of the college's freshman course in that subject.

Advanced Placement Program (APP) A College Board service that provides high schools with course descriptions of college subjects and Advanced Placement Examinations in those subjects. High schools implement the courses and administer the examinations on the basis of satisfactory grades. Students are then eligible for advanced placement, college credit, or both.

Advanced Standing Advanced status accorded to students who score high on Advanced Placement Tests or who have taken "advanced" or "college level" courses in high school. If qualified, a student may gain credit for a semester or a full year of collegiate study, or a student may be allowed to skip certain introductory courses.

American College Testing Program A non-profit membership organization headquartered in Iowa City, Iowa, that provides tests and other educational services for students, schools and colleges.

American College Testing (ACT) Program Assessment Test battery of the American College Testing Program, given at test centers throughout the year. It includes tests in English usage, mathematics usage, social studies reading, and natural sciences reading. The composite score referred to in some colleges' descriptions is the average of a student's scores on these four tests.

Application A document submitted by a student who wants to be admitted to the college.

Approval The process by which a governmental or non-governmental agency or association gives official recognition to an educational program. Usually, approval does not include standards or inspections as rigid as those in accreditation, although approved programs or schools may or may not be superior to those with full accreditation.

Associate Degree The degree given for finishing a two- or three-year program of college work (most often a two-year program). In some colleges, associate degrees are given for partial completion of work in a bachelor's degree program.

Bachelor's Degree The degree given for finishing a college program of at least four but not more than five years of academic work. Usually this degree is either a BA (bachelor of arts) or BS (bachelor of science). There are also a number of specialized bachelor's degrees for certain fields such as BArch (bachelor of architecture).

Certificate An award for finishing a one- or two-year post-secondary school program. It usually certifies competency in a specific job field. Example: certified welder.

College Board A non-profit membership organization, headquartered in New York City, that provides tests and other educational services for students, schools and colleges.

College Fair A large gathering of college recruitment officers to provide information about admissions to their respective institutions. Some public schools have college nights which are similar to college fairs, but are conducted on a smaller scale. Usually, the college night is restricted to an area of a county or region.

College-Level Examination Program (CLEP) A program of examinations in undergraduate college subjects and courses that provides students and other adults with an opportunity to show college-level achievement for which they have not previously received credit. The examinations are used by colleges to evaluate the entering freshmen and the status of students transferring from other colleges.

Common Application An admission application that, when completed, can be sent to several institutions.

Community College A two-year college offering courses that are supposed to fit the needs of the local community. Occupational, adult, and general education courses are included along with liberal arts transfer courses. Though the terms *junior* and *community* colleges are often used interchangeably, junior colleges are more often limited to liberal arts transfer courses.

Cooperative Education A combination of classroom study and work experience directly related to the classroom study.

Curriculum A planned sequence of activities that helps students gain special skills or a certain body of knowledge. Most curricula also lead to a degree, diploma, or certificate in the particular field of study.

Deferral A term used by the college to handle early-decision candidates who were not accepted in December but have a chance in regular admissions.

Degree A title given as official recognition for satisfactorily completing a curriculum. This is an "earned" degree. ("Honorary" or "unearned" degrees don't count as academic achievement, but rather as a school's recognition of people with special achievement, or who have donated money to the school.)

Diploma A document that states a person has satisfactorily completed a curriculum.

Doctor's Degree (Doctorate) The highest degree in a field of study or profession. The doctor's degree usually requires three or more years of work beyond the bachelor's degree and a dissertation (lengthy written work based on original research). PhD (doctor of philosophy) and LLD (doctor of laws) are two examples of doctor's degrees. Do not confuse this degree with MD (doctor of medicine), which is a first professional degree in medicine.

First Professional Degree The degree that shows all academic requirements have been completed for practicing a profession. A first professional degree requires five, or more often, six years of college work, sometimes seven or eight. Examples: MD (doctor of medicine), PodD (doctor of podiatry).

Grade-point Average or Ratio A system used by many colleges to evaluate the overall scholastic performance of students. GPA is found by first determining the number of grade points a student has earned in each course completed and then dividing the sum of all grade points by the number of hours of course work carried. Grade points are found by multiplying the number of hours given for a course by the student's grade in the course. The most common system of numerical values for grades is A=4, B=3, C=2, D=1, and E or F=0.

Graduate School The part of a university that offers programs for advanced degrees.

Liberal Arts College A college in which the emphasis is on a program of liberal arts and basic sciences, usually leading to a bachelor's degree. Some preprofessional programs such as prelaw and premedicine may also be offered.

Major A student's main field of study.

Master's Degree The degree given for finishing one year (sometimes two) of academic work beyond the bachelor's degree. Some master's degrees are MA (master of arts), MS (master of sciences), MBA (master of business administration).

Matriculation Admission to, and attendance at, a post-secondary institution working toward a degree.

Open Admissions The college admissions policy of admitting high school graduates and other adults generally without regard to conventional academic qualifications, such as high school subjects, high school grades, and admissions tests scores. Virtually all applicants with high school diplomas or their equivalent are accepted.

Pass-fail Grading System Some colleges rate students' academic performance in their courses as either passing or failing instead of giving grades to indicate various levels of passing work. The college's entire grading system may follow this pattern, or it may be an optional one for individual students in specific courses.

Rejection The rejection letter usually starts: "There are a large number of well-qualified candidates for the few places in next year's freshman class. . . ." If rejected by a school, you may want to apply there later as a "transfer" or a prospective graduate student.

Reply Date Date that an accepted student must indicate desire to attend. Failure to reply means acceptance will be withdrawn by the college.

Student-designed Major An academic program that allows a student to construct a major field of study not formally offered by the college. Often non-traditional and interdisciplinary in nature, the major is developed by the student with the approval of a designated college officer or committee.

Undergraduate School The part of a university offering programs leading to the bachelor's degree.

University An institution of post-high school education that has these main aims: (1) teaching graduate and undergraduate programs; (2) conducting research to find new knowledge and more ways to use old knowledge; (3) making its findings and teachings available to society. The university grants advanced degrees as well as bachelor's degrees in many fields including liberal arts, sciences, and professions.

Waiting List A kind of limbo that leans closer to rejection than acceptance. If placed on such a list for a school that still appeals to you, let the school know of your interest. It may sway a decision when openings appear.

APPENDIX B

MATCHING YOURSELF WITH THE WORLD OF WORK*

The following guide was designed to help you compare job characteristics with your interests and skills. Listed and defined are 17 occupational characteristics and requirements that are matched with 200 occupations.

The table can be used in at least three ways. First, if you already have some idea of which occupation you wish to enter, you can use the table to find out the general characteristics of that occupation. Second, if you've decided on a general field of work—such as health or sales—but not on a particular occupation, the table can help you learn about the different jobs in that field. Third, if you haven't thought much about occupations, but you do know what skills you have, the table can introduce you to several occupations you might be good at.

One note of caution: The chart can be helpful in organizing occupational information, but it is intended only as a general exploratory tool. Before you eliminate an occupation from consideration because of a single characteristic, you should realize that the job characteristics presented in the table refer only to a typical job in the occupation.

All jobs in an occupation are not alike. Most accountants, for example, work alone, but accountants who are auditors or investigators may work with others. Therefore, if you have an interest in an occupation, you should not disregard that career simply because one or two of its characteristics do not appeal to you. You should check further into the occupation—either through reading or by talking to your counselor—to find out how particular jobs in the occupation or occupational cluster might match up with your personality, interests, and abilities.

*This appendix is excerpted from the Fall 1986 issue of *Occupational Outlook Quarterly.* It was written by Melvin Fountain, editor of the *Occupational Outlook Quarterly,* U.S. Department of Labor, Bureau of Labor Statistics.

Key to Letter Codes in Columns 14, 15, and 17

Column 14—Earnings:
Three categories of earnings, based on 1985 averages, are shown:

L = lowest (10 percent or less)

M = middle (11 to 19 percent)

H = highest (20 percent or more)

Column 15—Employment growth:
Three categories of projected growth from 1984 to 1995 are shown:

L = lowest

M = middle

H = highest

Column 17—Entry requirements:
Three categories of education and training requirements are shown:

L = high school or less education is sufficient, and the basics of the job can usually be learned in a few months of on-the-job training

M = post-high school training, such as apprenticeship or junior college, or many months or years of experience are required to be fully qualified

H = 4 or more years of college usually required

	Job requirements								Work environment			Occupational characteristics					
	1. Leadership/persuasion	2. Helping/instructing others	3. Problem-solving/creativity	4. Initiative	5. Work as part of a team	6. Frequent public contact	7. Manual dexterity	8. Physical stamina	9. Hazardous	10. Outdoors	11. Confined	12. Geographically concentrated	13. Part-time	14. Earnings	15. Employment growth	16. Number of new jobs, 1984-95 (in thousands)	17. Entry requirements
Executive, Administrative, and Managerial Occupations																	
Managers and Administrators																	
Bank officers and managers	●	●	●	●	●	●					●			H	H	119	H
Health services managers	●	●	●	●	●	●								H	H	147	H
Hotel managers and assistants	●	●	●	●	●	●								[1]	H	21	M
School principals and assistant principals	●	●	●	●	●	●								H	L	12	H
Management Support Occupations																	
Accountants and auditors		●	●		●	●					●			H	H	307	H
Construction and building inspectors		●	●	●	●		●			●				M	L	4	M
Inspectors and compliance officers, except construction		●	●	●	●		●			●				H	L	10	M
Personnel, training, and labor relations specialists	●	●	●	●	●	●								H	M	34	H
Purchasing agents	●		●		●	●								H	M	36	H
Underwriters			●											H	H	17	H
Wholesale and retail buyers	●	●	●	●	●									M	M	28	H
Engineers, Surveyors, and Architects																	
Architects			●	●	●	●	●							H	H	25	H
Surveyors	●				●		●	●		●				M	M	6	M
Engineers																	
Aerospace engineers			●	●	●							●		H	H	14	H
Chemical engineers			●	●	●									H	H	13	H
Civil engineers			●	●	●									H	H	46	H
Electrical and electronics engineers			●	●	●									H	H	206	H
Industrial engineers			●	●	●									H	H	37	H
Mechanical engineers			●	●	●									H	H	81	H
Metallurgical, ceramics, and materials engineers			●	●	●									H	H	4	H
Mining engineers			●	●	●									H	L	[2]	H
Nuclear engineers			●	●	●									H	L	1	H
Petroleum engineers			●	●	●							●		H	M	4	H

[1] Estimates not available.
[2] Less than 500.

	Job requirements								Work environment				Occupational characteristics				
	1. Leadership/persuasion	2. Helping/instructing others	3. Problem-solving/creativity	4. Initiative	5. Work as part of a team	6. Frequent public contact	7. Manual dexterity	8. Physical stamina	9. Hazardous	10. Outdoors	11. Confined	12. Geographically concentrated	13. Part-time	14. Earnings	15. Employment growth	16. Number of new jobs, 1984–95 (in thousands)	17. Entry requirements
Natural Scientists and Mathematicians																	
Computer and Mathematical Occupations																	
Actuaries			●	●							●	●		H	H	4	H
Computer systems analysts	●	●	●	●	●						●			H	H	212	H
Mathematicians			●	●										H	M	4	H
Statisticians			●	●										H	M	4	H
Physical Scientists			●	●										H	M		H
Chemists			●	●										H	L	9	H
Geologists and geophysicists			●	●	●					●		●		H	M	7	H
Meteorologists			●	●	●									H	M	1	H
Physicists and astronomers			●	●										H	L	2	H
Life Scientists																	
Agricultural scientists			●	●										[1]	M	3	H
Biological scientists			●	●										H	M	10	H
Foresters and conservation scientists		●	●	●	●			●	●	●				H	L	2	H
Social Scientists, Social Workers, Religious Workers, and Lawyers																	
Lawyers	●	●	●	●	●	●								H	H	174	H
Social Scientists and Urban Planners																	
Economists			●	●										H	M	7	H
Psychologists		●	●	●		●								H	H	21	H
Sociologists			●	●		●								H	L	[2]	H
Urban and regional planners	●		●	●	●	●								H	L	2	H
Social and Recreation Workers																	
Social workers	●	●	●	●	●	●								M	H	75	H
Recreation workers	●	●	●	●	●	●	●	●		●			●	L	H	26	M
Religious Workers																	
Protestant ministers	●	●	●	●	●	●								L	[1]	[1]	H
Rabbis	●	●	●	●	●	●								H	[1]	[1]	H
Roman Catholic priests	●	●	●	●	●	●								L	[1]	[1]	H

[1] Estimates not available.
[2] Less than 500.

	Job requirements								Work environment					Occupational characteristics			
	1. Leadership/persuasion	2. Helping/instructing others	3. Problem-solving/creativity	4. Initiative	5. Work as part of a team	6. Frequent public contact	7. Manual dexterity	8. Physical stamina	9. Hazardous	10. Outdoors	11. Confined	12. Geographically concentrated	13. Part-time	14. Earnings	15. Employment growth	16. Number of new jobs, 1984–95 (in thousands)	17. Entry requirements
Teachers, Counselors, Librarians, and Archivists																	
Kindergarten and elementary school teachers	●	●	●	●	●	●	●	●						M	H	281	H
Secondary school teachers	●	●	●	●	●	●		●						M	L	48	H
Adult and vocational education teachers	●	●	●	●	●	●	●	●					●	M	M	48	H
College and university faculty	●	●	●	●	●	●		●					●	H	L	−77	H
Counselors	●	●	●	●	●	●								M	M	29	H
Librarians	●	●	●	●	●	●		●					●	M	L	16	H
Archivists and curators			●	●	●									M	L	1	H
Health Diagnosing and Treating Practitioners																	
Chiropractors	●	●	●	●	●	●	●							H	H	9	H
Dentists	●	●	●	●	●	●	●							H	H	39	H
Optometrists	●	●	●	●	●	●	●							H	H	8	H
Physicians	●	●	●	●	●	●	●						●	H	H	109	H
Podiatrists	●	●	●	●	●	●	●							H	H	4	H
Veterinarians	●	●	●	●	●	●	●	●	●					H	H	9	H
Registered Nurses, Pharmacists, Dietitians, Therapists, and Physician Assistants																	
Dietitians and nutritionists	●	●	●	●	●	●								M	H	12	H
Occupational therapists	●	●	●	●	●	●	●	●						[1]	H	8	H
Pharmacists	●	●	●	●	●	●					●			H	L	15	H
Physical therapists	●	●	●	●	●	●	●	●						M	H	25	H
Physician assistants	●	●	●	●	●	●	●							M	H	10	M
Recreational therapists	●	●	●	●	●	●	●	●		●				M	H	4	M
Registered nurses	●	●	●	●	●	●	●	●	●				●	M	H	452	M
Respiratory therapists	●	●	●	●	●	●	●							M	H	11	L
Speech pathologists and audiologists	●	●	●	●	●	●								M	M	8	H
Health Technologists and Technicians																	
Clinical laboratory technologists and technicians			●		●		●				●			L	L	18	[3]
Dental hygienists		●			●	●	●	●					●	L	H	22	M

[1] Estimates not available.

[3] Vary, depending on job.

	Job requirements								Work environment			Occupational characteristics					
	1. Leadership/persuasion	2. Helping/instructing others	3. Problem-solving/creativity	4. Initiative	5. Work as part of a team	6. Frequent public contact	7. Manual dexterity	8. Physical stamina	9. Hazardous	10. Outdoors	11. Confined	12. Geographically concentrated	13. Part-time	14. Earnings	15. Employment growth	16. Number of new jobs, 1984-95 (in thousands)	17. Entry requirements
Dispensing opticians		•	•	•	•	•	•							M	H	10	M
Electrocardiograph technicians		•	•		•	•	•							[1]	M	3	M
Electroencephalographic technologists and technicians		•	•		•	•	•							[1]	H	1	M
Emergency medical technicians	•	•	•	•	•	•	•	•	•	•				L	L	3	M
Licensed practical nurses		•			•	•	•	•	•				•	L	M	106	M
Medical record technicians					•						•			L	H	10	M
Radiologic technologists		•			•	•	•		•					L	H	27	M
Surgical technicians		•			•	•	•							L	M	5	M
Writers, Artists, and Entertainers																	
Communications Occupations																	
Public relations specialists	•		•	•	•	•								H	H	30	H
Radio and television announcers and newscasters	•	•		•	•	•					•			L	M	6	H
Reporters and correspondents	•		•	•	•	•								[1]	M	13	H
Writers and editors	•		•	•	•						•		•	[1]	H	54	H
Visual Arts Occupations																	
Designers			•	•	•	•	•							H	H	46	H
Graphic and fine artists			•	•			•								H	60 M	
Photographers and camera operators			•	•		•	•						•	M	H	29	M
Performing Arts Occupations																	
Actors, directors, and producers			•	•	•	•	•	•				•	•	L	H	11	M
Dancers and choreographers			•	•	•	•	•	•				•	•	L	H	2	M
Musicians			•	•	•	•	•	•				•	•	L	M	26	M
Technologists and Technicians Except Health																	
Engineering and Science Technicians																	
Drafters					•		•				•			M	M	39	M
Electrical and electronics technicians			•		•		•							M	H	202	M
Engineering technicians			•		•		•							M	H	90	M
Science technicians			•		•		•							M	M	40	M
Other technicians																	
Air traffic controllers		•	•	•	•		•				•			H	L	[2]	H
Broadcast technicians			•		•		•				•			M	H	5	M

[1] Estimates not available.
[2] Less than 500.

	Job requirements								Work environment			Occupational characteristics					
	1. Leadership/persuasion	2. Helping/instructing others	3. Problem-solving/creativity	4. Initiative	5. Work as part of a team	6. Frequent public contact	7. Manual dexterity	8. Physical stamina	9. Hazardous	10. Outdoors	11. Confined	12. Geographically concentrated	13. Part-time	14. Earnings	15. Employment growth	16. Number of new jobs, 1984–95 (in thousands)	17. Entry requirements
Computer programmers			●		●						●			H	H	245	H
Legal assistants				[3]	●	[3]								M	H	51	L
Library technicians		●			●	●	●						●	L	L	4	L
Tool programmers, numerical control			●				●		●					M	H	3	M
Marketing and Sales Occupations																	
Cashiers		●				●	●				●		●	L	H	566	L
Insurance sales workers	●	●	●	●		●							●	M	L	34	M
Manufacturers' sales workers	●	●	●	●		●								H	L	51	H
Real estate agents and brokers	●	●	●	●		●				●			●	M	M	52	M
Retail sales workers	●	●		●		●							●	L	M	583	L
Securities and financial services sales workers	●	●	●	●		●							●	H	H	32	H
Travel agents	●	●	●	●		●								[1]	H	32	M
Wholesale trade sales workers	●	●	●	●		●								M	H	369	M
Administrative Support Occupations, Including Clerical																	
Bank tellers					●	●					●		●	L	L	24	L
Bookkeepers and accounting clerks					●						●		●	L	L	118	L
Computer and peripheral equipment operators			●		●		●				●			L	H	143	M
Data entry keyers					●		●				●			L	L	10	L
Mail carriers						●	●	●		●				M	L	8	L
Postal clerks					●	●	●	●			●			M	L	–27	L
Receptionists and information clerks		●			●	●					●		●	L	M	83	L
Reservation and transportation ticket agents and travel clerks		●	●		●	●					●			M	L	7	L
Secretaries				●	●	●	●							L	L	268	L
Statistical clerks					●						●			L	L	–12	L
Stenographers				●	●	●	●							L	L	–96	L
Teacher aides	●	●			●	●	●	●					●	L	M	88	L
Telephone operators		●				●					●			L	M	89	L
Traffic, shipping, and receiving clerks			●	●	●									L	L	61	L
Typists							●				●		●	L	L	11	L

[1] Estimates not available.
[3] Vary, depending on job.

	Job requirements								Work environment			Occupational characteristics					
	1. Leadership/persuasion	2. Helping/instructing others	3. Problem-solving/creativity	4. Initiative	5. Work as part of a team	6. Frequent public contact	7. Manual dexterity	8. Physical stamina	9. Hazardous	10. Outdoors	11. Confined	12. Geographically concentrated	13. Part-time	14. Earnings	15. Employment growth	16. Number of new jobs, 1984–95 (in thousands)	17. Entry requirements
Service Occupations																	
Protective Service Occupations																	
Correction officers	●	●			●			●	●		●			M	H	45	L
Firefighting occupations		●	●		●	●	●	●	●	●			●	M	M	48	L
Guards						●	●	●	●		●		●	L	H	188	L
Police and detectives	●	●	●	●	●	●	●	●	●	●				M	M	66	L
Food and Beverage Preparation and Service Occupations																	
Bartenders				●		●	●	●			●		●	L	H	112	M
Chefs and cooks except short order				●			●	●			●		●	L	H	210	M
Waiters and waitresses				●		●	●	●					●	L	H	424	L
Health Service Occupations																	
Dental assistants		●			●	●	●	●					●	L	H	48	L
Medical assistants		●			●	●	●		●					L	H	79	L
Nursing aides		●			●	●	●	●	●				●	L	H	348	L
Psychiatric aides		●			●	●		●	●					L	L	5	L
Cleaning Service Occupations																	
Janitors and cleaners								●					●	L	M	443	L
Personal Service Occupations																	
Barbers						●	●	●			●		●	L	L	4	M
Childcare workers	●	●		●		●		●					●	L	L	55	L
Cosmetologists and related workers					●	●	●	●			●		●	L	H	150	M
Flight attendants		●			●	●	●	●						M	H	13	L
Agricultural, Forestry, and Fishing Occupations																	
Farm operators and managers	●	●	●	●	●		●	●		●				M	L	−62	L
Mechanics and Repairers																	
Vehicle and Mobile Equipment Mechanics and Repairers																	
Aircraft mechanics and engine specialists			●		●		●	●	●	●		●		H	M	18	M
Automotive and motorcycle mechanics			●			●	●	●	●		●			M	H	185	M
Automotive body repairers			●				●	●	●		●			M	M	32	M
Diesel mechanics			●			●	●	●	●		●			M	H	48	M
Farm equipment mechanics			●				●	●	●	●				M	L	2	M
Mobile heavy equipment mechanics			●				●	●	●		●			M	M	12	M

	Job requirements								Work environment			Occupational characteristics					
	1. Leadership/persuasion	2. Helping/instructing others	3. Problem-solving/creativity	4. Initiative	5. Work as part of a team	6. Frequent public contact	7. Manual dexterity	8. Physical stamina	9. Hazardous	10. Outdoors	11. Confined	12. Geographically concentrated	13. Part-time	14. Earnings	15. Employment growth	16. Number of new jobs, 1984–95 (in thousands)	17. Entry requirements
Electrical and Electronic Equipment Repairers																	
Commercial and electronic equipment repairers			●	●		●	●							L	M	8	M
Communications equipment mechanics			●	●		●	●							M	L	3	M
Computer service technicians			●	●		●	●							M	H	28	M
Electronic home entertainment equipment repairers			●	●		●	●		●				●	M	M	7	M
Home appliance and power tool repairers			●	●		●	●							L	M	9	M
Line installers and cable splicers			●		●		●	●	●	●				M	M	24	L
Telephone installers and repairers			●		●	●	●	●	●					M	L	–19	L
Other Mechanics and Repairers																	
General maintenance mechanics			●				●		●					M	M	137	M
Heating, air-conditioning, and refrigeration mechanics			●				●		●					M	M	29	M
Industrial machinery repairers			●				●	●	●					M	L	34	M
Millwrights			●				●		●					H	L	6	M
Musical instrument repairers and tuners							●							L	L	1	M
Office machine and cash register servicers			●	●	●		●							M	H	16	M
Vending machine servicers and repairers			●	●			●							[1]	M	5	M
Construction and Extractive Occupations																	
Construction Occupations																	
Bricklayers and stonemasons			●		●		●	●	●	●				M	M	15	M
Carpenters			●		●		●	●	●	●				M	M	101	M
Carpet installers			●		●	●	●	●	●					M	M	11	M
Concrete masons and terrazzo workers			●		●		●	●	●	●				M	M	17	M
Drywall workers and lathers			●		●		●	●	●					M	M	11	M
Electricians			●		●		●	●	●	●				H	M	88	M
Glaziers			●		●		●	●	●	●				M	H	8	M
Insulation workers			●		●		●	●	●					M	M	7	M
Painters and paperhangers			●		●	●	●	●	●	●				M	L	17	M
Plasterers			●		●		●	●	●			●		M	L	1	M
Plumbers and pipefitters			●		●	●	●	●	●	●				H	M	61	M
Roofers			●		●		●	●	●	●				L	M	16	M
Sheet-metal workers			●		●		●	●	●					M	M	16	M
Structural and reinforcing metal workers			●		●		●	●	●	●				H	M	16	M

[1] Estimates not available.

	Job requirements								Work environment					Occupational characteristics			
	1. Leadership/persuasion	2. Helping/instructing others	3. Problem-solving/creativity	4. Initiative	5. Work as part of a team	6. Frequent public contact	7. Manual dexterity	8. Physical stamina	9. Hazardous	10. Outdoors	11. Confined	12. Geographically concentrated	13. Part-time	14. Earnings	15. Employment growth	16. Number of new jobs, 1984–95 (in thousands)	17. Entry requirements
Tilesetters			●		●		●	●						M	M	3	M
Extractive Occupations																	
Roustabouts					●		●	●	●	●		●		M	L	[2]	L
Production Occupations																	
Blue-collar worker supervisors	●	●	●	●	●		●		●					M	L	85	M
Precision Production Occupations																	
Boilermakers			●				●		●					M	L	4	M
Bookbinding workers		●			●		●	●	●		●			L	M	14	M
Butchers and meatcutters						●	●	●	●		●			L	L	−9	M
Compositors and typesetters							●	●	●		●			L	M	14	M
Dental laboratory technicians								●			●			L	M	10	M
Jewelers	●	●	●	●	●	●	●				●	●		L	L	3	M
Lithographic and photoengraving workers		●	●		●		●	●			●			H	M	13	M
Machinists			●				●	●	●		●			M	L	37	M
Photographic process workers							●				●			L	H	14	L
Shoe and leather workers and repairers		●			●	●	●							L	L	−8	M
Tool-and-die makers			●				●	●	●		●	●		H	L	16	M
Upholsterers							●	●			●			L	L	6	M
Plant and System Operators																	
Stationary engineers			●				●	●	●					M	L	4	M
Water and sewage treatment plant operators			●	●			●		●	●				L	M	10	M
Machine Operators, Tenders, and Setup Workers																	
Metalworking and plastic-working machine operators							●	●	●		●	●			L	3	L
Numerical-control machine-tool operators			●				●	●	●		●			M	H	17	M
Printing press operators		●	●		●		●	●	●		●			M	M	26	M
Fabricators, Assemblers, and Handworking Occupations																	
Precision assemblers					●		●	●			●			L	M	66	L
Transportation equipment painters							●	●	●		●			M	M	9	M
Welders and cutters							●	●	●	●				M	M	41	M

[2] Less than 500.

	Job requirements								Work environment			Occupational characteristics					
	1. Leadership/persuasion	2. Helping/instructing others	3. Problem-solving/creativity	4. Initiative	5. Work as part of a team	6. Frequent public contact	7. Manual dexterity	8. Physical stamina	9. Hazardous	10. Outdoors	11. Confined	12. Geographically concentrated	13. Part-time	14. Earnings	15. Employment growth	16. Number of new jobs, 1984–95 (in thousands)	17. Entry requirements
Transportation and Material Moving Occupations																	
Aircraft pilots			●	●	●		●				●			H	H	18	M
Busdrivers				●		●	●	●			●		●	M	M	77	M
Construction machinery operators					●		●	●	●	●	●			M	M	32	M
Industrial truck and tractor operators				●			●	●			●			M	L	−46	M
Truckdrivers				●			●	●			●			M	M	428	M
Handlers, Equipment Cleaners, Helpers, and Laborers																	
Construction trades helpers					●		●	●	●	●				L	L	27	L

INDEX

Q

R